Maḥmúd's Diary

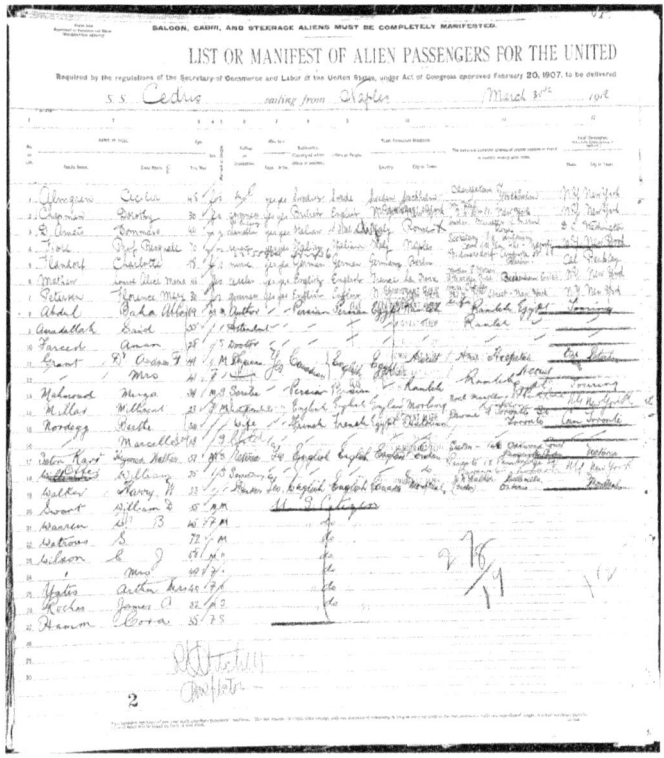

The ship's manifest on the Cedric *on its voyage to New York in April 1912, listing the names of 'Abdu'l-Bahá and those travelling with Him*

Maḥmúd's Diary

*The Diary of Mírzá Maḥmúd-i-Zarqání
Chronicling 'Abdu'l-Bahá's Journey
to America*

translated by
Mohi Sobhani

with the assistance of
Shirley Macias

George Ronald
Oxford

George Ronald, Publisher
www.grbooks.com

© This translation Mohi Sobhani 1998
Reprinted 2012, 2023
All Rights Reserved

A catalogue record for this book is available
from the British Library

ISBN 978-0-85398-659-1

Cover design: Steiner Graphics

CONTENTS

A Note from the Publisher	vii
Maḥmúd's Diary	1
Preface	3
Introduction	9
The Diary	11
Biographical Notes	429
Bibliography	453
References and Notes	457

A NOTE FROM THE PUBLISHER

In the spring of 1912 'Abdu'l-Bahá set off from Alexandria on His historic journey to America. Among his small entourage was Mírzá Maḥmúd-i-Zarqání, who became, in the words of Shoghi Effendi, 'the chronicler of His travels'.

Mírzá Maḥmúd had made a number of teaching trips through Iran and in 1903 began to teach the Bahá'í Faith in India. He was, therefore, already a seasoned traveller by the time 'Abdu'l-Bahá asked him to journey with Him to the West. Mírzá Maḥmúd went everywhere with 'Abdu'l-Bahá, making extensive notes not only of the Master's many public talks and conversations with individuals but also of the new sights and experiences they found in America as well as the daily routines of eating, writing letters and travelling. Maḥmúd remarks on the novelty of the New York skyscrapers, electric lights and American foods and customs for 'Abdu'l-Bahá's party as well as the picturesque spectacle provided to the Americans by His entourage in their *'abá*s and Persian hats.

'Abdu'l-Bahá's journey across America was remarkable. He was 68 years old and had been a prisoner most of His life. When He set out from Egypt He was unwell and planned only to travel to the American East coast and to Chicago. However, the American Bahá'ís begged Him to visit their communities and He undertook the strenuous three thousand-mile journey across the continent by train, sitting up most nights in a chair rather than spending money on a sleeping compartment. He spoke at public meetings nearly every day, sometimes three times a day, and gave hundreds of private interviews. His hectic and exhausting schedule is well-documented by Mírzá Maḥmúd, who frequently alludes to the anxiety of the Master's companions over His health. Maḥmúd's telling references to the simplicity of 'Abdu'l-Bahá's lifestyle – 'For dinner 'Abdu'l-Bahá ate only a little bread and cheese and went to bed' – contrast with the opulent lives lived by many of the Americans who visited Him.

The present work is a translation of the first volume of Maḥmúd's *Badáyi'u'l-Áthár*, an impressive documentary which he appears to have written from his notes on his return to the Middle East in 1913. Maḥmúd made extensive notes of many of 'Abdu'l-Bahá's major talks and various private conversations. The translations of 'Abdu'l-Bahá's words recorded in the present volume were read and revised at the Bahá'í World Centre. The publisher is grateful to Kalimát Press, who undertook the original translations of these passages, for their kind permission to use these translations in the present volume.

The Universal House of Justice, in a letter of April 30, 1984 to the National Spiritual Assembly of the Bahá'ís of the United States, stated that it

> . . . attaches great importance to this work which, as you may know, is regarded as a reliable account of 'Abdu'l-Bahá's travels in the West and an authentic record of His utterances, whether in the form of formal talks, table talks or random oral statements. Mírzá Maḥmúd was a careful and faithful chronicler and engaged in assembling and publishing his work with the permission of the beloved Master, as he states in the Introduction. Indeed, Shoghi Effendi drew upon it for details about the Master's visit to the West in writing *God Passes By* . . .

Maḥmúd wrote in Persian in an ornate style not often used for English prose. Certain phrases common in Persian are inelegant when translated into English and these have, for the most part, been omitted, for example, 'His Luminous Presence', 'His Blessed Person' and so on. The Universal House of Justice itself, in a letter of July 24, 1987, to a publisher advised that the word 'Ḥaḍrat', meaning 'His Holiness', 'should not be used in this translation, especially when referring to 'Abdu'l-Bahá'. However, without burdening the work with many of the flowery descriptions that may seem peculiar to a reader of English, the translator has tried to retain the flavor of the original Persian. Mírzá Maḥmúd was, after all, a Persian and brought his own culture to bear on his American experience.

To assist the reader, the publisher has added explanatory endnotes and biographical notes on many of the people mentioned in the diary. These do not form part of the original text.

The names of some of the people mentioned in the text are unclear. Maḥmúd recorded in Persian the names of Americans as he heard them pronounced. As not all vowels are written in Persian, it is not always possible to be sure which name is meant. For example, the name of Mr and Mrs Killius when written in Persian script could also be read as Clives and it is only by careful research that the correct spelling has been found. Some of the people mentioned are not named in English-language Bahá'í histories and we cannot therefore be certain how their names should be rendered.

Maḥmúd occasionally mistakes the date of a particular event or talk by 'Abdu'l-Bahá. This may be due to his unfamiliarity with the Gregorian calendar or that he was apparently writing some time after his return from the West.

The sheer volume of 'Abdu'l-Bahá's activities and the pace He set Himself as He traveled made Mírzá Maḥmúd's work more difficult than that of most diarists. That he wrote so comprehensively and so accurately under such circumstances is a tribute to his devotion to 'Abdu'l-Bahá and to his skill as a chronicler.

Maḥmúd's Diary

PREFACE

In the Name of God, the Most Exalted, the Most Glorious

Praise and gratitude be to the Lord of the Kingdom of attributes and names for the Manifestation of His Greatest Name [Bahá'u'lláh], through whom the principles of peace and the tranquillity of humankind have been revealed and the foundation for the salvation of the peoples of the world has been laid; and for the appearance of the Mystery of God ['Abdu'l-Bahá],[1] who has raised the standard of universal peace and pitched the tabernacle of unity for all humankind. He has delivered the people of Bahá from the darkness of prejudice and blind imitation and illumined them with the light of divine knowledge and unity. He has safeguarded them from the idle fancies of the people of negation and discord and protected them from the mischief and rancor of the Covenant-breakers. Thus under the banner of His mighty Covenant, diverse peoples have become united and with the utmost zeal have arisen to spread abroad the light of unity and love. They are spreading the principle of the unity of religions and discovering the secrets of harmony and fellowship. They have become the lovers of humankind and the propagators of peace and tranquillity in the world of humanity. They have burned the veils of vain imaginings and of religious, political, national and gender prejudices, and with heart and soul are serving the children of men, who are all citizens of one country and members of one family.

The people of Bahá have unveiled the shortcomings of the material world, knowing a divine civilization to be the highest honor and best mantle for humankind. With God's assistance and through the power of His Covenant, they have made extraordinary progress and in this enlightened age have transformed the thoughts and caused the upliftment of human character. May God increase their power, might, perfection and grandeur and assist them through the Concourse on High and the Hosts of the Abhá Kingdom! Verily, He is mighty over all things. Light and glory, salutation and praise be upon the Dawning-Places of His Cause among His people and the Day-Springs of the revelation of His grace to His creation, through whom the sovereignty of God is manifested in this world and His guidance provided by One through whose exalted efforts the signs of glory and might have been spread and the banners of power and grandeur have been raised: the Greatest Branch of God, the Ancient Mystery, the Will of God, who has branched out from the Ancient Root; He whom God has chosen for His Cause in this century of light, appointed to protect the world and succor all who are on earth and in heaven. O God, cause us to circle round His desire, to be obedient to His will, to hold fast to the robe of His bestowals and to remain steadfast in His Covenant and Testament. Verily, He is Victorious, the Self-Subsistent, the All-Knowing, the All-Wise.

This humble servant [Maḥmúd Zarqání] was the recipient of such great bounty and love from the One round whom circle all Names, the Source of all generosity and grace – 'Abdu'l-Bahá (may my life be a ransom for His friends who are steadfast and firm in His Covenant) – in whose company he traveled in Europe and America as part of His entourage. As I wrote to share the glad tidings of the Master's talks with the friends in the East, to inform them of the great events taking place – the spread of the teachings of God, the majesty of God's Covenant in both America and Europe, the onrush of many highly respected people, men and women alike, the reverence shown to Him by the clergy of all denominations and the praise of many philosophers – I was overwhelmed. I felt compelled to speak and my pen trembled in my hand. Although brief and inadequate, this chronicle attempts to describe the majesty and grandeur of the Center of God's Covenant and the power and authority of the words of God He uttered in both public and private gatherings. Recently, the most great Mystery of God, with complete and perfect joy and enthusiasm, returned to Port Said. Once again the emanations of His light illumined the horizon of the East. The hearts of the Eastern friends were filled with joy and elation. A few of the believers, especially Ḥájí Mírzá Ḥaydar 'Alí (may my life be a ransom for his humility before the presence of 'Abdu'l-Bahá) asked me to collect and organize 'Abdu'l-Bahá's talks, to describe the events related to His journey in the West and to publish this for the delight of the believers and as an aid for those who seek truth. After obtaining permission from the Center of the Covenant, I began collecting and organizing all the papers and notes so that the readers might obtain a clear understanding of the importance and significance of this journey and, in particular, that the people of the East might pay due respect for this great event and be everlastingly thankful for this heavenly blessing and honor. At the present time, the peoples and governments of America and Europe, who are extremely proud of their material and technological progress and civilization, look upon the inhabitants of the East with disdain and prejudice and consider them to be a most uncivilized and ignorant people, as demonstrated by the imposition of their unjust rule over them. At such a time has a majestic Sun shed its light from the horizon of the East and a brilliant Star appeared over the Eastern horizon in such wise that these proud and so-called civilized peoples have become humble and been inspired to pay homage to the Light from the East.

The first point to consider is the effect that 'Abdu'l-Bahá had when He traveled from the East and directed His attention towards the thousands of eminent men and women of the West, clergy of all denominations and highly regarded philosophers of America and Europe who paid the highest respect to Him at the many gatherings in churches, synagogues and large halls, and who praised Him and acknowledged the greatness and the excellence of His character.

Second is to observe the wisdom, perfection and style of His speech and discourse as He answered questions, whether from individuals or at public gatherings. The manner of His response was so flawless and His reasoning so profound that inquirers were completely satisfied, without a hint of objection.

Third is the transformation that occurred in the hearts of the people who were attracted by the penetrating power of His utterance. In every meeting, both public and private, there was great exhilaration in people's hearts. How many eyes wept through joy and happiness, and how many lips, wreathed in smiles, praised Him most highly!

Fourth is the large number of clergymen and presidents of societies who felt highly honored to have Him in their midst and who openly acknowledged His high station, His vast knowledge and the greatness of His teachings.

Fifth is the recognition of the greatness of the Cause of God and loftiness of the station of God's Covenant as published in several journals, newspapers, books and articles written by scholars and philosophers of both America and Europe. Because the translations of these articles and publications are by themselves sufficient to fill a book, they will be published separately.

Sixth is His courage, the potency of His utterances and the power of reasoning in His talks, talks which demonstrated the validity of the Christian teachings in Jewish synagogues and the reality of Islam in Christian churches; His elucidation of the proofs of the existence of God and the immortality of the human soul to the materialists and agnostics; and the offering of solutions to the complex economic problems of the world to gatherings of socialists, the promulgation of the teachings and principles of this new Dispensation with the glad tidings of the appearance of the promised Manifestation of God and the establishment of His dominion in the world and His command to spread this Cause throughout the world. 'Abdu'l-Bahá's talks and discourses will eventually make an enormous collection. Now they are being gradually compiled and will be presented to Him for His approval, after which they will be published.[2]

Seventh is the Master's renunciation of all comfort, rest and concern for His own health in spreading the teachings of God. How many nights He could not sleep despite His overwhelming exhaustion and how many days He found not a moment's rest owing to the rush of people, the gathering of such large numbers and His continuous discussions with them about the Cause of God! His travels over long distances across land and sea left Him no rest or comfort. Each day a new physical weakness and suffering appeared. Nevertheless, He always preferred servitude to the threshold of the Abhá Beauty above His own comfort and health. His constant joy and enthusiasm amazed us. These qualities are not attainable except through the power of the Holy Spirit and assistance from on High.

Eighth is the progress of the Cause and the increase in the numbers of new believers in both Europe and America resulting from 'Abdu'l-Bahá's journey. Many prominent people became aware of the need to investigate the Cause of God and were willing to accept its independent nature.

And ninth is 'Abdu'l-Bahá's selflessness, His refusal to accept assistance, gifts, funds or recompense from anyone; rather, He bestowed aid on the poor and needy in the cities He visited. This had a powerful impact on many souls and amazed them. Before setting out on this journey, 'Abdu'l-Bahá often admonished His entourage that 'In these travels, we shall conform to the saying of Christ that when you leave a city you should be so detached as not to allow even the dust of that place to settle on your garment.'[3]

When 'Abdu'l-Bahá accepted the invitations from the organizers of the peace congresses to travel to America, believers from all parts of the country offered to contribute towards His expenses. They collected a large sum [$16,000] and sent it to Him in two separate drafts. When the first draft arrived, He immediately returned it to its sender. From Alexandria, Egypt, He wrote to Mírzá Ahmad Sohrab, who was then in Washington DC, and firmly instructed him to return the funds immediately to the contributors, telling them that 'Abdu'l-Bahá had sufficient money for the journey, otherwise

He would have accepted their offer. 'Abdu'l-Bahá later revealed many Tablets on this subject which He sent to the friends in America. 'Abdu'l-Bahá's action was widely publicized in various newspapers in Egypt and many non-Bahá'ís were witness to His selflessness and detachment from material wealth.

What follows are some of the great and important results of this historic and blessed journey, the contemplation of which brings great joy and happiness to those who witnessed them. For the sake of brevity, the less important events and daily routine are omitted (even though their sweet savor is greatly appreciated by the friends). The major events of the Master's journey are being recorded daily and will be presented in two volumes. The first volume concerns 'Abdu'l-Bahá's journey to America [this volume]; the other will describe His journeys in Europe.[4] I beseech the Omnipotent God to protect me from errors and omissions, to assist me to elevate His great Cause and to expound His everlasting, mighty Covenant. Verily, He is the Merciful, the Loving and the Most Kind.

INTRODUCTION

Following the Turkish Revolution in 1909, which, among other things, resulted in 'Abdu'l-Bahá's release from the Most Great Prison in 'Akká, Palestine [then a part of the Ottoman Empire], and after He had received many letters from the friends in America, including a booklet with notes and signatures from the believers entreating Him to visit America, He consented to take this momentous journey.

When a number of leaders of churches, synagogues and societies became aware that the Bahá'ís had asked 'Abdu'l-Bahá to visit America, they too sent invitations to Him to attend peace congresses and to meet their congregations. Owing to 'Abdu'l-Bahá's physical condition and health, caused by His long years of imprisonment, He remained in Haifa for some eleven months. Then, exhausted and with many difficulties, He traveled to Egypt and resided in Port Said, Alexandria and Zaytoun for eleven more months. His health improved and He gained His physical strength but still He did not specifically promise to travel to America. Instead, He decided to take a short journey to Switzerland to teach the Cause and for a change of climate. While the Master was there, the Bahá'ís in Paris and London pleaded with Him to visit them. For a period of four months He traveled throughout Europe, bringing the glad tidings of the Cause, and raised the call of Yá Bahá'u'l-Abhá in various gatherings in halls, churches and synagogues.[5]

When the American believers learned of 'Abdu'l-Bahá's travels in Europe, they felt sure that He also would come to America.

Many believers joyfully went to London to be in His presence. They pleaded with Him to continue His journey to America. He did not consent to their request at that time but instead returned to Egypt. During the five months of His stay in Alexandria, each week brought many more invitations from America, until, at last, He said that He would accept. This announcement brought a new spirit to those anxious souls. He often mentioned that, 'This journey is a long one and my body is very weak. We shall remain at sea for more than two weeks; it will be difficult for my body to bear. But as it is for the sake of diffusing the divine fragrances, I shall undertake it, trusting in God and severing myself from all else save Him.'

Some believers suggested that if 'Abdu'l-Bahá traveled to England, His arrival would coincide with the maiden voyage of the *Titanic*, which was believed to be the finest and largest English vessel in the world, and that if He would make His journey on that ship, He would arrive in New York in only five days in comfort and ease. Most of the friends approved of this suggestion. But after brief reflection, 'Abdu'l-Bahá said, 'No, we will go direct, trusting in the assistance and protection of the Blessed Beauty. He is the true Protector and the divine Keeper.' Later, when the tragic news of the sinking of the *Titanic* reached the friends and believers, they were exceedingly grateful that He had not accepted their suggestion.

The Diary

Monday, March 25, 1912
'Abdu'l-Bahá's departure from Ramleh, Alexandria

When 'Abdu'l-Bahá was saying farewell amid the tears, lamentations and sadness of the friends and members of the Holy Family who watched their beloved's departure, one of 'Abdu'l-Bahá's daughters, Rúḥá Khánum, was seriously ill. It was evident that this deeply affected the Master. It was in these circumstances that 'Abdu'l-Bahá left Alexandria on the morning of Monday, March 25, 1912. Although He had already bidden the friends farewell and had embraced most of them, many accompanied Him to the ship, expressing their sadness and anguish at their impending separation from Him. After visiting, walking about the ship and receiving His cabin assignment, 'Abdu'l-Bahá went to the main hall where He bestowed His love, affection and assurance on each of the friends. After an hour, the friends left the ship in tears. Then the S. S. *Cedric*, an Italian liner from the White Star Line,[6] set sail, honored to be the means of transporting the Most Holy Being and becoming the focus of the envy of the whole earth.

The ship left the port of Alexandria with a burst of steam and great fanfare. 'Abdu'l-Bahá's companions numbered six: Shoghi Effendi, Siyyid Asadu'lláh-i-Qumí, Dr Amínu'lláh Faríd, Mírzá Munír-i-Zayn, Áqá Khusraw and this servant, Maḥmúd-i-Zarqání. After the ship left, 'Abdu'l-Bahá went to the first class dining room and gave permission to His companions to have lunch with Him. Although our cabins were in second class, arrangements had been made for us to dine in the first class dining room with Him. 'Abdu'l-Bahá remarked at lunch:

> The doctor of this ship is an Italian and, as Italians are at war with the Turks, the doctor, imagining us to be Turks and

wanting to go to war with us, says that K͟husraw's eyes are affected with a disease which will make him unfit to land in America. He wished to examine the eyes of all, but Dr Faríd prevented him.

Then He told K͟husraw not to worry, that He would try to intercede on his behalf and not allow them to prevent his travel. He said, 'Don't worry; to the extent possible I will not allow you to be sent back. We are ready to give our lives for one another.' 'Abdu'l-Bahá then went to His cabin in the upper deck and rested for awhile. Afternoon tea was served in the main salon of the ship. 'Abdu'l-Bahá spoke about the excessive drinking and eating habits of the Europeans. 'It is hardly two hours since they took their lunch and now they are having a full meal with their tea.' Then He spoke about the Italians, saying that at the time of the Romans they were famous for their knowledge and virtues but now their character seems to have declined like the Greeks. And similarly the Egyptians. He said:

> During the last days of our stay in Egypt, we went to Tanta for the repair of the tomb of Ḥájí Abu'l Qásim and from there went to Mansurih. In Tanta one of the English officials was our friend, who held us in great honor and showed us great respect everywhere. Observing this, the natives were more respectful and polite to us than even to the said officer, and throughout the town, everyone, young and old, even the policemen in the street, saluted us. But, at another time when we went alone to Mansurih, because the people did not observe outward riches, they did not pay any attention to us. This is the condition of hypocritical people who only look to outward appearances.

This evening 'Abdu'l-Bahá did not dine in the main hall but instead the waiter brought His dinner to the cabin. After eating He went to the lounge, rested on a comfortable couch for a short time and then returned to His cabin to sleep.

Tuesday, March 26, 1912
[aboard the *Cedric*]

On the morning of March 26 when I was close by His cabin, 'Abdu'l-Bahá came out and said: 'Last night I slept comfortably. For a long time I could not sleep well on account of the ache in my bones but now it is gone altogether.' I mentioned that the humidity in Port Alexandria was very high and that it must not have been good for His health. 'Yes,' He said, 'the climate here is better because at sea the humidity ascends and thus is not harmful, whereas there is more humidity in coastal regions and this is harmful to health. Besides, an electro-magnetic force is produced by the moving and surging of the water which is very beneficial to health.' Then He added, 'Despite the sea and weather being a bit rough, the rolling of the ship is slight owing to its huge size. Vibration is caused by its being powered by steam and one feels the vibration of the engine more than the movement of the ship.'

When we had all gathered the Master asked Shoghi Effendi to chant a prayer. After the prayer, He went to the dining room for morning tea. He commented, 'This is a divine table. Outwardly it is well adorned. Náṣiri'd-Dín Sháh did not have such a table. Praise be to God that divine confirmations are with us. Those who were hated by the nations of the world are now seated at such a table. One must be grateful.'

One of the servants asked why man is not thankful when in comfort. 'Abdu'l-Bahá replied, 'It is due to negligence. Otherwise one must be aware and thankful when immersed in the sea of bounties.' Then He said, 'I have not had a good bath for several months.' The ship's attendant was then asked to prepare a warm fresh water bath for Him. Afterwards, He said, 'I am much better now. For a long time I have not had leisure to take a real bath.'

When Mírzá Munír stated that one of the Arab travelers had spoken to him about Mírzá Kheiralla's arrogance and heedlessness, 'Abdu'l-Bahá replied:

The poor man has become nameless and debased both in this world and in the Kingdom. What a high honor he had! But as he did not appreciate the fact, it all came to naught. He wished to be made the leader of America and wrote plainly to me to this effect. One of the answers I gave him was, 'Cast aside all mention of the ruler and the ruled, the governor and the governed.'

Siyyid Asadu'lláh remarked that 'leadership must be wielded with obedience to the Cause of God'. 'Abdu'l-Bahá said: 'If a man considers himself humble and lowly in the Cause of God, he becomes glorified in all eyes. On the other hand, the moment he aspires to personal greatness, he falls into disgrace and oblivion.'

At this point a refined lady approached 'Abdu'l-Bahá and with the aid of an interpreter said that she lived in New York City and had heard something about the Bahá'í teachings. 'I knew you were in Egypt,' she said, 'and when from a distance I saw your august personage on this ship, it occurred to me that you might be 'Abdu'l-Bahá.' 'Abdu'l-Bahá said, 'The heart, when pure and free, becomes inspired. It is evident from your having been transformed in such a short time that there is a spiritual link between pure hearts.' The woman told the Master that she was a Unitarian and requested Him to send a message through her to the Unitarian congregation. 'Abdu'l-Bahá replied:

> The most important of all intentions is to spread the love of God, to establish harmony and oneness among the people. This is what distinguishes man from animals. Hence, tell your community in America:
>
> Glad tidings, glad tidings,
>   the Sun of love has dawned.
> Glad tidings, glad tidings,
>   the table of fellowship is spread.
> Glad tidings, glad tidings,
>   the standard of the Kingdom is hoisted.

Glad tidings, glad tidings,
  the divine springtime has appeared.
Glad tidings, glad tidings,
  the clouds of mercy have rained.
Glad tidings, glad tidings,
  the trees of the garden of humanity have become green and verdant.
Glad tidings, glad tidings,
  the Herald of the Kingdom has raised His voice.

The woman was so impressed and moved that she came into His presence every day and shared with many passengers the teachings and principles of the Bahá'í Faith.

Lunch was usually served at 1:00 p.m. At the table, 'Abdu'l-Bahá showered His love and blessings on His companions. In the afternoon, the same lady again entered His presence and heard from Him a detailed explanation of the extraordinary forces which govern the material world, although the human kingdom, He explained, is above the laws of nature.

Afternoon tea was served in 'Abdu'l-Bahá's cabin but owing to the extreme motion of the ship, He had no appetite.

Wednesday, March 27, 1912
[aboard the *Cedric*]

The following morning 'Abdu'l-Bahá visited the cabins of His companions while some were still asleep. He stopped at each cabin for a few minutes to inquire about its occupant's health and condition, bestowing upon each His love and affection. When we were all gathered at the table in the dining room on the upper deck, 'Abdu'l-Bahá directed Shoghi Effendi to chant a prayer. During the prayer, many passengers became interested in the gathering and watched 'Abdu'l-Bahá as He sat with His companions. They listened to the chanting of prayers with complete concentration, respect and courtesy. Observing this scene and the manner in which 'Abdu'l-Bahá would rise, sit and speak, they became interested and all their attention was directed towards the majesty and beauty of the Center of the Covenant.

At lunchtime the Master came to the table and said, 'Your cabins below are not good, you must move up.' We explained that although there were better cabins on the second deck, because we were from the East, they had not given them to us. 'They treat us as poorly as they can because they do not believe in God or in salvation.' 'Abdu'l-Bahá replied: 'If some of them appear to behave with trustworthiness and honesty, it is merely for personal esteem, in order to be held in favorable regard, and for name and fame, rather than for the sake of promoting humane values, righteousness, the fear of God and love of truth.'

The Russian Consul, who was on the ship, came into 'Abdu'l-Bahá's presence while He was speaking about Sufism and how the leaders of the Ishraq doctrine believed they could discover the reality of the material world through spiritual inspiration whereas the Peripatetics believed that comprehension of the reality of the material world depends on education and training.[7] 'Abdu'l-Bahá gave a description of Sufism, explaining that the Sufis believe the world of existence to be like the sea and all creation the waves of that sea. When the Russian Consul asked 'Abdu'l-Bahá about the soul, He gave a description of its nature and progress, explaining that the abstract is not comprehended by the senses and that the lesser kingdoms can never understand the higher ones. 'Abdu'l-Bahá then described the signs and indications of the existence of the soul. The Consul was quite fascinated. As he was traveling only as far as Naples, he said his farewells with extreme courtesy and sincerity.

An American came to see the Master in the late afternoon and spoke to Him about his travels around the world. 'Abdu'l-Bahá told him, 'You have traveled in this world; I hope you will now traverse the world of the Kingdom and become a wayfarer in the realms of the spirit.' The American asked whether the Bahá'í Faith accepted the Bible. 'Abdu'l-Bahá replied:

This Cause acknowledges the truth of all the Books and all the Manifestations of God. The heavenly teachings are composed of two kinds of commandments. One kind is concerned with spiritual verities, with the perfections and virtues of the world of humanity. These commandments never change or alter. Each of the Books and the Prophets was the promulgator of these principles upon which all the religions are based, hence the foundation of all the divine religions is one. The second category of commandments is concerned with material principles and social issues. These are altered according to the exigencies of the age. For example, at the time of Christ the social laws of the Torah were changed.

The American then asked about reincarnation. 'Abdu'l-Bahá answered:

> It is not as people have understood. What is intended is the return of pre-existent attributes and perfections in new forms. Moreover, in all realms of existence the spirits are in a state of development; for instance, the mineral spirit ascends and progresses to the vegetable kingdom, and the vegetable spirit to the animal kingdom, and the animal spirit to the human kingdom. In like manner, the human spirit ascends into the divine worlds and the exalted realms.

On another occasion this same person came to 'Abdu'l-Bahá and brought with him some Chinese and Japanese idol figurines to show Him. The Master remarked:

> What a great difference exists between men. One person degrades himself to such a degree that he idolizes and worships stones, lifeless images, motionless effigies, notwithstanding that God has given him understanding and favored him with the honored robe of humanity! Another person reaches such a pinnacle of perfection that he becomes a sign of God and an

educator of the world of humanity! Consider what a great distance there is between the one and the other. Although the object of both Buddha and Krishna was the one God and they proclaimed the unity of God, yet now their followers cling to and believe in idols and images.

During 'Abdu'l-Bahá's conversation many others joined us and were moved by His words. Several visitors asked for permission to arrange a large meeting where He could speak. They prepared a poster and placed it on the main bulletin board of the ship: 'His Honor, 'Abbás Effendi, will speak on the subject of the Bahá'í Faith in the first class main auditorium.' This announcement attracted many passengers, men and women alike.

After dinner, 'Abdu'l-Bahá gave a comprehensive talk to an audience of well over five hundred people. First He described the potential of the human race and the high station and virtues of the human kingdom. 'In spite of these potentialities,' 'Abdu'l-Bahá said, 'humanity has not attained maturity, and human beings, depriving themselves of these divine favors, seek glory in war and bloodshed.'

'Abdu'l-Bahá then spoke about the new Manifestation of God, the teachings of Bahá'u'lláh and His spiritual influence on the world. After His talk everyone was happy. Many shook the Master's hand, all, with the exception of a few priests and prejudiced Italians, delighted to be in His presence. From then on, more and more people came to see 'Abdu'l-Bahá in both public and private gatherings and His talks were translated sentence by sentence.

In the afternoon the ship approached the Strait of Messina and volcanoes could be seen in the distance. 'Abdu'l-Bahá remarked:

> The real volcanoes which lay waste the cities and towns are the battleships which are aptly named in Arabic 'Mudammir', that is, 'destroyer'. Without doubt these are the destroyers of the edifice of humanity. When will the time come that these battleships will be diverted from performing such ruinous tasks and become vessels for the transportation of people?

When the city of Messina appeared on the horizon, nestling in the bosom of the mountain, illuminated by lights, that piece of earth appeared to be a heaven with stars shining brightly. It was a majestic sight, the more so because it was being observed and enjoyed by 'Abdu'l-Bahá.

Thursday morning, March 28, 1912
[aboard the *Cedric*]

Naples, one of Italy's most important cities, appeared on the horizon and was seen by 'Abdu'l-Bahá. The ship docked. At this time Italy and Turkey were at war; the hatred between them was so intense that if the enemy were observed in one country, he would be harmed and abused by its inhabitants without question. Because of this, the friends urged the Master and His companions not to disembark at Naples because their Eastern attire and Turkish fezes would incite the hatred of the local people. Thus 'Abdu'l-Bahá did not leave the ship at Naples but instead looked at the city, its gardens and buildings from the deck of the ship. He spoke much that day about the hardworking laborers and workers' rights, about how hard they work and how desperate and needy their lives are:

> What hardship these coal miners have to suffer, how poor and needy they are! It is necessary for the directors of companies and the owners of factories to allot a certain share, however small it may be, to their laborers so that their condition may be improved and they may be deterred from striking.

Friday, March 29, 1912
[aboard the *Cedric*]

Some American Bahá'ís who were waiting for the steamer boarded the ship to see 'Abdu'l-Bahá. Among them were Mr and Mrs [Percy] Woodcock and their daughter from Canada, Mr and Mrs Austin from Denver, Colorado, and Miss [Louisa] Mathew, a friend from London, who made the rest of the journey with them to New York.

It became known that a group of physicians from Naples was to board the ship to examine the eyes of the passengers. The ship's doctor had already given his opinion about the infection of Áqá Khusraw's eyes. When these physicians examined the passengers' eyes they said that the eyes of Shoghi Effendi and Mírzá Muníri-Zayn were also infected and that they must leave the ship. The efforts of 'Abdu'l-Bahá, His companions and the American friends were of no avail and apparently were not in accord with God's mysterious will and plan. The physicians insisted that even if these friends continued their journey to New York, they would not be allowed to disembark and would have to return. Therefore 'Abdu'l-Bahá asked the three to obey.

Saturday, March 30, 1912
[aboard the *Cedric*]

'Abdu'l-Bahá bestowed upon those three souls His utmost kindness and blessings and bade them farewell. With great sadness and dejection they left the ship. The Master's heart was broken and all of the companions were very sad. 'Abdu'l-Bahá said, 'There is a wisdom in this matter which will become known later.' Much of His time that day was spent on this issue until the steamer left Naples for New York in the afternoon.

'Abdu'l-Bahá's companions were now three Persians – Siyyid Asadu'lláh-i-Qumí, Dr Faríd and myself – and the six Americans – Mr and Mrs Woodcock, Miss Woodcock, Mr and Mrs Austin and Miss Mathew, who with great joy remained in the presence of their beloved Lord. We were all of us now in first class near 'Abdu'l-Bahá.

In the afternoon the Master invited us to His cabin for tea. He later took His dinner in the main salon and said, 'I have come to the table tonight out of regard for you and have even taken a hearty meal.' Then He remarked:

*Mírzá Maḥmúd-i-Zarqání, the chronicler
of 'Abdu'l-Bahá's journey to the West*

Dr Amín Faríd, right, *with Chicago Baháʼís, 1903. He translated many of ʻAbduʼl-Baháʼs talks in the West but later disgraced himself*

Shoghi Effendi, indicated by an x, in 1913, around the time of ʻAbduʼl-Baháʼs return from His Western travels

Siyyid Asadu'lláh-i-Qúmí, a member of 'Abdu'l-Bahá's entourage

Louisa Mathew, who traveled on the steamer with Abdu'l-Bahá to American in 1912

Juliet Thompson, who was devoted to 'Abdu'l-Bahá and was permitted to paint His portrait

'Abdu'l-Bahá with Edward and Carrie Kinney and their children in New York. The Master gave His first talk in America in their home on April 11, 1912

Above left: *Mountfort Mills, a prominent New York lawyer in whose home 'Abdu'l-Bahá spoke.* Above right: *Howard MacNutt, whose misunderstanding of the station of 'Abdu'l-Bahá caused disunity in the Bahá'í community. He publicly repented in November 1912*

Arthur P. Dodge, left, *with 'Abdu'l-Bahá and His entourage, taken along Riverside Drive, New York*

At Grand Central Station, New York

John and Louise Bosch. John Bosch came from California to New York especially to see 'Abdu'l-Bahá

Edward Getsinger, who traveled as part of 'Abdu'l-Bahá's retinue

'Abdu'l-Bahá standing before Agnes Parsons's house in Washington DC

Mrs Agnes Parsons with 'Abdu'l-Bahá. Mrs Parsons was the Master's hostess during His stay in Washington DC

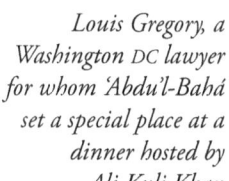

Louis Gregory, a Washington DC lawyer for whom 'Abdu'l-Bahá set a special place at a dinner hosted by Ali Kuli Khan

'Abdu'l-Bahá with Ali Kuli Khan and Madam Florence Khan, taken in New York City. Ali Kuli Khan was the Persian Charge d'Affaires

'Abdu'l-Bahá with Yúsuf Ḍíyá Páshá, the Turkish Ambassador,
left, *and Siyyid Asadu'lláh-i-Qúmí,* center

*Ahmad Sohrab, who translated many of
'Abdu'l-Bahá's Tablets into English*

Left to right: Zia Bagdadi, unknown man, unknown woman, Mírzá Valíyu'lláh Khán, Pauline Hannen, Ambassador Yúsuf Ḍíyá Páshá of Turkey, Fanny Knobloch, 'Abdu'l-Bahá, unknown woman, Siyyid Asadu'lláh, Ali Kuli Khan

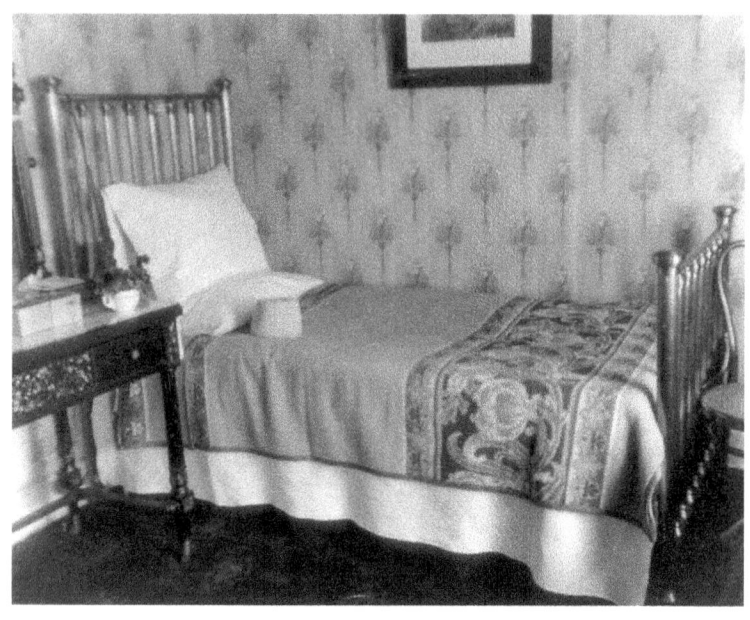

The bed used by 'Abdu'l-Bahá at the Plaza Hotel, Chicago

Dr Zia Bagdadi, who represented the Arab Bahá'ís at the laying of the corner-stone of the Wilmette House of Worship

'Abdu'l-Bahá addresses the Bahá'ís gathered at the Temple site, Wilmette, May 1, 1912

Breaking the ground at the Temple site, each race and nation taking a turn

A souvenir of some soil from the excavation at the Temple site

These Italians took us for Turks. They sent a report to this effect and stopped three of our party from proceeding. One was a secretary, the other a cook. If they had stopped only these two it would have mattered little. But why should they treat that tender youth Shoghi Effendi so harshly? They have treated us with injustice; nevertheless I have always helped and am still helping them, whether at Alexandria or at Haifa. It has invariably happened that the friends of God have been afflicted. How sorely the disciples of Christ were persecuted on the ship and with what great affliction they were carried to Rome.

That evening the Master and His company of friends and believers presented a very unusual and beautiful sight, the intermingling of the Eastern and Western friends attracting all eyes.

Sunday, March 31, 1912
[aboard the *Cedric*]

The Master visited the cabins of His companions and inquired about each person's health. He then took tea in His cabin. When He came out, the American friends remarked that today was Sunday and that every Sunday morning the salon was converted into a church for prayers. He replied, 'You should also go and join in.' Therefore the friends attended the prayer services. Afterwards 'Abdu'l-Bahá spoke to us about Mrs [Phoebe] Hearst and said that she had contributed £500 to repair the road to the Shrine of the Báb. 'Abdu'l-Bahá, in turn, had sent her a very valuable ring that He had been able to purchase for a modest price. However, as she was very wealthy, the enemies of the Cause [the Covenant-Breakers] imagined that she had helped the Cause, although, as a matter of fact, she had received much more than she had given.

Today 'Abdu'l-Bahá took His meal in His cabin. After a taking little rest, He invited the American friends to His cabin and spoke to them about His journey from Ṭihrán to Baghdád made during the severe winter without proper accommodation or clothing.[8]

'There was so much snow and it was so cold', He said, 'that my feet were frostbitten. To this day my toes are affected by cold weather.' Later He gave an account of Mírzá Yaḥyá and his followers and of the complaints they made to Edward G. Browne:

> They tampered with the contents of the history of Ḥájí Mírzá Jání by removing some of its passages and inserting others. They sent it to the libraries of London and Paris and through such falsehood induced him [Browne] to translate and publish the document. In order to achieve his own selfish desires, he had it printed.

In the afternoon 'Abdu'l-Bahá invited all the believers to His cabin for tea. He then sent a cable to Ramleh in Alexandria informing them of His good health and inquiring after the well-being of the Greatest Holy Leaf [Bahíyyih Khánum]. At the dinner table in the evening 'Abdu'l-Bahá's conversation centered around the point that every created thing is subject to change. 'All created things', He said, 'are subject to change and transformation. Every youth will grow old and every sapling will become an old tree and everything old will decay and perish.' Similarly, He said, each one of the religions of the world has at one time been the cause of progress but each has become like an old tree, devoid of truth. The people of this age hope that these trees will again bear flowers and fruits but this is impossible. Thus, for instance, the Hindu and Buddhist expect to regain the progress of the times of Brahma and Buddha.

Monday, April 1, 1912
[aboard the *Cedric*]

A narrow-minded clergymen on board came to visit the Master. 'Abdu'l-Bahá spoke extensively to this visitor according to his capacity and discussed in detail the problems of people who veil themselves from reality. The visitor left Him most reverently.

The health of the Master is improving daily. The sea has

become even more calm and the winds more favorable and the friends and companions are even more honored and thankful to be in His court of bounty and favor.

In the afternoon, as 'Abdu'l-Bahá was walking in front of His cabin, Mr and Mrs Austin joined Him. They told Him about the founder of the famous school in Rome, Mrs Montessori. The majority of the students are orphans whose parents perished in the earthquake in Messina. She has managed the school in such a way that now most of the schools in Europe and America are following her standards. 'Abdu'l-Bahá said:

> The more the Catholics showed prejudice, the more they were debased. Only now have they shown willingness to accept the new measures. Otherwise, these persons are the most prejudiced of all religions. At present, in every quarter of Paris, the Catholic clergymen observe only trifling religious rituals. Officially they are engaged in attending to funerals and other ceremonies and have nothing at all to do with other matters. God has disgraced the ministers of religions. Whatever they do debases them more and more. The decay of the nations and the degradation of the people have always proceeded from the ministers of religion.

Tuesday, April 2, 1912
[aboard the *Cedric*]

The Master again spoke on the subject of the spiritual illness and self-serving motives of the heads of various religions. One of the friends asked Him about the leaders and Hands of the Cause in this Dispensation. He said:

> The Blessed Perfection has extirpated superstitions, root and branch. The Hands of the Cause in this dispensation are not heirs to any name or title; rather, they are sanctified souls, the rays of whose holiness and spirituality throw light on the hearts

of all. Hearts are attracted by the beauty of their morals, the sincerity of their intentions, and their sense of equity and justice. Souls are involuntarily enamored of their praiseworthy morals and laudable attributes. Faces turn in spontaneous attraction to their outstanding qualities and actions. 'Hand of the Cause' is not a title that may be awarded to whomever it may please to have it, nor is it a chair of honor upon which whoever wishes may sit. The Hands of the Cause are the hands of God. Therefore, whomsoever is the servant and promoter of the Word of God, he is the hand of God. The object is a matter of the spirit and not one of letters or words. The more self-effacing one is, the more assisted he is in the Cause of God; and the more meek and humble, the nearer he is to God.

'Abdu'l-Bahá took His midday meal in His cabin. In the afternoon He invited the believers and the Western ladies for tea in the library, serving them tea and sweets. He then spoke to them about various types of transportation such as ships, trains, carriages and so on. 'They are', He said, 'good for long and tedious journeys; but for recreation and holiday trips, horseback riding in the spring season in the country, which is full of flowers and green foliage and sparkling waters, is the best of all, and gives a unique pleasure.' The friends also spoke about dirigibles and airplanes. 'Abdu'l-Bahá said:

> Those who have provided the means for transporting arms and ammunition and the instruments of wars and massacres on earth will do so in the air. There will come to exist such instruments as to cause all the means of destruction in the past to be looked upon as children's playthings.

At the table that night Mr Woodcock asked about the difference between the soul and the spirit. 'Abdu'l-Bahá said:

> The soul is a link between the body and the spirit. It receives

bounties and virtues from the spirit and gives them to the body just as the outward senses carry to the inward senses what they receive from the outer world in order that it may remain deposited in the memory and may be made serviceable by man through his power.

Wednesday, April 3, 1912
[aboard the *Cedric*]

Gibraltar, an important naval center for the European powers, came into view and the steamer entered the straits. 'Abdu'l-Bahá looked towards the left with field glasses. He then spoke about Gibraltar, Spain, Algiers and about the Muslim victories, giving an account of their sincere religious leaders. 'What a magnificent honor', He said, 'God bestowed on the Muslims in the beginning, and what a disgrace they accepted for themselves in the end.'

Our American friends requested that the Master ask us, the Persians, to alter our attire to suit the circumstances of the time and place, changing everything except our Persian hats and coats. He replied, 'What harm is there in it? I do not care much about what is unimportant and what is not harmful to the Cause. They are trifles.' Then He began to stroll back and forth, as was His custom every morning and evening on the deck, and continued to speak:

> In past ages crossing the ocean was not as easy as it is now. Up to the present time no one has traveled, with a purpose like ours, from Persia to America. Some have made the journey but it was for their personal gain or for trivial motives. Ours may be said to be the first voyage of Easterners to America. I have strong hopes of divine assistance – that He will open the doors of victory and conquest on all sides. Today, all the nations of the world are vanquished, and victory and glory revolve around the servants of the Blessed Perfection. All aims will come to naught except this mighty aim. Hardship and

debasement in this path are, therefore, comfort and honor, and affliction a blessing.

Thursday, April 4, 1912
[aboard the *Cedric*]

The Master was slightly indisposed today. He took a little mineral water. Later in the day the conversation was mainly about Columbus, who, intending to reach India, traveled by sea in a straight line from east to west, and, on reaching land, found himself on the shores of the American continent. 'Really,' 'Abdu'l-Bahá said, 'how much trouble these people undergo merely for outward benefits. How many lives have been lost only in an effort to explore the North Pole and for worldly renown.' He related a story:

> Once one of the Europeans fell overboard in a storm at sea and his fellow passengers saved him. However, he lamented to himself, 'Oh, why wasn't I drowned so that the publications of the incident in the newspapers would have spread my name in all countries?' These people accept death for trifling affairs but they never take a step in the path of the Cause of God.

Then the Master spoke about Nabíl-i-Zarandí, saying, 'The true worth of such personages will be appreciated in the future.' He described the disloyalty of the Covenant-breakers and the people of sedition. Later that afternoon, He revealed a long Tablet in honor of Afnán-i-Yazdí.

For dinner a little soup especially prepared for 'Abdu'l-Bahá was brought to the table. His general condition improved after dinner and He sat on the deck for a long time. That night He praised the music, which is always heard after breakfast and dinner, and He sent the musicians four pounds as a tip.

Friday, April 5, 1912
[aboard the *Cedric*]

Very early in the morning the Master called some of us to His cabin and said that He was tired. After taking a bath and drinking some tea He felt better and came out of His cabin. The weather was fine and the sea very calm. In the distance one could see the Atlantic islands. The Master strolled up and down the deck observing the islands through field glasses. He breakfasted in His cabin on chicken cooked especially for Him.

In the afternoon some of the friends and other passengers gathered around Him in the salon. Among them was an American gentlemen, a newspaper publisher. The conversation with him was first about Persia and then he inquired about 'Abdu'l-Bahá's journey. 'Abdu'l-Bahá replied:

> I am going to America at the invitation of peace congresses, as the fundamental principles of this Cause are universal peace, the oneness of the world of humanity and the equality of the rights of men. As this age is the age of lights and the century of mysteries, this lofty purpose is sure to be universally acknowledged and this Most Mighty Cause is certain to embrace the East and the West.

The Master's talk was very expressive and the listeners were delighted, especially the newspaper publisher, who said farewell to the Master with the utmost reverence. He even wanted to kiss the Master's hand but 'Abdu'l-Bahá stopped him and instead gave him His own prayer beads.[9]

Day by day the admiration of the passengers and the ship's personnel for the Master increases. Whenever they pass by Him, they bow, removing their hats in respect. After supper the Master sat for awhile and spoke about a universal language.

Saturday, April 6, 1912
[aboard the *Cedric*]

While having tea in His cabin 'Abdu'l-Bahá gave instructions concerning our arrival in New York City: 'We shall reach New York in a few days. We shall stay in hotels at each place and not trouble the believers. However, if meetings are arranged in their homes, it will not matter.' He continued, 'Go to the table and have your tea.'

The Master spent the morning writing Tablets until noon and then went to the dining room table. He was asked for guidance about food. He said, 'We shall not interfere with their bodily food. Our concern is with spiritual food.'

In the afternoon He invited the Western friends to His presence and related a history of the Cause and the difficulties and persecutions of the early days. One the Tablets revealed today was a long prayer, a Tablet of visitation in honor of Hájí Muḥammad-Taqí, the Afnán, and another was a Tablet in His own hand. Regarding this Tablet He summoned us, saying:

> Come here and consider this important question. A person from Ṭihrán has written that the Universal Will is always manifest; that is to say, God is always manifest in human form. I have sent him an emphatic reply and urge you also to remember that between two Manifestations there are days of concealment. There is no doubt that for the Sun of Reality there is no rising or setting in its own sanctified center but, owing to the exigencies of the contingent world, it rises and sets. Those persons who say in the days of concealment and interval that God is manifest in human form and that 'He always shows Himself in different forms like an artful beloved'[10] are the sources of difference in the Cause and create discord among the people. All these evasive statements of theirs are mere pretensions. Their only object is to get themselves known as persons in whom divine signs are centered. We must, therefore, adhere to the explicit text, to the literal meaning of

what is written in the Tablets, and must not deviate from this even to a hair's breadth.

While walking in the stern of the ship in the afternoon 'Abdu'l-Bahá said: 'It is the twelfth day of our voyage. We have traveled a quarter of the way around the globe and have traversed six degrees of longitude. Here it is afternoon, while in Egypt it is the middle of the night at this time.'

In the evening some clergymen announced a meeting to observe the crucifixion of Christ. The Master remarked, 'Their speeches in the meeting will be to the effect that Christ sacrificed Himself in order to redeem us from our sins. But they do not understand the inner meaning.' After the meeting He spoke extensively on this subject. 'The redemption of sins', He said, 'depends on our acting upon the admonitions of Christ, and the martyrdom of Christ was to cause us to attain praiseworthy morals and supreme stations.'

Sunday, April 7, 1912
[aboard the *Cedric*]

Before His morning tea 'Abdu'l-Bahá requested that prayers be chanted. He offered thanks for the protection and assistance of the Abhá Beauty. When all of the Western and Persian friends were seated at the table for tea, He reverently expressed His thanks and gratitude for the divine favors. Each one of the friends was honored to be in His presence and asked themselves, 'What am I seeing? Is it a dream or reality?'

In the afternoon some of the Western friends and a few passengers came to meet Him. He spoke in detail about the Bahá'í teachings of the oneness of humanity, universal peace and the raising of the tent of brotherhood and union. Everyone was interested and their hearts filled with joy and happiness to an even greater extent than before.

Monday, April 8, 1912
[aboard the *Cedric*]

Although tired from the sea voyage, the Master wrote Tablets to the Bahá'ís in Ṭihrán. He took no food except milk until midday.

Wireless telegrams were received from the Bahá'ís in California and Chicago, expressing their joy at the Master's journey and conveying their happiness and devotion to the Cause.

Some of the passengers brought their children to visit 'Abdu'l-Bahá. He showered them with His blessings and loving-kindness, so much so that the children did not want to leave Him. 'The Blessed Beauty', He said, 'has taught us to love children and to be the lovers of the whole human race.'

The Master's discourse today was mainly on the advantages and benefits of love and unity among humankind and the harm and terrible results of prejudice, blind imitation and disunity.

Tuesday, April 9, 1912
[aboard the *Cedric*]

While having His morning tea the Master remarked:

> We shall be at sea for another day. Steam power is truly a wonderful thing. If there were no such power, how would the vast oceans have been crossed? What wonderful means God has supplied and what confirmations the Blessed Beauty has conferred. Otherwise, how could we be here? What have we in common with these places?[11]

As the post was being readied to send 'Abdu'l-Bahá's letters to the friends in the East from New York, a wireless arrived from the friends in New York congratulating Him on His arrival and welcoming Him.

An American doctor came to visit 'Abdu'l-Bahá. The Master spoke with him for about an hour on the history of the Faith, the persecutions and afflictions suffered by the Ancient Beauty, His imprisonment, the teachings and other subjects.

At the breakfast table the Master said, 'I will take only a little soup. I have no appetite for the shipboard food.'

In the afternoon the believers and some Western ladies found great spiritual joy in the Master's presence as He told them of the influence of the Cause in promoting unity, love and fellowship among the peoples of the world.

The Italian physician, mentioned above, noticing the devotion of those surrounding the Master, became more respectful and even bowed when passing Him; in the evening He came into 'Abdu'l-Bahá's presence with the utmost reverence. When the Master mentioned Shoghi Effendi, Mírzá Munír and Áqá Khusraw, the doctor said that he did not know anything about Shoghi Effendi's eyes, that he had only examined Khusraw's eyes and that the fault lay with the group of doctors from Naples. He begged the Master's pardon.

Later in the evening the Italian Consul and other passengers, group by group, visited 'Abdu'l-Bahá. They were pleased with the teachings of Bahá'u'lláh and expressed their hope that these principles and doctrines would make great progress in America. Some expressed their faith and asked for 'Abdu'l-Bahá's address in New York. As this was the last night of the voyage, one by one they bade farewell to the Master and took their leave. At 9:00 p.m. the lights of New York appeared shimmering in the distance and the steamer anchored offshore near the breakwater to enter the harbor the next morning.

Wednesday, April 10, 1912
[Wednesday, April 10, 1912][12]
'Abdu'l-Bahá's arrival in New York City

After morning tea, the Master instructed that telegrams be sent to the Assemblies in both the East and the West informing the believers of His safe arrival. Then He said:

No one thought at the time of our departure from Ramleh that this voyage would be so enjoyable, that the great ocean would be crossed so easily and that my health would withstand the voyage in such manner!

One of the companions remarked that the confirmation of the Abhá Kingdom is ever with the Supporter of the Covenant and that all the people on the ship had remarked that the great ocean had never been so calm at this time of the year.

While the Master was having breakfast in the dining room, telegrams were pouring in from the American Bahá'í Assemblies expressing their great joy and congratulating Him upon the safe arrival of the steamer. The Statue of Liberty, standing majestically in mid-water, came into the Master's view.[13] He ordered the luggage to be kept in readiness. As the ship came alongside the wharf, many tall buildings, including two enormous buildings 45 and 35 stories high, loomed into view.[14]

Many Bahá'í friends from New York and surrounding areas were waiting in line on the jetty, waving their hats and handkerchiefs in happiness. The Master, however, did not come out from His cabin.

When the boat anchored, some newspaper reporters came on board to see 'Abdu'l-Bahá to ask Him about the purpose of His journey. He replied:

> Our object is universal peace and the unity of humankind. I have traveled to Paris and London and now I have come to America to meet with those who seek universal peace and I hope that the peace societies of America will take the lead in promoting this end.

They asked, 'How can universal peace be achieved?' 'Abdu'l-Bahá answered:

Its realization is through the attraction and support of world public opinion. Today universal peace is the panacea for all human life.

They questioned, 'What are these ills?' He answered:

One of these ills is the people's restlessness and discontent under the yoke of the war expenditures of the world's governments. What the people earn through hard labor is extorted from them by the governments and spent for purposes of war. And every day they increase these expenditures. Thus the burden on men becomes more and more unbearable and the tribulations of the people become more and more severe. This is one of the great ills of the day. What a great tribulation there is in the countries of Italy and Turkey in these days! The fathers hear of the death of their sons and the sons are distressed on hearing the news of the death of their fathers. What cities are laid to ruin and what rising fortunes are thrown to the winds! The antidote for this great ill is world peace, which is the source of universal tranquillity.

They then asked: 'Is it not possible that peace can become the cause of trouble and war the means of progress?' He replied:

No. It is war which is today the cause of all trouble. If all would lay down their arms, they would be freed from all difficulties and every misery would be changed into relief. However, this cannot be brought about except through education and the development of people's thoughts and ideas.

This sort of exchange continued, the Master giving full and thorough answers to their questions. The reporters then asked for permission to take photographs of the Master for their newspapers, and 'Abdu'l-Bahá agreed.

The friends were waiting impatiently to see the Master but He instructed them to go to Mr [Edward] Kinney's house where He would see them in the afternoon. Thus the friends departed, except for a few who had already come on board and were honored to meet Him.[15]

After distributing gifts among the crew, 'Abdu'l-Bahá disembarked, thereby blessing American soil, the recipient of everlasting honor, with the footsteps of the Beauty of the Divine Covenant. I wrote an ode in tribute to this blessed voyage:

> The Beloved of the East and the Supreme Spirit of Persia
>   crossed the Atlantic Ocean,
> Each second replete with joyful acclamations
>   exclaiming from the *Cedric*
> That the King of Kings of the Covenant and the Monarch
>   of Devotion
>   had consented to come to America.
> He was welcomed with open arms
>   and the earth became the envy of heaven.
> Existence itself nudged the world of being.
> The sea raised its ceaseless voice
>   that the King of Kings of the Covenant
>   had consented to come to America.
> On the tenth of April 1912 the illustrious and
>   beauteous Beloved
>   reached New York to a great and wondrous welcome,
> While heavenly angels proclaimed the glad tidings
>   that the King of Kings of the Covenant
>   had consented to come to America.

The first meeting between the believers and the Master was that afternoon at Mr Kinney's home.

After leaving the ship the Master went to the Hotel Ansonia. After some tea, He went to the meeting with the friends. And what a wonderful meeting it was![16] The friends were so full of joy and happiness that it seemed the very walls were immersed in rapture and ecstasy. Because it was so crowded, many had to stand. When the initial excitement abated, the Master gave thanks and gratitude to the Blessed Beauty for His assistance and then spoke about the power and influence of the holy utterances to attract and cement the hearts, unifying the East and West.

Because of the crowded conditions and excessive heat, the Master left the meeting and returned to His hotel. As He left the gathering, each believer approached Him, greeted Him with 'Alláh-u-Abhá', shook His hand and took hold of His *'abá* [cloak], requesting prayers for assistance and confirmation.

They continued to surround Him until He entered His carriage and left for the hotel. Upon His arrival, He again offered thanks for the assistance of the Blessed Beauty and gratitude for the help and protection of the Abhá Kingdom.

The Hotel Ansonia is one of the landmark buildings in New York and is 17 stories high. The Master's suite was on the seventh floor and had two bedrooms, a drawing room, a kitchen and a bathroom, all completely furnished. The rent for the Master's apartment was £4 per day, exclusive of board and incidental expenses.

Thursday, April 11, 1912[17]
[New York]

Some friends came to visit 'Abdu'l-Bahá. A newspaper reporter came and asked about the purpose of the Master's journey. He replied:

> I have come to visit the peace societies of America because the fundamental principles of our Cause are universal peace and the promotion of the basic doctrine of the oneness and truth of all the divine religions. Differences between religions are due to misunderstanding and imitation. If these imitations were to be eliminated, all religions would be united.

The Master gave many such eloquent responses to the reporter's questions and ended with a discussion about the rights of women, the discouragement of polygamy and other social ills.

As 'Abdu'l-Bahá had been mentioned in the newspapers as 'The Prophet of the East', He said to the correspondent, 'I am not a prophet; I am a servant of God. My name is 'Abdu'l-Bahá [the servant of Bahá]'. Although the Master disclaimed the station of a Prophet, many newspapers, in describing His many qualities and attributes, continued to refer to Him as the 'Prophet of the East' and the 'Messenger of Peace'.

After He had revealed several Tablets in honor of some of the assemblies in America and had given instructions regarding the arrangement of meetings, He granted an audience to other representatives of the press who had earlier telephoned asking permission for an interview. He spoke at length about the unity of the principles of religions, the necessity for universal peace, the importance of a spiritual civilization, as well as the importance of education and the progress of women. The reporters took down all of His statements and published them in the newspapers. Representatives from other magazines and journals took more photographs of the Master and printed them in their publications. As a result, there were continuous calls requesting public and private meetings with Him. The friends also telephoned inquiring about the Master's health and well-being.

There was a public meeting in the afternoon at the home of Mr Howard MacNutt[18] and another meeting that evening at the home of Miss Phillips.[19] The Master expressed His happiness at meeting with the friends, exhorting them to be obedient to the Will and Testament of Bahá'u'lláh and to distinguish themselves among the peoples and nations of the world. Hundreds of people attended each meeting, all standing as the Master entered and calling out 'Alláh-u-Abhá'. When the time came for Him to leave, each went forward with great joy and happiness to shake His hand and to beg confirmation from Him. When 'Abdu'l-Bahá went to the waiting carriage, they stood surrounding it until He drove away.

Friday, April 12, 1912[20]
[New York]

Group after group of believers from New York and the surrounding areas came to visit. There were also many seekers who were interested and desired to visit the Master. Some clergymen also visited. The Master spoke to them, saying:

> Material and spiritual matters have always advanced hand in hand but at the present time the material side is predominant and the divine principles have been neglected and thrown aside and forgotten. One of the chief reasons for this growing apathy is that the ministers of religion have taught that religion is opposed to science and reason and have thus enforced imitation. You must, therefore, relate religious verities to science.

Then He added:

> The appearance of the divine Manifestations is like the coming of springtime. It is self-evident that spring does not remain forever. We pray that the divine Spring may again be the cause of the rejuvenation of the garden of existence.

At the end of His talk 'Abdu'l-Bahá discouraged everyone from war and disunity and urged all to peace and unity. The clergymen were so transformed that they remarked as with one voice, 'We have attempted for many years to portray and promote the spiritual teachings with such pleasing and tangible proofs.' They then requested the Master to come to their churches to speak. The Master replied, 'I have already promised others and I shall stay here only a week for the present. I may speak on my return from Chicago.'

In the afternoon there was a public meeting at the home of Mrs [Alexander] Morten.[21] Because the Master had spoken so much today, He was tired and rested for a little while in an upstairs bedroom before the meeting. When He came down the staircase to face the crowd below, He gave a wonderful, compassionate talk in an eloquent and melodious voice on the subject of the spiritual springtime. Apart from the many believers, there were also about a hundred newcomers present who shook His hand and expressed their joy and happiness. When He started to go upstairs, the crowd pleaded with Him to stay for a few more minutes. They approached Him, group by group, and then left, extremely happy and with great devotion. Some believers requested blessings for their children. The Master has a great love and affection for children. Some of the friends showed Him Tablets that He had written for them, overjoyed to have been so honored by Him. It is surprising to see how much the Cause of God has influenced them and the power of God's Covenant. The believers in America are extremely devoted to the Center of the Covenant and are obedient to His words and commands.

On the return to the hotel the carriage drove through the park roads. The Master remarked, 'America will make rapid progress in the future but I am fearful of the effects of these high buildings and such densely populated cities; these are not good for the public health.'

Saturday, April 13, 1912[22]
[New York]

Among the prominent people who called upon the Master were the President of the New York Peace Society [Mr W. H. Short][23] and an important inventor of armaments [Mr Hudson Maxim].[24] It happened that both were visiting 'Abdu'l-Bahá at the same time. It was interesting to see the power and majesty with which the Master spoke to these two about serving the world of humanity and public welfare. Both left His presence with joy and devotion.

In the afternoon the public meeting was at the home of Mr [Mountfort] Mills.[25] Several clergymen, professors and dignitaries were present. The Master first spoke on the superior power of the human kingdom over nature. Then in another room He spoke to the clergymen about the necessity of a power that will cause spirituality to be victorious over materialism. 'This power', He said, 'is the power of Bahá'u'lláh. We used that power and thus have succeeded in this great Cause.' The meeting and the attention and joyful devotion of those present gave 'Abdu'l-Bahá much satisfaction. In the carriage returning to His hotel, He said:

> I have made the subject of my talks here only one of the principles of the Blessed Beauty. I have not as yet touched upon others of greater importance. It is because I perceive the pulse of the people and the needs of the present circumstances that the confirmations of the Blessed Beauty successively rain down and assist me. These effects that you see are not only the result of addresses but are due to the assistance of the Blessed Beauty. Of course, everyone says that peace is desirable but the power to influence and conform is what is required. The Blessed Beauty is indeed my helper and protector, to the degree that were I, for example, even to make war the subject of my talks, the same effects would become apparent. It is indeed the confirmations of the Blessed Beauty that aid us. Otherwise how would Westerners show such consideration to us Easterners?

The Persian servants and American believers were with 'Abdu'l-Bahá when He was at His hotel. A photographer with a movie camera received permission to photograph Him, together with His companions.

We also received news today of the disaster of the *Titanic*.[26] The believers said prayers in gratitude that the Master had not acceded to their request that He travel on the ship.

Sunday, April 14, 1912
[New York]

The Master went to the Church of the Ascension.[27] This was the first church in America to be honored by the presence of the Master. He had previously received an invitation to visit this great edifice.

He entered the church from a special side door opening into a room in the church and rested for a while. The clergymen came in and expressed their warm gratitude for His presence. After prayers, the Master went to the podium from the upper door. At the insistence of the minister, the Master sat on the tall chair especially reserved for the Viceroy of Christ. After more prayers, the minister spoke about the history and teachings of the Cause and, with great courtesy and respect, introduced the Master. The believers attending the services were elated. The Master rose from His seat and gave a comprehensive talk on the meaning of divine civilization. He presented the Bahá'í teachings and spoke about the Revelation of Bahá'u'lláh and the unification of humankind. The audience sat spellbound like iguanas sitting in the sun,[28] overwhelmed by the Master's talk, especially at the end when the Master chanted a prayer in a most melodious voice. The prayer greatly affected the hearts of the listeners. As He left the church, group after group rushed towards Him. The Bahá'ís sang 'Alláh-u-Abhá' and many asked for His blessings. From among the crowd a woman's voice was heard. Tears poured from her eyes as she held fast to the hem of the Master's robe. She was so overcome she could not speak. The Master showered her with His love and kindness and calmed her with loving words of assurance. It was a great day and a most impressive meeting. Not one of the two thousand people was disappointed and everyone left smiling in warm appreciation.

That afternoon the Master spoke at the Advanced Thought Center.[29] His talk was on the unity of God, the unity of the world of humanity and the need for greater capacity to receive the divine blessings. As He left the meeting hall, many people surrounded Him and asked what they could do to become united. The Master showered them with His love and kindness. They asked to see Him again and left Him with great courtesy and humility.

Monday, April 15, 1912
[New York]

The Master was shown several newspapers that had published His picture and articles about His talks and yesterday's meetings. So great is the influence of the Cause of God that a zealous clergyman has made objections to Dr [Percy Stickney] Grant, the minister of the Church of the Ascension who had invited 'Abdu'l-Bahá to sit in the chair reserved for the Viceroy of Christ. He asked why the minister had permitted 'Abdu'l-Bahá to sit on the chair. Although he objected to the Master's talk, he could find no justification for his complaint. Other clergymen replied to his objections in a newspaper article, referring to his discourteous attitude. Thus he was obliged to write an article himself in which he stated that he had no doubt about the knowledge and importance of the teachings of 'Abdu'l-Bahá and that his intention had been only to point out that the church's rules and regulations had been broken.

The bishop of the church was introduced to 'Abdu'l-Bahá by Mr Mills. The bishop expressed his gratitude and appreciation for the Master's visit to the Church of the Ascension, saying, 'I am very optimistic and pleased about the teachings of this Cause. You are the first great visitor from the East who has brought such important tidings to the West. Until now no one could imagine that such a great cause could exist in the East. This blessed journey is the cause of praise and gratitude.'

As the bishop listened to the Master's remarks about the dangers of blind imitation and prejudice, and on the fundamental unity of all religions, the necessity for universal peace, the agreement between science and religion, and a divine civilization, and so on, he became very respectful, and left with gratitude and humility.

In thanking the Master the bishop said, 'You are the first great traveler from the East to the West to come with such noble principles.' I then recalled the statement of the Master on the ship when He said, 'Up to the present time no one has traveled, with a purpose like ours, from Persia to America . . . Ours may be said to be the first voyage of Easterners to America.'

Tuesday, April 16, 1912
[New York]

From early morning until late afternoon many believers and seekers came by requesting permission to see 'Abdu'l-Bahá. Many sat on the porch waiting their turn and were extremely grateful if they could see Him for just a few minutes and be personally addressed by Him.

The public meeting today was held at the home of Mr [Arthur Pillsbury] Dodge. After lunch, 'Abdu'l-Bahá spoke on the subject of the unity of nations brought about by the power of God, the influence of the words of Bahá'u'lláh and the ascendancy of His Cause. Because a large number of people were present, they entered through one door and, after greeting the Master, shaking His hand and seeking His blessings, left by another. Some were tearful while others were smiling and elated, asking for His assistance that they might be successful in teaching and in serving the Cause. This was the state of the people at all the public meetings. If I were to write about this in detail, it would take many volumes.

Wednesday, April 17, 1912
[New York]

Among the dignitaries visiting the Master were several New York clergymen who invited Him to speak to their congregations. The Master told them, 'I am going to Chicago in two days and therefore am unable to accept your invitation.'

Owing to the prejudice and hatred that has existed between blacks and whites, it has been impossible for white people to invite black people to their homes. Therefore 'Abdu'l-Bahá has repeatedly encouraged the believers to promote fellowship and unity among these two races.

An important meeting was held today at the home of Mr Kinney.³⁰ It was attended by many Bahá'ís and non-Bahá'ís and demonstrated a strong bond of unity between whites and blacks. The Master said that the East has always been the dawning place of light, that this gathering of blacks and whites is like the gathering of many colored flowers and that the variety of colors enhances the beauty of the garden and brings about the loveliness of each.

In the evening the Master invited everyone to dinner, which He Himself prepared. He spoke about unity and love and demonstrated to everyone how to serve at the threshold of the Blessed Beauty. Indeed, it was a blessed evening and a wonderful example of generosity and bestowal in the highest degree.

Thursday, April 18, 1912
[New York]

Besides the individual meetings of the friends with 'Abdu'l-Bahá, there were two public meetings held today. One was at the home of Mrs [Marshall] Emery,³¹ where He spoke about the life of the Blessed Beauty, His glory, His many afflictions and hardships and the triumph of the Cause of God despite His imprisonment by His enemies. This account brought tears to the eyes of the listeners and caused them to ponder deeply. Many asked that they might be assisted to serve the Cause.

The other meeting was held at the Bowery Mission Hall³² to help and assist the poor and destitute. First 'Abdu'l-Bahá spoke on the subject of the station of poverty and gave the men hope for the future. His words were so penetrating that even those who were not poor became envious at 'Abdu'l-Bahá's description of the station of poverty. The report of this meeting was publicized in many newspapers. When 'Abdu'l-Bahá finished His talk, He said He wished to serve the poor. The chairman announced that 'Abdu'l-Bahá would stand near the door so that they could come to Him from one side and then leave from the other. It was an impressive sight. The Master showered His kindness on each one and gave each of them some coins. Because there were about four hundred people, some said that the Master's money would not suffice; there would not be enough for all of them. Instead, some money was left over, which was given to other destitute people and children outside the Bowery.

Friday, April 19, 1912
[New York]

It was the last day of 'Abdu'l-Bahá's stay in New York. From early morning until noon there were the usual comings and goings of numerous friends and believers at the Master's hotel. In the evening a large meeting was arranged for the Master's talk at Earl Hall at Columbia University.[33] In addition to students and professors, there were many other interested people, as well as the Bahá'ís. 'Abdu'l-Bahá's talk was most penetrating and dealt with the supernatural powers of human nature and the results achieved from education and knowledge, and gave an explanation of peace and so on. After the meeting, those who had already met 'Abdu'l-Bahá brought other seekers to meet Him in another room. These meetings were so long that the professors' plan to give the Master a tour of the university had to be abandoned.

From both the friends and inquirers was frequently heard the remark, 'Oh, that this meeting would never end, for we do not want to leave Him.'

As it was 'Abdu'l-Bahá's last night in the city, many believers remained longer than usual in His company. Each was a Majnún,[34] enchanted with the beauty of the Center of Bahá'u'lláh's Covenant and attracted to the divine fragrances.

The friends continued to arrive until late at night. 'Abdu'l-Bahá bade farewell to all and promised to be back among them when He returned.

Saturday, April 20, 1912
[en route to Washington DC]

In the early morning after prayers, meditations, morning tea and receiving some of the believers, 'Abdu'l-Bahá left the Hotel Ansonia for the railway station [Grand Central Station]. A large group of friends and well-wishers were there to bid Him farewell. One by one they came to Him and in their own ways expressed their respect, attraction and humility.

When He arrived at the station, 'Abdu'l-Bahá walked around the building, praising its beauty and construction. We were informed that it is one of the finest in the world, its construction costing about six million dollars. The train began its journey and for the first few miles it traveled by the great river. As well as His usual companions, two American Bahá'ís traveled with the Master. One was Mr John Bosch from California, who had come to New York specifically to see Him. He had asked for a Persian name and was given the name Núrání ['the Luminous'] by the Master. The other American was Dr Edward Getsinger, who begged 'Abdu'l-Bahá that he be allowed to be a part of His entourage. As most American trains have but one class of travel, except for sleeping compartments, we were all accommodated in one cabin.

After a journey of about five hours the train reached Washington DC. Before the journey the Master had sent a telegram to the friends in Washington requesting that a house be rented for Him. Mrs [Agnes] Parsons had invited the Master to stay at her home but He did not at first accept her invitation. However, after He was told by the friends that her home had been especially prepared for His visit, for which she had been anxiously waiting, He agreed to her request; for had her invitation not been accepted, she would have been heart-broken and deeply saddened. The Master and a translator went to Mrs Parsons's home and 'Abdu'l-Bahá instructed the other members of His entourage to stay at the house rented for Him. Thus Mrs Parsons's house was the first home in America in which the Master resided; He stayed there for several days.[35]

That evening 'Abdu'l-Bahá attended the annual meeting of the Orient–Occident Unity Conference at the public library.[36] It was a vast gathering and the hall was filled to capacity. As the Master entered the hall, the audience was awe-struck. All stood and remained standing until He bade them be seated. It was amazing to witness how spontaneously these people paid Him their respect, even though most were not Bahá'ís. He spoke on the importance of the relationship between the East and the West, the unity of people and about the Revelation of the Greatest Name. His talk was so moving and inspiring that afterwards everyone wanted to meet Him but because He was too tired to greet everyone, He decided to return home.

Sunday, April 21, 1912
[Washington DC]

The highlight of the day was a very important and well-attended meeting at the Universalist Church.[37] The minister of the church introduced 'Abdu'l-Bahá with a most glowing tribute to His life and teachings. Then the Master rose from His seat and delivered an address on the need for cooperation, love, friendship and universal peace. He stressed Christ's statement that 'I have yet many things to say unto you, but ye cannot bear them now. Howbeit when he, the Spirit of truth, is come, he will guide you into all truth' [John 16:12–13], and added, 'And now that time has come and the Divine Spirit has spoken, revealing all truth.'

I have reproduced here the whole of that address:[38]

> What the minister of the Church delineated before us just now testifies to his high sense of morality and his efforts to serve the world of humanity. It is truly praiseworthy and deserves commendation for it opposes the ingrained prejudices of man. These prejudices have kept the human world in a state of chaos for the past six thousand years. How many wars have taken place; how many battles have been fought; how much discord has been

caused by them! Inasmuch as this century is the century of the manifestation of truth – praise be to God! – the thoughts of men are turned to truth and the souls are prepared for the oneness of humanity. The ocean of reality is surging more tumultuously and the mirage of imitation is daily passing away. All the existing religions have had one foundation of truth. This foundation has led humanity to love, accord and progress. However, after each of the divine Manifestations, that light of reality was gradually beclouded and the darkness of superstitions and imitations came in its place. The world of humanity was encircled in that darkness. Day by day, enmity waxed great until it reached such a pitch that each nation rose against the other. Were it not for political obstructions, the nations would have completely destroyed and overthrown one another. Now it is enough! We must investigate the truth. We must pass by these vain imaginings. Praise be to God that we are all the servants of one God. We are all under the protection of His favors and are recipients of His bestowals. God is kind to all. Why should we be unkind? God is at peace with all; why should we war with one another? At most it is this: that some are ignorant; they must be educated. Some are as children; they must be trained. Some are sick and infirm; they must be healed. But the ill patient must not be detested. The child must not be considered bad. We must strive to remedy and heal. All the Prophets of God came for the education of humanity in order that the immature souls might become mature and to establish love and amity among mankind. The Prophets have not come to this world to cause discord and enmity. For God wants good for all His servants, not ill; and he who wishes the servants of God ill is opposed to God. He is not on the right path; rather, he has followed the footsteps of Satan, inasmuch as the attribute of God is mercy and that of Satan is rancor. Therefore, every man who is merciful and kind to his fellow man is following God's way and every man who bears hatred toward his fellow man is opposing Him. God is absolute mercy and pure love, and Satan is absolute enmity and utter hatred. Therefore, in whatever meeting you see love, know that it is a manifestation of God's mercy; and wherever you see enmity, know that it is the outcome of the evil suggestions of Satan. The Prophets of God have come to this world to make human souls the expressions of the All-Merciful and to instill friendship and love in the hearts of men. The animal is a captive of nature and does what its nature prompts it to do. It has not consideration for good or evil. But the Prophets have come to teach man that which is good, not evil, so that he may act in conformity with justice and equity and not follow the demands of his natural instincts. He should act in accord with reason and justice, even though that be against his natural inclination. Whatever he should find contrary to reason and equity, that should be considered unworthy, even though it be propitious to his natural impulse. Therefore, man must follow the attributes of the All-Merciful. However, the imperfect members of society follow their natural instincts. They obey these instincts. They are captives of physical susceptibilities. They are not aware of the spiritual bounties. Man is possessed of two aspects, the physical and the divine. The divine aspect consists of reconciliation, purity, love and faithfulness but the animal aspect consists of war, contention, bloodshed and massacre. If the animal side in man should overcome, he becomes more degraded than animals. If the divine side should triumph, he becomes an angel. The teachings of the Prophets were solely directed to educate humanity in order to subdue the animal side so that persons under the yoke of nature may find salvation and the heavenly aspect may rule victorious. This divine aspect is the bounty of the Holy Spirit, it is the second birth. He who possesses the divine aspect is a well-wisher of mankind and is most kind to all. He will entertain no enmity toward any Faith and will not belittle any religion, for the foundations of the religions of God are one. If we refer back to these foundations, we shall become united. But if we turn toward imitations, we shall be at variance, for imitations differ but the foundations of the divine religions are one and the same. Imitation leads to differences and trouble but the foundations of the divine religions cause love and union.

Christ once said, 'When he, the Spirit of Truth, is come, he will guide you into all truth.' He also said, 'There are many things which you cannot bear hearing now, but when the Spirit of Truth is come, he will expound all truth unto you.' Now is the century in which the Spirit of Truth has spoken and has revealed the whole truth. He has laid bare the truth of the religion of Christ and has redeemed people from superstitions so that the edifice of ignorance and enmity may be destroyed and the foundation of love may be established. We must all endeavor with heart and soul in order that this enmity and spite may disappear entirely from the midst of humanity, that this hatred and strife may pass away absolutely. The Holy Spirit admonishes us to follow the example of Christ, to read the Gospels and to see that Christ was pure love. He even prayed for His executioners when He was on the cross. He prayed, 'O Lord, pardon them, for they know not what they do. If they knew, they would not perform such deeds.' See how loving the divine Manifestations are that even on the cross they pray for the forgiveness of their oppressors. Therefore we must emulate the Prophets of God; we must follow in Their footsteps; we must free ourselves from the darkness of dogmatic imitations. I ask you, did God create us for love or for enmity? Surely He has created us for love and friendship. Therefore, we must be aware because self-interest prompts people to shut their eyes to the truth. They want to pursue their own self-interest and they move but in the darkness of desire. Consider what hardships Christ suffered when He appeared. In spite of all this He in the end united diverse people and different religions. The Romans, Greeks, Assyrians and Egyptians were most hostile toward each other. Christ, through the breath of the Holy Spirit, united them all, established fellowship among them all, so that differences were cast aside and strife and disputes were forgotten. They were united under His standard and lived in peace through His teaching. Which was preferable? To have followed Christ or to have followed satanic and hostile instincts? I hope that the people of the East and the West shall be quickened by the breath of the Holy Spirit, in this, the blessed century of Bahá'u'lláh, and become united, that all may cling to the essential reality of the divine religions – that truth is one and that it is indivisible and not multiple. When all investigate the truth, all will be united, the light of the oneness of humanity will shine and universal peace will come into being. I will now pray on your behalf:

> O Lord! These Thy servants have assembled here out of pure love. They have gathered together in perfect accord and harmony. O God! Illumine their faces, make joyous their souls with Thy most great glad tidings. Brighten their eyes with the verses of Thy guidance and delight their ears with the melody of Thy sweet voice.
>
> O Lord, we are wrongdoers; forgive us. We are sinners; grant us Thy pardon. Shelter us in Thy refuge. Satisfy the needy through Thy forgiveness. Free us from the world of vain imaginings and guide us to the Truth, that we may seek the divine reality, shun the mortal world, approach the divine kingdom and, withdrawn from the world of darkness, enter the realm of light.
>
> Deliver us from the darkness of material existence and illumine us with the rays of the infinite realm. Make us the manifestations of Thy light and the dawning places of Thy signs. Turn us from all else save Thee and cause us to become the recipients of Thy mysteries. Thou, O God, art the Compassionate, the Wise, the Forgiving, the Mighty.

After this wonderful talk, the minister rose to thank the Master and said to the congregation, 'If anyone wishes to shake hands with 'Abdu'l-Bahá, he should come from one side of the podium and leave by the other.' The Master stood near the pulpit and members of the audience approached Him with great respect and reverence. They bowed, shook His hand and offered their thanks to Him. Later the Master said, 'The people in the church pressed my hand to such a degree that it is now aching.' In addition to these public gatherings, from morning to evening people from all walks of life came to the Master's residence to visit Him.

Monday, April 22, 1912
[Washington DC]

A meeting was held with the Bahá'ís.[39] When the Master arrived, the friends greeted Him with poems and songs written in His praise. He spoke about the events during His long travels, the union of peoples from the East and the West, the greatness of this century and the appearance of the Greatest Name. He concluded the meeting by chanting a beautiful and moving prayer. The friends rushed to His side; one shaking His hand, another holding onto the hem of His robe and yet another shedding tears of joy and in the utmost happiness. When the Master left the gathering, the friends formed two rows as He passed through their midst. He approached His automobile and again the friends rushed towards Him like moths circling around the candle of the Covenant.

In the afternoon, the Master spoke at another gathering about the sinking of the *Titanic*.[40] He prayed for the souls of the passengers and expressed His condolences to their survivors. In the evening, Mrs Parsons held a dinner in His honor to which all the friends were invited.[41] At the table, 'Abdu'l-Bahá said:

> Consider the confirmations of the Blessed Beauty, what He has done, how He has brought us to the house of such a personage, who in the utmost love has prepared such a feast in our honor. The power and influence of the Word of God have united the East and the West! How perfect are His heavenly favors and how all-embracing His divine bounties!

Tuesday, April 23, 1912
[Washington DC]

Today the Master went to Howard University, an educational institution for blacks.[42] The hosts (mostly black with a few whites) had made special arrangements so that when the Master arrived He was welcomed by music from a band while the audience applauded with excitement and exuberance. It is difficult to describe the scene adequately. The president of the university was very cordial and introduced 'Abdu'l-Bahá as the Prophet of Peace and the harbinger of unity and salvation. Then the Master rose from His seat and spoke on the subject of the harmony between blacks and whites and the unity of humankind.[43] The audience repeatedly applauded Him during the talk, delighted at His words. At the conclusion, the president of the university thanked 'Abdu'l-Bahá on behalf of all those gathered. As He left the auditorium, group after group formed two lines, one on each side, all showing their highest respect by bowing and waving their hats and handkerchiefs in farewell to the beloved Master.[44]

'Abdu'l-Bahá had lunch at the home of Ali Kuli Khan. Several believers were present, including ourselves.[45]

There was a public meeting in the afternoon at the same house.[46] The majority attending the meeting were ladies from high society. At this meeting the Master spoke about the education and improvement of women and the promotion of unity and peace in the world of humanity.[47] After the meeting several new people arrived[48] and sat for a brief time in the Master's presence. They so enjoyed His company they did not want to leave.

In the evening, close to bedtime, when the Master was alone and extremely tired from the day's activities, He prayed, praising and thanking the Blessed Beauty. On one occasion He said:

> We must offer thanks to the Blessed Beauty because it is His help that has stirred the people; it is His grace that has changed the hearts. The assistance of the Abhá Kingdom has

transformed a drop into a mighty ocean. The aid of the Most High has turned a gnat into an eagle, has invested an ant with the power of a Solomon and has caused the debased one to become a source of eternal honor.

A third meeting was held this evening in a black church.[49] All those present paid Him the highest respect and were delighted to hear about the new teachings. The Master's talk, they felt, gave them honor and would cause them to progress. As is customary at churches, there was a collection and the Master made a contribution.

Wednesday, April 24, 1912
[Washington DC]

In the morning 'Abdu'l-Bahá went to a Bahá'í children's conference.[50] As He entered the hall, the children sang songs in praise of 'Abdu'l-Bahá in unison, accompanied by the piano. When the Master saw the children, He said, 'Praise be to God. These children, like flowers, are in a state of utmost purity, freshness and delicacy!' After He spoke and recited prayers for the children, the Master kissed and embraced each child and gave them some sweets. The immensity of His love and affection for the children was clearly obvious.

A second meeting[51] was held that evening at the home of Mr and Mrs Andrew J. Dyer, a mixed race couple.[52] Those present were in such unity and love that the Master remarked:

> Before I arrived, I felt too tired to speak at this meeting but at the sight of such genuine love and attraction between the white and the black friends, I was so moved that I spoke with great love and likened this union of different colored races to a string of gleaming pearls and rubies.

After He spoke and showered His love on each one, He left in His carriage for a third meeting.[53]

'Abdu'l-Bahá was so filled with joy and happiness and His voice resonated so loudly that even the people walking along the street could hear Him:

> O Bahá'u'lláh! What hast Thou done? O Bahá'u'lláh! May my life be sacrificed for Thee! O Bahá'u'lláh! May my soul be offered up for Thy sake! How full were Thy days with trials and tribulations! How severe the ordeals Thou didst endure! How solid the foundation Thou hast finally laid, and how glorious the banner Thou didst hoist![54]

'Abdu'l-Bahá continued in this manner until the carriage reached the home of Mr [Alexander Graham] Bell. This great individual is the inventor of the telephone and the head of a scientific society. The day before, this venerable and inventive old gentleman had visited the Master and invited Him to attend the meeting of the scientific society. When the Master entered, all rose and each in turn shook His hand. Those who had met the Master previously introduced Him to the others with the greatest respect and honor. After the Master was seated, discussion of scientific issues continued. Each spoke of his experiences and discussed his discoveries. After several people had spoken, Mr Bell asked Ali Kuli Khan, the Persian ambassador,[55] to relate the history of the Faith. Then Mr Bell thanked the Master for coming to his home and asked Him to address the guests.

    The Master began His talk by praising their good manners and praiseworthy qualities. He then spoke of the importance and the results of science, the greatness of this age and the interdependence of society, and paid a glorious tribute to the new Dispensation. Mr Bell was extremely delighted and rose to thank the Master for His talk. The hearts of those present were so moved that when the next member arose to give his talk, he could only say, 'The talk of the Master from the East was so wonderful that I find myself inadequate to say anything' and sat down. A few others spoke briefly and the meeting ended.

Mr Bell invited the Master and his guests to go into the dining hall. It was midnight, and as it is customary for people in the West to eat late at night before going to bed, the table was spread with bread, meat, candies, cookies, fruit and beverages. Although the Master had not yet had dinner, He spoke through Mr Bell to his wife and daughter. Mrs Bell is deaf and mute and communicates through sign language. Sign language is similar to writing, with lines, points and stops, just as in telegraph technology, and is now so well developed that people can speak easily with the deaf.

As is well known, Mr Bell's main purpose was to invent an instrument that would enable the deaf to communicate. Out of his deep love for his wife, he devoted himself to this day and night and in the end invented the telephone. But this did not fulfill his intended purpose. The Master said:

> Yes, most of the great inventions were made in a similar way. For instance, the search for alchemy has brought into being thousands of useful medicines and the desire of finding a direct route to India from Europe became the cause of the discovery of America.

Thursday, April 25, 1912
[Washington DC]

There was a special meeting for the Theosophists[56] in the morning. The Master spoke on the distinction and superiority of human beings to the rest of creation, the various faculties of the soul, the unity of God, the need for spiritual progress and divine civilization. There were many guests and after the Master's talk some went into a private room to ask Him personal questions. Another meeting was held in the afternoon at the Master's residence.[57] As with the other meetings, it was attended by the public. The living room on the ground floor was filled to capacity. 'Abdu'l-Bahá spoke on the importance and necessity of spiritual teachings and their renewal in every age. He also discussed the principles of this great Cause. After the talk, many received permission to ask Him questions in an adjoining room. Most of them first apologized, aware that He was extremely tired, but said that just being in His presence was for them their greatest joy and that to listen to Him was a source of happiness and honor.

Today the Master said to Mrs Parsons:

> Such a traveler and guest is the cause of much bother. You need to leave the house and run away. The usual guest in a city meets certain people at specific times but you have had to host the public from morning until evening.

In the evening the Turkish Ambassador, his honor Ḍíyá Páshá, invited the Master to a royal feast.[58] Most of us were also invited, as were many dignitaries, all of whom were dressed in formal attire. The Master gave a short talk at the table with the utmost majesty and beauty on the subject of the influence of the words of the Manifestations of God and their all-conquering power. The Ambassador then read from a prepared statement written in praise of the Master and presented it to Him:

> The light of His honor's quality and knowledge in this new land and new world is now shining upon all peoples, showering them with His encouragement and enlightenment. He has suffered and sacrificed everything for the purpose of disseminating good qualities for humanity. He has now honored us by His presence. His Honor, 'Abdu'l-Bahá, is unique in our age and is highly esteemed and treasured by all of us. With prayer to the Lord of the worlds, I wish Him a long life and good health.
>
> Ḍíyá Páshá

When the Ambassador completed his statement, the Master spoke:

> This night is a very blessed night, worthy of the utmost praise and joy for many reasons. First, praise be to God, we are in a

country which is famous for its prosperity and freedom. Second, we are in a house which is connected to the great Ottoman Power. Third, we are the guests of His Excellency the Ambassador who shines like the sun in the world of morality. Fourth, this meeting provides a tangible demonstration of the love and unity that is possible between the East and the West.

His Excellency the Ambassador is from the East, while his wife is an American. Similarly, His Excellency the Ambassador of Persia is from the nobility of the Orient, while his wife is also an American. This is a proof that the Orient and Occident can meet, love and unite. The greatest wish of people of thought and broad vision and sound understanding is the oneness and unity of humanity. This reality was not so apparent in former times but in this enlightened age which is the age of science and the progress of the world of humanity, this important fact has become manifest through the help and assistance of God: that all peoples are related, that all are from one family, citizens of one country and one world. This is the century of the oneness of the world of humanity and of the decline and abrogation of the superstitions of past ages. Every learned person is persuaded that this is the century for oneness and unity and the time for fanciful prejudices to fade away. We pray that misunderstandings among nations may disappear completely so that it may be evident that the foundation of all divine principles is the oneness of mankind and that the real purpose of all divine Manifestations has been to educate humanity. Divine religions are not the cause of dissension, nor do they beget enmity and hatred, for the foundation of all of them is truth and truth is one, it has no plurality.

The differences which we find are the results of imitations. As the imitations vary one from another, they become the cause of animosity and difference. The gloom of these imitations has wholly obscured the Sun of Reality. But, praise be to God, day by day these clouds are being dispersed and dissipated; ere long, they shall be wholly removed and the Sun of

Reality shall be seen to shine most brilliantly. The standard of the oneness of humanity will be unfurled, the tabernacle of the universal peace will be raised, and this world will become another world.

I thank His Excellency the Ambassador who brought about this meeting of people of different nationalities in his home. Such meetings, in truth, deserve much praise and commendation.

At the close of the meeting the Ambassador again arose to show his respect and appreciation. He accompanied the Master to His carriage with the utmost humility and esteem.

During these days, many dignitaries and important people visited the Master. Even President [Theodore] Roosevelt[59] came, with humility and respect, especially to see the Master.

Friday, April 26, 1912
[Washington DC]

In addition to the usual receptions at the home of Mrs Parsons, there were three public meetings: one in the morning, another in the afternoon and one in the evening. At the first gathering, at the All Saints Unitarian Church, the Master spoke on the subject of the varieties of light, the effulgence of the Sun of Reality in its original essence, and of the waiting souls with pure hearts who are like unto clear spotless mirrors, whose eyes and ears become enlightened by the appearance of the Sun of Reality.[60] So great was the respect and devotion of the audience that 'Abdu'l-Bahá wrote in a cable He sent to the Orient: 'Today three thousand persons visited with the utmost harmony.'

At every gathering, whether for Bahá'ís or non-Bahá'ís, several stenographers, as well as the Persian secretaries, were in attendance. The English translations were published soon after the address itself but the Persian originals taken down by us verbatim had to be submitted to 'Abdu'l-Bahá for correction. Because of His heavy schedule, He had little time for this, so the originals were often delayed in their publication.

The afternoon meeting was held at the home of Mrs Parsons.[61] The subject of the talk was the interpretation of the Old Testament statement concerning the creation of man in the image of God. At the conclusion 'Abdu'l-Bahá took His leave of the friends, promising to return to Washington DC from Chicago. On hearing this, the friends hastened to shake hands with Him and showed great reverence and humility to Him, joyful that soon He would return to their midst. After the meeting, 'Abdu'l-Bahá went for a stroll in a park to recuperate.

In the evening 'Abdu'l-Bahá went to a third gathering, held in a very large building, to speak to a group of young women from the suffrage movement.[62] This was the largest meeting held thus far and the most spacious and majestic hall. 'Abdu'l-Bahá delivered a most impressive address which He began by saying:

> One of the teachings of Bahá'u'lláh is equality of rights for men and women. When He promulgated this principle in the Orient, the people were astonished.
>
> One of the proofs of the advancement of women is this magnificent and imposing building and this large gathering.

'Abdu'l-Bahá's talk centered on the subject of equality of men and women and the necessity of giving women the same training as men. Many praised Him, both before and after His talk. The meeting closed with a song of praise.

The chairman of the meeting, Mr Hoover from New York, introduced the Master most eloquently. When 'Abdu'l-Bahá came to the pulpit, He was received with a standing ovation and a burst of enthusiasm. Then, with a motion of His hand, all seated themselves.

As the Master arose to give His talk, everyone began to clap so loudly that the sound echoed around the great hall. Everyone was thrilled as the beloved Master stood and the hearts of the believers were relieved of all grief and anxiety. Indeed, the appearance of the Center of God's Covenant in these meetings is worthy of the highest praise and will undoubtedly be of the greatest benefit to all. Instead of the harsh treatment meted out to the Manifestations of God, here was the advancement and elevation of the Cause of God. To listen to the melodious, resonant voice of the Center of the Covenant in such auditoriums fills one with excitement and raises the banner of everlasting honor. The presence of the Eastern friends was sorely missed.

At the end of the meeting, people again filled the room to capacity so they could glimpse 'Abdu'l-Bahá's beautiful face and shake His hand.

Saturday, April 27, 1912
[Washington DC]

Mrs Parsons offered the Master a sum of money but He said that she should distribute it among the poor. No matter how much she supplicated, He would not accept it, saying, 'If we had not had the money necessary for the expenses of the voyage, we would have accepted your offer.'

The Treasurer of the United States had lunch with the Master.[63] This gentleman was very happy and smiling as he bade farewell to the Master. Later, the Master went to the home of an official to say goodbye. The man embraced Him, weeping with joy. When I saw the smile of the Treasurer and the tears of the official, I recited this poem: 'The smiles and tears of the lovers are from another world.'

The Bahá'í meetings and the outstanding qualities of the Master have received such acclaim that today, out of jealousy, some narrow-minded Christian clergymen spoke out against the Cause.

Since this was the last night of the Master's stay in the this city, Mrs Parsons held an elegant reception for dignitaries and city officials in honor of 'Abdu'l-Bahá and on behalf of the Orient-Occident Unity Society.[64] Three hundred people in formal attire assembled in the spacious rooms, which were beautifully decorated with flowers and ornaments. When the Master came downstairs, each guest, man and woman alike, approached Him with the utmost reverence to shake His hand. They introduced one another and paid Him their respects. The guests then went into the dining room to partake of the repast prepared for them, including beverages, cakes, ice cream and coffee.

After they had eaten the guests were ushered into the music hall while the Master sat in another room to receive those who wished to see Him. He answered all their questions. To a Washington judge He said: 'It is possible to establish among the powers of the whole world the unity which is found among the states of the United States of America.' To some doctors He stated, 'I hope that you will raise the standard of universal peace.' To a mathematician He said, 'I hope that you will try to teach the truth and principles of divine religions to different nations just as you are teaching mathematics to different persons in your school.' To Admiral Peary, the explorer of the North Pole, He said, 'I hope you will discover the mysteries of the Kingdom of God.'[65] The Master spoke to a bishop, saying, 'My hope is that you will abandon harmful imitations, spread the truth of the teachings of Christ and remove all those dogmas that are against science and reality.' To the chargé d'affaires of Switzerland, the Master described His sojourn in that country. To some relatives of the President of the United States [William Howard Taft] He spoke about divine civilization. To a member of Congress, He said, 'Just as you are exerting yourself for the good of America, so must you expend your energy for the benefit of all the nations of the world.' He also spoke to the head of the United States Patent Office and the General Consul, the President of the Peace Congress and other well-known personages.

When this magnificent meeting ended, the guests came to 'Abdu'l-Bahá one by one to shake His hand and to say goodbye. The night was one of the most blessed nights and that meeting one of the most great and important meetings.

Sunday, April 28, 1912
[Washington DC, en route to Chicago]

The Master prepared to leave for Chicago. Among those who came to see Him was the ambassador of Great Britain,[66] who was very humble and reverent while in His presence. Many friends, believers and seekers were with 'Abdu'l-Bahá until His departure at 5:30 p.m. As He was leaving He said to Mrs Parsons:

> This was the springtime; we had good meetings at your home; I shall never forget them. I shall pray for divine confirmation for you that you may be assisted both materially and spiritually. This material world has an outward appearance, as it has also an inner reality. All created things are interlinked in a chain leading to spirituality and ultimately ending in abstract realities. I hope that these spiritual links will become stronger day by day and that this communication of hearts, which is termed inspiration, will continue. When this connection exists, bodily separation is not important; this condition is beyond the world of words and above all description.

To others He said, 'I hope these meetings of ours will bring forth everlasting results. The greatest of all benefits is the oneness of humanity and universal peace.'

Some friends came to the railway station to see 'Abdu'l-Bahá off and to gaze once more at the Master's beautiful countenance.[67] Some were to accompany Him to Chicago. Among them was Mrs Moss, a stenographer, who had requested a Persian name and was given the name Marzieh Khánum.

After crossing the Potomac River, the train entered the state of Virginia, which is exceedingly fertile and green. The scenery on both sides was charming, with a verdant expanse of land as far as the eye could see. 'Abdu'l-Bahá praised the scenery and said it was most beautiful but His face showed signs of an inner sorrow. After a few minutes He said, 'Whenever I see such scenes, I feel great sorrow, for the Blessed Beauty liked verdure and greenery very much. God shall never pardon those who imprisoned Him in that place.[68]

The conversation then turned to the train. The Master praised the sleeping car room, the cleanliness of the compartments and the electric lights in them; however, owing to the speed of the train, the Master was not able to sleep.

Monday, April 29, 1912
[Chicago]

In the morning the Master again praised the beauty and fertility of the countryside; a more fertile land had never before been seen. He had breakfast in the dining car. Today He spoke mostly about the days of the Blessed Beauty and had Him constantly in mind.

The train reached Chicago at night.[69] The city was so bright with lights it was as though it were the Feast of Lights. When the friends saw the Master at the train station, they were filled with excitement, crying out 'Alláh-u-Abhá' and 'Yá 'Abdu'l-Bahá', their voices resounding throughout the station.

The Master went to the Plaza Hotel. After a brief rest, He was visited by some of the Bahá'ís, to whom He said:

> You have a good city. The call of God was first raised in this city. I hope that in Chicago the Cause of God will progress greatly and that it may be illumined by the light of the Kingdom just as it is brightened by electricity.
>
> In Washington we always had audiences of one to two thousand in large meetings. Day and night I had no rest. A close friendship was created between the black and white people. Many came to the Faith. Even those who are not believers drew much closer. Notwithstanding all this, I like Chicago more because the call of Bahá'u'lláh was first raised in this city. I hope you will be assisted to do great service and to live together in the utmost love and harmony.

When the believers begged for protection from tests and trials, 'Abdu'l-Bahá said to them:

> The severest tests were in Persia where properties were pillaged and the friends were martyred. They had not a moment's security. In short, I had a great desire to see you. If I hadn't this desire, the assistance of Bahá'u'lláh would not have encompassed me. It is His assistance that has brought me here, for, at the time of leaving Alexandria, when I boarded the ship, I was not well at all.

Some newspaper reporters telephoned, asking permission to interview the Master. He agreed that they could interview Him the following morning. After dinner, He looked out at the park and, gazing at the scenery before Him, said, 'This building commands a good view; most of the parks, streets and the city's lights can be seen.'

Tuesday, April 30, 1912
[Chicago]

Several friends and inquirers gathered in one of the rooms of 'Abdu'l-Bahá's suite and went in two or three at a time to speak with Him through an interpreter. Each returned transformed, soaring high in the atmosphere of happiness and joy. A few newspaper reporters were announced and He addressed them:

> We believe Bahá'u'lláh to be the supreme educator of humanity. When the gloom of contention was spread over the Orient; when the nations of the East were steeped in enmity and hatred; when its religious sects shunned one another, denouncing one another as impure, and the people were ever engaged in war and the shedding of blood, Bahá'u'lláh appeared as the sun from the horizon of the East and summoned all to fellowship and harmony. He devoted Himself to

their education and upliftment. He guided people from all nations and religions, cemented different denominations and united diverse nationalities to such an extent that if you attend their meetings you cannot say who is a Jew, who is a Muslim, who is a Parsi or who is a Christian. The despotic king of Persia with the legions of his 'ulamá [Muslim clergymen] arose against Him and inflicted the severest persecution upon Him. They imprisoned Bahá'u'lláh and killed His followers. The oppression intensified to such a degree that all those who dared obey Bahá'u'lláh would lose life and property. But with all this, they could not resist Him; His teachings spread more and more. Then His persecutors exiled Him to Baghdád, whence He was sent to Rumelia[70] and finally to the penal city of 'Akká. He passed away in that city. I myself was in the same prison until the declaration of liberty by the Committee of Union and Progress when all prisoners were set free.

As to the teachings of Bahá'u'lláh, they are, first, the investigation of truth. The fundamental principle of all the Prophets is Truth. Truth is one. Abraham was the promulgator of truth; Moses was the servant of truth; Christ laid down the cornerstone of truth; Muḥammad was the propagator of truth; the Báb was the herald of truth; and Bahá'u'lláh was the light of truth. Truth is the foundation of all the divine religions and is one. In truth there is no dissension. Imitations are different and are a cause of dissension and division. If people investigate truth and set aside imitations, all the nations will unite, for there exists no difference in religious truth; the differences lie in imitations only.

The second principle of Bahá'u'lláh is the unity of mankind. Bahá'u'lláh proclaims that all are the servants of one God; He has created all and provides for and sustains all. All are immersed in the ocean of His mercy and God is kind to all. Why should we be unkind to one another? We must follow the polity of God. Can we conceive a better polity than that of God?

The third principle He gave us is the harmony of science

and religion. Both science and religion are truth. If religion is against reality and truth it is mere superstition. Every religious tenet that conflicts with true knowledge and sound reasoning is not worthy of belief. Thus the dogmas and imitations that stand in the way of science and progress must be removed.

The fourth principle is that religion must be the cause of unity, it must connect hearts to one another. Christ and all the other divine messengers came to create unity and love. Therefore, if religion becomes the cause of differences, its nonexistence is preferable.

The fifth principle is that all religious, racial, patriotic and political prejudices are the causes of war and the destroyers of the edifice of humanity. All these must be discarded and abolished.

The sixth principle is Universal Peace. Humanity must achieve this peace. Until its light illumines the decisions of the leaders and governments of the world, humanity will find no rest.

The seventh principle is the equality of rights for men and women. The education of women must be equal to that of men so that they may advance and achieve the same status as men. Teachings of this kind are numerous.

In addition to the visits of large numbers of people at the hotel both day and night, three large meetings were held, attended by almost three thousand people, all of whom were honored to see 'Abdu'l-Bahá. The first meeting was held at Hull House and was attended by both blacks and whites.[71] The Master spoke on the subject of the unity and oneness of humanity; that God has given faculties and powers equally to all and that the different colors of humankind are like the various colors of the flowers of a garden, which increases the beauty and charm of the garden. His eloquent and impressive talk thrilled His listeners.

There exists among the whites in America a marked animosity for the blacks, who are held in such low esteem that the whites do not allow them to attend their public functions and think it beneath their dignity to mix with them in some of the public buildings and hotels. One day, Dr Zia Bagdadi invited Mr [Louis] Gregory, a black Bahá'í, to his home. When his landlord heard about this, he gave notice to Dr Bagdadi to vacate his residence because he had had a black man in his home. Although such prejudice was intense, the influence of the Cause of God and the power of God's Covenant is so great that in many cities in America hundreds of black and white Bahá'ís mingle together and associate with each other as brothers and sisters.

Another meeting was held at Handel Hall especially to bring together the blacks and the whites.[72] The Master offered a commentary on a verse from the Old Testament, 'Let us make man in our image, after our likeness': 'By "image and likeness"', He said, 'is meant human virtues and perfections and not the black or white color of the skin.' The Master's impressive talk transformed and deeply affected the gathering.

The Master then went to a third meeting, addressing some two thousand people at the Convention of the Bahá'í Temple Unity[73] held at the spacious Drill Hall. The entire audience stood when the Master entered, even though not all were Bahá'ís. The friends were full of excitement and cried 'Alláh-u-Abhá' so loudly that the hall resounded with their voices.

After a song of praise and glorification, the Master gave a detailed and eloquent talk on the purpose of the Temple and the unification of all under one standard. He concluded His talk by chanting a prayer in Persian in a most melodious voice. Some of those attending the convention met Him outside and asked whether they could visit Him at His residence. The crowd gathered around Him until He got into His carriage.

Wednesday, May 1, 1912
[Chicago]

In the morning 'Abdu'l-Bahá looked at some buildings from His balcony and enjoyed the lovely view of the park. He spoke to us, until visitors arrived, about the early days of the Most Great Prison and the sufferings of the Blessed Beauty. He sent several telegrams today to the assemblies of the East, sharing with them the glad tidings of the assistance of Bahá'u'lláh.

He spoke with the friends for a time and bestowed upon them His love. About an hour later He went to the proposed site of the Mashriqu'l-Adhkár[74] located outside the city, where property had been purchased for the construction of this great building. By the time He arrived the friends had already assembled and had pitched a large tent for the meeting.

'Abdu'l-Bahá first drove around the site, inspecting its boundaries, and then entered the tent. The friends stood all about Him, their eyes intently fixed on His luminous face. It was in these circumstances that 'Abdu'l-Bahá gave His talk on the power of the Cause of Bahá'u'lláh to unite the people of the East and the West beneath the shadow of the Word of God. He also spoke about the Mashriqu'l-Adhkárs of 'Ishqábád and America.[75] He then went to the spot where He was to lay the cornerstone with His own hands. Miss Holmes presented Him with a golden trowel especially prepared for the occasion. He took it in His hand and dug the earth for the foundation stone.[76] Then the delegates from the American assemblies, followed by representatives of the Eastern friends, each took the trowel and continued digging the foundation. Among them were Mihtar Ardishír Bahrám Surúsh representing the Bahá'ís of Pársí background,[77] Siyyid Asadu'lláh representing the Bahá'ís of Muslim origin, Zia Bagdadi representing the Arabian friends and Ghodsieh (Qudsíyyih) Khánum Ashraf representing the Bahá'í women of the East. When the digging was completed, the Master set the stone in place with His own hand.[78] He then showered His love and affection on the friends and left the site. Most of the friends remained and had lunch inside the tent.

There was a reception at the Plaza Hotel later that afternoon at which the Master spoke on divine civilization and spiritual qualities.[79] Both before and after the meeting friends and inquirers requested interviews and asked Him questions on several subjects.

Thursday, May 2, 1912
[Chicago]

From morning until noon 'Abdu'l-Bahá received successive waves of visitors, both friends and inquirers, in His private room. When the numbers grew too large, He went into the outer room and spoke to the visitors about unity, fellowship and the importance of overcoming hatred and enmity. He began by saying:

> The object of my undertaking such a long journey with all its inconveniences has been to bring about spiritual illumination in the Occident, for the Occident has great capacity and its people are less fettered by vain imaginings and imitations. Lofty ideals find a quick acceptance among them and today the loftiest ideal of all is devotion to the unity of mankind and universal peace.

In the afternoon there were two public meetings at the LaSalle Hotel. One was for the Federation of Women's Clubs[80] and the other for the Unitarian congregation.[81] 'Abdu'l-Bahá's first talk was on education and the rights of women and in the latter He spoke about human powers and gave proofs of the existence of God. Both talks were so impressive, charming and attractive that all the friends from the East and West offered thanks and glorification to the Abhá Kingdom, with smiles on their faces that were like roses in bloom.

Back at the Plaza Hotel, 'Abdu'l-Bahá responded to questions about the differences in capacities and talents among people, saying:

> Souls possess two types of capacity: one is derived from innate powers and the other is acquired through the education imparted by the Teacher of the world of humanity. The development of innate capacity is completely dependent on education and on man's own exertions. In other words, innate

capacity is not realized without education and exertion on the part of man and its perfection demands effort and training.

Question: 'How should one associate with people of bad character?' 'Abdu'l-Bahá replied:

> This, too, has two aspects. There are certain evils whose consequences affect the doer only and do not extend to others. Of course, with discretion and tact, we must try to warn and educate wrongdoers. They are sick; we must bring healing to them. But there are actions which are injurious to others. Association with persons who commit such deeds leads to a deterioration of morals and therefore to mingle with them is not advisable, except for persons of perfect integrity, who can also impart education. They should be exhorted to exert themselves to modify their morals and refine their behavior. The public should be protected from such harmful conduct by the institutions which administer justice. Thus, in the Tablets of the Blessed Beauty, although He commends association with people of all religions and races, He also forbids fellowship with the wicked, admonishing us to shun the people of negation and denial.

Several learned men, scientists, engineers and government officials visited 'Abdu'l-Bahá today.

Friday, May 3, 1912
[Chicago]

From early morning friends and inquirers visited 'Abdu'l-Bahá in twos and threes, all profusely offering their thanks and praise for the favors they had received from Him.

Today the members of an association of Indians residing in Chicago, who had previously attended 'Abdu'l-Bahá's receptions, arrived as one body and after obtaining His permission, read Him an address of welcome:

From the Society of Indians Residing in Chicago to His Holiness 'Abdu'l-Bahá 'Abbás. In the Name of God!

We, the members of the Society of Indians Residing in Chicago welcome you to this country. The Cause that has brought your Excellency to this country is most surely a source of honor and grace to us. Asia has always been the dawning-place of religions: Muḥammad, Christ, Buddha and Confucius were born in that enlightened continent; and we confidently believe that at this time, too, Asia will again usher in the universal principles of accord. The Bahá'í Cause, like the Cause of the Buddha, will be a source of uniting nations and will be a fulfillment of the teachings of our forefathers. Although Asia presently is in a state of backwardness, we console ourselves with the thought that although we are lacking in material progress, yet, concerning spirituality, we are the pride of the world.

We feel happy when we realize that through your Excellency, the means for the acquisition of Western arts and sciences will become available for those in the East and that the youth of Persia will come to these parts to acquire material knowledge and broaden their thinking and will return to their homes to benefit their brothers and sisters in the East on the road to progress.

Further, we believe that our country, India, will greatly benefit from a visit from your Excellency. The lack of unity between the Hindus and Muslims has kept them in the utmost contention and strife. As your Excellency's teachings are very much like the teachings of our religious leaders, they will undoubtedly unite them and make these contending nations one. We are certain that you will receive the same warmth and honor in India as here in America.

We pray to God to give your Excellency long life so that you may be enabled to convey your message to all mankind.

We are, most beloved Master, your sincere friends, the members of the Society of Indians Residing in Chicago.

More people gathered, forming a large group. The Master gave a public talk at the hotel on the gradual weakening of man's physical and material powers and the effect on man of divine civilization and spiritual education. All were struck with the charm of 'Abdu'l-Bahá's expression and the power of His argument. They openly expressed their conviction that the true salvation of the world of humanity lay in following the teachings of Bahá'u'lláh. The address by the Society of Indians and the testimony of others are examples for the fair-minded of the degree of attachment and attraction of the people, just as 'a drop expresses oceans'.

In the evening the Bahá'ís consulted. 'Abdu'l-Bahá sent us there and later joined us. He spoke briefly to the meeting but on the subject of the Ma<u>sh</u>riqu'l-A<u>dh</u>kár, the Master said, 'I will not discuss this matter. It is the business of the consultative assembly.' Later He added: 'If I were to speak about the Ma<u>sh</u>riqu'l-A<u>dh</u>kár, it would have to be built at once.'

In the early evening 'Abdu'l-Bahá gave a very eloquent and impressive address to the Theosophical Society,[82] which fascinated the audience, especially the members of the society.

Some of the friends had asked whether they could take photographs of 'Abdu'l-Bahá. Several photographs were therefore taken in the park across from the hotel by Mr [Albert C.] and Mrs Killius, two of the devoted believers. In one of the photographs 'Abdu'l-Bahá is standing with a flower in His hand. In another He is with His entourage and in the third He is standing among the believers. Although photographs of the Master had been taken in other cities, these are better and more lifelike.

Saturday, May 4, 1912
[Chicago]

As 'Abdu'l-Bahá's stay in Chicago was drawing to a close, there were numerous meetings and receptions. In the morning some clergymen visited Him in His hotel room. At the usual daily reception, He spoke about the three kingdoms of nature and the need for comprehensive education. He then went to the Plymouth Congregational Church, which was magnificent and most beautifully decorated. Its rector, Dr [Joseph A.] Milburn,[83] had seen the Master several times and was greatly attracted to Him. After the customary service, the rector introduced 'Abdu'l-Bahá:

> Having heard of the teachings and the peerless qualities of 'Abdu'l-Bahá, I arranged to leave for 'Akká. Then I was informed that 'Abdu'l-Bahá, Himself, was coming to America. Now God has endowed us with a great blessing that 'Abdu'l-Bahá has graced us with His presence here.

He then went on to give a detailed history and teachings of the Cause and introduced the Master as the Herald of Peace and the Son of God, 'Abbás Effendi.

As the Master approached the pulpit, the congregation rose to their feet, and although they were in church, they greeted Him with prolonged applause and cheers of joy. 'Abdu'l-Bahá called them to order then spoke about the manifestation of the center of illumination and the Sun of Truth which appears at different times at different points of the zodiac, thus illustrating the renewal of religions and the unity of the Messengers and the Holy Books. At the end of His talk He chanted a prayer in Persian in a melodious voice.

The hearts of the listeners were so attracted that the church seemed to be filled with the Holy Spirit. The people crowded around 'Abdu'l-Bahá to the extent such that it became difficult for the Master and His companions to leave. Groups of people surrounded Him to shake His hand and to ask for His blessing. The most surprising thing about these meetings was that although most of the people had never before heard of the Bahá'í teachings, they were so attracted and fascinated that they would follow the Master in their cars from one meeting to another.

'Abdu'l-Bahá had lunch at the home of Dr Forde and after meeting with a few people, He left for the hotel, saying, 'Let us walk for a while, and then take the tram.' Our host and some of us suggested that the distance was great and pointed out that Mr Forde's car was available. At our insistence, 'Abdu'l-Bahá rode in the car but as it twice punctured its tires, He took the tram.

When 'Abdu'l-Bahá arrived at the hotel, many people were already waiting for Him. He answered their questions, for which they were filled with gratitude. One person asked him about the future affairs of Asia and the countries in the East. 'Abdu'l-Bahá gave a detailed answer:

> No progress is possible except through the power of the Holy Spirit and the Cause of God. Each of the Manifestations of God appeared amongst a nation and in a country which outwardly had no means of salvation or progress. But no sooner had those nations come under the shelter of the Cause of God than they excelled all the civilized countries of the world. Today, whichever nation raises the standard of the oneness of humanity and comes under the shelter of this divine power will ultimately lead the whole world.

Question: 'What is the difference between the Bahá'í religion and the other religions of the world?'

> The foundation of all the religions is one and this foundation is truth. In this respect there is no difference between either the divine religions or their Founders. The subsidiary laws that pertain to the affairs of society differ. These social laws are subject to the demands of time and place, so they are modified in each age.

Question: 'What are evil and bad qualities?'

> There is no evil in the world of existence; rather, evil is the absence of goodness just as darkness is the absence of light.

Speaking of the exigencies of the material world and its creation, 'Abdu'l-Bahá said:

It [the world of creation] calls for change and transformation. Without change there can be no composition or development. Change and transformation, decomposition and composition produce opposites. In the realm of reality, however, there are no opposites. Consider the world of the sun, which has neither darkness nor east and west. But owing to the exigencies of this world, there is night and day, light and darkness.

After answering these questions, 'Abdu'l-Bahá went with Mrs [Corinne] True and other friends to a Chicago cemetery to offer prayers for the departed.[84]

In the early evening 'Abdu'l-Bahá went to the All-Souls Church.[85] A great excitement was also created among the people of this church. His eloquent address, given in sweet and melodious tones, concerned the missions of the Divine Manifestations of God and the peace and unity of humanity. He concluded His talk with a detailed account of the Most Great Manifestation, Bahá'u'lláh, and the influence of His exalted Word.

After members of the audience came to Him to shake His hand and express their thanks and devotion, He went to the home of Dr Milburn, the rector of the Congregational Church. There He gave a most impressive and eloquent talk on the benefits of peace and harmony and the harm caused by war and strife. He discussed the requisites for prosperity and the unity of humankind. It was the last night of His stay and the effect of His words was so deep and far-reaching that it is beyond description.

Sunday, May 5, 1912
[Chicago]

As it was the last day of the Master's stay, there was much commotion among the friends visiting the Master's apartment. A large number of Bahá'ís and their children had gathered in the hotel's salon.[86] 'Abdu'l-Bahá embraced and kissed each child with love and kindness. Giving them flowers and sweets, He said to them:

According to Christ you are the children of the Kingdom and according to Bahá'u'lláh, the candles of the world of man, for your hearts are in the utmost purity and your spirits are sanctified. You are not soiled with the things of this world. Your hearts are pure and clean like the mirror. Your parents must bring you up with great kindness and must educate you in morals and praiseworthy attributes so that the virtues of the world of man may be exemplified perfectly in your characters and conduct, that you may progress in all fields of endeavor, may acquire knowledge of the arts and sciences, and may become the cause of the manifestation of eternal bounties and universal advancement.

Then addressing the entire assembly, He said:

I am going, but you must rise up to serve the Cause of God. Endeavor to keep your hearts sanctified and your intentions pure so that you may attract divine bounties. Remember, although the sun shines equally on all things, yet in the mirror its effulgence is intense, and not in the dark stone. The cause of this intensity and heat in the glass is its purity; without purity and cleanliness, these effects would never appear in it. Similarly, if rain fall on barren land, it produces nothing, but if it fall on pure fertile land, it makes it verdant and causes it to yield a harvest. This is the day in which only pure and chaste hearts can derive benefit from the eternal bounties and only pious souls can receive light from the ever-existent splendors. Praise be to God that ye believe in God, have faith in His words and are turned to His Kingdom. You have heard the voice of God and your hearts are delighted with the breezes of the Abhá paradise. Your intentions are good; your object is the will of God; and your desire is to render service to the Kingdom of God.

Therefore, you must gird up your loins with unswerving determination, you must be united among yourselves and you must not be irritated by one another. Your eyes must be turned always to the kingdom of God and not to the world of man. You must love His creation for His sake and not for your own. When you love one another for the sake of God you shall never be perturbed. No human being is perfect, every person has some flaw. If you look to your fellowman you will always be upset; but if you look to God it shall not be so, because the world of God is a world of perfection and endless mercy; therefore, you will love and show kindness to all for His sake. You must not look to the faults of others; you must look with the eye of forgiveness and pardon. The eye that regards faults sees nothing but faults and the eye that overlooks faults is fixed on the Creator of the souls. It is He Who has created all, has nurtured all, has endowed all with life and spirit and has given to all eyes and ears. Thus all are the signs of His power and for His sake we must love all, and show kindness to all, assist the poor, render help to the weak, heal the sick and educate the ignorant.

It is my desire that the union and harmony of the friends of Chicago may be an example for all the friends in America and that all creation may derive benefit from their behavior; that they may lead all. Then and only then shall the confirmations of the Abhá Kingdom and the bounties of the Sun of Reality encircle you.

Monday, May 6, 1912
[Chicago – Cleveland]

'Abdu'l-Bahá left Chicago for Cleveland in the morning. As He was leaving, Bahá'ís and non-Bahá'ís surrounded Him like moths around a light, their hearts burning with thoughts of separation and tears flowing from their eyes.

The train reached Cleveland in the afternoon.[87] Many friends and newspaper reporters were at the station to welcome Him. The reporters photographed Him with His companions and asked for an interview.

After making arrangements at the Euclid Hotel for His stay,

'Abdu'l-Bahá gave the reporters permission to visit. He gave them an account of the history and teachings of the Cause. One of them questioned Him about His mission. He replied:

> My message is the oneness of humanity and universal peace; the harmony of true science and religion; the equality of rights; the elimination of religious, racial and political prejudices; the truth of all the divine religions; the removal of religious imitations and superstitions; the education of women to such a degree that they may have equal rights with men; the adjustment of the economic condition of all people so that if a rich man enjoys honor and affluence, the poor man may also have a mat to lie on and a house to dwell in; the establishment of spiritual civilization; the reformation of human morals; the unity of all religions, so that when the people of the world recognize the truth of all religions, they may become united since truth is one – if they follow imitation, war and dissension shall remain, because imitations are the cause of differences.

After an hour, He left the hotel for Dr Swingle's home for a meeting with the Bahá'ís.[88] After He had some tea, He entered a room that was filled to capacity. He spoke to the friends about the prosperity of America and the perfecting of material civilization with spiritual refinement, the rising of the Sun of Truth, the raising of the divine call and spreading the teachings of God. The friends were deeply moved and full of admiration. Through their meeting with Him, they had found new life. At the beginning of the meeting, a photograph was taken of Him with His companions and some of the friends.

In the evening, the auditorium of the Euclid Hotel was full and there was standing room only.[89] About five hundred Bahá'ís and non-Bahá'ís were enchanted by His charm and speech. The meeting began and ended with music. The audience was most appreciative of 'Abdu'l-Bahá's talk on the necessity of religion, the dangers of war and the benefits of love, unity and harmony.

Tuesday, May 7, 1912
[Cleveland – Pittsburgh]

Early in the morning 'Abdu'l-Bahá received newspapers giving news of His arrival, His addresses and the meetings of the Bahá'ís, and describing the respect shown to Him, each report having a photograph of Him taken with us.

Shortly afterwards He received a letter from a dignitary of the city, who stated that after reading the newspapers and reflecting on the teachings of the Cause, he was convinced of its truth and greatness and wished to submit to 'Abdu'l-Bahá a statement of his conviction and recognition of the Faith.

We left Cleveland at 8:00 a.m., arriving in Pittsburgh around noon. The friends in Pittsburgh, who had been informed by telegram of 'Abdu'l-Bahá's arrival, were waiting at the station. When the train pulled in, they were overjoyed to see Him and followed Him to the Hotel Schenley where He was staying.

After an hour's brief rest, 'Abdu'l-Bahá received many people who had been invited by the friends to meet Him. Some were leaders of the Jewish community who invited Him to address their congregations. However, owing to a previous commitment at the Peace Congress in New York City, He was not able to accept their invitation.

There was a large meeting in the evening at the hotel for the friends in Pittsburgh.[90] 'Abdu'l-Bahá spoke on the teachings of Bahá'u'lláh, His address ending with these words: 'The East must acquire material civilization from the West and the West must learn divine civilization from the East.' Everyone expressed their appreciation of the teachings with the utmost sincerity.

A little later a group of philosophers, doctors and journalists met with 'Abdu'l-Bahá. He spoke to them in detail about composition and decomposition and the diagnosis of disease:

> If one is fully cognizant of the reason for the incursion of disease and can determine the balance of elements, he can cure

diseases by administering the food that can restore the normal level of the deficient element. In this way there will be no need for medicines and other difficulties will not arise.

After a detailed discussion of this subject, He asked them, 'Although animals do not know the science of medicine, why, when they are sick, do they abstain instinctively from what is injurious to them and eat foods that are beneficial, while man, when ailing, inclines more to that which is injurious to him?' They had no answer to this question and stated that the Master knew the answer better than they.

'Abdu'l-Bahá then gave a description of the extraordinary power of the world of humanity and the freedom of man from the limitations of nature:

> Since man's attention is not confined to one interest, his negligence is greater; while his comprehension is greater than that of all other creatures when it is focused and fixed on one subject.

Thus did the Master speak to the group of journalists, philosophers and doctors, who thanked Him for His discourse.

Wednesday, May 8, 1912
[Pittsburgh – Washington DC]

Early in the morning, as the Master was having tea, preparations were underway to continue our journey. We received copies of some of the newspapers carrying accounts of 'Abdu'l-Bahá's visit and His explanations of the most intricate problems of life and the influence that the Cause had had in that city. Every day the call of the Cause of God was awakening the inhabitants of Cleveland and Pittsburgh who had been asleep on the bed of negligence and this was increasingly reported.

The time for the Peace Congress, which the Master had

promised to attend, was fast approaching. He moved like lightning from place to place and at each He tore asunder the veils of vain imaginings. In a very short time He accomplished many great tasks. Because the meetings in these cities had been scheduled in advance, several were held in one day and thousands of people were attracted and transformed by Him.

'Abdu'l-Bahá left Pittsburgh at 9:00 a.m. and at 9:00 p.m. the friends in Washington DC, who were anxiously awaiting His arrival at the railway station, were overjoyed to see Him.[91] At every stop He had been shown such great respect that it was like the bowing and bending of the cypress trees, demonstrating the power of the spiritual springtime and the tranquillity and flourishing of the garden of humanity. After lunch on the train, some of the friends pleaded with Him to secure a cabin that He might sleep and get some rest. He replied: 'I make certain expenditures only to help people and to serve the Cause of God; and since my childhood I have never liked distinctions.' He spoke for some time on this subject and warned us against making such personal distinctions.

When the Master arrived in Washington DC He was driven to a house especially rented for Him at 14 Harvard Street,[92] which was near Mrs Parsons's home. Joining us today were Dr Zia Bagdadi of Chicago, the son of Muhammad Mustafa Bagdadi, and Mírzá Ahmad Sohrab of Washington DC, both of whom were given the tasks of translating and writing.

The Master spoke today about the meaning of the prophecies and signs of the Day of the Manifestation of God:

> Through their ignorance of these meanings people have always remained veiled from the manifestations of the bounties of Him Who is the Causer of Causes. Although in the divine scriptures mention is made of a heaven and an earth other than the physical heaven and earth, yet they have interpreted these signs literally and have deprived themselves of spiritual worlds and divine knowledge.

'Abdu'l-Bahá then went to Mrs Parsons's home where He spoke about the teachings on economics to the friends, who were extremely pleased with His explanation.

Thursday, May 9, 1912
[Washington DC]

There was a continuous going and coming of visitors at the Master's house from morning until noon. 'Abdu'l-Bahá had lunch at Mrs Parsons's, where in the afternoon He received many people. In the evening He addressed a well-attended meeting, speaking on the principles and tenets of the Faith and counseling the friends to pay no attention to those who objected to the Cause. As the fame of 'Abdu'l-Bahá and the Cause spread, certain narrow-minded ministers had, out of jealously, raised their voices in opposition. At the end of the meeting the Master said:

> Although I pay great respect to the feelings of people in order that they may not run away or make the least objection, yet the religious ministers of Washington have denounced us.

Then He said:

> The denunciation by the leaders of religion is a proof of the greatness and influence of the Cause because no one pays any attention to something insignificant.

Today various clergymen invited the Master to honor their churches by addressing their congregations. He told them that He was unable to accept because He had limited time but that He would be returning to Washington DC.

Friday, May 10, 1912
[Washington DC]

Several distinguished people came to visit 'Abdu'l-Bahá in the morning. After a private interview involving lengthy questions and answers, He spoke in detail on the preeminence and progress of this century and the decrease in the tendency of people to blindly follow tradition.

In the afternoon 'Abdu'l-Bahá spoke to a gathering of distinguished women on the rights and education of women. Later, after a drive in the park, He visited a home for the poor which had been established through the efforts of Mrs [Alice Barney-] Hemmick. In the evening, He spoke about the influence of the Cause of God, the spiritual power of Bahá'u'lláh, ending His talk with loving exhortations to the Bahá'ís.

The Master dined at the home of Mrs Hemmick and Mme Dreyfus-Barney. Everyone was delighted to be in His presence and floated in a sea of happiness until late at night listening to His loving admonitions and exhortations.[93]

Saturday, May 11, 1912
[Washington DC – New York]

The Master made preparations to leave for New York. Some people who had not been able to see Him previously came to visit and He spoke to them about His journey and the spreading of universal peace, which is one of the commandments of Bahá'u'lláh.

'Abdu'l-Bahá left for the railway station, where several believers were waiting to bid Him farewell. They were down-hearted at being separated from their Beloved, who had showered them with such kindness and blessings.[94]

In New York, the friends who were waiting for the Master took Him to the Hudson building on Riverside Drive where He was to stay.[95] He said to them:

We went to Chicago and Washington and now we have come back again. Time passed very pleasantly. The people of America are highly accomplished. They desire to acquire understanding and they wish to make progress. When one sees a tree growing, one should feel hopeful that it will give flowers and bring forth fruits. People asked questions and on hearing the answers they contended no more. Most of the ministers who came would express agreement. Those who asked us questions on important topics were delighted on hearing the answers. The religious leaders of other countries are not so inclined but are more bent on contention. We met very good ministers in Chicago. Some invited us to their churches and we had lengthy conversations with them. One of them, Dr Milburn, invited us to supper at his home. My purpose in mentioning all this is to convey that all showed agreement and acceptance.

Just yesterday we spoke in Washington with a number of notable persons, judges, and also a friend of Roosevelt.[96] As we were talking about the unifying influence of different religions, and concord among nations, this friend said that Christ was a source of differences. But when we explained to him the coming together of different nations under the canopy of the word of Christ, he smiled and accepted the point. Others, too, expressed great delight. When I asked him if he had any other question or objection, he replied that he had none at all. When asked if he accepted all these statements, he said, 'All right.'[97]

When the Master spoke the words 'all right' in English, the friends were amused and a ripple of laughter went around the room. He then spoke about the unification of the blacks and whites of America.[98]

That evening at a public reception at His home, 'Abdu'l-Bahá spoke about the divine favors bestowed on the people of Bahá and encouraged the friends to be grateful for such bestowals and blessings.

Sunday, May 12, 1912
[New York – New Jersey – New York]

In the morning, after prayers, the Master had tea and remarked that 'Although we have not had sufficient rest yet we have to go to Montclair today to speak at the Unity Church there.'

He left with His companions, took a ferry for New Jersey and later boarded a train for Montclair. After an hour's journey, we arrived at the home of Mr [Charles] Edsall, through whom the rector of the church had invited the Master. After greeting the friends, 'Abdu'l-Bahá went to the church where the rector, Dr Edgar S. Wiers, was waiting for Him at the entrance. He took the Master's hand most reverently and accompanied Him to the pulpit, as well as showing us to our seats. After the service, he introduced the 'Great Mystery of God' saying, 'Today we shall read from the New Gospel, that is, from the teachings of Bahá'u'lláh instead of the Bible.' The minister then read a few selections from previously translated Tablets and said:

> A few years ago a monument was erected in Genoa, Italy. Its purpose was to commemorate the memory of a Protestant martyred by the Catholics through religious prejudice. On the statue was engraved these wise words, 'The greatest achievements of the last centuries have been the elimination of religious prejudice and the extension of human thought.' But now I say that these words have not been fully realized and prejudice continues to hold its sway to a degree.
>
> Now there comes a matchless Cause which does away with all prejudices. It is the new teaching of the Bahá'í Faith, which has stirred the religions of the world and has sacrificed some twenty thousand persons to root out prejudice. The East has always been the dawning-point of divine religions. That land is the mother of all religions. The West is in extreme need of such peace because of its excessive armaments and its many wars.
>
> Although it has spread only recently to the West, the Bahá'í

Cause will erelong encompass the entire hemisphere. And now from the leader of this mighty Cause you will hear an important message. It is truly our good fortune that this holy man is journeying in many parts of the world and has now come to this church to deliver the news of the great peace to us. I am greatly honored to introduce His Holiness 'Abdu'l-Bahá 'Abbás and to say that He is one of the great prophets of the world and one of the chosen ones of God.[99]

After this introduction the Master stood up and the entire congregation, out of respect, immediately rose and remained standing until He bade them be seated with a wave of His hand. He spoke in a melodious and eloquent voice, beginning His speech by discussing the oneness of God and His Holy Manifestations and concluding with the statement that in every age the Sun of Truth appears within a sign of the zodiac. At the end He chanted a very touching prayer. As at every such meeting, the effect of 'Abdu'l-Bahá's talk had to be seen, for it is difficult to describe.[100]

As 'Abdu'l-Bahá left the church, many surrounded Him and shook His hand, each one attracted, each heart full of eagerness, each soul inclined towards the Master and every eye turned towards Him, each supplicating and yearning for the confirmations of the Kingdom. Not one mind was bereft of eagerness and no heart failed to be immersed in the sea of joy.

'Abdu'l-Bahá returned to Mr Edsall's home where several Bahá'ís and seekers had gathered, including the minister and his wife, to have lunch with Him. All were overjoyed to be with Him. 'Abdu'l-Bahá was exceedingly happy and the gathering became the envy of heaven.

After lunch and a little rest, another group came to visit 'Abdu'l-Bahá and another meeting was held with eagerness and excitement. The Master spoke with animation, encouraging the friends and guiding the true seekers. Before He left, the minister brought out the church's guest book, requesting that the Master write a prayer in His own hand. He did so at once:

> He is God! O Lord! O Pure One! Thanks be to Thee that, traversing mountains and deserts and crossing the great ocean we were enabled to reach this country and utter Thy Name and manifest Thy signs in these regions. Even in this church we have raised our voice to Thy Kingdom like unto Elijah. O God! Attract the members of this church to Thy beauty, protect and shield them in Thine own shelter and bless them.
>
> Signed 'A 'A[101]

Time passed so happily that the Master promised the friends in Montclair a second visit. He then returned to New York.

In the evening 'Abdu'l-Bahá went to the Grace Methodist Church in New York to speak to the public meeting of the Peace Forum.[102] He spoke on the purpose of the Prophets of God, the peace and unity of humankind and the coming of Bahá'u'lláh who would establish and promote these divinely-ordained teachings. His talk ignited such a fire in the listeners' hearts that all became as moths with scorched wings. In this meeting, too, the members of the audience, with one accord, stood when the Master appeared before them, which seemed extraordinary to everyone. 'Abdu'l-Bahá gave this address:

> If we look at history, we find that from the beginning to the present day strife and warfare have existed among mankind. It has either been religious warfare, warfare of races, warfare among nations or a war between two countries. All these wars were due to the ignorance of humanity, were the product of misunderstandings or were the results of the lack of the education of humankind.
>
> The greatest wars and massacres were perpetrated in the name of religion. Yet the sole purpose for which the divine Prophets appeared was none other than the establishment of love and goodwill among mankind. These Prophets were shepherds and not wolves. Shepherds are to protect and collect their flocks and not to scatter them. Every divine shepherd has

gathered together a certain flock which had been scattered. Moses was one of them. He assembled the various tribes of Israel and created love among them and led them on their way to the Holy Land. From their scattered state, He drew them together, united them and caused their development. Hence their degradation was transformed into glory, their poverty changed into wealth, their vices were replaced by virtues and finally they established the Kingdom of Solomon and the fame of their glory reached the East and the West. Therefore, it is obvious that Moses was a divine shepherd, for He assembled the scattered tribes of Israel and united them.

When Christ appeared, He too became the cause of the gathering of the scattered sheep. He united the dispersed flock of Israel with those of the Greeks, Romans, Chaldeans, Syrians and Egyptians. These nations were in a state of war and strife with one another, shedding one another's blood and tearing one another apart like ferocious animals.

But Christ united, assembled and cemented them together by creating affinity among them so that strife and warfare were entirely extirpated. Therefore, it is manifest that the divine religions were the cause of love and affection. Divine religion is never a cause of discord and disagreement. If religion be the cause of strife, its nonexistence is preferable because religion must be the source of life. If it be the cause of death, its absence is desirable and irreligion is preferable. Religious teachings are like unto remedies. If a remedy be the cause of disease, the absence of such a remedy is desirable.

Likewise, when the Arabian tribes were in a state of rancor and strife, engaged in shedding one another's blood, plundering one another's property, imprisoning one another's wives and children and leading a warlike life in the peninsula of Arabia, and when no solitary soul enjoyed composure nor a single tribe was at ease, at such a time Muḥammad appeared. He gathered, reconciled, united and cemented the different tribes so that all strife and warfare vanished from among them.

The Arabian nation developed to such a degree that they founded the sovereignty of Andalusia [Spain] and established the mighty Caliphate.

From these evidences we must infer that the basic purpose of divine religion is to promote peace and not war. The foundation of the religions of God is one reality. It is love; it is truth; it is the promotion of fellowship and amity. These wars are the outcome of imitations which crept in subsequently. The essence of religion is one reality which constitutes the foundation Truth of the religions of God. There is no difference in the essence; the difference lies in imitations. Due to this difference in imitations, discord and strife take place. If imitations are eliminated from religions and the foundation Truth alone is followed, all of them would agree, and strife and discord would disappear, for religion is reality and reality is one and does not admit of plurality.

Racial distinctions and national differences are purely imaginary. Humanity is one in essence; it is one progeny of a common ancestor inhabiting the same globe; and there is no difference in the original genesis and creation of God. God has created all humanity. He has not created Frenchmen, Englishmen, Americans or Persians. There is no difference in regard to race. All are the leaves of one tree, the waves of the same sea, the fruit of one tree and the flowers of the same garden. Let us turn to the animal kingdom, where there is no distinction among them with regard to kind. The sheep of the East and the West graze together; no sheep of the East will regard a sheep of the West as a stranger and an alien. They graze together in the same pasture most harmoniously and affectionately. There are no racial dissensions or disputes regarding kind among them. Likewise the oriental and occidental birds, for example, the pigeons, will be found to live together in genuine love and amity. There is absolutely no racial distinction among them. Such fanciful concepts do not exist among animals, although they lack the faculty of reason.

Is it becoming for man to observe such vain thoughts, notwithstanding the fact that he is endowed with reason, perceptive faculty and thinking power and is the repository of the divine trust? With all these bestowals how does he permit himself to yield to these erroneous superstitions by saying 'I am a German', 'I am a Frenchman', 'I am an Englishman' or 'I am an Italian'? Through these superstitions they wage war against one another. Is this becoming? God forbid! It is not. If the animal does not condescend to follow such superstitions, why should man be willing to stoop to such low ideas which are nothing but superstition and pure imagination?

Is it proper to foster wars and feuds on account of nativity – such as Eastern and Western, Northern or Southern? No, by God! These, too, are sheer superstitions and mere fanciful imaginations. The whole earth is but one land and one home. Therefore, man must not allow himself to adhere to these superstitions.

God be praised! I have come from the East and find the American continent is prosperous, its climate is most delightful, its inhabitants are extremely courteous and its government is fair and just. Is it becoming for me to say, 'This land is not my country and therefore it does not deserve any consideration?' This would be utter prejudice to which man must not yield. He must, instead, investigate reality, which consists in that all humanity is one in kind and the whole earth is one home. Hence it is proven that the cause of every warfare and bloodshed is purely imaginary and has absolutely no foundation.

Consider what is taking place in Tripoli owing to Italy's disregard for law. Many of the helpless are being killed, thousands of men are being slain every day on both sides. How many are the children who become fatherless, the fathers who become childless and the mothers who bemoan the loss of their dear children. What is the result after all? Nothing. Is it just that man should be so reckless? Consider how animals with a blessed disposition are entirely free from war and strife.

Although thousands of sheep graze together and thousands of flocks of pigeons fly together, war never takes place among them. But ferocious animals, such as wolves and dogs, are always fighting and attacking one another. However, these ferocious animals are necessarily compelled to hunt for food, whereas man does not stand in such need. He is capable of earning his livelihood. Men shed blood from greed, love for self-glory and desire for fame. The leaders of the nations enjoy delightful luxuries in their palatial buildings and only the poor are sent to bear the brunt in the battlefield. Every day new instruments are invented for destruction of the very foundation of the human race. The leaders are utterly devoid of all feelings of mercy toward those helpless ones and show no pity to the mothers who have tended their children so lovingly, having passed many sleepless nights and spent many laborious days in nurturing and bringing their children to maturity. Is it becoming that parents should be made to see thousands of the dear young ones torn to pieces in one day in the battlefield? What savagery! What heedlessness! What ignorance! What hostility! What animosity!

Ferocious animals rend only that which is necessary to meet their requirements; for instance, the wolf kills only one sheep a day. But an unjust man slaughters one hundred thousand of his kind in a day and glorifies in this action, saying, 'How brave I am! What a feat of courage I have shown! I have killed in one day one hundred thousand of my kind and have destroyed a whole country.' Consider to what extent man is ignorant and heedless! If a man kills another person – one single soul – he is called a murderer and he receives capital punishment or life imprisonment. But the man who kills one hundred thousand of his kind in one day is extolled as the greatest general and the greatest hero of the world. If a man steals a single dollar, he is called a cruel thief, whereas if a general ransacks the whole country, he is pronounced a conqueror of the world. What ignorance! What heedlessness!

Among the various religions and denominations in Persia there existed animosity, envy and hatred. In Asia religions were hostile toward one another, the sects sought to murder one another, the races were filled with hatred and the tribes were constantly at war. They considered that the greatest glory for man was to be able to kill, to slaughter many of his kind. If one religion succeeded in prevailing over another religion and in killing the adherents thereof, the first took pride in such deeds. This was the time when Bahá'u'lláh appeared in Persia. He founded the oneness of the world of humanity and established the foundations of universal peace. He declared that all men are the servants of God Who created all and provides for all. He is kind to all. Why should we be unkind? God is compassionate and merciful to all His creatures. Why should we entertain animosity or spite? God loves all. God provides for all. He trains us all and He is kind to all. Our duty is to be kind and loving to all. This is the divine polity. We must follow the polity of God. Is it possible that the human polity should be better than the divine polity? Certainly, it is not. Therefore we must emulate the divine polity. As God deals with all humanity affectionately and kindly, so must we deal with each and every one. Bahá'u'lláh laid the foundation of universal peace and proclaimed the oneness of mankind. He preached throughout the East the lessons of peace and goodwill. On this subject He sent to all the kings epistles encouraging and admonishing them. He made it evident that the glory of humanity lies in peace and reconciliation. This occurred about sixty years ago. Because He promulgated universal peace, the kings of the Orient rose against Him, as they regarded such teachings to be in conflict with their personal ambitions and interests. They arose to persecute and molest Him in divers ways, exiled Him and eventually confined Him to a fortress. They arose against His followers as well. For the sake of this teaching, which sought the abandonment of superstitions and imitations and promoted the establishment of the unity of mankind, the blood of twenty thousand Bahá'ís was spilled. How many homes were destroyed! How many persons were slaughtered and killed! Yet the friends of Bahá'u'lláh stood firm and steady, and up to this date they have endeavored with head and heart to promulgate peace and harmony, having shown their adherence to this principle by their actions.

Men of all denominations who have accepted the teaching of Bahá'u'lláh invariably support the cause of international peace and practice the principle of unity of mankind. They have the utmost love for all men because they know that all are the servants of God, that they belong to one kind and that they have a common descent. At the utmost, those who are ignorant must be educated, those who are sick must be treated, those who are children must be educated and trained. We must not regard children as enemies, we must not be annoyed with patients but we must treat the sick and must teach and educate those who are ignorant. Therefore the essentials of the foundation of the religions of God are love and amity among all humanity. If a divine religion should be productive of discord and hatred, it is not divine; for religion must be the cause of binding together and the means of infusing love and amity. Mere knowledge of anything is not sufficient. We all know that justice is good but there is the need for volition and executive power to carry it out. For example, we know it is good to construct a place of worship but the mere knowledge will not bring about its existence. We should exercise our will to build it. Wealth is needed for its erection; knowledge alone will not suffice. All of us know that peace is good, that it is conducive to the existence of humanity but this needs to be put into effect, it needs action. As this is the century of light which has the capacity for peace, these ideals will necessarily spread and attain the status of fulfillment and action. Time, itself, will raise up those who will promote the cause of peace. Within all countries peace exists. When I came to America I found its people supporters of peace and possessing great capacity, its government just, and equality established among its people. I desire that the light of peace be first shed abroad from America to the rest of the world. The people of America have greater competence to perform this task; that country is not like others. If Great Britain should come forward in support of this cause, it is apt to be interpreted that she is doing so for the preservation of her own interests. If France should stand up in its support, it may be said that she has done so in order to ensure the safety of her colonies. If Russia should proclaim it, she would be supposed to have done so in pursuance of the interests of her sovereignty. But the American nation, it is admitted, does not have such colonial possessions, is not anxious to extend its dominion and is not designing the invasion of other countries. Therefore, if America takes steps in this direction, all are certain to acknowledge that this is solely the outcome of her moral courage, her zeal and sense of honor, and that she has no ulterior motives.

Therefore, it is my desire that you may hold aloft this banner because you are preeminently fit for it. All countries are in readiness for this and the demand for international peace is very high everywhere because the people are in distress. Every year the powers increase the expenditure of war and so the people are tired. At this moment the subterranean storehouses of Europe are full of arms and ammunition and hellish armaments are about to exterminate the foundation of mankind.

The basic foundations for peace and amity are found in the principles of divine religions. If misunderstandings among religions disappear you will see that all work for peace and promulgate the oneness of humankind, for the foundation of all is one; it is truth, and truth is neither multiple nor divisible. The light of this reality shone forth in all the Prophets. For example, Moses promulgated this reality, Jesus established this reality, Muḥammad advocated this reality, the Báb proclaimed this reality, Bahá'u'lláh upheld the standard of this reality and He promulgated universal peace and the unity of mankind. In the prison He rested not until He planted the banner of peace in the East. All the people who have accepted the teachings of Bahá'u'lláh are peace-lovers and are ever ready to sacrifice their lives and properties for it. As America is renowned for her material progress and for her scientific inventions and colossal undertakings, may she also exert noble efforts for the realization of universal peace, so that she may receive Divine help in this undertaking. May this great principle spread from her to other countries. I pray that all of you may succeed and be confirmed.[103]

Monday, May 13, 1912
[New York]

From morning until the afternoon there was a constant stream of visitors and friends. Then the Master went to another meeting of the New York Peace Society.[104] The moment He entered the spacious hall of the Hotel Astor, the audience broke into such hearty cheers that the very walls of the building echoed. There were some two thousand people in the audience and when Mírzá Valíyu'lláh Khán-i-Varqá and I wished to enter, there was no room. However, the Persian fezes we wore were like crowns of honor and signs of respect. Whoever saw us knew at once that we were the servants of His threshold and assisted us to pass through the crowd until we reached 'Abdu'l-Bahá so that we could record His words.

Many people welcomed 'Abdu'l-Bahá with beautiful flowers of varying hues. The beauty of this great peace congress and the eloquence of all the speakers are tributes to 'Abdu'l-Bahá.

Mrs [Anna Garland] Spencer introduced 'Abdu'l-Bahá, describing Him as the Prophet of the East and the Messenger of Peace. Dr Grant spoke of the calamities that had befallen the Master and His imprisonment for the sake of establishing peace among the peoples of the world. The Consul General of Persia [Mr Topakyan] referred to 'Abdu'l-Bahá as the Beauty of God and the Glory of the East. Professor [William] Jackson, who had visited Persia, said that peace, prosperity and security would only be attained through this blessed Cause. The president of the society [Dr Stephen S. Wise] then gave an explanation of 'Abdu'l-Bahá's name and welcomed Him most warmly. The Master stood and a great excitement rippled through the audience. Although the Master was tired owing to His many speaking engagements and the difficulties of the journey, and His voice was hoarse, He delivered an incomparable speech. First He thanked the audience for its great love and kindness. He then spoke about the problems associated with peace, giving an explanation of some of the verses and commandments of Bahá'u'lláh regarding unity and the oneness of humanity. The audience was deeply moved. Every eye beheld that gathering as a court of power and majesty where all, like poets, praised in the most beautiful words and verses the Temple of Servitude. Verily, no desire remained unmet for us, the servants of His threshold. We witnessed with our own eyes the victory and confirmation of the Abhá Kingdom. 'Abdu'l-Bahá repeatedly said, 'Although I say always that I am 'Abdu'l-Bahá, a servant of God, still people refer to me as a messenger and a prophet. It would be better if they would not attribute such titles to me.'

In the evening there was a meeting at 'Abdu'l-Bahá's residence with people from India and Japan. He spoke to them in detail, saying:

> India had a great civilization in former times. That civilization spread from that part of Asia to Syria and Egypt; from Syria it was extended to Greece from whence it found its way to Arabia and Spain. Again, from Spain it spread over most of Europe. The world of man, however, has not yet reached its maturity. The time will come when this material civilization will be infused with divine civilization. Universal peace will be realized and people will become angelic. That will be the time of the world's maturity.

Tuesday, May 14, 1912
[New York]

As 'Abdu'l-Bahá was invited to Lake Mohonk, the venue for the conference of the International Peace Society, He made preparations to leave. This conference was the greatest of all the peace conferences in America. It was held in a most ideal location and many dignitaries and delegates from various countries had been invited to attend. Lake Mohonk is four hours away from New York by train. At the train station special landaus[105] were waiting to take the guests to the conference site. The Master took one of these and went to the Hotel Lake Mohonk. He praised the beauty of the place and the scenic grandeur of the route as His carriage drove for about an hour amidst green valleys, wooded hills, woodlands, waterfalls and natural springs. The conference was to last for three days. Each day two long sessions were held in the spacious hall of the hotel facing the lake, the hall having been especially built for the conference.

On the first evening, 'Abdu'l-Bahá's name was at the head of the program. All the members and delegates were anxious to hear His address. The president [of the International Peace Society, Mr Smiley] introduced the Master with the utmost respect and glowing words of praise. Then 'Abdu'l-Bahá stood and spoke. A new spirit and a new excitement seemed to prevail over the gathering. During the day most of the delegates had been engaged in materialistic issues. The highest level that their discussions had reached was the issue of the internal unity of countries and the problems of the United States of America. In the evening, however, they found themselves puzzled when they heard the eloquent, elegant address of the Master concerning the unity of all people, the reformation of the whole world and the Manifestation of the Greatest Name which would bring about the oneness of the world of humanity and the promulgation of the teachings of universal peace. He spoke for about 20 minutes, the time allotted to Him in the program. According to the custom of the West, the audience applauded for a long time when He ceased speaking. They requested that He continue but because He was tired He apologized and with a gesture of His hand bestowed kindness on all. One by one, dignitaries and delegates from many countries came to shake His hand. Some of them embraced Him and expressed their thanks. The president again stood, offered thanks and spoke with great reverence on the importance of the teachings, praising and commending 'Abdu'l-Bahá on behalf of the audience. Mr Smiley's wife then gave the Master a pendant especially made for the peace conference and thanked Him most joyfully.

Wednesday, May 15, 1912
[Lake Mohonk]

The Master remained at Lake Mohonk. Many came into His presence and to each He taught the Cause of God, answering their questions in the way best suited to the understanding of the listener. Concerning the peace conference, He related a story:

> Once I wrote to the Persian friends that if the workers of peace conferences do not apply in their own lives what they advocate, they are like those wine sellers who convene and make emphatic speeches regarding the harmfulness of wine and proposing its prohibition. But when they go out of the meeting, they begin again to sell wine and to do what they were doing in the past. Therefore it is necessary for the power of execution and effect to spiritually penetrate the body of the world.

The Master gave two addresses at this conference. At the request of the president, He wrote in detail explanations of the divine questions, which were to be published in a book recording the proceedings of the conference. A copy of the other address which He gave on the first evening was written by us.

Thursday, May 16, 1912
[Lake Mohonk – New York]

Photographs of 'Abdu'l-Bahá and His party were taken. Many dignitaries visited Him and were attracted and ignited by His love. He then expressed His intention to return to New York. The president of the conference was reluctant for Him to leave. The Master replied, 'As I have to see numerous people and speak to many audiences, I must leave.' The president remained in the presence of the Master with great reverence until He left. The Beloved presented the president with a good quality Persian carpet, for which he was very thankful.[106]

When the Master returned to New York, the friends came to see Him. They were delighted to hear that so many at the conference were attracted and paid attention to the Master's address. A few days later the talks He had given at the conference were published in a New York newspaper and thus provided guidance to many.

Friday, May 17, 1912
[New York]

Many friends came to visit Him and when their numbers increased, the Master went into the assembly room and gave a lengthy talk that began with a description of the Lake Mohonk conference. He said that the influence and practice of peace and the unity of nations could only be accomplished through the power of the Holy Spirit.

When He was tired during these days He would often go alone in the afternoon to the park near Riverside Drive. He explained: 'When I sleep on the grass, I obtain relief from exhaustion and am freed from cares. If I am not alone, I will talk and perspire and will not become relaxed and free of cares.' As always, people were continually coming and going both day and night. Everyone was anxious to see Him and He spoke to them continuously. It was impossible for Him to get any rest except when He went out alone.

Saturday, May 18, 1912
[New York]

Among those visiting 'Abdu'l-Bahá were some New York clergymen. One of them, Dr John H. Randall, had, while the Master and His retinue had been absent, spoken to his congregation about the life and teachings of 'Abdu'l-Bahá. He expressed the hope that he would follow in the footsteps of the Master. So effective was his talk that many of his listeners burst into tears. He came with great humility to ask 'Abdu'l-Bahá to deliver an address in his church. 'Abdu'l-Bahá replied that since He had been invited to speak that week at several gatherings in Boston, He was not able to accept the invitation until after He returned.

This morning 'Abdu'l-Bahá spoke to the people in the Church of the Divine Paternity.[107] The minister of the church, Dr [Frank Oliver] Hall, spoke at length on the manifestation of the Báb and Bahá'u'lláh, giving a detailed account of the appointed successor and the Covenant of God. He explained that the meaning of the name of 'Abdu'l-Bahá was that He was under the canopy of the Cause of Bahá'u'lláh and concluded by saying that this Cause is the same reality that underlies all the religions of God and will become the cause of brotherhood, concord and universal peace.

The beloved Master stood and delivered an address about the unity of religions and the teachings of the new Manifestation in such a way that all were attracted to the divine fragrances. After His talk the audience pleaded with Him to allow them to line up on one side of the podium in order to shake His hand and then leave from the other side. Although they were permitted to do this, there was still such a crowd around the Master's carriage that it was difficult to proceed.

Sunday, May 19, 1912
[New York – New Jersey]

The landlord [of 'Abdu'l-Bahá's house] had complained about the excessive comings and goings of the visitors, therefore the Master chose the house of Mr and Mrs Kinney for the gatherings of the friends. Among the new people visiting 'Abdu'l-Bahá were some Jewish rabbis.

That evening 'Abdu'l-Bahá went to the Brotherhood Church in New Jersey. At the opening of the service, Dr [Howard Colby] Ives,[108] who was greatly respected and sincere, highly praised 'Abdu'l-Bahá. He stated that this great teacher and proclaimer of the Cause of God, since His arrival in America, had stayed at the Hotel Ansonia and had not accepted any assistance from anyone, bearing all of His expenses personally. Indeed, He had even liberally contributed to institutions and churches serving the poor. When Dr Ives finished speaking on the bounties of the Cause of God and the majesty of God's Covenant, the Master rose and delivered an address on spiritual brotherhood and the unity of the world of humanity. His talk increased the interest and yearning in the hearts of the listeners. Although all came to Him, one by one, to shake hands and depart, afterwards when He went into an inner room of the church, a crowd of people, after receiving permission, came to see Him and were delighted to hear the Master's explanations in response to their questions. All offered Him thanks and praise.

Monday, May 20, 1912
[New York]

Among those visiting the Master at the Kinney's home were some narrow-minded Christian ministers. He spoke to them about the misunderstandings among Christians about Islam. After the Master spoke emphatically with reasoning and proofs to establish the reality of Islam, the ministers left humbly and joyfully, impressed by His explanations.

In the evening an enthusiastic gathering of women suffragists gathered to hear the Master's address.[109] While riding in Mr Mills's automobile, the Master said: 'You will learn of the value of this automobile later because it will be said that the servants of the Blessed Beauty sat in it.'

When He entered the gathering, the entire audience stood with great joy and excitement. The chairman of the meeting [Mrs Penfield] first gave an introductory account of the persecutions and imprisonment of the Master and explained the meaning of the name 'Abdu'l-Bahá. The Master then spoke at length about the education and rights of women. There was great excitement in the audience, and, as in other gatherings, the people were deeply moved and both men and women shook His hand, supplicating for assistance.

Tuesday, May 21, 1912
[New York]

In the morning and afternoon the Master delivered addresses at two public meetings.[110] One consisted of admonitions from the Abhá Beauty, and the other, owing to His impending journey to Boston, was a farewell address to the friends, promising them a speedy return.

This afternoon many of the believers' children came to visit. He embraced them all with the utmost kindness and affection. He exhorted the friends to provide Bahá'í education and spirituality for these newborn trees of the Garden of Favor. To witness such meetings is a real joy. With great devotion, the young and old circled around 'Abdu'l-Bahá like moths.

Wednesday, May 22, 1912
[New York – Boston]

At 10:00 a.m. the Master left New York for Boston, arriving at the Hotel Charles at 4:30 p.m. Many delegates from organizations and groups had gathered at the railway station to greet and welcome Him. The believers had decorated a house with colorful flowers, having made all necessary preparations to receive Him.

That evening the first meeting in Boston was held at 8:00 p.m. for the American Unitarian Association Conference at the Tremont Temple, the largest of all of the churches in the region. The President of the Republic, Mr Taft, is also a member of this important association. Present at the conference were some 800 Unitarian ministers representing the Unitarian churches in America and Canada. In addition, there were nearly two thousand others assembled. The presiding officer of the meeting was the Lieutenant-Governor of Massachusetts [Robert Luce], who introduced the Master to the audience, saying:

> Tonight we express our highest respect and heartfelt gratitude in this great gathering for this highly revered and peace-loving personage who has come from the East to the West to promote the principles of the oneness of humanity and universal peace. Indeed, it is a great joy and supreme honor that this esteemed personage has graced our meeting with His presence. It is my great honor to introduce to you His Holiness 'Abdu'l-Bahá.

When the Master stood up, the entire audience gave Him a prolonged standing ovation. Although in all meetings the audience has risen when the Master appeared, this gathering had a particular importance. The group was composed of elected representatives and leaders of many congregations from several countries and it was they who stood, demonstrating their reverence and to honor Him. The Master spoke about the progress and evolution of creation. It was so impressive that the audience applauded with elation and joy.

Thursday, May 23, 1912
[Boston]

Many Bahá'ís and non-Bahá'ís came group by group to visit the Master. His bestowals and favors revived their souls and brought joy to their hearts. In but five minutes one of the journalists was so impressed that he accepted the Cause and decided to write and publish articles on the Faith. As he left the gathering, he wept at the feet of the Beloved and most reverently supplicated to be confirmed in dedicating the rest of his life in service to the Cause.

At noon 'Abdu'l-Bahá visited the house [Denison House] maintained for the poor of Syria and Greece [the Greek-Syrian Relief Society]. Members of this association had prepared lunch for Him with great care. The lady who was the president of the association had been busy making preparations for His reception. In one of the large rooms there was a table laden with various Eastern dishes. The Master was given the seat of honor to the right of the hostess, which, according to Western etiquette, is a sign of respect. Many association members were also present. Among the Master's comments at the table was this: 'Happy are you who are engaged in serving the poor. My greatest happiness is this, that I may be counted among the poor.'

After lunch the Master gave an elegant address about poverty and detachment, filling the hearts of all those present with hope and delight. All, both young and old, expressed their heartfelt gratitude.

Upon leaving the meeting, He gave ten pounds for the poor. Later, sitting in Professor Blacks's[111] home surrounded by admirers, He showered kindness upon all. The professor accompanied the Master to the town of Worcester, located about 50 miles from Boston.

Passing through green and verdant plains and breathing the invigorating and pleasant air, 'Abdu'l-Bahá spoke sorrowfully in remembrance of the Blessed Beauty and the Greatest Name, saying: 'Would that the Blessed Beauty could have come to these regions! He loved such scenery very much.' Whenever He saw the green and fragrant countryside, He asked the driver to stop. At one place, near the shore of a lake, the greenness of the landscape, the translucence of the water and the purity of the air so pleased Him that He instructed the driver to stop for long time. The entire group stood and waited. No one dared say anything about the delay.

The Master spoke of the Blessed Beauty in mournful terms, which deeply moved us all. In two hours we reached Worcester. The Master accepted the professor's invitation to rest for a while in his home. After tea 'Abdu'l-Bahá went to the meeting at the university, which had been arranged especially for His visit. More than one thousand students, faculty and others had assembled. Professor Hall thanked 'Abdu'l-Bahá for coming to the meeting.

The Master spoke on the value and importance of science. The hearts of those present were attracted and their souls enkindled with the fire of love to such a degree that they soared in the heaven of knowledge, their minds indelibly engraved with the words of the Master.

After His address, some distinguished individuals and seekers were invited to a magnificent reception prepared for the Master. As the chancellor of the university had himself invited 'Abdu'l-Bahá, he himself served the Master. A number of Japanese, Chinese and Turkish students came into His presence and greatly appreciated His words.

When it was time to leave, the Master took both the president's hands in His and said:

> I am very pleased with you and delighted to see your university. You are, indeed, serving the world of humanity and expending your life for mankind. Above all, I wish for you the blessings of the Kingdom and desire that you will be a cause of the spread of sciences and arts. I will pray on your behalf that God may make you a standard of guidance and that the love of God may shine upon your heart. I have seen a great love and affection in you, as well as in the professors and scholars. I shall never forget this meeting, and I shall always remember and mention your services.

Later He returned to Boston in the automobile especially provided for Him by the chancellor. The Master went directly to the home of Mrs Alice Breed. As that evening was the commemoration of the

Declaration of the Báb as well as the birthday of 'Abdu'l-Bahá,[112] the Bahá'ís, with the utmost happiness and joy, had arranged a magnificent feast. When 'Abdu'l-Bahá arrived, He rested for a while and then joined the gathering of the friends, illuminating the meeting with His presence. With joyful and shining faces, all eyes were directed towards the Master. The freshness and verdure of that gathering was like a flower garden and was proof that the Tree of the Cause of God has been firmly rooted in American soil and that it has produced leaves and blossoms of the utmost beauty.

The Master spoke briefly about the greenery of the surrounding countryside, the magnificence of the city of Boston, as well as the university. He then gave an account of the life of the Báb that gladdened the hearts and cheered the souls.

Tea, drinks and sweets were served in another room. Mrs Breed brought before the Master a birthday cake with 68 candles, representing His age. At her request, He lit the first candle and then each of the friends in turn lit a candle, each person like a moth burning with the fire of love. When the cake was cut, each guest took a slice as a sacred relic. Mrs Breed, indeed, lit the candle of servitude and steadfastness that evening and, in doing so, became the recipient of bounty from 'Abdu'l-Bahá's presence.[113]

Friday, May 24, 1912
[Boston – Brookline – Boston]

Both believers and non-Bahá'ís came in groups to visit the Master. Among them were journalists who asked various questions and received specific answers from 'Abdu'l-Bahá. The Master had been invited to a conference sponsored by the Free Religious Association.[114] He quickly left for the meeting at Ford Hall. More than a thousand people were in the audience. The subject of His talk was the unity of the teachings of the Messengers of God and the oneness of religions.

Because another lecturer had spoken just before the Master criticizing religion, 'Abdu'l-Bahá's talk seemed extraordinary and produced a great effect. Another speaker, a zealous minister, had announced that a false Christ, a denier of Christ, had come to America. But when the people heard the Master's address establishing the truth of all the Prophets and especially that of Christ, they were surprised, astonished and extremely interested. Moreover, the dignity of 'Abdu'l-Bahá as He left the meeting became a further cause of attracting the hearts. The members of the association, as well as the Association of Unitarians, had offered to pay the expenses of the Master's journey but the offer was not accepted.

As they left the conference, the chairman held the Master's hand while the audience applauded. He expressed his gratitude and appreciation to the Master. As 'Abdu'l-Bahá left the hall He bestowed His favors upon all.

From that conference 'Abdu'l-Bahá went to Brookline, at the request of Mrs White, Mrs Jackson's sister. A banquet was held in a magnificent palace surrounded by resplendent gardens, situated on the summit of a hill and overlooking a large lake, the beauty of which is beyond description. Here a great number of visitors came to see the Master. He was pleased with the meeting and the surroundings. After a delightful talk, attracting all to Him, He returned to Boston to accept a previous invitation. After an hour's journey in an automobile especially sent for Him, He arrived at the hotel [the Boston Hotel] for a brief rest. He then went to the meeting which was held at the home of Mrs Nichols, who had sent an automobile for Him. A group of learned and eminent scholars and philosophers was waiting for Abdu'l-Bahá to ask Him many important questions, the comprehensive answers to which impressed and satisfied all. The discussion lasted about two hours. Their hearts were transformed by His explanations about universal peace among nations, the equality of rights of men and women and the education of girls. Then, after tea, punch and sweets, the meeting ended.

Saturday, May 25, 1912
[Boston]

Among the visitors this morning was a group of Unitarian ministers who asked many questions and who received important answers. They took their leave with great humility. Another visitor, Rabbi Fletcher, remained for over an hour in the Master's presence, asking various questions and receiving answers. He was so grateful and enthralled that it is difficult to describe his attraction. Dr Jack, the editor of an important London journal, also came for an interview. With great fervor and interest, he wrote down the answers to his questions for his journal. Besides the visits of these interested people, the Bahá'ís, who were in spiritual ecstasy and excitement, continuously begged for admission to 'Abdu'l-Bahá's presence.

At a meeting in the afternoon at the Master's residence with philosophers and learned men of Boston, one visitor asked about the immortality of the soul. In response, 'Abdu'l-Bahá delivered a most unique discourse on the subject, which left everyone astonished. Those leaders of science and knowledge were captivated with the beauty of the Covenant. The talk was so impressive that the Master Himself remarked as He left the meeting: 'Until now there has never been such a discourse about the immortality of the soul.' This was purely the result of His authority and power. He had had no intention of speaking on this subject but when He was questioned, He answered without hesitation.

After the meeting He went to a public park in Boston. Later that evening, in the Huntington Chambers, the Bahá'ís held a farewell gathering with over one thousand in attendance. The Master spoke on the signs of progress in the 20th century. He then chanted a prayer in such an imploring manner that tears sprang to all eyes. The meeting ended with the utmost beauty and dignity.[115]

Sunday, May 26, 1912
[Boston – New York]

'Abdu'l-Bahá left Boston today but before leaving He attended a meeting of the Golden Circle [al-Ḥalqata<u>dh</u>-<u>Dh</u>ahabíyyah], the largest Syrian society in America. One of the learned men, Dr Georgi, introduced the Master and praised Him in the most beautiful words. Another gentleman, a poet of the Arabic language, read, with great reverence and respect, an ode he had written in praise of the Cause of God and the Master. Then 'Abdu'l-Bahá rose and delivered a most eloquent address, which made the Syrians very happy. No one could have imagined that they would have been so attracted and moved to such a degree. When 'Abdu'l-Bahá stepped from the pulpit, all rushed towards Him to shake His hand. An Arab woman struggled out of the crowd with great difficulty and threw herself at His feet, saying, 'I testify that in Thee is the spirit of God and the spirit of Christ.'

The meetings in Boston pleased the Master, especially the meeting with the Syrians, which He mentioned in particular, saying: 'What a meeting it was! How the confirmations of the Blessed Beauty transformed the people!'

This was the last meeting in Boston. He left the hotel at noon, reaching New York by 6:00 p.m. Without any rest He went directly from Mr Kinney's home to the Mount Morris Baptist Church. Standing under the arch of the church and leaning exhausted against a pillar, He addressed the meeting. He spoke of baptism and of the need of the soul to be ready to receive the breaths of the Holy Spirit. At the close of His talk He chanted a prayer.[116] That night all saw with their own eyes the spirituality and innocence of Christ and the influence of the Holy Spirit. Let no one think that these are mere words; rather they are the expressions and feelings of all those who witnessed this. My premise is this: that in all the gatherings in America, the non-Bahá'ís look upon 'Abdu'l-Bahá as a Prophet of God. Even though they are not Bahá'ís, their manners and conversations with Him are the same as they might use for their own Prophet and leader. All who come into His presence are seen in this condition. They all refer to the Blessed Being as the Messenger of Peace and the Prophet of the East in their speeches and writings. Although there are a few narrow-minded clergy who burn with the fire of jealousy, a large number of just ministers in every city have accorded Him the utmost reverence. Among them is the translator of those who spoke in praise of the Master. Their words indicate the quality of the audience and societies addressed by 'Abdu'l-Bahá and are a clear proof of the grandeur and power of the Greatest Branch.

Monday, May 27, 1912
[New York]

More than a thousand people assembled at the Metropolitan Temple in the afternoon to hear the Master.[117] Dr Hill, one of the ministers previously mentioned, stood and said:

> We are honored at this occasion by the presence of a distinguished guest who is the representative of universal peace. His fame has spread throughout the East and the West. Humanity has reaped great benefits from His teachings. Such an august personage deserves a genuine and sincere reception. Past ages necessitated the formation of nations but the present time requires a unity among the existing nations. I am greatly honored to introduce you to the founder and promoter of this universal peace and harmony.

Mr Frederick Lynch, the author of the book *International Peace* and an active member of the peace movement, stood and said:

> Since the arrival of 'Abdu'l-Bahá in America, I have had the honor of hearing and meeting Him several times; I have read with great interest His speeches and addresses in the newspapers. My ardent wish is that I may see here, too, the great

impact of His teachings and the influence of His manifest signs. I was present at the Peace Conference at Lake Mohonk and had the pleasure of listening to the most remarkable address given there. The principles of His teachings, as given in that address, are the oneness of humanity, universal peace and the unity of religions. All His talks vibrate with the spirit of these principles and their influence is felt by all. How I welcome this dear person, whose presence has inspired the minds and hearts of the Americans! He receives inspiration from the breaths of the Holy Spirit. His spirit is infinite, unlimited and eternal. I am delighted to have been invited to this great occasion and to have the opportunity publicly to express my heartfelt testimony.

'Abdu'l-Bahá then stood and spoke on the subject of the Fatherhood of God and the oneness of humanity. The greatest proof of the majesty and power of the Covenant of God was the talk given by Rabbi Silverman, which followed the Master's talk. Previously he had been opposed to the Cause and argued against it. But from the moment he came into the presence of the Master he was transformed and became entirely humble. Rabbi Silverman said:

> We have seen today the light with our own eyes. We are accustomed to seeing the sun rise from the East so we no longer regard it as a miracle. Spiritual light, too, has always shone from the East upon the West. The world is in need of this light, and we, too, are in need of this life-giving light. The fountainhead of this light has today spoken to us. This great personage, with a pure heart and chaste spirit, has attracted the hearts of the Americans and has made them His captivating lovers. His love and teachings have made a great impression upon the hearts and minds. The outward forms of religions are like shells, while the teachings and love are like unto the kernel. We need the shell so that the kernel may be protected. O people, distinguish between the shell and the kernel, the reality and the

form. As stated by this respected prophet, 'We must not err in distinguishing the light from the lamp.'[118]

Tuesday, May 28, 1912
[New York]

At a gathering of Bahá'ís, the Master recounted His journey to Boston, speaking on the capacity of souls and the need for divine education. Friends and inquirers were also continuously coming and going to visit Him in His room. Today He moved from the house facing the Hudson River to Mrs Kinney's home. He had instructed us to rent a house for Him because the owner of the apartment hotel considered that the comings and goings of so many diverse people was unusual and felt that the additional work and difficulty [for the staff] was too great. There had been so many people visiting from morning to night that the hotel management had been obliged to respond to incessant inquiries. However, when the staff saw the Master's great kindness as He left the hotel they became ashamed of their conduct and begged Him to stay longer, but He did not accept.

Wednesday, May 29, 1912[119]
[New York]

A public meeting was held today by the Theosophical Society where 'Abdu'l-Bahá spoke on matters relating to the spirit and its passage through the world of existence.[120] The effect of His address was such that the president of the society said, in the presence of 'Abdu'l-Bahá, that his greatest desire was to bring about a perfect harmony between the Bahá'ís and the Theosophists. The happiness of Master increased day by day through the influence of the Cause of God. Whenever He was asked about His health, He said with the utmost happiness, 'My health and happiness depend on the progress of the Cause of God. Nothing else merits attention. This happiness is eternal, and this life is life everlasting.'

Thursday, May 30, 1912
[New York]

After meeting with some of the friends and a few seekers, the Master went to a hall at the University of New York and gave an address on scientific questions and divine philosophy. His talk influenced many prominent people, all of whom were deeply moved and fascinated. Seeing the influence of the Cause in these sorts of large gatherings, the Bahá'ís offered thanks and gratitude for the confirmations of the Abhá Kingdom.

During this time the Master occupied Himself by writing Tablets in response to questions from both the Eastern and the Western friends. Today He gave an account of the lives of Varqá and Rúḥu'lláh. He showed His great kindness to the sons of this martyr in the path of God, Mírzá Azíz'u'lláh Khán and Mírzá Valíyu'lláh Khán. The Master then told the friends about some of the precepts of the Cause. During these discourses, He said often:

> I am the interpreter of the Writings of the Blessed Beauty, as explicitly designated by the Supreme Pen. All must obey. All matters pertaining to the Faith must be referred to the authorized interpreter. In the future all must turn to the divine House of Justice.

Friday, May 31, 1912
[New Jersey]

At the request of Mr [William H.] Hoar, the Master visited a sanatorium,[121] visiting with the friends and holding two meetings, one in the morning and the other in the afternoon. In both meetings He proclaimed the Word of God and spoke of the teachings of the Blessed Beauty.[122] Many were attracted to the Divine Voice. As the village of Fanwood is a summer resort and its fields and countryside very green and refreshing, it was very much enjoyed by the Master. But when they pleaded with Him to prolong His stay for a few days, because of the excessive heat and soot in New York, He said: 'We have no time for amusement and fresh air. We must engage ourselves in service to the Threshold of Oneness.' The services and devotion of Mr Hoar and his family were much appreciated by the Master and were spoken of frequently at the Holy Threshold.

Saturday, June 1, 1912
[New Jersey – New York]

In great humility a group of Bahá'ís came to the railway station to bid farewell to 'Abdu'l-Bahá. Everyone was weeping as the train left. When He left, the Master was in a devout and meditative mood.

Upon His return to New York, He spoke to a gathering of friends about the harm of intoxicating beverages and also related some historical stories to the friends. In the afternoon some Bahá'ís and inquirers visited Him in His room, one after the other. Among them was a socialist. 'Abdu'l-Bahá said in part:

> Tell the socialists that sharing of property and land in this mortal world is the source of strife and warfare but sharing and inheritance in the Kingdom is the cause of love and unity. If you put your efforts into understanding the precepts of the Kingdom instead of into acquiring worldly shares and rights, you will gain perpetual joy and happiness. The Kingdom of God is vast. He will give you whatever you desire and there will be no place for strife and conflict. Is this not preferable and more pleasing?

Each visitor with a particular interest was addressed similarly and each departed in joy.

Sunday, June 2, 1912
[New York]

At a large and beautiful gathering at the Church of the Ascension, many were honored with the bounty of hearing the addresses and explanations of the Master and were thus turned towards the Kingdom of God. This was the second time this church was graced by Him around Whom all names revolve. He said:

> At the time of my arrival at the church I was in no condition to speak; but when I stood before this great gathering I found the atmosphere of the church filled with the Holy Spirit and so a state of wonderful happiness and joy came over me.

He began His address by saying:

> In the terminology of the Holy Books, the church is a symbol of the Covenant, in other words it is a gathering place for different peoples and races so that it may become a sign and token of the true Temple and the Divine Law.[123]

It was an exposition about the Cause of God as the collective center, the manifestation of the Prophets and the coming of Bahá'u'lláh.

Through the pastor, Dr Grant, some in the audience requested permission to ask some questions, which was granted. Everyone who wished wrote a question on a piece of paper and submitted it through an usher. Through an interpreter, the questions were translated and the answers given to the inquirers. Oh, that the Eastern friends could have been in these churches and gatherings in the West to see with their own eyes the beauty and glory of their Master! They would have rejoiced in perceiving that which no spoken or written words can adequately describe.

Monday, June 3, 1912[124]
[New York]

Mr Penshoe, a cabinet member of the United States government, invited 'Abdu'l-Bahá to Milford [his estate outside the city]. For a day and a night many prominent statesmen and dignitaries of the Republic were enraptured, fascinated by the Master. His address to one of the meetings has been recorded separately.[125] A compendium of the addresses and His answers made during that time would be in itself a complete book.

In response to a question about the war among nations, the Master said:

> It will certainly come about but America will not participate in it. This war will be staged in Europe. You are in a corner and have nothing to do with others. You have no desire to gain territories in Europe, and no one lusts after your land. You are safe because the Atlantic Ocean serves as a great natural protection for you. Europe and most other areas will be forced to follow your system. Tremendous changes will take place in Europe. The great centralized powers will break up into smaller independent states. In reality it is not just that vast countries should be governed from a single center, for no matter how great the ability and wisdom of the statesmen of that center, or how developed their sense of justice, they will still not be fully informed of the needs of every town and village and cannot exert themselves justly for the betterment of their surrounding dependencies. For example, all parts of Germany concentrate their efforts to serve a single center, namely Berlin; and the whole of France is to serve Paris. Similarly, each of the colonial countries serves to adorn one great capital. But your government has a good system.

Tuesday, June 4, 1912
[New York]

When the Master left Milford, as well as the influence of His explanations, His kindness and gifts to the servants of the household made a great impression. Calling them before Him, He thanked them and gave each two gold coins.[126] Much affected, all bowed their heads then turned their faces towards 'Abdu'l-Bahá as He left with majesty and grace. As He turned to observe the lush greenery of that place, tears suddenly poured from His eyes. He was thinking about the Blessed Beauty and was grieved and saddened, recalling the afflictions and sufferings of the Pre-Existent Face.

When the Master returned to New York in the evening, He went to a house built on the shore of the Hudson River which had been rented at His request.[127] Here, at a gathering of the friends, He spoke about the achievements of American civilization in education, agriculture and commerce and the high standard of its government and people, saying:

> Their material civilization resembles a glass of the utmost transparency and purity but divine civilization is like a shining lamp. When these two combine, the utmost perfection will be realized. The light of the oneness of humanity, of universal peace, of equality of human rights and of divine morals will emanate from this country to all the regions of the world and will illumine them all.

Someone asked whether, with all these worldly occupations and physical labors, it is possible that such a spiritual condition can be realized. 'Abdu'l-Bahá replied:

> Provided they behave moderately, the more people advance in the material realm, the more their capacity for attaining spirituality is augmented. The sounder the body, the greater is the

resplendency and manifestation of the spirit. Truly, what impedes spirituality are the dogmas and imitations that are contrary to true science and a sound mind.

Wednesday, June 5, 1912
[New York]

In the morning, the Master, together with some of His servants, went to Brooklyn to attend a children's event given by the Unity Club. The gathering included dignitaries, civic leaders and national statesmen. After exchanging greetings in the drawing room, the Master went to the dining room. All of the rooms, as well as the salon, were exquisitely decorated with flowers of various hues. Many kinds of dishes were brought, most of which the Master did not touch. At the table some of the eminent people spoke to Him. Among them was Admiral Peary, the famous explorer of the North Pole, who gave an account of the voyage he undertook to further his exploration. Admiral Peary then praised the Master and spoke of his good fortune in meeting Him and the importance of the teachings. He asked the Master to make a short speech. Although 'Abdu'l-Bahá had not planned to speak, He delivered a discourse on the perfection of creation, its present defects and the need for education capable of producing great results by removing these imperfections. He also spoke on the importance of the education of children. Although there had been many speeches, this address created a great excitement, capturing everyone's attention. When it was time for 'Abdu'l-Bahá to leave, He was persuaded to have His photograph taken with His retinue.

In the evening there was a meeting at the Women's Union. A number of men were also present. 'Abdu'l-Bahá spoke on the education of women, service to humanity and the freeing of oneself from ego and desire. His address strongly impressed the audience, giving wings to both their hearts and minds.

Thursday, June 6, 1912
[New York – Brooklyn – New York]

In the morning, a group of the friends gathered in the Master's residence. He spoke to them about the Unity Club's children's event, explaining divine education and morals. He then went to Mrs Newton's home in Brooklyn. The servants of 'Abdu'l-Bahá were also invited to accompany Him for lunch at the home of Mrs Newton and Mrs Rivers.

Today a new guest came from the East to see the Master and to be in His presence, Mírzá 'Alí-Akbar Nakhjavání. At the table the Master asked him about conditions in the East. 'Abdu'l-Bahá gave a brief discourse at the table:

> Nothing in the world of existence is greater than such gatherings as these because they have been called solely for the love of God. Observe with what love people from the East are seated at the same table with people from the West. Such love and unity were previously impossible. The power of Bahá'u'lláh has created an affinity in these hearts and has drawn these souls under the canopy of one Word. No family ever gathers with such love and associates with such happiness and joy. It is through the divine power and through the potency of the Word of God that we are assembled here with such gladness and delight. We are turned towards the Abhá Kingdom and like the plants of the flower garden we are swayed by the breezes of His kindness and favor. Today is a day which shall never be forgotten, for we are under the shadow of the Blessed Beauty. Our hearts are joyous with His glad tidings; we breathe the fragrant breezes of the Abhá Kingdom; our ears are delighted with the divine summons, and our spirits are alive through heavenly bounties. Such a day shall never be forgotten.

In the afternoon, after a short ride in Brooklyn's large public park, 'Abdu'l-Bahá returned to New York. A group of people had assembled at His residence to see Him. Saying that He wanted to be alone for a while, He went to a small garden by the bank of the river near His residence. After a few minutes He returned and spoke to the friends of the heavenly melodies.

Friday, June 7, 1912
[New York – Philadelphia]

One of our companions showed such grave negligence and impudence that the heart of the beloved Master as well as our own hearts were saddened.[128] However, observing his behavior and the forbearance of 'Abdu'l-Bahá, we have not written about his actions, which were often the source of grief to the Master.

'Abdu'l-Bahá had accepted an invitation from church leaders in Philadelphia and left New York, even though He was exhausted and greatly grieved.[129] Nevertheless, He gave two talks to the friends in Philadelphia, one during the day and the other in the evening.[130] He spoke on the importance of the steadfastness of the friends and their devotion and sincerity to the Cause and acceptance of afflictions in the path of God. He stated that the purpose of the Supreme Manifestation of Abhá in enduring the severest persecutions and afflictions, and the troubles and martyrdoms suffered by so many innocent souls, was for the purification of the souls, the detachment of the hearts, the happiness of the spirits and the spirituality of the friends.

Because of His extreme exhaustion, 'Abdu'l-Bahá did not attend some of the meetings and gave His apologies. But the friends, with increasing fervor and ardor, resembling moths in the court of union, sang His praises and glories like unto enchanted nightingales, desiring neither sleep nor rest.

Saturday, June 8, 1912
[Philadelphia]

There were two large public meetings held in two churches.[131] In the morning, at the Unitarian Church, 'Abdu'l-Bahá spoke on the reality of divine existence and the meaning of the words of Christ that 'the Father is in the Son'. He gave the glad tidings of the Manifestation of the Greatest Name and explained some of the new teachings, concluding with a prayer chanted in Persian. The audience was so transformed that everyone wanted to be near Him, if only for a moment. But it was impossible for all.

The second meeting was held in the evening at the Baptist Temple. As the distinguished pastor had previously announced the visit of 'Abdu'l-Bahá and the address He was to deliver, and had also invited dignitaries and statesmen from Washington DC and vicinity, this meeting was of great significance. The Master delivered a detailed address on the methods of natural philosophy and of divine religion and then explained the teachings of the Supreme Pen. His explanations made a great impression, attracting all to His presence, such that everyone expressed humility and sincerity. They appeared to be very happy and honored to be in His presence. The Master's heart was elated with the meetings in Philadelphia and often made mention of them.

Sunday, June 9, 1912
[Philadelphia – New York][132]

As the Master intended to leave Philadelphia for New York in the morning, many friends were saddened at their imminent separation from Him. They came to the railway station in great sorrow to see Him off and all along the way supplicated assistance and guidance from Him.

In the evening in New York, the Master gave the friends a poignant account of His journey to Philadelphia, outlining the objective of His visit. He also spoke on spiritual stations and the inner progress of the soul, which are the ultimate fruits of human life.

Today the Master revealed many important Tablets. One of them was to Monsieur Dreyfus:

> O thou kind Friend,
> I visited Philadelphia, for a few days, at the invitation of two ministers and at the request of the friends of God. Two large congregations gathered in the two churches and I spoke within the measure of my incapacity. But the confirmations of the Abhá Kingdom, as evident as the sun, descended and enfolded us. Although we are powerless, He is Mighty. Although we are poor, He is All-Sufficient. The importance of this blessed verse became truly manifest: 'We shall aid whosoever will arise for the triumph of Our Cause with the hosts of the Concourse on high and a company of Our favored angels.'[133]
> I hope that both you and the maidservant of Bahá will be able to render important services on this journey and will become the cause of proclaiming the Word of God. Convey my respectful greetings to the maidservant of Bahá. I pray God for confirmations and assistance for her.
> May the Glory of the All-Glorious rest upon thee.

During this time, both day and night, many people besides these servants were present at the table and enjoyed the presence of the Master.

This evening He spoke of the days in Baghdád, saying:

> The Blessed Beauty did not make any more public speeches after leaving Baghdád and Adrianople. The mode of His discourse and the style of His utterances were a cause of wonder and were without peer or likeness. However, out of respect, I do not wish to give my speeches in that manner.

Monday, June 10, 1912[134]
[New York]

After prayers and meditations in the morning, the Master called us into His presence and requested that we chant some prayers. Later He was occupied managing His affairs. In the meeting with the friends today He spoke about differences that arise within religions after the ascension of their Founders, the Manifestations, to the heavenly abode.[135] But the Blessed Beauty has shut the door on such differences and has referred all affairs to the House of Justice so that whatever the House of Justice commands, all must obey and submit to it. He said that if the Bahá'ís should become divided into two branches, each establishing a House of Justice of its own in opposition to the other, both would be false. Bahá'u'lláh wrote His Covenant with His own Pen and, prior to the establishment of the House of Justice, He appointed and confirmed the Center of the Covenant, 'Abdu'l-Bahá, directing that 'whatever He does is correct'.

The Master spoke with great emotion at the meetings of the Bahá'ís, His exhortations accompanied by sighs of grief. His condition during this time was such as to cause great sadness.

In the afternoon He went to the house of the Persian Consul, Mr Topakyan. When He returned home, one of the friends questioned Him about the influence of dreams, saying that it has frequently occurred that two people from widely different places would call out to each other, recognizing each other's voices in the state of sleep. The Master responded:

> It is obvious that a very deep relationship exists between the spirit of man and the world of existence. It often happens that what we see in a dream comes to pass in wakefulness; indeed, even in wakefulness when the soul is unfettered, matters come to mind which later appear in visible form. This shows that between the reasoning power of man and that visible appearance there is a spiritual connection. Furthermore, the spirit of man has the power of discovering facts. When this power is

realized, problems become easily resolved. Amusingly, while materialists are engaged in making discoveries concerning the strata of the earth, they are immersed in the very spiritual power whose potency and influence they deny. They also claim to forecast coming events.

Such themes were frequently discussed in the Holy Presence.

Tuesday, June 11, 1912[136]
[New York]

After the morning obligatory prayers and meditation, many came to see 'Abdu'l-Bahá. Seekers and those with special petitions visited Him in His room. He then went into the sitting room and spoke to the visitors regarding the insincere faith and blind imitation of people of various religions and their branches, about the ultimate purpose of the Prophets and the penetrating influence of the Cause of Bahá'u'lláh.[137] Before the meeting ended He was asked how to reconcile two contradictory statements in the writings: that detachment from worldly affairs is enjoined and that it is incumbent upon all to engage in a trade or profession. 'Are not these commandments contradictory?' The Master replied:

> In the Cause of Bahá'u'lláh it is obligatory for the individual to engage in a trade or profession. For instance, I know mat weaving and you know another trade. The service we perform is equivalent to worship if we perform it with truth and trustworthiness; it is a cause of human advancement. If the heart is not bound and attached to the world, if it is unaffected by the vicissitudes of life, unhampered by worldly wealth from serving humanity and not dejected because of poverty, then this is a human perfection. Otherwise, to profess generosity if one is poor, or justice when one is powerless to extend it, is easy enough, but this will not establish one's spiritual education and awareness.

Another asked that if, after the Master left, some of the believers considered themselves superior to others, how they could be known. The Master replied:

> I have already spoken about this matter. You should, according to the saying of Christ, recognize them by their deeds. Those who relate themselves to me will be known by their deeds.

Wednesday, June 12, 1912[138]
[New York]

As so many people come every day requesting to see 'Abdu'l-Bahá alone, it is more than the Master can bear in His state of fatigue and exhaustion. Therefore, He instructed us in the morning:

> If anyone has not yet met me, or if anyone has some urgent business, call them. All others I will meet in the public gatherings because I have no time and it is impossible to see everyone individually.

After seeing a few seekers and settling the affairs of some friends, He came downstairs and delivered a public address on one of the great teachings of Bahá'u'lláh not found in previous dispensations, which is the prohibition of cursing enemies and to pray for their forgiveness.

At another meeting in the afternoon, one of 'Abdu'l-Bahá's discourses was on the importance of spiritual relationship, intellectual affinity and sincere affection. 'Although the nations and tribes', He said, 'have material bonds between them, yet in the world of the heart and soul they are in conflict. But those souls that have close spiritual ties and affinities of the heart are always ready to sacrifice their lives for one another, though they are not outwardly related.'

He also spoke of the greatness of this dispensation:

In the Shí'í tradition concerning this dispensation it is recorded that knowledge is composed of twenty-seven letters and that the divine messengers of the past from first to last have revealed but two letters; however, when the promised Qá'im comes, He will appear with all twenty-seven.

Aside from the true meaning of this passage which pertains to the power and might of the Cause of God, to the revelation of verses and signs, to the solution of divine problems, to the disclosure of the mysteries of the Holy Book and to the spread of knowledge – each of which is a hundred times greater in this mighty revelation than in any previous one – materially, too, all the learned men of this age agree that the advancements in knowledge, the arts, industries and inventions of this century are equal to those of the last fifty centuries, indeed, even greater than that.

Thursday, June 13, 1912[139]
[New York]

In the morning and afternoon several prominent ministers visited the Master to invite Him to their churches. They left happy and submissive after receiving the bounty of being in His presence and witnessing the effulgence of His countenance. After they left, the Master spoke to the friends and newcomers about the power and majesty of the Blessed Beauty. With great power and dignity He related the story of the last days of 'Abdu'l-Ḥamíd[140] and the malicious accusations of the enemies and adversaries:

> In spite of all these persecutions and afflictions, the Cause of God triumphed and the Covenant of God gained influence. In fact, even members of the Commission of Inquiry,[141] who every hour ordered a more severe persecution and spread a fresh calumny and who had joined our enemies and adversaries at 'Akká with the aim of destroying and effacing us, were overtaken by the wrath of God while returning to Constantinople.

Affairs changed; all the tyrants were debased; some of the members of this very commission were killed or murdered; and some fled away. Finally, one of them went to the believers in Egypt and begged for minimum subsistence.

The Master gave two talks in the afternoon to the gatherings of the friends. The first was about the differences among the Bahá'ís. 'Bahá'u'lláh', He said, 'declared that should Bahá'ís dispute, even if it be regarding Bahá'u'lláh Himself, both are wrong. He has enjoined all to turn to the House of Justice. But prior to its being established, all matters should be referred to the Center of the Covenant whom all are commanded to obey.'

After a brief rest, the Master went to another meeting where He spoke on the distinguishing characteristics of the world of humanity.[142] His introductory words were as follows:

> I was tired and so I slept. While I was sleeping, I was conversing with you as though speaking at the top of my voice. Then through the effect of my own voice I awoke. As I awoke, one word was upon my lips – the word *imtíyáz* ('distinction'). So I will speak to you upon that subject.

Friday, June 14, 1912[143]
[New York]

The beloved Master called these Servants of His Threshold into His presence, served us tea with His own hand and showered us with great kindness. After a prayer was chanted, He described the devotion, servitude, sincerity and trustworthiness of some of the early believers and expressed great kindness for Siyyid Muḥammad-Taqí Manshádí.[144] 'His station and worth', He said, 'will be appreciated in the future.'

In the afternoon at a public meeting He explained the first verse of the Bible and spoke on the reality of the Manifestations of God and the effulgence of the Sun of Supreme Oneness. In the evening He spoke with majesty and grandeur about the days of the Blessed Beauty:

> Although He was a prisoner, He pitched His tent with glory on Mount Carmel. Even outwardly His power and majesty were such that for five years the governor of 'Akká wished to attain His presence but was not permitted to do so by Him; indeed, He took no notice of him.

Later He gave an account of His many addresses in churches and public gatherings in America, saying, 'What I have spoken is according to the capacity of the people and the exigency of the time. "The father makes gurgling sounds for the newborn infant, although his wisdom can measure the universe."'[145] The Master gave a detailed account of the signs of the Báb and of the Tablets of the Abhá Beauty, relating them to the exigencies of the time.

Saturday, June 15, 1912[146]
[New York – Brooklyn]

'Abdu'l-Bahá had been invited to two large churches in Brooklyn and left New York at 10:00 a.m. Some of the Persian and American friends accompanied Him. At 11:00 a.m. the Unitarian Church was graced with His presence.[147] As the carriage approached, we saw outside the church an announcement in large letters saying 'The Great Persian Prophet, His Holiness 'Abdu'l-Bahá, will speak at 11:00 a.m. in this church on the 15th [sic] of June.' What created in us such a sense of wonder was that the pastor of the church had placed the sign announcing the prophethood of 'Abdu'l-Bahá on the door of his church! The moment the Master arrived, the pastor came out, and taking 'Abdu'l-Bahá's arm with great reverence, accompanied Him to the pulpit. The Master's address was on the degrees of oneness and unity. At the close of His talk, He chanted, with His hands uplifted and in a melodious tone, a prayer in eloquent Arabic that was translated sentence by sentence.[148]

Afterwards, at the request of the pastor, 'Abdu'l-Bahá visited the school, which is conducted in connection with the same church. Here, after the children sang and paid their respects to the Master, He encouraged them and spoke to them regarding their education.[149]

'Abdu'l-Bahá had lunch in Brooklyn at the home of Mr Mac-Nutt.[150] There He spoke to a gathering of the friends about the admonitions and exhortations [of Bahá'u'lláh], saying that they should be thankful for the bestowals and favors of God.

Later that day He went to the Congregational Church in Brooklyn.[151] The gathering and setting of the church were impressive and magnificent and the breaths of the Holy Spirit were felt by all. 'Abdu'l-Bahá left nothing undone in conveying the teachings of the Cause of God. He delivered a comprehensive address, speaking with authority and majesty on the freedom of conscience, the unity of religions, dogmatic imitations, the deprivation of people and the reality of Islam. He concluded by declaring the appearance of the Greatest Name and by explaining the teachings of Bahá'u'lláh. Notwithstanding that the address was primarily about the truth of Islam, everyone came to Him to express their gratitude and thankfulness. Each person, pastors and professors, rich and poor, men and women, and especially representatives from the press, praised Him. No one offered a single objection. The pastor of the church was so earnest and overwhelmed by the love of 'Abdu'l-Bahá that he repeatedly requested the promise of another visit. Owing to the Master's many engagements and little time, the invitation could not be accepted. On the following day, the *Brooklyn Eagle* newspaper published 'Abdu'l-Bahá's address and a description of the gathering.

Sunday, June 16, 1912[152]
[New York]

In the morning the Master spoke about the meeting held the previous evening at the church in Brooklyn. 'This is how we establish the truth of Islam in synagogues, churches and great temples. And see what the Muslims say about us?'

He gave a detailed account of the new teachings to an eminent American author, who was to write about them and who had requested permission from 'Abdu'l-Bahá to publish the work.

The subject of 'Abdu'l-Bahá's talk in a public meeting today was, 'However the material world may advance, it is still in need of the teachings of the Holy Spirit'.

These days He often encourages the friends to teach the Cause of God and to travel to neighboring countries. 'You must teach the Cause of God', He said, 'with great humility. Just as I feel myself humble before all, even before children, so must you be.' He then spoke about the various degrees of devotion.

> In the days of the Blessed Beauty, I never had a desire to write. The friends even complained about it. In reply I finally wrote to Varqá[153] saying, 'When the shrill of the Supreme Pen can be heard, what is the need of my writing?' However, in the days of the Most Great Luminary others wrote, referring to themselves, as the great sun of God.

Monday, June 17, 1912[154]
[New York – Brooklyn – New York]

At the request of the friends to take a motion picture of Him, 'Abdu'l-Bahá went to Mr MacNutt's home in Brooklyn.[155] The first scene is a hurried one, showing a ride in an automobile and the respectful reception of the friends. The second scene shows the Master walking, moving gracefully about and talking with His servants, saying:

> Observe the power of the Ancient Beauty and the influence of the Greatest Name through which He has united us with the people of America in this way. If all the powers of the world had joined forces, still it would have been impossible that

hearts could be attracted to such a degree and that we should be assembled in a meeting such as this with so much love, loving one another heart and soul. See what the power of Bahá'u'lláh has done! He has made the people of the East and of the West love one another. But for His power, the holding of such an assembly would have been impossible. Praise be to God that we are united and that we are of one heart and soul.

In the third scene 'Abdu'l-Bahá is shown walking alone, speaking in a melodious voice, saying: 'His signs are manifest, His might is established, His bounty encompasses all and His mercy is infinite.'

A fourth scene shows the beloved Master sitting among the children of the American friends, both black and white, while the Persian friends stand near Him.

The fifth scene shows a public meeting as 'Abdu'l-Bahá moves about addressing the audience. Then follows a scene of farewell, with the friends shaking His hand.

The friends were very happy at this large meeting. 'Abdu'l-Bahá's address was this:

> Rejoice! Rejoice! The Sun of Reality has dawned.
> Rejoice! Rejoice! The New Jerusalem has descended from heaven.
> Rejoice! Rejoice! The glad tidings of God have been revealed.
> Rejoice! Rejoice! The mysteries of the Holy Books have been fulfilled.
> Rejoice! Rejoice! The Great Day has come.
> Rejoice! Rejoice! The banner of the oneness of humanity is hoisted.
> Rejoice! Rejoice! The tent of universal peace is pitched.
> Rejoice! Rejoice! The Divine Lamp is illumined.
> Rejoice! Rejoice! The breezes of the Merciful are wafting.
> Rejoice! Rejoice! The joyful tidings and promises of the Prophets have come to pass.

> Rejoice! Rejoice! The Glory of Carmel has shed its effulgence on the world.
> Rejoice! Rejoice! The East and the West have embraced.
> Rejoice! Rejoice! America and Asia like unto two lovers have joined hands.

After the meeting the Master went to visit a Jewish friend, a believer, who was ill at his home 40 miles from Brooklyn. He returned to New York at night exhausted.

Tuesday, June 18, 1912[156]
[New York]

At a public meeting 'Abdu'l-Bahá again spoke on the Tablet of the Branch.[157] His talk centering around the Covenant and its promise. After the meeting, many pleaded for a private interview and continued visiting Him until noon.

Today He received the manuscript of *The Brilliant Proof* written by Mírzá Abu'l-Faḍl, which had been written in answer to the objections of a minister in London. Being pleased with the book, the Master instructed that it be translated and published.

He also spoke of the malice, mischief and misdeeds of the Azalis.[158]

In the afternoon several friends visited and described the picturesque scenery and interesting places of America. 'Abdu'l-Bahá said:

> We love meetings of fidelity and not picturesque scenes. We must first be faithful to God, to His ordinances and Covenant and to His servants. If we wish to see places of interest and picturesque scenes, we do so when we go visiting or when we pass through such places and scenes.

Sometimes during these days 'Abdu'l-Bahá would evince a mood similar to that He had when He was staying in Egypt, when He wished for martyrdom, desiring to be sacrificed at the Threshold of God. Among the many Tablets revealed at this time was one in honor of Áqá Riḍáy-i-Shírází, Qannád, who had recently ascended to the Abhá Kingdom.[159] Some of the verses of the Tablet were on this same theme:

> Fidelity demands roaming over deserts and mountains. True fidelity is attained when a wanderer, nameless and traceless, becomes a target for the arrows of oppression on the plain of martyrdom. O Lord! Ordain for Thy servant the realization of his utmost wish, this bounty which shines resplendent upon the horizon of fidelity, like unto the sun arisen at dawn. One request I have to put to the loved ones of Bahá, that they prostrate themselves before the holy threshold, lay their heads on the ground and ask that the sinful 'Abdu'l-Bahá be granted the cup of immolation, so that he may, in servitude to the threshold of Bahá, taste the sweet savor of a drop from the ocean of fidelity.

Wednesday, June 19, 1912[160]
[New York]

As 'Abdu'l-Bahá is to go to Montclair tomorrow, He bade farewell to the friends. Today He admonished and encouraged the friends, exhorting them to love and unity and to refrain from differences and disagreements.[161] Then, at the request of Miss Juliet Thompson, He went to a photography studio where several photographs were taken. As she is an artist herself, she drew 'Abdu'l-Bahá's likeness with her own hands in a few days.

Many people were present in the afternoon. 'Abdu'l-Bahá spoke with a minister about the prosperity of humankind and the oneness of the world of humanity.

Mrs Smith, a member of one of the distinguished families in Philadelphia, had recently embraced the Cause and had requested a Persian name. She was given the name Tábandih [Light-giver] by the Master. As she had a headache, He prescribed some medication for her, saying:

You must always be happy. You must associate with joyous and happy people and be adorned with divine morals. Happiness has a direct influence in preserving our health while being upset causes illness. The basis of eternal happiness is spirituality and divine virtue, which is not followed by sorrow. But physical happiness is subject to a thousand changes and vicissitudes.

Have you heard the story of the emperor who looked into the mirror and became very sad and despondent? He said, 'Oh! What a healthy and vigorous body I had but how worn it has become now! What a handsome face I had but how ugly it has become now! What graceful stature I had but how bent my body has become with age!' Thus he spoke one by one of the physical conditions of his youth and expressed his sadness at their loss. Such is the end of the physical happiness.

Another friend asked about tribulations and unexpected accidents. 'Abdu'l-Bahá replied:

> The chain of creation is interwoven in a natural law and divine order. Everything is interlinked. A link cannot be broken without affecting that natural order. Everything that happens is in conformity with this order and is based on consummate wisdom. Because it is decreed by God that every plant that grows must wither, all flourishing vegetation must fade away, every combination must disperse and all compositions must disintegrate. These are the necessary consequences of that universal law and of all relationships and is interpreted as divine decree.

In every meeting 'Abdu'l-Bahá gives this kind of philosophical explanation to complex problems, thus illuminating the hearts.

Thursday, June 20, 1912[162]
[Montclair]

The Master went to a house rented for Him in Montclair. Since the weather in New York was hot and humid at this time, the Montclair friends had begged Him to visit. Mr Edsall's relatives were elated and grateful for the beloved Master's visit. This servant told the Eastern friends that there was a possibility that 'Abdu'l-Bahá would remain there to rest from His arduous journey and overcome His fatigue, which would alleviate the many troubles and hardships of the past.

That night the Master spoke of the Blessed Beauty's stay in Baghdád and of His Declaration, about His teaching and educating the servants of God.

Friday, June 21, 1912[163]
[Montclair]

In the morning 'Abdu'l-Bahá spoke to the Bahá'ís and seekers of Montclair about the difference between the kingdom of the Manifestation of God and the kingdom of the material world. In the afternoon many believers from near and far were honored to visit Him. He spoke about some spiritual matters and counseled the friends that it is forbidden to interfere in political matters and that they should obey the laws of their country. Later, several friends arrived with the minister of the Unity Church, who invited the Master for a ride that they might receive His love and bestowals. Today a courier arrived with a special invitation from the Society of the Annual American Celebration [Independence Day, the 4th of July]. However, the Master did not promise to attend and deferred the matter depending on His schedule.

Saturday, June 22, 1912[164]
[Montclair]

In the morning 'Abdu'l-Bahá spoke about the followers of Yaḥyá, saying:

> These people are following their false imaginings. They say that the letter from the Báb to Yaḥyá begins thus: 'From God, the Mighty, the Beloved, to God, the Mighty, the Beloved.' But this passage is also written at the beginning of the letter to Dayyán[165] and to others. In Tablets revealed by the Blessed Beauty there are also many such passages. The intent is an address from the Manifestation to Himself. What does this have to do with Yaḥyá? In a Tablet from the Báb to Yaḥyá and written in Yaḥyá's own handwriting, he is directed by the Báb to ascertain God's intention by asking Siyyid Ḥusayn, the amanuensis.

The Master then gave various accounts of their vain imaginings and the mischief they caused in both the spiritual and material affairs of Persia. He also spoke about their malicious calumnies against the sincere and trustworthy Bahá'ís of the East and the West. He ended His talk with an exposition on the erroneous notion prevailing among some religious leaders that science is opposed to religion, a belief that leads people to false dogmas and to adhere to vain imaginings.

In the afternoon the Master gave an exposition on the words of Christ: 'He that desireth to follow Me, must bear his own cross.' He then mentioned the martyrs of this great Cause and, referring to 'Abdu'l-Vahháb-i-Shírází, said:

> Before he left the prison to go to the altar of divine sacrifice, he came first and placed his head on Bahá'u'lláh's feet and kissed them. Having embraced all the friends, he hastened to the plain of sacrifice, dancing and snapping his fingers in ecstasy.[166]

As the Master recounted this event, His voice became so resonant and powerful that it caused the friends to tremble, and then His mood changed. His body dancing and His fingers snapping, He made such ecstatic cries it seemed that the scene of martyrdom had been reenacted before our very eyes.[167] Afterwards, He said: 'Compare the condition and firmness of the martyrs of this Revelation with those of the disciples of Christ, taking into account the station attained. How great is the difference between this Day and the past. How far the one is from the other.'

Friends and seekers gathered in the evening. 'Abdu'l-Bahá's response to Mr Edsall's father-in-law was very inspiring and impressive.[168]

Sunday, June 23, 1912
[Montclair]

After morning prayers of thanksgiving, the Master, with some of these servants, went to the market to purchase food and utensils. 'Abdu'l-Bahá Himself supervised the arrangements in the kitchen. During this journey He often cooked and prepared the meals, especially when there were special guests. When there were no guests, He would not permit us to go to the trouble of preparing special meals but instead was satisfied with a piece of bread and some cheese. With all this, His glory and majesty caused many to bow humbly before Him. In fact, it was seldom that many did not sit at His table both mornings and evenings to receive the blessings and honor of His presence. After returning from the market and completing His chores in the kitchen, He spoke of the development of Europe:

> The material progress of Europe is approaching its zenith. Everything that reaches its zenith undoubtedly begins to decline. I hope that spiritual progress will be bestowed on them and that they will be protected.
>
> It is obvious that whatever is growing, like a tree, is in the

process of development. When we were going from Ṭihrán to Baghdád, there was not a friend to be found on the way but as the tree of the Cause of God was in its infancy and growing, it was apparent that the divine Cause would surround the East and the West and the reign of Náṣiri'd-Din Sháh would come to naught. Observe what has become of his sovereignty and consider where we are.

In the afternoon the hall of the building was full of people. Many were standing in adjacent rooms to hear 'Abdu'l-Bahá. He began by saying:

> It is not the place that should be looked at but the illumined faces and hearts of the friends. In Baghdád there was a small room, about one-third the size of this one, in which a number of the believers were living – but under the shade of the kindness of Bahá'u'lláh and they were very happy.

Monday, June 24, 1912
[Montclair]

In the morning 'Abdu'l-Bahá said to us:

> After the Ascension of Bahá'u'lláh I did everything within my power to promote the Cause of God. I clung to spiritual methods and rendered such servitude at the Threshold of God so that the divine Cause might advance throughout the world. And my correspondence was so heavy that, at the time of the death of an American maidservant of God, my letters to her were counted and numbered sixty-seven; so you can imagine the situation!

When asked about His health at a gathering of the friends, He replied:

Bodily health is not important. What is more important is spiritual health which gives eternal pleasure and has everlasting effect. The more the body is cared for, the worse it becomes. Thus denial is preferable for the body. I took only a cup of milk today and I feel much better. Why should man undergo so much trouble and hardship merely for the purpose of eating?

In the afternoon He gave detailed answers to questions relating to His talks at Green Acre. He then spoke on the blind imitations and prejudices of people.

Tuesday, June 25, 1912[169]
[Montclair]

The Master was invited to breakfast at Mr Edsall's home. When He returned home, He found a number of Bahá'í women, who had come from New York, wearing aprons and cleaning the house. These elegant ladies were washing dishes, sweeping, dusting the furniture and arranging the carpets. They did this with such love and zeal that it is beyond description. 'Abdu'l-Bahá said:

> See what the power of the Blessed Beauty does! What might and sway, what bounty and favor is this! He has inspired these persons to serve with such sincerity and love! They are washing dishes and sweeping the room. They are serving with heart and soul.

He bestowed great favor on one of the ladies by inquiring about her husband, Dr Krug, a prominent physician in New York. She said to the Master, 'From the moment He met you, he has not only ceased his opposition but is now helping me to serve the Cause.'

Later 'Abdu'l-Bahá narrated the story of the conquest of Islam in Persia and spoke about the prohibition of the drinking of wine in the Qur'án. He said:

> When the Muslims arrested the leader of the Zoroastrians and flogged him for drinking wine, under the whip he cried, 'O Muḥammad of Arabia, what have you done! What an influence you have shown!' Now they must say, 'O Bahá'u'lláh, what have you done! With what power You have made the proud ones the captives of love and have united the East with the West!'

At a meeting at His home that afternoon, the Master answered many questions. Among His pronouncements was the prohibition of self-mortification. He directed that the health and strength of the body be preserved, saying that the more the physical body improves, the more it is capable of making spiritual progress.

In the evening the drawing room and adjacent rooms were filled with people. Because the friends opened the gathering with singing and playing the piano in praise of the Master, He spoke about spiritual music which can enrapture the spirit and influence spirituality.

Wednesday, June 26, 1912
[Montclair – Newark]

To some people visiting the Master for the first time, He spoke about Christ's words to His disciples:

> 'Whatsoever thou shalt loose on earth shall be loosed in heaven' [Matt. 16:19]. The Christians have not understood its meaning. They imagine that it means the redemption of sins through the Christian leaders. The intention of Christ was to permit His disciples to elaborate or abrogate the laws of the Torah, as He had altered only two, those of the Sabbath and divorce. But, alas! The spiritual leaders of the Christians did not grasp His meaning, so that when the Greeks and Romans became Christians, some of the idolatrous customs were incorporated into Christianity. For example, the adornment of

churches with images, self-mortification, abstinence, monks' habits, the lighting of candles in church, the ringing of the bell in the steeple and others. These are all from idolaters.

Another group came into 'Abdu'l-Bahá's presence asking about the mysteries of Sufism and reincarnation. Receiving satisfactory answers, they left happy and pleased.

In the afternoon in Newark, near Montclair, both new and old friends gathered at the home of Mrs Kerry.[170] The Master spoke to them on the life of the spirit and its effect on the world of humanity and set aglow the fire of the love of God in their hearts. He then went to the Military Park and gardens, which is the best public place in the town. His walk with His companions presented a magnificent sight. Attired in our Persian *kuláhs*[171] and Eastern dress, and accompanying the Master and the several American men and women who followed Him with great reverence and humility, we formed a unique scene. All eyes turned towards the dignity, beauty and glory of 'Abdu'l-Bahá and to that gathering of the East and West.

The Master then went to Mr Harris's home where the friends had gathered before dinner. The Master urged and encouraged the friends to associate in love and unity with all the peoples and nations of the world. After dinner, because it was late and the distance was great, He rested there for the night.

Thursday, June 27, 1912
[Newark – Montclair]

'Abdu'l-Bahá returned to Montclair today and was in the best of health and happiness. He was engaged all morning explaining religion, dispensing the glad tidings of the Most Great Manifestation and expounding on the veils that envelop the people. Group after group came to Him, and each left with the utmost devotion and humility.

In the afternoon, at the request of Mr Edsall and other friends,

'Abdu'l-Bahá went to the park to rest for a while. He said, as He left the tram at the entrance of the park, 'What great changes have occurred! What waves have swept over us and brought us here! Let us see what waves are still to come.'

A gazebo was set on a small rise in the center of the park. There the Master sat on a bench, inviting Mr Edsall, his son-in-law and us to sit near Him. He stated, 'The Committee of Union and Progress in Constantinople is very good but both internal and external enemies are laying plans to imprison me again on my return to the Holy Land.' When we said that it might have been better had He remained in Egypt, He replied:

> My beginning and my end, the place from which I start and the place to which I return is the Holy Threshold. What I have is from that Threshold and to it I shall return. Had it not been for His aid and assistance, would these people sitting on your right and left have any concern about you and me? We must be just and speak the truth. Who are we that we should be showered with these favors? Compare the position of Persia with that of America.

Later He spoke about certain verses in the Qur'án, saying:

> In reality these verses are the most convincing proof of the all-sufficing greatness and nobility of the Prophet of God [Muḥammad], Who, triumphant and powerful, yet sets forth God's address to Him with the words: 'Thou didst not understand, ere this, what "the Book" was, nor what the faith was' [Qur'án 83:52]. And, 'Unless we had confirmed thee, thou hadst certainly been very near inclining unto them [the unbelievers] a little. They would have taken thee for a friend' [Qur'án 17:73–4]. All such verses are proofs of the truth and greatness of Muḥammad. An imposter does not express weakness and ignorance when in a state of power and majesty. However, the people of desire interpret these verses otherwise.

Again, He said:

> Once I said to Mírzá Muḥammad Qulí, 'Do you remember the days in Baghdád when we had not even fifteen paras[172] to have a hot bath? We must now appreciate the favors of the Blessed Beauty and, in thankfulness, gird up our loins to serve Him. He has guided, assisted and made us victorious in this world as well as in His Kingdom.'

The Master spoke at length about the withdrawal of the Blessed Beauty from Baghdád.[173] He told of the prayers of the friends of God who recited, 'Yá Alláh-ul-Mustaghath',[174] the receipt of the news of the bequest of Áqá Abu'l-Qásim-i-Hamadání,[175] their eventual tracing of Bahá'u'lláh to the place in Sulaymáníyyih where He had taken abode, and then their dispatching a petition to the Blessed Beauty for His return.

The Master then got up and went towards the hotel. When He entered it, two wealthy ladies, guests at the hotel, were seated in the lobby. As soon as they saw Him they requested permission to be introduced to Him. The Master returned to the lobby a littler later and took a seat near them. They asked His purpose and He related to them a brief history of the Cause, something of the prison of 'Akká and the spread of the fragrances of God. They remarked that He appeared to be very wealthy. He replied, 'My riches are of the Kingdom and not of this world.' They said that the signs of wealth were very evident. The Master then said, 'Although I have nothing, yet I am richer than all the world.' Then He spoke about true wealth and the transient nature of worldly affairs, citing passages from the Bible. During this discourse an elegant couple passed by and, hearing 'Abdu'l-Bahá's voice, stopped to listen to His explanations. The two ladies and the couple were so astonished and charmed that the believers were spellbound by their transformation. The ladies gave their names and addresses to Mr Edsall so that they might meet with the friends and be counted among the people of Bahá.

What can I say? Every morning and evening hearts are fascinated and souls attracted to the Abhá Kingdom by 'Abdu'l-Bahá. This is accomplished even though He had neither rest nor relaxation. He used to say, 'If my happiness and spirituality could come to the fore and my mind be at rest, then you would see how hearts could be attracted and souls set ablaze.'

When He returned home, He found a multitude waiting for Him. The gathering was even larger than before, with both new and old friends coming from New York, Newark and Montclair. As it was the last evening of the Master's stay, the hearts were especially attracted and the minds full of a unique spirit. He spoke on the need for the breaths of the Holy Spirit in the material world and about the education of humanity through divine power.

Friday, June 28, 1912[176]
[Montclair – West Englewood]

As the Master had previously invited the friends in New York to a Unity Feast in Englewood, He prepared to leave Montclair in the morning. Although most Americans do not awaken until after sunrise, some of the friends and their children were waiting an hour before dawn to see Him and to receive His blessings. Then another group arrived and received His bestowals.

'Abdu'l-Bahá left Montclair at half past eight in the morning, passed through New York, and after changing trams four times and passing twice by the river, He reached Englewood. Tired from the journey and the warm weather, having traveled from morning to noon, He briefly rested at the home of Mr [Roy] Wilhelm.[177] Meanwhile, the friends began to arrive from the surrounding areas and gathered on the lawn adjoining the house. The meeting was arranged in a circle under the trees, with almost two hundred people seated at the table and being served by the Bahá'ís. Everyone enjoyed the delicacies and was extremely happy.

The green lawn under the shade trees was strewn with flowers so that it seemed as if an embroidered carpet had been spread, every

'Abdu'l-Bahá speaking at Plymouth Congregational Church, Chicago, May 5, 1912

'Abdu'l-Bahá at Dr Swingle's Sanatorium, Cleveland, Ohio, May 6, 1912. Edward and Lua Getsinger are at the center rear

Valíyu'lláh and Azíz'u'lláh Varqá, sons of the Persian martyr-poet Mírzá 'Alí-Muḥammad-i-Varqá

Howard Colby Ives, pastor of the Brotherhood Church, Jersey City, who became a Bahá'í after meeting 'Abdu'l-Bahá

William Hoar, whose services to the Bahá'í Faith were much appreciated by 'Abdu'l-Bahá

Scenes from the moving picture taken in New York City at the home of Howard MacNutt, June 17, 1912

Scenes from the moving picture taken in New York City at the home of Howard MacNutt, June 17, 1912

The Unity Feast in West Englewood, New Jersey, June 29, 1912

'Abdu'l-Bahá with a few of the Bahá'ís attending the Unity Feast at Roy Wilhelm's home in West Englewood. Edward Kinney is at the rear left, Lua Getsinger in the center back and Roy Wilhelm on the far right.

Unity Feast at West Englewood

At the Unity Feast, June 19, 1912

Roy Wilhelm, at whose home in New Jersey 'Abdu'l-Bahá hosted the Unity Feast

'Abdu'l-Bahá walking near His residence in New York

Visit to Mr Topakyan, Persian Consul General, at Morristown, New Jersey, June 20, 1912

Barbecue in honor of 'Abdu'l-Bahá given by Consul General Topakyan

Lua Getsinger, who was given the title 'Herald of the Covenant' by 'Abdu'l-Bahá

Grace Robarts Ober and Harlan Ober. 'Abdu'l-Bahá suggested that they marry each other and blessed their marriage in July 1912

Hippolyte Dreyfus, the first Frenchman to become a Bahá'í

Portrait of the Master taken at Dublin, New Hampshire, in the summer of 1912

'Abdu'l-Bahá in a carriage in front of Day-Spring, the Parsons' summer house in Dublin, New Hampshire

Left to right: Mírzá Maḥmúd-i-Zarqání, Edward Getsinger, Mírzá 'Ali-Akbar Nakhjavái (?), Dr Amín Faríd, Ahmad Sohrab, Ali Kuli Khan, 'Abdu'l-Bahá, Mírzá Valíyu'lláh-i-Varqá, Siyyid Asadu'lláh. Taken by Elize Cabot on August 15, 1912 on the lawn of the Parsons' home.

'Abdu'l-Bahá with the boys at Dr Henderson's camp, August 1, 1912. Ahmad Sohrab, standing left, and Valíyu'lláh Khán-i-Varqá, right, are in fezes.

Fanny Knobloch in 1909. She was the guest of 'Abdu'l-Bahá in Dublin, New Hampshire

Alfred E. Lunt, a prominent lawyer from Boston

Sarah Farmer, the founder of Green Acre

Abdu'l-Bahá with His interpreters at Green Acre

design indicative of the power of the Covenant of the Ancient Beauty. To see the Master walking in this green, flower-covered garden, with a gentle breeze blowing, the purity of the air, the cleanliness of the surroundings and the rejoicing of the friends, was most pleasing; all seemed to vie with one another to please the Master.

When 'Abdu'l-Bahá entered the circle, He delivered a very eloquent address on the greatness of the Cause, the influence of the Word of God, the importance of the meetings of the friends and the need for unity among the friends of God. He counseled them to be truthful and faithful.[178] Afterwards He strolled in the rose garden. 'Abdu'l-Bahá gave His permission for His photograph to be taken and was photographed with two groups. In one He is seated in the garden with His Persian servants standing around Him and in the other He is seen with the friends, some of whom are seated while others are standing.

A minister and another important personage came to visit 'Abdu'l-Bahá. He invited them into Mr Wilhelm's house and spoke with them until dinner was ready. He later left the house to take a brief stroll. When the friends were seated at the table, He took vials of attar of rose in His hand and anointed, perfumed and blessed them all, one by one. He thus made them the anointed of the Court of Servitude and the recipients of the spirit of devotion to the Threshold of God, for the bounties of the Holy Spirit had descended and the favors of God encompassed all. Standing in the center of this assemblage of lovers, He spoke to them in a voice that was sweeter than honey then returned to Mr Wilhelm's house.

That the friends were ecstatic today need not be stated, since their Host was the Beloved of the Covenant, their meeting was an assembly of love and amity, and the surroundings were green and verdant with trees in full bloom perfuming the air. There was a pilaf, a very delicious Persian dish that had been prepared for the occasion, sherbet, a Persian drink and many sweets. Everyone was happy at the unity of the gathering. The Master said:

This meeting will be productive of great results. It will be the cause of attracting a new bounty. This day in which we have come together is a new day, and this hour a new hour. These meetings will be mentioned in the future and their results will be everlasting in all the divine worlds.

There were two more meetings: one in the afternoon and the other in the evening in Englewood for some of the friends who were not able to take part in the first meeting. They took their seats in the garden adjoining Mr Wilhelm's house, sitting on chairs and benches in rows. After a short walk, 'Abdu'l-Bahá joined the visitors, sat down among them and requested the chanting of a prayer. He then spoke eloquently, encouraging the friends to spread the fragrances of God. As He was about to leave, one of the seekers asked Him, 'What are the new teachings of this Cause that are not to be found in the other great religions?' The Master stood in the center of the garden and summoned all to come near. They came and stood in two rows. The Master walked between the rows and spoke. His explanation was so magnificent that everyone was astonished. During His discourse a carriage and automobile passed near by. As they neared the gathering and saw 'Abdu'l-Bahá, the carriage passengers stopped, alighted and they, too, heard His speech and were attracted to the teachings. The Master described, one by one, the teachings of the Manifestation: the unity of humankind, universal peace, association with all religions, forgiveness of enemies, the prohibition of cursing foes, the equality of rights of men and women, the establishment of the House of Justice and the International Tribunal, compulsory education for both boys and girls, the prohibition of wars between nations and governments, and the harm of all forms of prejudice, be they racial, religious, sectarian, patriotic, political and so on. He spoke on these teachings extensively and in detail. At the end, He asked the audience whether these principles had been brought by past religious dispensations and recorded in their books. They all responded 'No'. The inquirer was so overwhelmed that he clapped his hands in delight, expressing his joy and gratitude.

Because it was a moonlit night, this talk was given in the garden, so it was not recorded but these explanations can be found in 'Abdu'l-Bahá's other addresses. After the meeting, He remarked, 'If these persons were to be confronted with the question, what new teachings did Christ bring other than changing the laws of the Sabbath and divorce, they would be utterly confounded.'

'Abdu'l-Bahá stayed in Englewood for the night.

Saturday, June 29, 1912[179]
[West Englewood]

'Abdu'l-Bahá and we were invited to the home of the Persian Consul General, Mr Topakyan.[180] On the way the Master stopped by the home of the minister who had visited Him the previous day. When he saw the Master approaching from the distance, he rushed out of his house and with great humility and reverence thanked the Master for gracing his home. His zeal and joy increased minute by minute as he listened to the Master's encouraging words.

'Abdu'l-Bahá then continued the journey by automobile through the wooded countryside and went directly to the home of the Persian Consul General in Morristown, which is one of the most delightful places in the region. One of its charming features is the creek that runs through the green-clad hills whose trees and verdure face the Consul General's house. This beautiful setting appealed both to the heart and the soul. After the arrival of the Master, who was welcomed by the Consul General and his staff, several important people were invited to meet 'Abdu'l-Bahá. A number of reporters also interviewed Him and expressed their delight in His answers to their questions. Around lunch time, a photographer arrived and took two photographs of the Master, one before lunch was served and the other while He was seated at the table. In brief, the Consul General was most courteous and humble in the Master's presence, to such an extent that he refused to sit without permission. He recorded 'Abdu'l-Bahá's talk and conversations for publication in the newspapers and was honored to host the Master.

After the Master had a brief rest and a stroll in the afternoon, another reporter came to the house. As he listened to 'Abdu'l-Bahá's explanations about the teachings, he recorded them for publication. Then with great majesty, dignity and grandeur, 'Abdu'l-Bahá left for New York. When He arrived home, He did not permit us to prepare dinner for Him. Instead, He ate some watermelon and bread and retired for the night.

Sunday, June 30, 1912[181]
[New York]

In the morning, after His obligatory prayer and supplications, the Master invited us into His presence and served us tea with His own hand. He spoke of the blessings and confirmations of the Ancient Beauty, the Greatest Name:

> This help and assistance are from Him and these confirmations are through His bounty and favor; otherwise, we are nothing but weak servants. We are as reeds and all these melodies are from Him. We are ants and this dignity of Solomon is from Him. We are servants and this heavenly dominion is from Him. We must, therefore, offer our constant gratitude to Him for His favors and must join heart and soul to praise Him for His blessings.

As His home[182] is always filled with a continuous stream of visitors, 'Abdu'l-Bahá did not accept invitations from societies or organizations to speak at public meetings. Instead He spoke to the people gathered in the evenings, gave special audiences during the day and attended to other tasks. This evening He spoke about His long stay in New York. 'As it is the meeting place of the East and the West,' He said, 'I desire to make it a center of signs, and pray that the friends may advance and gain precedence in spirituality.'[183]

Apart from these gatherings and meetings, the Master's walks outdoors attract everyone and His graciousness captivates all.

Monday, July 1, 1912[184]
[New York]

During the Master's stroll in the park near the house, a person of Greek descent walked by. When he saw 'Abdu'l-Bahá, he was attracted and approached Him. The passerby immediately summoned his friends, who were in the park, to gather round. In those green surroundings the Master spoke to them about Greek philosophers and about the progress and civilization of their country in ancient times. He then exhorted and encouraged them to acquire the virtues of the world of humanity. He was so compelling that they were immediately influenced. That evening they came to the Bahá'í gathering and became yet more links in the chain of lovers.[185]

Every night after the public meeting, seekers are invited to visit 'Abdu'l-Bahá in His own room. As they listen to His solutions to complex spiritual problems, to His convincing arguments and to answers to their questions, they are drawn towards the Kingdom of God and attracted to the Abhá horizon. Although it is summer and intensely hot, every day and night a new group of inquirers is introduced.

Tuesday, July 2, 1912[186]
[New York]

After the usual morning prayers and thanksgiving to God, 'Abdu'l-Bahá sent for us and offered thanks and praise to the Most Great Name for the assistance and protection vouchsafed by the Ancient Beauty.

The Master spoke with seekers and visited with friends until noon. After some milk and bread for lunch, He rested for a while but the friends and 'Abdu'l-Bahá's companions remained to enjoy the generous lunch.

In the afternoon, a prominent gentlemen invited the Master to the Plaza Hotel, which is one of the most elegant hotels and a gathering place for the American elite. We went there to see the building. The Master sat in one of the small rooms. When the manager of the hotel offered to show Him the rest of the hotel, He did not accept. Afterwards the Master said to the friends: 'When I see magnificent buildings and beautiful scenery, I contrast them with memories of the prison and of the persecutions suffered by the Blessed Beauty and my heart is deeply moved and I seek to avoid such sightseeing excursions.'

Tonight He spoke about God and creation: 'The Kingdom of God', He said, 'is pre-existent and, since He is the Creator, without doubt He has always had a creation.'

Wednesday, July 3, 1912[187]
[New York]

Today was the anniversary of the independence of the United States from England. There were celebrations everywhere. The Master was invited to attend the Fourth of July parade to which the mayor was also invited. A special messenger had been sent to the Master at Montclair with the invitation. He replied then that He would come if His schedule would permit. As it was not a spiritual occasion, the Master did not go but in order to show His interest, He sent us, His companions, wearing our Persian hats and *'abás*. We arrived before the mayor, were received with great honor as representatives of 'Abdu'l-Bahá, and were given seats near the mayor's chair. There were people there from many nations including China, Japan, Turkey and India, as well as members of the American military and businesses carrying flags and decorations for the celebration. All of these passed before the mayor and were followed by parades of men, women, boys and girls in gala dress and singing sweetly. As they passed by the mayor's stand, he spoke to all gracefully and kindly. After the parade it was the turn of the poets and speech-makers.

When we returned from the event to the Master, we described all that had taken place. It was well that He did not go because the excessive heat and crowds would have been a strain to His strength and health. Whenever it is beneficial to the interests of the Cause, He endures every kind of hardship. For example, on certain days during this journey, in spite of exhaustion and fatigue, He went to faraway places and attended many gatherings in the course of one day. He said, 'I am continually speaking from morning until evening. Not even the strongest person would have such patience and fortitude.'

In the afternoon, at the request of friends, He went for an automobile ride into town. In the evening He spoke at length in His home about the coming of the Promised One.[188]

Thursday, July 4, 1912[189]
[New York]

A number of people met 'Abdu'l-Bahá in the morning. He spoke to them about divine knowledge and the spiritual stations which lead to eternal life – the ultimate goal of human existence. A black youth was there, to whom the Master gave the name 'Mubárak' ['happy'], and to a black woman He gave the name 'Khush Ghadam' [a person who brings good fortune, welcome news, good omen]. He spoke to them about the importance of harmony between the white and black races of America and described the various meetings attended by both blacks and whites and the talks given at them which dealt with this question.

Mrs Kaufman asked about the influence of heavenly bodies on human affairs. 'Abdu'l-Bahá replied:

> The words of the astrologers are for the most part doubtful and unreliable. But the whole of creation is interrelated like the different parts of the human body which have a complete affinity from the toenail to the hair on the head. Every part is perfectly connected with the other. Similarly, the whole of

creation forms a chain composed, as it were, of many links connected with each other. It is therefore obvious that they all greatly influence each other and are part of organized, regular cycles.

He was then asked about the connection between the soul and the body. He replied, 'It has the same connection as the sun has with the mirror. Death consists of the severance of this connection.'

'Some say that your prayers and promises for us have come true and are being completely fulfilled.'

'I always pray with complete self-effacement and humbly implore confirmations from the Kingdom of Abhá.'

'Do you feel the excessive heat? Does it affect your health?'

'I am so absorbed that I feel neither the heat nor the cold. It is all the same to me.'

Today the Master was occupied in revealing Tablets for the Eastern friends. Notwithstanding the heavy pressure of work, He does not delay answering important questions.

There was a large crowd in the evening to whom He spoke about the various kingdoms of creation and the virtues of the world of existence. After the meeting several seekers visited the Master in His room. He answered their questions regarding the stations of divinity and the journey in the path of knowledge and servitude. Everyone was pleased and delighted and joined us in offering praise and glory to God.

Friday, July 5, 1912
[New York]

Some Tablets were revealed for friends in California, consoling them because of their separation from Him since He was not traveling to that state at the present time. Most of the friends on the West Coast of America had not yet had the honor to see Him. When they learned of His intention, they were saddened and sent telegrams begging Him to visit their state.

Today, at the invitation of Juliet Thompson, 'Abdu'l-Bahá went to a museum near His house.[190] On the first floor there were statues, figures of animals and a collection of relics of early American civilization. On observing these objects, 'Abdu'l-Bahá said, 'From these things it appears that America had a great civilization in ancient times.'

In the evening, He spoke to a large number of friends and seekers at His home about detachment from physical desires and the attainment of everlasting life. Everyone was delighted.[191]

Saturday, July 6, 1912
[New York]

After morning prayers and visits with some Bahá'ís and non-Bahá'ís, the Master went for a long walk. It was His custom to go out for a walk before lunch and dinner.

A person of Greek ancestry invited the Master to go to a park outside of the city where a number of his friends, who desired to meet 'Abdu'l-Bahá, had gathered. The Master went to the park. While traveling on the subway, He said:

> In man's nature there must be a desire to ascend and not to descend. The underground air is suffocating. It would have been better if we had gone by road above. The Blessed Beauty used to say that it is even a pity that the dead body of man should be buried under the ground.

When the Master entered the park, He sat on the grass and those who wished to meet Him came to Him.

Much of the time was spent listening to a translation of a long article that appeared in today's issue of *The Sun* concerning 'Abdu'l-Bahá's talk at a church. The reporter had been present when the address was given and had published the translation, adding a brief history of the Cause. In his article, he emphasized the force of 'Abdu'l-Bahá's reasoning in establishing the truth of all of the Manifestations of God, and in particular of Islam and this mighty Cause.

The newspaper was sent to the Assemblies in the East so they would be informed of the influence of the Cause and the prestige of 'Abdu'l-Bahá. In addition to such articles and comments in the newspapers of many cities, both Bahá'ís and non-Bahá'ís wrote eulogies and poems in praise of the Master. Everyone was full of praise for Him, which demonstrates the influence of the Cause in the West. There were even short, sweet poems written in English about His manners and mode of speech. Foremost among such poets was Mr [Frank K.] Moxey. When 'Abdu'l-Bahá was staying in New York, Mr Moxey had written a booklet eloquently praising Him, which he intends to publish in the near future.

This evening the Master explained that the distinction of the world of humanity is due to its relationship to the world of the spirit.[192]

For some time the Master had repeatedly instructed Lua Getsinger to return to California. She delayed her journey and then became ill. When the doctor's medications proved of no avail, the Master gave her pomegranate preserve with an apple and she recovered.[193]

Sunday, July 7, 1912
[New York]

Lua Getsinger was again instructed by the Master to leave for California. His words to her were very emphatic and clear; among them was this admonition:

> The Blessed Beauty entered into this Covenant for obedience and not for opposition. I say this merely for the protection of the Cause of God and for the purpose of safeguarding unity among the friends. Were it not for the removal of vain imaginings and the eradication of differences, I should not have asserted that I am 'the Center of the Covenant'. We must obey

the Blessed Beauty. We must never forget His favors and exhortations. If even a breath of egotism is found in us, we shall perish at once. The friends must be alert. Everyone who expresses a word not from the texts sows discord among the believers. The Blessed Beauty entered into this Covenant for obedience; that is, that no one should utter a word from his own self or cause any conflict. If it were not so, everyone would open a way for himself and expound the Words of God in his own manner. One would say, for instance, 'As I have the power of the Holy Spirit, I have a greater capacity for understanding.' Others, even these old ladies, would at once retort, 'We, too, have the power of the Holy Spirit.'

The power of the Holy Spirit is limited to the Blessed Beauty and the interpretation thereof to none but me. If it is so, then there will be no differences. We must occupy ourselves with thoughts of spreading the Cause. Know that whoever has any thought other than this will become the cause of discord among the friends.

'Abdu'l-Bahá sent Lua with Mrs [Georgia] Ralston, a new believer who had been very much welcomed by the Master. He gave Mrs Ralston a beautiful small Persian carpet.

In the evening at a public meeting 'Abdu'l-Bahá spoke of the animosity shown by a Catholic priest towards the Cause of God. The Master called the friends to His presence and emphatically exhorted them to associate with one another with love and unity.

Monday, July 8, 1912
[New York]

After His prayers, 'Abdu'l-Bahá called to Him, one by one, the friends, old and new, who had assembled at His house. Each had a particular request or question. They came into His presence and each had a portion of this bounty. Mr Hoar's family was invited to dine at 'Abdu'l-Bahá's home. As it was very warm and because of His heavy schedule, the Master did not get any rest until the afternoon when He went for a walk in a park adjacent to His house. He walks in the park, situated on the bank of the river, every day. Mr Moxey described 'Abdu'l-Bahá's walks in that park in a beautiful poem.

Several friends came to see the Master in the afternoon. The name of Mr Barakatu'lláh of India was mentioned. 'Abdu'l-Bahá said:

> This man culls the teachings of the blessed Cause and publishes them in the name of Islam in the illusive hope of building an imaginary castle and of deriving some profit by deceiving the Muslims. But in the long run he will see nothing but manifest loss.

At the public meeting this evening 'Abdu'l-Bahá's talk was on the dual nature of man. He said: 'There are two natures in man. The realization of human virtues and perfections depends on the ascendancy of the spiritual over the animal nature in him.'

Tuesday, July 9, 1912
[New York]

A number of friends were waiting for 'Abdu'l-Bahá when He arrived with a paper from Mírzá Abu'l-Faḍl in His hand. He gave it to us and said, 'Read it. It is very interesting.' It was an answer to criticisms of one Siyyid 'Abdu'lláh, an enemy of the Cause. These criticisms are themselves more proof of the greatness of the Center of the Covenant than are the praises of the friends. Mírzá Abu'l-Faḍl has recorded the very words of this critic in his book.[194]

Although that Siyyid had embraced Christianity, thus retrogressing, he appeals in his pamphlet to the peoples of the world, even the Zoroastrians and Jews, to cooperate with him in his opposition to the Bahá'í Faith. The English press of Cairo published his pamphlet in the month of Naisan[195] 1912. In his pamphlet, he attributes the success of the Cause to the virtues and perfections of the Center of the Covenant. Below is a passage from the second chapter of his pamphlet:

> And when we reflect upon his [the Master's] work and the work of his father, we find a great difference between the two. The foundation laid down by Bahá'u'lláh did not rise except very little. It was not even apparent to the eyes of outsiders. But what has been built upon it by 'Abbás ['Abdu'l-Bahá] since the time of the passing of his father, which does not exceed twenty years, is really striking. We see millions of people of various religions and diverse denominations such as Muslims, Christians, heathens, Buddhists and Hindus drawn and attracted to His Cause from such remote countries as America, Caucasia, Russia, Great Britain and the shores of India.

In the fifth chapter, he wrote:

> What vast genius, striking intelligence, consummate opulence and tried virtue has enabled 'Abbás Effendi to attract multitudes of people from diverse denominations and languages? Even this month he received hundreds of letters from his American friends, supplicating him to visit them. They sent 1,000 guineas[196] to defray the expenses of his journey. He granted their request as he had promised them last year, but sent back their guineas with thanks and apology, saying that it was not his custom to accept such things. Consider this great opulence which was related to me by one of his followers and also spoken of by some Egyptian papers. Look to this virtue and piety which is the cause of love and affection as is said by our ancestor, the author of Islamic law: 'Be indifferent to what the people possess and the people will love you.'

At the table the Master read this paper and smiled. He remarked that according to the words of the Qur'án, the deniers said to the Messenger of God, 'Verily, Thou art an insane one.' But now, according to the words of the deniers of the Cause, 'vast genius, striking intelligence, consummate opulence, tried virtue' and the majesty of the Center of the Covenant have become a cause for the attraction of hearts. The preeminence and power of the Cause is established even by the words of its enemies. Today the services of Mírzá Abu'l-Faḍl were mentioned repeatedly by 'Abdu'l-Bahá.

Wednesday, July 10, 1912
[New York]

People from many different backgrounds continuously visited the Master. It seemed He was not silent for a moment. At one time He spoke of the discord among the various branches of Christianity, and at another, the degrees of divine oneness. He spoke of the despair of the material world and advanced decisive proofs of the necessity for divine power. The next moment He discussed the tribulations and persecutions suffered by the Ancient Beauty and the eventual victory of the Cause of God over all the powers of the world. At yet another moment He spoke of the veils which obscure the people at the time of the appearance of the Manifestation of the Preexistent Beauty. One of the explanations given today concerned the meaning of the Tablets of chrysolite mentioned in the *Hidden Words*,[197] about which one of the friends had asked. The Master replied:

> What is meant is one of the holy Tablets. But it also alludes to the fact that the divine Tablets should be engraved on precious stones. In addition, there is a saying in the East by which the color white symbolizes divine will; red, divine decree and martyrdom; green, predestination; and yellow, execution of the decree.

The day was cloudy and rainy. The weather in New York is like the rainy season in India. The evening was cooler, and when the rain stopped, a large number of friends and seekers came to visit the

Master. He spoke to them about the outpouring of the showers of mercy and divine bounty and the fact that the bounties of the All-Bounteous God will never cease.

Today Mr and Mrs Clark said they wished to visit the Master and to obtain permission to go to Tabríz in Persia. The Master asked Valíyu'lláh Khán-i-Varqá to write and ask them to wait a little while. But as they came so eagerly and quickly to New York to secure permission, saying that they had been invited by the people of Tabríz, He permitted them to leave for Persia.

Thursday, July 11, 1912 [198]
[New York]

After morning prayers and meditation, 'Abdu'l-Bahá bestowed His favors upon the friends and well-wishers, especially on Mrs Goodall and Mrs Cooper and other friends from California, confirming and assisting them. While He conversed with the friends, He also wrote Tablets in response to petitions from the believers.

Among those who visited Him today were two eminent clergymen: one was Dr Grant, the minister of the Church of the Ascension, and the other Dr Ives of the Brotherhood Church of New Jersey. They have frequently visited the Master, showing Him the utmost respect and reverence.

In the afternoon there was a meeting of the friends at the home of Miss Juliet Thompson.[199] 'Abdu'l-Bahá encouraged them to hold as many meetings as possible. 'Promise each other', He said, 'to visit one another's homes so that it may be the cause of promoting love and happiness.' After His eloquent discourse, sherbet and sweets were served and then He left the meeting.

At the evening gathering at His house 'Abdu'l-Bahá spoke on the degrees and station of creation, the maturity of the world and the magnitude of the Dispensation of the Ancient Beauty. The meeting lasted until dinner was ready. He sat at the table and invited all the friends from America to dine with Him. At this point a lady asked, 'Up to the present time, not a single woman has appeared as a Messenger from God. Why have all the Manifestations of God been men?' 'Abdu'l-Bahá replied:

> Although women are equal to men in abilities and capacities, there is no doubt that men are bolder and physically more powerful. This distinction is also apparent in the animal kingdom, for example among pigeons, sparrows, peacocks and others.

Friday, July 12, 1912
[New York]

As the heat was excessive and because He had been revealing Tablets and visiting with the friends, 'Abdu'l-Bahá was tired. We said that there was a bath in the house and that the Master could have His bath every day. He said: 'We are like soldiers; we must not form any habits or have a care for anything.'

At another time He was asked how He liked the tall buildings of America. He replied:

> I have not come to see very tall buildings or places of interest in America. I look always for the foundation of the love of God in the realm of the hearts. I have no inclination to see other sights.

At a meeting with the friends in the afternoon He explained the uniqueness of the divine teachings of this great Cause. Among them are the establishment of the Covenant and the Expounder of the Book ['Abdu'l-Bahá], thereby closing the door on the differences that have arisen at the inception of past Dispensations; association with all religions; the prohibition of cursing or execrating other sects; the commandment to forgive enemies; the oneness of humanity and universal brotherhood; the giving and taking in marriage from all nationalities; the injunctions to parents to educate their children, whether boys or girls; the equality of the rights of men and women; the establishment of the supreme House of Justice as the center of authority; and finally the relinquishing of religious, patriotic, racial and political prejudices. His talk was long and very detailed.

In the evening 'Abdu'l-Bahá was invited to Brooklyn and we accompanied Him. On the way He spoke about New York's large population and the occupations of the people:

> This city with its suburbs has about half the population of Persia. If Persia had a population and an affluence like this, and had she turned herself to progress, she would have far excelled this country in all respects. There can be no comparison whatsoever between these people and the manners, love, hospitality, intuition and sagacity of the Persians.

He then described the days of the Blessed Beauty's sojourn in Constantinople, the self-subsistence and grandeur of the Ancient Beauty and the testimony of Mírzá Ḥusayn Khán, who had said in Ṭihrán that there was only one person, Bahá'u'lláh, who had been the cause of glory and exaltation of the Persians in foreign lands and who did not court anyone's favor in that city.

After approximately an hour's drive, the carriage stopped at the home of Mrs Newton and Mrs Rivers. After a short rest, 'Abdu'l-Bahá went to the table for dinner. Afterwards, He thanked the hostesses, spoke briefly and then returned home. On the way back He spoke about the difference in time between the East and the West. 'Here it is almost midnight', He said, 'while in the East it is midday and in other countries it is afternoon. Here we are going to sleep, while in the East they are busy doing work.'

While the carriage was in motion it felt less hot but the long distance and the exceedingly hot weather took their toll on 'Abdu'l-Bahá. The carriage crossed the Hudson River, passing through the length of the city, which was bedecked with gas and electric lamps of red, yellow and green and colorful advertisements along its wide streets and in the shops. The light emanating from them threw a luster on the greatness of this mighty century. Then the carriage reached home.

Saturday, July 13, 1912[200]
[New York – West Englewood]

Today was a very happy day. The Master had been invited to speak at the Unitarian Church of New York. The pastor of the church [Rev Leon A. Harvey] advertised the talk in the newspapers and also posted announcements outside the church to the effect that the 'Great Persian Prophet will speak at 11:00 a.m. on July 13, 1912 [sic]'.[201] A large multitude assembled. 'Abdu'l-Bahá was welcomed by the pastor, who escorted Him into his office. When the music and singing began, the Master came out. The pastor gave a short and interesting account of the history of the Cause and spoke of 'Abdu'l-Bahá's incarceration in the Most Great Prison in 'Akká, after which he introduced the Master to the audience.

'Abdu'l-Bahá stood and spoke on the oneness of the world of humanity and the principles of divine religion. His talk gave everyone fresh insight, opened new vistas before every eye and engendered a new spirit in every heart. At the end of His talk He chanted a prayer in a melodious voice, which stirred the souls and made everyone long to offer their prayers and supplications to the Kingdom of God. Not wishing to greet the audience one by one owing to the excessive heat and the strain of His exertions, the Master went into the pastor's office and waited. The pastor told 'Abdu'l-Bahá that people from the audience were waiting outside to shake hands with Him and to thank Him so the Master came out and stood on the platform. In great humility and reverence the people came one by one in a file from one side, shook His hand and left from the other side. Those who had not known of His presence in America asked for His address so they could visit Him.

On the way home from the church, the carriage passed through the spacious parks and gardens of the city. While the carriage was crushing the flowers and grass under its wheels, it seemed as if it were exacting tribute from the kings and bestowing crowns and thrones upon the poor.

In the afternoon 'Abdu'l-Bahá spoke about the distribution of wealth and the means of livelihood, thus correcting some of the erroneous notions of the socialists.

At night 'Abdu'l-Bahá went to Mr Wilhelm's home in Englewood where a group of seekers, after hearing His talk, stated that they had been longing for such teachings for years. He then went to the home of Mr [Louis] Bourgeois for dinner.

Sunday, July 14, 1912[202]
[West Englewood – New York]

The Master returned to New York in the morning and went directly to Mrs Sieglar's home to see her mother, who was unable to walk because of a foot ailment but who longed to see the beloved Master and attain His presence. When her desire was made known to the Master, He immediately decided to visit her. The ailing woman was very pleased and happy and found in 'Abdu'l-Bahá the fruit of her life and a feeling that she had been newly born.

When He returned to His residence the Master conversed until noon with the many seekers who had come to visit Him. Several distinguished ladies met with Him later in the afternoon at Mrs Krug's home. He spoke to them about the education and training of women and after a period of questions and answers He left the gathering.[203]

In the evening 'Abdu'l-Bahá's talk at the meeting at His home centered on two groups – the materialists and theists. He spoke about divine power and demonstrated its outward influence on human souls in every cycle. After the meeting other seekers arrived and remained for some time before departing.

Being greatly exhausted and fatigued, the beloved Master did not take dinner but instead went directly to bed.

Monday, July 15, 1912
[New York – Brooklyn]

'Abdu'l-Bahá held in His hand a copy of the address He delivered at the Baptist Church in Philadelphia. He said: 'I present my subjects and explanations in such a way that no one can refute or argue with them. They are accepted by people of understanding and wisdom.' Later He went downstairs where several people were waiting to see Him. Among them were some friends from California. He stressed the fact that all activities should be undertaken only with His permission so that no breach of the love and unity of the believers might occur.

There was a cheerful and animated gathering at Mr MacNutt's home in Brooklyn during the afternoon and evening. The greatest blessing and bounty at the meeting was the manifestation of fellowship and unity among the Bahá'ís under the shadow of the banner of the Covenant of God. 'Abdu'l-Bahá's great joy was reflected in His face and all the friends were enthralled and enraptured. The Master spoke several times. After He had explained some spiritual matters, He would leave the house to take a short walk and then return to speak to them again. He encouraged the friends to serve the Faith, then explained the meaning of the signs of the fulfillment of prophecies. He expressed His joy at the unity and harmony of the Bahá'ís and bestowed His blessings on them. His stay in New York brought about great results and effected the fellowship and unity of the friends.

Tuesday, July 16, 1912[204]
[Brooklyn – New York]

'Abdu'l-Bahá returned to New York to find a large group gathered at His home, waiting for Him. At the meeting the Master shone as a lamp and burnt away the veils of superstition. One eminent woman, a doctor, asked him: 'What is the cause of all these calamities and troubles in the world of creation?' He replied:

Calamities are of two kinds. One kind results from bad morals and misconduct such as falsehood, dishonesty, treachery, cruelty and the like. Surely, misdeeds bring forth evil consequences. The other kind is the result of the exigencies of the contingent world, of consummate divine law, and of universal relationships, and is that which is bound to happen, as, for instance, changes, alterations, life and death. It is impossible that a tree should not wither or that life should not end in death.

Answering questions from the audience, 'Abdu'l-Bahá explained that God is holy beyond comprehension, appearance, ascent and descent, ingress and egress, thereby correcting the erroneous notions of some philosophers and ascetics. The Master's explanations were long and very convincing.

A wonderful meeting was held in the evening. Two very dear friends, Mr Harlan Ober and Miss Grace Robarts were married.[205] Besides the many friends, many others were present, including a very devoted Christian minister [Howard Colby Ives]. The Master had instructed that the wedding be performed according to the law of Christianity and it was performed by the minister. After the ceremony, 'Abdu'l-Bahá rose and chanted a prayer, blessing the marriage of the two devoted believers. Congratulations were given and everyone praised the ceremony.

Wednesday, July 17, 1912[206]
[New York]

In the morning, 'Abdu'l-Bahá said:

> The holding of last night's meeting was done with wisdom and it produced great love. The marriage of the Bahá'ís was also performed according to Christian rites, so that the world may know that the people of Bahá are not confined by trivial customs, that they respect all nations and their peoples, that they are free from all prejudices and associate with all religions with utmost peace and happiness.

He then said:

> My discourses in various gatherings have been founded on principles that are in conformity with reality as well as with the utmost wisdom. For instance, I say that the foundation of all divine religions is the same and that the Prophets are the dawning places of truth. No one can take exception or say that the principles of the Prophets and the truth of their teachings are different. Then I state that the basic teachings of Bahá'u'lláh are universal peace; the oneness of humanity; prohibition of execration and calumny; association with the followers of all religions in harmony and unity of nations, of races and of governments; and such like. I ask, did any of these principles exist in former books and religions? At the end of the talk I say that the laws of the divine religions are of two kinds: the first deals with spiritual verities which are one and the same in all religions; the other with laws which change according to the exigency of the time. For example, it is written in the Torah that if one breaks the teeth of another, his teeth must also be broken; and if one blinds the eyes of another, his eyes must also be blinded. For the sake of one dollar the thief's hand was to be cut off. Now, can such laws be permitted and enforced in this age? Surely, no one can say it is permissible. In this way, all answers to important questions have been elucidated perfectly and none can deny them or protest against them.

Thursday, July 18, 1912[207]
[New York]

'Abdu'l-Bahá's talk today centered on the persecutions and tribulations of the Blessed Beauty and the triumph of the Cause of God in the face of opposition from the most powerful enemies.

When the Master later expressed His intention to move from New York to Dublin [in New Hampshire], the friends were stirred by emotion and excitement. He said:

My weakened condition and excessive work hamper me, otherwise many extraordinary souls would have arisen among these friends. As long as such souls do not arise, the real object will not have been accomplished. A certain amount of enthusiasm and ability can be discerned among them, it is other persons who are to arise.

He then mentioned the names of Mullá Ḥasan and Mullá 'Abdu'l-Laṭíf,[208] saying:

> They were deputized by the mujtahid[209] to see the Blessed Beauty in Mázandarán. The moment they approached Him, they were transformed and became a new creation, not seeking rest for a moment whether by day or night. After undergoing great suffering and persecutions in Mashhad, Mullá 'Abdu'l-Laṭíf sacrificed his life in the field of martyrdom and hastened to the Abhá Kingdom. Similarly, a blind Indian Shaykh[210] attained the presence of Bahá'u'lláh in Mázindarán and danced and sang ecstatically from night till morn. Thus are people required to arise for the Cause of God. Such are the people who are worthy of the field of service and sacrifice.

In the evening the Master spoke on the importance of unity and amity among the friends, on the composition and decomposition of elements, and on the existence and disappearance of matter.

Friday, July 19, 1912
[New York]

A letter was received from Mrs Parsons in Dublin, New Hampshire, begging Him to go there to meet some seekers after truth as well as for a change of surroundings and climate. 'Abdu'l-Bahá, although very tired and weak, spent the afternoon receiving friends and revealing Tablets for the believers. At the evening meeting He spoke about the martyrs of the Faith and visited the son of Varqá, the martyr, Mírzá Valíyu'lláh Khán, who was the recipient of the Master's loving kindness. He then spoke of the martyrdom of Varqá and his son Rúḥu'lláh in a most impressive and dignified manner, paying tribute to and demonstrating His great loyalty to these servants of the threshold of the Blessed Beauty. He then said, 'It is my last night with you and I exhort you to be loving and united.'[211] When He finished His talk, all the friends demonstrated their great joy and happiness.

Saturday, July 20, 1912[212]
[New York – New Jersey]

'Abdu'l-Bahá received an invitation from the Consul General of Turkey. After meeting with the friends and expressing His happiness at their devotion and unity, He left for the Consul's home. He took the ferry across the water, then a tram and arrived at the Consul General's house. The Consul himself had gone to meet the Master by another route but his wife and relatives received Him with the utmost respect and reverence until the Consul General returned.

A number of prominent men and statesmen, as well as the Consul General, were present. The Master rested for a short time in one of the rooms. Then the Consul General, praising 'Abdu'l-Bahá, introduced Him to the audience. The Master came to the table and spoke on the danger of wine and alcohol. He then considered some philosophical subjects and answered questions from the Consul's wife about misconduct and its harmful consequences. She was pleased and when He was about to depart expressed her gratitude by kissing His hand. Everyone begged His pardon for any lack in their service to Him.[213]

The Consul General's brother-in-law requested and obtained permission to take the Master's photograph. The Consul General then accompanied the Master to the railway station to see Him off, even though 'Abdu'l-Bahá had asked him not to do so.

At a gathering of Armenians in the evening the Master gave a stirring and impressive talk concerning the attributes of the world of humanity, spiritual courage and valor. His talk was not recorded because we arrived at the meeting late.

Sunday, July 21, 1912
[New York]

The esteemed Bahá'í Monsieur Dreyfus of Paris came to visit the Master. One of the Master's talks at the meeting of the friends was about services beneficial to the world of humanity. 'Universality is of God,' He said, 'while every limitation is human.' Continuing, He said, 'The Sun of Truth has risen always in the East and yet it has shone with greater luster in the West.' Mr Kaufman remarked that he had read in the newspapers about the Master's journey to the West and understood that the purpose of His journey was for the upliftment and education of the West as well as of the East. Mr Kaufman then asked, 'Will the East regain its former glory?' The Master replied, 'It will be greater than before.' The Master then spoke about eternal life and everlasting honor and said:

> How many great men have come into the world! What wealth they have owned! What kings have sat on the thrones of glory and riches! What beautiful and comely people have adorned the world of man! But what has been the outcome? Honor, life, luxury and pleasure have all perished. But the fame of the beauty of Joseph is still universal and the honor of the disciples of Christ still endures; their sufferings are the cause of life everlasting.

At dinner a number of the Eastern and Western friends were at the Master's table. Mrs True and some other friends asked His permission to serve the guests, which He gave.

Monday, July 22, 1912
[New York]

At the morning gathering of the friends one asked about the longevity of life in ancient times. The Master replied:

> Some think that is a third motion of the earth which is the cause of the length or shortness of life. This motion, they say, is different from the diurnal and annual motions and is the cause of change in the condition of the globe. But the long lives mentioned in certain books and narratives have a different basis. For instance, it was a custom in former times to mention a dynasty or family by the name of one person only. However, the people in the following ages thought that the length of time that a family survived was the length of the life of that family's founder.

'Abdu'l-Bahá had planned to leave for Boston and Dublin today but because of the arrival of the brother of the Khedive of Egypt,[214] the great Amír, Prince Muḥammad-'Alí Páshá, the Master's departure was delayed. The Master paid him a visit which was returned by the prince. On each visit this eminent, enlightened man received the utmost love and showed great interest. When the prince returned to Egypt he published an account of his journey, describing his visit with the Master, which is available everywhere in Egypt and elsewhere. On page 414 of his account he describes his visit with 'Abdu'l-Bahá:

> Monday morning, July 22. I was informed that His excellency, the venerable oriental sage, 'Abbás Effendi, the head of the Bahá'í Movement, wished to see me. I therefore set 3:00 p.m. today for a conversation with him. 'Abbás Effendi arrived at the appointed hour. I received him with respect and regard for his reverence and honor.

Age has not altered his extraordinary sagacity and infinite intelligence. He stayed with me for an hour and conversed on diverse subjects of great importance and usefulness, which amply testified to his vast knowledge and wide experience. Truly, he is a man of science and knowledge and is one of the exalted personages of the East. We paid 'Abbás Effendi a return visit. He was living in a small but well-furnished house. Everything to insure his comfort was available. He had a suite of ten persons with him wearing Persian *kuláhs* on their heads. From this orderly and well-organized reception, I understood that this revered personage, because of the weakness of the Americans, had brought such a large number of Persians with him so that he might draw attention to himself. I do not mean this to lower the dignity of this great man, nay, on the other hand, it shows his great intelligence and indicates his vast knowledge of the way by which he may impress the minds of the people so they may turn towards him. His numerous, most impressive speeches have found a wide circulation in America. Indeed, the newspapers and periodicals are still publishing them with commentaries by the learned men of their religion. His influence has reached to such a prominence that bigoted and jealous people are protesting vigorously against him. I stayed with him for a long time and we talked with each other on various subjects. He made me happy by his delightful talks. I departed from his presence with his love and reverence preserved in my heart.

From such writings those with perception can see that although the Khedive's brother was not a Bahá'í, he was drawn to and affected by the Master. His words are a brilliant testimony to the effectiveness of the Master's talks, the impressiveness of His addresses and the vigour with which 'Abdu'l-Bahá promulgates the teachings of God.

Tuesday, July 23, 1912
[New York – Boston]

'Abdu'l-Bahá left New York at 8:00 a.m. for Boston and Dublin, reaching Boston at 3:30 p.m. A number of friends were at the train station to receive Him. As soon as they saw Him, they hovered around Him like moths around a candle, anxious to sacrifice themselves before Him. As He did not plan to stay in Boston for more than two nights, He instructed everyone in His entourage except an interpreter and a secretary to go directly to Dublin.

He then went to the Hotel Victoria where the public meeting was held at 6:00 p.m.[215] There were both Bahá'ís and non-Bahá'ís present as well as some journalists who questioned Him about His purpose in coming to America. The Master replied:

> I came for the peace gatherings in America. They are good. But their efforts must not end in words alone. I pray that they may receive confirmation so that this country may become the center of efforts for peace.

His address was on economic problems.

In the evening He was invited to dine at the home of Mrs [Alice Ives] Breed. As the Master left the hotel, crowds of people stood in rows as He passed through them. That evening He spoke about the persecutions and tribulations of the Manifestations of God, the reconciliation of the hearts and the victory of this blessed Cause of God. After dinner He made the long and tedious journey back to the hotel.

Wednesday, July 24, 1912
[Boston]

From 8:00 a.m. until noon, the Master spoke to friends and seekers who came to visit. Newspapers carrying accounts of the previous day's meeting were brought to Him. Both His talk and the questions and answers were published.

In the afternoon He gave a public address about the beauty and perfection of the world of being.

He was invited later to the Golden Circle Club where He was asked whether Arabic might become the universal language. He said that it would not. He was then asked about Esperanto. He replied:

> A few weeks ago, I wrote a letter from New York to one of the promoters of Esperanto telling him that this language could become universal if a council of delegates chosen from among the nations and rulers were established which would discuss Esperanto and consider the means to promote it.

He gave a public address on the subject of the relationship between the East and the West. The president of the club and its members were enchanted and reverently and humbly bid Him farewell. Some even continued to listen to His explanations in the automobile as it traveled for one and a half hours through parks, gardens and green fields, all beautifully landscaped. When He reached the hotel, He found another group waiting. After greeting the members of the Bahá'í Assembly, He spoke with the group at length.

Later that day the president of the Boston Theosophical Society invited the Master to speak to his association that evening. Although He was tired, seeing that the meeting place was not too far away, He accepted and gave a detailed and comprehensive talk on the immortality of the spirit of man.[216] When the meeting ended, the people ran to the door to shake hands with the Master and to express their joy and devotion. Some were in ecstasy.

Thursday, July 25, 1912
[Boston]

As 'Abdu'l-Bahá had said He intended to leave Boston for Dublin, the friends and seekers gathered at the hotel. He encouraged them to lead fruitful lives and to overcome self and desire.[217]

Consenting to a request of Mr Kinney, the Master paid a visit to Green Acre. When He got there, two Arab seekers fell at His feet crying, 'O Thou the Prophet of God'.[218] He lifted them with His own hand, saying: 'I am 'Abdu'l-Bahá [the Servant of Bahá].'

At 4:00 in the afternoon 'Abdu'l-Bahá left Boston and by 7:00 p.m. He was gracing the gardens of Dublin.[219] The Master took up residence in one of the two houses Mrs Parsons had especially prepared for Him, which was furnished with every comfort; however, the Master said that we must bear our own expenses. Mrs Parsons had hoped that the arrival of the Master would remain private so that He might rest a little. When 'Abdu'l-Bahá learned of this He said:

> We have come for work and service and not for leisure. We must render service to the Threshold of the Blessed Beauty and must make such servitude the cause of our solace and the joy of our souls. As this place is a summer resort and many prominent people are present, therefore, unless they should themselves ask, the friends should not teach openly. They must deal with them with perfect dignity and honor.

Continuing, He said:

> Consider where we came from and where we are now in Dublin here in America. We must offer thanks for the assistance and protection of the Abhá Beauty that we may breathe a breath in the path of servitude.

He then gave an account of the life of Ḥájí Abu'l-Qásim, an indigo merchant, and the restoration of his grave. 'He was', He said, 'one of the servants of the Blessed Beauty. My first thought on my arrival in Egypt was to repair his tomb.' Similarly, He spoke of the good intentions and sincerity of Áqá Muḥammad Taqí Iṣfahání, who is residing in Egypt. In the evening he enjoyed His dinner and ate in good health and happiness.

Friday, July 26, 1912
[Dublin]

Early in the morning, while having tea, 'Abdu'l-Bahá spoke about the Tablet of the Báb to Náṣiri'd-Dín Sháh when he was the Crown Prince and the answer of the 'ulamá.[220] 'It must be compared', He said, 'with the Lawḥ-i-Sulṭán[221] which issued from the Supreme Pen so that the injustices of the followers of Mírzá Yaḥyá might be exposed.'

In the afternoon 'Abdu'l-Bahá spoke of Ḥájí Muḥammad-Taqí Vakíl'ud Dawlih, the Afnán. He also showed great kindness to some of the American Bahá'ís. About one of them He said:

> Write this in the margin of the book: The time will come when her whole family will be proud of Mrs Krug and her faith. Her husband is still distant and heedless; the time will come when he will feel himself exalted on account of Mrs Krug's faith. I see what they do not see. Ere long the whole of her family will consider the faith of that lady as the crown of honor on their heads.

That evening 'Abdu'l-Bahá spoke of the days of the Blessed Beauty and of His kindness towards Shaykh Salmán. He praised the sincerity and constancy of that messenger of the Merciful and described some of the events in his life.

This day was also a blessed day and passed in the utmost joy and happiness.

Saturday, July 27, 1912
[Dublin]

In the early morning 'Abdu'l-Bahá went out onto the balcony. On one side was a view of an extensive field of some 40 miles and on the other a vista of green plains and verdant mountains ranging for some 16 miles. He remarked:

If there is any justice, then what I have done for the friends will become apparent. I have done all this through the bounty and assistance of the Blessed Beauty. Otherwise, what have we Persians in common with the Americans on top of this mountain and valley in Dublin?

A likeness of Ṭáhirih which had been published by one of the Germans was shown to 'Abdu'l-Bahá, who said, 'This picture is not at all authentic.' He then spoke of the life of Ṭáhirih.

At the invitation of Mrs Parsons, 'Abdu'l-Bahá went to her home for lunch. In the afternoon, several of Mrs Parsons's friends came by and were deeply impressed by the Master's talk. From this day forward, visitors began to come in great numbers. In the afternoon Mr Parsons brought his carriage to take the Master for a ride. They drove to Lake Dublin where 'Abdu'l-Bahá spoke to the members of the club about spirituality and the progress of this new age. When He returned He instructed that cables be sent to the Assemblies of the East.

In the evening Mr [W. W.] Harmon, a leader of the Theosophists, came from Boston to see the Master, who spoke to him about divine civilization, the influence of the Word of God and about this great Bahá'í Dispensation:

> One of the martyrs of this Cause, at the time of his martyrdom exclaimed, 'Christ said that the spirit is willing but the flesh is weak; but I say that my flesh is as happy as my spirit.'

He spoke of the spread of civilization from the East to the West, saying:

> What a blessing God bestowed upon the Persians but they could not appreciate it! Had they not been ungrateful, the government of Persia would have ranked first in the world. I wrote to Muḥammad 'Alí Mírzá[222] that if he would compensate for the spilled blood of the Bahá'ís and govern with justice,

he would receive confirmation; otherwise, God doeth what He pleaseth. He did not listen to me. Again I wrote to Persia that so long as the nation and the government do not combine like milk and honey, prosperity and happiness are impossible. Persia will become desolate and the end result will be intervention by neighboring powers.

Sunday, July 28, 1912
[Dublin]

After prayers the Master revealed several Tablets. A lengthy one was addressed to Mírzá Abu'l-Faḍl (may my life be a sacrifice to him). The Master's affection and love for him was such that when Mr MacNutt presented Him with a picture of Mírzá Abu'l-Faḍl, He took it at once and kissed it with such love and warmth that all saw how dear he was to the Master.

The Master sat in the drawing room and spoke to Mr Harmon about the sanctity of God, who is beyond emanation and appearance, ascent and descent, ingress and egress, and about the reflection of His attributes on the mirrors of the hearts of the Manifestations. His talk was brief but comprehensive and impressive. He also explained the meanings of the holy books and discussed the saying that 'everything is contained in everything', that is, every atom of creation passes through infinite forms and every molecule is transformed and passes through everything else. He then said:

> The Theosophists are educating a boy in the schools of Europe and say that he will become the promised one of all nations. How ignorant this is! God must select the Promised One, not men. The lamp that men ignite will be put out; but the Lamp of God is ever bright. He who is educated by men is always dependent on men. How can he give eternal prosperity? It is as if a person wishes to make a sun out of oil and wick.

'Abdu'l-Bahá was asked about the conditions in Turkey. He replied, 'Do not expect good news from that spot. But we have nothing to do with political affairs. Our work concerns spirituality, the knowledge of God and the acquisition of spiritual bounties.'

A group of prominent persons came to see Him in the afternoon at Mrs Parsons's home. The subjects concerned telepathy, the immortality of the spirit and related subjects. The guests were so impressed that they attended every meeting. After each day's meeting Mr and Mrs Parsons come with their carriage to take the Master out riding with them. Today He said He would rather go for a walk and instead sent some of His servants for a ride.

This evening Mr Harmon read to the Master passages from a book he had written on Theosophy and Buddhist teachings. He showed Him the illustrations he had drawn. He had illustrated truth as a circle, with God at its center, and divided the circle into seven segments representing the world of creation. The Master listened to him with love and patience while at the same time removing his superstitions with quotations from philosophers and sages in such a way that Mr Harmon was astonished. The Master explained the seven segments so beautifully that he cried, 'Oh, your explanations have opened the doors of understanding before me!' The Master then said, 'I have had no education. I have not even been to elementary school. These people know it.' Mr Harmon said, 'I feel that whatever you say comes from innate knowledge.'

Monday, July 29, 1912
[Dublin]

Sitting on the carpet, the Master spoke about Mr Harmon, saying:

> What captives of superstitions people are! What troubles they endure for the sake of name and fame! What fruit will these superstitions bear? All are transitory and perishable and no trace of them will remain. It will be as though they had never

existed. They are sowing seeds in a barren land. Man ought to sow pure seeds in a fertile soil.

Later in the day He spoke with Mr Harmon for a considerable time. Afterwards He reviewed some letters and prepared them for mailing.

He went to Mrs Parsons's home in the afternoon. He was asked about His health and the climate, to which He replied:

> The air of this place is good. But we are happy wherever we go; our happiness consists in service to the Most Holy Threshold. We have not come to America on a pleasure trip; we are here to serve the Court of the Blessed Beauty. Whenever we succeed in this purpose, that place is good. A merchant is happy whenever his goods find a market, wherever it may be.

Then He sat in the gazebo facing the garden and related the afflictions and trials of Bahá'u'lláh in Baghdád:

> In spite of all these troubles we were happy beyond description because under His shadow we were favored with the blessing of attainment to His presence.

Afterwards He went into the house. The drawing room was filled. His address to the visitors concerned both spiritual and material matters, including questions of economics which corrected some of the false ideas of the socialists. The audience was pleased. Each day a new spirit is seen in the meetings. It is difficult to believe that in this mountainous and scenic countryside, meetings that diffuse the fragrances of God can be held. All this is due to the power of the Center of the Covenant. 'Wherever our king is, it is Paradise, even if it is as small as the eye of a needle.'[223]

Tuesday, July 30, 1912
[Dublin]

Mírzá 'Alí Akbar Nakhjavání remarked that the enthusiasm of the people was due to the power of the Covenant and the influence of the Master's words. 'Abdu'l-Bahá replied: 'It is not due to my power but to my Father's; it is all His work.' Today He invited both Eastern and Western friends to be His guests.[224] Some stayed in His house while others were given accommodation at the hotel located in the warmer climate at the bottom of the mountain. The guests came to the hotel every morning to visit Him. Meetings were held in the afternoon at the home of Mr and Mrs Parsons. The audience of prominent persons was fascinated by 'Abdu'l-Bahá and His qualities. Several people invited the Master to their homes.

In His talk in the afternoon at Mrs Parsons's home He made clear that:

> Confirmation is not dependent on talent, knowledge or wisdom. Many unimportant persons have made significant discoveries. Many people labored for years to explore the North Pole but Admiral Peary reached it. One's efforts should be focussed on the object of one's quest. Because Columbus found confirmation, he discovered America with a minimum of difficulty. The disciples of Christ were apparently abased, yet they achieved something which Napoleon never did: they changed the whole aspect of the world. So it is evident that everything comes about through the assistance of God.

Wednesday, July 31, 1912[225]
[Dublin]

In the morning the Master went to the summer school that had been established by Mr Henderson 20 years ago. It is located some 25 miles from Dublin and classes are held in tents in a clear, open field. As soon as 'Abdu'l-Bahá's automobile arrived, the students, between the ages of 12 and 18, surrounded it and enthusiastically welcomed Him. They wore uniforms with knickerbockers and moved about busily but courteously. The headmaster then took 'Abdu'l-Bahá to the school hall and remained standing while the Master spoke to the students and teachers, praising the school and the good manners of its students. Later He visited each of the student's tents. Some of the children had cameras and requested permission to take the Master's photograph. Dr Henderson said that when he had established the school 20 years ago there was not a summer school in the whole of America and now there are hundreds of them. 'Abdu'l-Bahá remarked: 'Everything praiseworthy spreads rapidly. But the children must first be taught religion so that they may be sincere and trustworthy.'

After tea and refreshments, the pupils asked the Master's permission to show Him their gymnastic exercises. The Master remained there a long while and spoke at length about education. When it was time to leave, the headmaster and school staff expressed their heartfelt gratitude to 'Abdu'l-Bahá.

At the public meeting in the afternoon at Mr and Mrs Parsons's home, the Master spoke on spirituality and eternal happiness.

Thursday, August 1, 1912
[Dublin]

The Master related to us that 'One hundred years ago there was a school in Baghdád which was held during the summer but it was for the children of the wealthy only. The people of the West have adopted and perfected the customs of the East.' He also said:

> As charitable works become praiseworthy, people often perform them merely for the sake of fame and to gain benefit for themselves, as well as to attract people's admiration. But this does not render needless the teachings of the Prophets because it is spiritual morals that are the cause of training one's innate

nature and of personal progress. Thus will people offer service to one another with all their hearts for the sake of God and in order to fulfill the duties of devotion to Him and service to humanity and not for the purpose of acquiring praise and fame.

Then He spoke of Mashadí Amír Ghafghazí, a rich man from the Caucasus:

> Prior to his embracing this Faith, he was so dauntless and merciless that he had killed countless persons but after embracing this Faith he was entirely transformed, so much so that when once he was fired at by a pistol he did not even raise his arm in self-defense. Such people become educated under the shadow of belief. Similarly, the Bahá'ís of 'Ishqábád interceded on behalf of a man who had killed one of their members.[226]

At a gathering in the afternoon the Master spoke on the equality of the rights of men and women, the greatness of this cycle, the oneness of the world of humanity and God's creation. After the meeting several ministers spoke to Him. One was the pastor from the Dublin Unitarian Church who invited the Master to speak at his church.

Friday, August 2, 1912[227]
[Dublin]

A meeting for blacks was held near Lake Dublin. At this gathering the Master delivered an eloquent address regarding unity and amity between blacks and whites. He spoke of the approaching wedding of Miss [Louisa] Mathew, a white woman, and Mr [Louis] Gregory, a black man, which is to take place shortly in Washington DC. The white people in the audience were astonished to see the influence of the Cause and the blacks were pleased. Incidents like these are little less than miracles; in fact, 'splitting the moon in half'²²⁸ would be an easier accomplishment in the eyes of the Americans. This meeting was full of joy.

The guests rejoiced when the Master returned to Mr and Mrs Parsons's home. His words made a deep impression. He spoke on the oneness of the basic principles of the religions of God and the unity of His Manifestations. When questioned about Muḥammad, the Prophet of God, His proofs were clear and persuasive and his arguments decisive, uplifting every downcast heart. Everyone testified to the convincing nature of His argument and the greatness of this Cause. Some seemed to be disturbed at His Reference to Islam but no one said a word.

Saturday, August 3, 1912
[Dublin]

While a few of us were discussing the Master's explanations and the simplicity and decisiveness of His talks, He said to us:

> The explanations must be adapted to the capacity of the hearers and suited to the exigency of the time. Beauty of style, moderation in delivery and suitability of words and meanings are necessary. It is not only a matter of uttering words. In 'Akká, Mírzá Muḥammad-'Alí²²⁹ would hear me speak and would repeat my words exactly on other occasions but he did not understand that a thousand wisdoms and ingredients other than speech are necessary. In the days of Baghdád and Sulaymáníyyih, Shaykh 'Abdu'l-Ḥusayn²³⁰ was told that the Blessed Beauty was attracting the Kurds to Himself by quoting Ṣúfí and gnostic terms. This poor Shaykh obtained a copy of the Futúḥát-i-Makkíyyih [Conquests of Mecca]²³¹ and committed its passages to memory. But wherever he quoted them, he saw that none lent an ear to him. He was greatly puzzled as to why people did not listen to him. The Blessed Beauty said, 'Tell the Shaykh that We are not in the habit of reading the Conquests of Mecca (Futúḥát-i-Makkíyyih) but We impart to

them the verses of True Civilization. We are not propounding the writings of the <u>Sh</u>ay<u>kh</u> [Ibn al-'Arabí], we are propounding the Holy Writ.

In the afternoon He spoke about how the secondary laws of religions change in every age according to the exigencies of the time and the harmfulness of the materialistic world and the benefit of religion. The meeting ended with a series of sincere questions and answers.

Sunday, August 4, 1912
[Dublin]

When He had finished writing Tablets in response to petitions from the friends in the East and the West, the Master had a little time to rest. He then went for lunch at the home of Miss [Fanny] Knobloch. Her friends and relatives were fascinated with His explanations and enchanted by His manner.

In the afternoon He spoke in Mr and Mrs Parsons's drawing room about the power of the Cause of Bahá'u'lláh and the assistance and confirmations of the Greatest Name. Mírzá 'Alí Akbar [Na<u>kh</u>javání] related that during the troubled times in 'Akká the Master used to say that a great event would take place in the very near future: it would be as though this lamp would go away and then come back to its original place. Now we understand that this assertion of 'Abdu'l-Bahá was a reference to His travels and His return to the Holy Land. The Master then said:

> The assistance of the Blessed Beauty brings about extraordinary things. Every act of the Blessed Beauty constitutes in itself a consummate proof. In one of my early writings I wrote that in the eyes of the possessors of insight the doings of Him Who is the Sovereign Truth have no equal. For instance, if the Blessed Beauty asked after someone's health, although outwardly a common expression, it could give to a person who

was perceptive hints as to the wisdom and mystery hidden in the words spoken on that occasion. Thus it is that God in all His actions is distinct from all others, just as a wise man displays in all his actions the signs of wisdom.

There were several people waiting to see Him. Two ladies, both of whom were hard of hearing, requested permission to sit near Him so that they might listen to His words through their hearing aids. He said, 'Yes, the nearer they come, the better they will hear the Words of God. They must hear the Voice of the Lord in whatever way possible or by whatever means.'

Today, the Master's talk on the immortality of the soul so impressed the hearts that from then on He was asked to speak on this subject at most of the meetings.

Monday, August 5, 1912[232]
[Dublin]

Standing on the lawn and facing the green and verdant hills and valleys, 'Abdu'l-Bahá said:

> How calm it is. No disturbing sound is heard. When a man observes the wafting of the breeze among these trees, he hears the rustling of the leaves and sees the swaying of the trees, it is as though all are praising and acknowledging the one true God.

Before the afternoon meeting a devoted lady told the Master that one of her friends, when informed that she was planning to attend the meeting, strongly advised her not to go lest she fall into a trap. He said to her:

> It has always been the practice of the heedless to hold back the sincere ones from the Cause of God. As for a trap, praise be to God that we have been trapped happily for sixty years and we

have no desire to escape. It is a trap that frees people from the shackles of prejudice and superstitions and delivers them from the prison of self and desire. It makes them the captives of the love of God and of service to the Cause of the oneness of humanity.

After delivering the message of God and explaining the divine teachings, the Master spoke humorously about the philosophers.

> They say that had there been a spiritual world they would have sensed it. But, as a matter of fact, inability to sense a thing is not a proof of the nonexistence of that thing. If inability to sense constitutes proof of perfection, the cow must be the greatest philosopher, for she does not realize anything beyond the animal world.

This amusing statement that the cow is the greatest of all philosophers caused everyone to laugh. After the meeting, some men and women invited Him to go for a ride in their automobile. While driving, a herd of cows passed in front of the automobile and, becoming frightened, began to run about every which way. The ladies in the car cried out, 'Oh Master, see the crowd of philosophers. How frightened they are running away from us.' 'Abdu'l-Bahá laughed so heartily that He tired Himself. As the Americans like such jests, it became an oft-repeated remark.

Tuesday, August 6, 1912
[Dublin]

In the morning while pacing back and forth in the drawing room of His residence, the Master said:

> When Persians want to record any important matter, they say, 'Write this down in the twenty-ninth section.' Now, as the Persians say, write this in the twenty-ninth section of your

book. Whatever occurs is the cause of the elevation of the Word of God and the victory of the divine Cause, even though outwardly it may appear to be a great affliction and hardship. What hardship, grief or affliction could be greater than that which occurred at the time when the Blessed Beauty was exiled from Ṭihrán? Hearts of stone were melted. All the relatives were weeping and lamenting. All were in utter despair. But that exile became the cause of the raising of the Call and exalting the Word of God, of fulfilling the prophecies of the Prophets and of guiding the people of the world. Had it not been for this exile, these things would not have appeared and these great events would not have occurred.

Consider the case of Abraham. Had He not been exiled, He would not have received that greatest blessing; neither a Jacob nor an Isaac would have risen; the fame of the beauty of Joseph would not have been spread throughout the world. He would not have become the ruler of Egypt; no Moses would have appeared; no Muḥammad, the divine Messenger, would have come. All these are a result of the blessings of that exile. It is the same now.

Later He spoke about the harmful effects of disunity and discord:

> For example, the separation between the eastern and western empires and the disagreement between the eastern and western churches in Christianity caused a great weakness. Notwithstanding this, the people still do not take heed.

In the afternoon He gave a talk on the oneness of the foundation of religion.[233]

Wednesday, August 7, 1912
[Dublin]

I shall content myself today with recording just one of the Master's addresses. He delivered this talk in the afternoon in home of Mr and Mrs Parsons. The audience was greatly moved and a wonderful spirit of sincerity spread throughout the gathering. The following is the transcription of His address as well as the questions and answers on the immortality of the soul.

> He is God! We must first prove that there is no annihilation in creation. Annihilation is only the decomposition of elements. For example, all these things we see in existence are made up of elements; that is, single atoms have combined and have formed infinite patterns. Every combination produces an entity. For example, through the combination of certain elements this flower has come into existence. Its annihilation means only the decomposition of this combination, it does not mean the destruction of the individual atoms or principal elements because these remain and will not be destroyed. When we say that this flower is destroyed we mean that its combination is decomposed but the principal elements remain; only their combination is destroyed.
>
> In the same way, man has come into existence as the result of the combination of certain elements. Although his death is the disintegration of these elements, the elements are not annihilated. Therefore, life consists of the combination of elements and death of their dissolution or transference from one state to another. The transference of the vegetable to the animal world is the death of the former. Draw your own conclusions from this. Similarly, the transference of man from this world of matter and the dissolution of his elements constitute human death. Thus, it should be known that for existence there is no death. At most there is a transfer from one state to another. As the soul of man is not the result of composition and does not come into being

through the affinity of molecular elements, it is not subject to disintegration. If it were, then we would say the soul has died. But because it is not composed, therefore it cannot be decomposed. And it is clear that even the basic elements are not subject to decomposition as they are not a compound composition. No doubt remains regarding this matter.

Second, the transference of the body from one condition to another brings about no change or alteration in the soul. For instance, the body is young but it grows old, while the soul remains unaffected; the body becomes weak but the soul does not; the body becomes diseased or paralyzed but the soul remains unchanged. It has often come to pass that one of the limbs of the body has been amputated; the soul, however, remains the same and is not affected at all. Therefore, it is clear that the changes experienced by the body do not affect the soul. As long as it is unchanged, it will remain eternal. The pivot of mortality is change and alteration.

Third, in the world of sleep, man's body is powerless and his faculties inactive. The eye does not see, the ear does not hear, the body does not move; but the soul sees, hears, moves and discovers realities. Therefore, it is proven that the soul is not destroyed with the death of the body; it does not perish after the death of the body; it does not sleep when the body is asleep; rather, it has perception, it discovers, it flies and it travels.

Fourth, the body is here but the soul is present in the East or the West. While in the West, it puts the affairs of the East in order; while in the East, it explores the affairs of the West. It manages and regulates the momentous affairs of the world. The body is in one single place but the soul is present in various places and countries. It discovers America while in Spain. Thus, the soul has a control and influence which the body has not. The body cannot see but the soul can see and has perception. Therefore, it follows that its existence is not dependent on the body.

Fifth, no effect occurs without a cause. It is impossible for a cause to be non-existent when its light and radiance are manifest, for fire not to exist when its heat is sensed, for light not to exist when illumined objects are witnessed, mind not to exist when the power of thought is present. Briefly, there can be no effect without a cause, for as long as there is an effect there must be a cause. Therefore, though Christ appeared one thousand nine hundred and twelve years ago, His signs still exist today and His sovereignty and influence are manifest. Is it possible for that divine Spirit to be non-existent and these great signs still to be present? Therefore it is established that the Cause of these signs is He Who is the source of eternal light and everlasting bounties.

Sixth, everything can have only one shape, whether it be triangular, square or pentagonal. An object cannot have different shapes at the same time. For instance, this carpet is rectangular; is it possible that it can have a circular shape as well? It cannot. That is possible only if it loses its first form and takes a new one. Nevertheless, while it is impossible for an object to possess diverse forms at one and the same time, the spirit of man possesses all forms and has manifold shapes simultaneously. It has no need to change from one form to another. As it is beyond change and forms, it is non-material and eternal.

Seventh, when a man looks at creation, he sees two things: that which is perceptible to the senses and that which is abstract. The things that are perceptible to the senses, such as vegetables, minerals and animals, that can be seen by the eyes, heard by the ears, smelled, touched or tasted, are subject to change. But rational powers are not perceived by the physical senses. The power of the mind and knowledge are intellectual realities and are not subject to change or alteration. The eye cannot see them; the ear cannot hear them. It is impossible that knowledge, which is an intellectual reality, be changed into ignorance. The soul, too, is one of the intellectual realities: it is unalterable and is not subject to annihilation.

A person who is endowed with perception has spirituality and heavenly attributes; he can recognize that the human soul has never been subject to annihilation and will never become so. He sees that all created beings are in harmony with the spirit and are under its influence. He knows himself to be eternal, everlasting, constant, imperishable and encompassed by the lights of God, the Lord of glory. For he has spiritual susceptibilities and is affected by conscience and spiritual impulses. He is not limited by rational constraints or human emotions and sentiments. However, the man who has no perception or inner sight finds himself always dejected and lifeless; every time he thinks of death, he is afraid, because he considers himself to be mortal.

Blessed souls are not of this category. They sense that they are eternal, luminous and imperishable like the disciples of Christ. It is for this reason that at the time of death or martyrdom Bahá'ís rejoice, because they know there is no death or annihilation for them. At most, the body disintegrates but the soul exists in the divine world and has everlasting life.

The audience was deeply moved by this address and all expressed their satisfaction and became devoted to 'Abdu'l-Bahá.

Tuesday, August 8, 1912
[Dublin]

One of the devoted friends asked the Master about imperfect realities and their immortality. He replied:

> All realities and spirits are immortal, even the spirits of nonbelievers and imperfect persons. But they cannot be compared in any way with the spirits of the sanctified souls and holy personages. Although this wood has existence, yet in comparison with the existence of man, it is as nothing.

In the afternoon 'Abdu'l-Bahá spoke at a public gathering. He touched on various aspects of love and unity among people and the necessity for cooperation and mutual assistance in human society. In answer to a question regarding vengeance, He replied that man has no right to seek vengeance but that the community is responsible for the protection of all life, property and honor. He then went on to say:

> The more material education advances, the more competitive is the race in aggression and injustice. But spiritual education is the cause of competition in praiseworthy actions and the acquisition of human perfections. We hope that day by day these injustices will diminish and the spiritual virtues increase.

The Master went into another room where a young man with a striking personality and pleasing appearance asked Him in what school He had studied philosophy. The Master answered: 'In the same school where Christ studied.' He then asked the Master, 'What is the relationship between God and nature?' The Master replied:

> Some of the philosophers believe that God is the Supreme Reality and that every human being has a spark of this divine reality within him; that He Himself is in a state of utmost power and that all things manifest Him according to their different capacities. Therefore they hold that the Supreme Being is dispersed into infinite forms. This is the position of Plato. But we say that existence as conceived by man or comprehended through human reason or intellect is a characteristic of matter. Matter is like unto essence, while existence is its manifestation. The body of man is essence and existence is dependent upon it. This human body is matter while existence is a power conditioned on matter.
>
> But it is not so with the Essential Self-Existent One. His existence is true existence which is self-subsistent, not an intellectually perceived and comprehended existence; it is an Existence by which all created things come into being. All

things are like unto His handiwork and are dependent upon Him. We refer to Him as Self-Existent because we need to make use of a term but we do not mean that that Being can be contained within our comprehension. What is intended is the Reality from Whom all things emanate, the Reality through Whom all things exist.

Not only was the questioner grateful and satisfied with this response but everyone else was also pleased.

Friday, August 9, 1912
[Dublin]

A number of the friends, both old and new, were present at 'Abdu'l-Bahá's house. One of their questions was whether the existence of evil proceeds from God. He replied:

> There is no evil in existence. Evil is non-existence. All that is created is good. Ignorance is evil and it is the non-existence of knowledge; it has no existence of its own. Hence, evil is the non-existence of good. Want of wealth is poverty; absence of justice is oppression; want of perfection is deficiency. All of these opposites imply non-existence and not existence.

At the public meeting in the afternoon 'Abdu'l-Bahá exhorted the audience to refrain from blind imitation, reminding them that the distinction of man lies in his ability to investigate reality and ascertain the truth. He spoke of the coming of Bahá'u'lláh and explained some of the teachings of the Supreme Pen.

After lovingly shaking hands with those present, 'Abdu'l-Bahá came into the room where we were and asked about our health, saying to us, 'Come here, be seated. Mrs Parsons has sent tea, sweets and some fruit for you. Eat and drink.' Then with a merry twinkle in His eyes, He continued:

> Oh! You are very badly off here! May God hear your complaint! Oh! It is so difficult to live in this manner, to dwell in such a house, to breathe such air! And to stay with such servants and respected friends is, of course, very hard for you! May God come to your help!

Then He said:

> Joking aside, what a wonderful table the Blessed Perfection has spread for His friends! Had kings come here they would have been served but this fervor and zeal of the friends would not have appeared for any one of them. These noble people who serve you love you with heart and soul and serve you without any fear, hope or expectation of reward. The poet spoke truly when he said that three things are scarce, namely, the demon, the phoenix and the faithful friend. Yes, like the demon and the phoenix, the true friend is rare. But under the shadow of the Word of God, the Blessed Beauty has produced such friends for you.

Saturday, August 10, 1912
[Dublin]

In the morning the Master explained and illustrated some of the verses of Bahá'u'lláh for the friends who had come from the surrounding area to see Him. The explanations ended with the statement that contentment in poverty is better than happiness in wealth but happiness in poverty is more praiseworthy than mere contentment. Above all is the rich man who, having sacrificed, emerges pure from tests and trials and becomes the cause of tranquillity to mankind. Gratitude is the cause of multiple blessings but the apex of gratitude is sacrifice. The station of sacrifice is the highest of all. For this reason it is said, 'You will never attain unto righteousness until ye sacrifice that which ye love.' The Master then narrated a story:

At the time of his death a king longed for the station of a poor man, saying, 'Would that I were a poor man so that I would neither have practiced oppression nor have had any regrets at the time of death.' A poor man heard this, and said, 'Praise be to God that at the hour of death kings desire to be poor. We poor people at the hour of death have no desire to be kings.'

Conversation of this kind continued for some time.

In the afternoon 'Abdu'l-Bahá addressed a meeting and spoke on the principles of the Cause, emphasizing universal peace among the nations. After the meeting a person in the audience said: 'The Bahá'ís do not believe in any one person but believe in the good teachings of all the Prophets and religions.' The implication of his statement was that believing in the Manifestation of God was of no consequence. But note the Master's reply to this remark:

> The basic principles of all religions are the same and the Sun of Truth is one, yet every day it appears from a different dawning point. Hence, the Bahá'ís believe in the fundamental truth of all the religions and turn to the Sun of Truth. From whatever dawning point it may appear they turn toward it. At one time, it appeared from the dawning point of Moses, then from that of Jesus and again from that of Muḥammad. But if all had looked only at the dawning points, they would have remained veiled like the Jews when the Sun of Truth appeared from another place. Today the Bahá'ís look at the Sun of Truth and not at the dawning point. From whatever place it may appear, they turn to it. You have rightly understood that the Bahá'ís do not believe in a person; rather they believe in the truth which shines from the divine dawning points.

Sunday, August 11, 1912
[Dublin]

A glorious meeting was held at the Unitarian Church in Dublin.[234] He went to the church at 11:00 a.m. and as He entered the entire audience rose to its feet. The pastor sang a beautiful song in praise of 'Abdu'l-Bahá. After the preliminary ceremonies, the Master was introduced by the pastor with the utmost reverence and esteem. He then stood and gave a detailed address on the necessity of true education and spiritual power and spoke of the coming of Bahá'u'lláh and His teachings. At the end of His talk He chanted a prayer, His life-giving melodies penetrating the souls and attracting the hearts. A wonderful spirit of humility seemed to permeate the building and the voice of acceptance seemed to issue from all sides.

Many who had not already had the honor of visiting 'Abdu'l-Bahá came to Him with such eagerness that the Master said, 'The Call of God has been raised here and the work is finished.'

He was invited for lunch at the home of Mr and Mrs Pumpelly. There He was asked about the Cause of God and about the new principles. Although He responded to the questions of those present, still they thought that the talk had been prepared beforehand and that the interpreter had committed it to memory. They felt no one would have been able to speak extemporaneously with such clarity and perception. The vastness of His knowledge is even more evident. My point is that His talk and explanations seemed extraordinary in the eyes of the people and that the unseen confirmations of Bahá'u'lláh assisted the Center of the Covenant.

After this meeting the people's spirits were raised. In the afternoon a multitude gathered at the home of Mr and Mrs Parsons. 'Abdu'l-Bahá spoke, encouraging everyone to think about His words, to meditate on the holy verses, to investigate truth and to gain a full knowledge of divine realities. It is merely owing to a lack of understanding among the leaders of religions, He said, and to their blind imitations and superstitions that statements contrary to science and common sense have crept in and caused intellectuals and scientists to deny religion and disputes to arise among the people, obscuring the true meaning of the laws of God.

Monday, August 12, 1912
[Dublin]

A group of Dublin residents had a picnic on the shore of Lake Dublin and invited the Master and His entourage to join them. After sitting for a while viewing the surroundings, the Master went for a short walk. Upon His return He went to the table and ate sweets and sherbet with the friends. He was pleased to see the simplicity of the repast and to feel the sincerity and warmth of the people.

In the afternoon a large gathering of people came to hear Him. They asked Him to speak on the immortality of the spirit. Everyone was so pleased, happy and filled with admiration that one by one each came to shake His hand and to express his or her gratitude. The Master's talk was so much appreciated that for many days afterwards He was asked to speak on the immortality of the spirit, economics and the new teachings. At each meeting He spoke on subjects He had already elucidated and on new topics, which greatly increased the admiration of the audience.

Tuesday, August 13, 1912
[Dublin]

Because some of the people who met 'Abdu'l-Bahá today were musicians, He gave an explanation of the science of music:

> Music is produced by vibrations of air which affect the tympanum of the ear. Although music or an ordinary pleasing voice is of the physical realm, yet it has an effect upon the spirit. In the same manner, freshness and purity of the air, the atmosphere, the scenery and sweet fragrances impart joy,

spirituality and comfort to the heart. Even though these are physical phenomena they have a great spiritual influence.

He then narrated stories of the great masters of music, gave an account of the famous Rúdakí[235] and read his famous poem which had caused Amír Náṣír Sámání to change his course from Herat to Bokhara:[236]

> The Júy-i-Múliyán[237] we call to mind
> We long for those dear friends long left behind.
> The sands of Oxus, toilsome though they be,
> Beneath my feet were soft as silk to me.[238]

The Master ended His explanations with beautiful songs and these verses:

> From whence comes this minstrel
> Who sings the name of my Beloved,
> That I lay down this life and soul
> For a message from my Loved One?
>
> To hear the message from the City of the Beloved
> Resuscitates the heart.
> The soul dances
> On hearing the Word of the Beloved.[239]

In the afternoon the Master spoke on the immortality of the soul and the teachings of the new Manifestation. Afterwards, many were eager to see Him alone. He said to them:

> My desire is greater than yours. Some of the disciples went to Rumelia and said, 'We had a desire to see you so we have come from Jerusalem to this place.' Now, behold what a desire I had to see you, that I traveled from the East to the West!

Wednesday, August 14, 1912
[Dublin]

All the friends had been informed that the Master would soon leave Dublin for Green Acre in Eliot, Maine, and that time was running out. They asked Him to speak on economics and to correct certain false ideas of the socialists. His explanations were so impressive that after He left they implored Him to reveal a Tablet on this subject and send it through Mrs Parsons so that it might remove doubts from the minds of the people. The following is a transcription of that Tablet:

> Dublin: To the maidservant of God, Mrs Parsons.
> Upon her be Bahá'u'lláhu'l-Abhá.
> He is God.

O thou, my spiritual daughter,

I am on a train on my way to San Francisco. I recalled your praiseworthy qualities and the dear face of little Master Jeffrey, so I wanted to write this letter. Know that my greatest pleasure will be when I shall see you, my dear daughter, enraptured and completely charmed by the paradise of Abhá, and aflame with the fire of the love of God. May my dear daughter burn and melt like a candle to enlighten all people. It is my hope that thou mayest be so.

Regarding the question of economics according to the new teachings, as this caused some difficulty for you because the report you received did not reflect what I said, I shall outline the essence of this matter so that it will be clearly proven that there is no complete solution for the economic question apart from that offered in the new teachings. It is absolutely impossible to resolve the problem by other means.

In solving this problem we must start with the farmer and end with other trades, because there are twice as many farmers, if not more, as there are people engaged in other trades. Thus it is right that we begin with them. The farmer is the primary factor in society.

In every village a council of wise men of the village should be established and the whole village should be placed under its jurisdiction. In addition, a public treasury should be established with its own administrator. At harvest time a specific quantity of the general produce of the village should be appropriated for the treasury. This treasury will have seven sources of income, namely: tithes, taxes on livestock, unclaimed inheritance, property that has been found but that has no owner, buried treasure (if found, one third of it should be paid to the council), mines (one-third of the natural resources taken should be levied by the council) and donations. Likewise, there are to be seven categories of expenditure: first, moderate public expenditures such as the expenses of the council and maintenance of public health; second, payment of government taxes; third, payment of taxes on livestock to the government; fourth, care of orphans; fifth, providing for the disabled; sixth, management of schools; and seventh, providing the necessary means of livelihood for the poor.

The first means of income is the tithe, which must be administered as follows: If a person's average income is $500 and his necessary expenses amount to the same sum, no tithe will be collected from him. If another person has an income of $1,000 and his necessary expenses amount to $500, he will be able to pay the tithe because he will have more than he needs. If he pays the tithe there will be no decline in his standard of living. Another has an income of $5,000 and his expenses are only $1,000, so he will have to pay one and one-half times the tithe because he has an even greater amount than he needs. Another has an income of $10,000 and his necessary expenses amount to $1,000; therefore he will have to pay two times the tithe because his surplus is larger. Another person has an income of $100,000 and expenses amounting to $4,000 or $5,000; he will have to pay one-fourth of his income. Another has an income of $200 but the expenses he requires to live at subsistence level amount to $500. He spares no pains in working and laboring for his livelihood but the fruit of his labor is inadequate. He must be helped from the treasury so that he may not be in want and may live in comfort.

In every village a certain amount should be allocated for the orphans there. The disabled must be provided for. The treasury must also provide for the needy who are unable to work. The council will also allocate a certain amount for the department of education and for public health. If there is a surplus, it will be transferred to the national treasury for general expenses. If it be thus arranged, every individual in society will live comfortably and pass his days happily.

Differences in station will also remain and no breach will occur in this respect. Gradations of rank are without doubt one of the essentials of society. Society is like an army. An army requires field marshals, generals, colonels, captains and privates. It is utterly impossible for all professions to be equal. Preservation of rank is necessary. But each individual in the army must live in perfect peace and comfort. Likewise, a town requires a mayor, judges, merchants, men of means, craftsmen and farmers. Of course, these ranks must be observed, otherwise the general order would be disrupted.

Convey my heartfelt love to Mr Parsons. I shall never forget him. If possible, have this letter published in one of the newspapers, as others are proclaiming these principles in their own names. Convey wondrous Abhá greetings to Qudsíyyih.[240]

Upon you be Bahá-u'l-Abhá.

'Abdu'l-Bahá Abbás.

Thursday, August 15, 1912
[Dublin]

Today was the Master's last day in Dublin. Mrs Parsons had asked a large number to attend and had invited the best musicians to play the piano and sing at the beginning of the meeting. The Master sat in an adjoining room enjoying the music. There was such a crowd in the large drawing room that although rows of chairs had been arranged, no seating was available. The Master entered the room to give His last talk in Dublin:

> I have explained every question for you, delivered to you the message of God, expounded the mysteries of the divine Books for you, proved the immortality of the spirit and oneness of truth and expounded for you economic questions and divine teachings.

As this was His last address everyone came to shake His hand and offer his or her thanks before leaving His presence. Mrs Parsons said that the people were usually happy but because they knew 'Abdu'l-Bahá was leaving they were sad and wanted to prolong His stay.

He replied, 'I, too, wished to stay longer but I must go to Green Acre and other places. I must raise the call of the Kingdom in all places. The days of my life in this world are limited, so I must pass through all regions and announce the glad tidings of the Kingdom of Abhá.'

'Abdu'l-Bahá spent the day saying farewell to many eminent people. After the afternoon meeting, one of the believers, Miss Knobloch, with His permission took several photographs of Him with His servants.

The automobile was ready and He was driven to the home of a friend where a meeting was held. The people were very enthusiastic and inebriated with love and affection. After speaking to them briefly and narrating a few stories, He left.

Friday, August 16, 1912
[Dublin – Green Acre]

At dawn, while we were still in bed, we heard the Master sweetly chanting a prayer. We at once got up, went to Him and were served tea and refreshments from the all-bountiful Sághí.[241] He instructed us to collect our belongings and prepare to leave. Around 10:00 a.m. Mr [Alfred E.] Lunt's automobile arrived and the Master left Dublin. En route He had lunch at Nashua, New Hampshire, and after a little rest continued on His journey. We reached Green Acre[242] in the afternoon where more than five hundred people were waiting for Him. Both sides of the entrance had been decorated with multicolored lanterns and a festive reception awaited His arrival.

After a short rest, the Master entered the main room of the Inn and gave a brief talk about the investigation of truth. From there He went to the home of Miss Farmer, the founder of the Green Acre Society.[243] This distinguished lady was revived by His visit and although she was not feeling well, she accompanied the Master back to the Inn.

In the evening at the hotel,[244] in response to questions from the audience, 'Abdu'l-Bahá delivered a most impressive address on the love of God, the immortality of the spirit and the divine teachings. Everyone was deeply moved and their hearts were transformed.[245]

Monday, August 17, 1912
[Green Acre]

The beloved Master's health was better and He was happy. He spoke of the pleasant climate of Green Acre and visited with friends and seekers until He left for a walk. On the way to Mr [Charles Mason] Remey's house the Master was accompanied by a group to whom He spoke about many spiritual truths. When He arrived, Mr Remey offered Him a cup of water, saying that he had longed for many years to invite the Master and that he thanked God for being given the honor to offer Him a cup of water. The Master said:

> Your home is simple and furnished plainly. People are captivated by the superfluities of the present generation. It is

impossible for a man to furnish his house in utmost perfection. The more he tries the more he finds it lacking because every day new products are manufactured. People have filled their lives with difficulties.

Later the Master went to the home of Mrs [Carrie] Kinney. There He spoke about material progress and the philosophers' lack of feeling for the spiritual kingdom, saying that 'This is befitting of animals. Truth must be sought and laid bare. No one should endeavor to force upon people what he conceives. The brilliant reality, which is the spirit of the world today, is one. It can never be multiple.'[246] He uttered such statements on numerous occasions and in various ways. Because Green Acre is known as a center for religious freedom and advanced liberal views, many fortune-tellers, spiritualists and ascetics come here every year to spread their superstitious views. The discourse of the Center of the Covenant completely swept away the cobwebs of their superstitions. They were checked to such a degree that some of the impostors, who in previous years had delivered lectures contrary to the Cause of God, now came to see Him, bowing before Him and repenting. Some of them begged Him to heal them, saying, 'You have healed many.' The Master replied:

> We pray but God bestows healing. We do not make claims for ourselves. We are only the expounders of the Word. We are all promulgating the Cause of Bahá'u'lláh. I am 'Abdu'l-Bahá. Bahá'u'lláh is the Dawning Place of Holiness. Address your needs to Him. I am only the expounder and promulgator of the Word. Bahá'u'lláh is the Source, the One Who has illumined this dark world, made corporeal into spiritual, quickened the dormant minds, changed the earthly souls into heavenly ones and given life to the dead and sight to the blind.

That night He delivered an address on the unity of mankind in the east hall of the Eirenian.[247] On His return to the Inn He spoke with the audience in jests which nevertheless touched on many important subjects. He offered sweets to some visitors who, following the superstitious ideas of the ascetics, did not eat certain foods. He dispelled their beliefs by saying, 'Food has nothing to do with faith. Rather, you should eat things to gain strength and you should acquire spirituality.'

Sunday, August 18, 1912
[Green Acre]

It was a rainy day. The Master was occupied until noon counseling the friends to devote their time in teaching the Cause of God and advising them not to interfere in the affairs of the Green Acre Fellowship. Lunch was prepared by Mrs Kinney. 'Abdu'l-Bahá said: 'A little soup would have sufficed me. A variety of foods makes me ill.'

In the afternoon 'Abdu'l-Bahá gave an impressive talk to a gathering of liberal-minded visitors concerning the renewal of religious laws and the oneness of the Manifestations of God.[248] A wonderful impression was produced on the whole audience as His melodious voice rang with majestic tones, moving the chairman of the conference to tears. As the Master was offering a prayer, one lady stood up and then fainted. When she regained consciousness she said that the power of the meeting overwhelmed her. It seemed to her that everyone in the audience was flying in heaven.

When the Master left this gathering, He met some people who were singing. He said to them, 'We listen always to your terrestrial music, now it would be well for you to give ear to our celestial songs.' After seeing to things in the kitchen, He came out to meet a number of the friends who had come to seek His advice on personal matters. He gave each His special attention. When Miss Edna McKinney, who had transcribed His addresses in English, came into His presence, He said to her, 'Thou art a maidservant who in the Kingdom of God is among the near ones. I desire the confirmation and protection of the Abhá Kingdom for you.' He also expressed extraordinary kindness for Mrs Parsons, Mrs Goodall, Mrs Cooper, Mrs Krug and Miss Juliet Thompson, who were not present. He advised Mrs Kinney not to wish for too rapid progress at once in the emancipation of women.

Monday, August 19, 1912
[Green Acre]

Among the friends was a lady who had come from Brooklyn to ask 'Abdu'l-Bahá's permission to go to Utica. He kindly said to her:

> Put your trust in the Blessed Beauty. Every momentous work that one undertakes has difficulties in the beginning. One should withstand such difficulties with the utmost steadfastness. We who wish to raise this magnificent edifice must be as brave as the soldiers who are intent on conquering strong fortresses.

Later He walked to Miss Taylor's home. Resting in the foyer, He praised the climate and beauty of the surroundings, saying,

> Here on a moonlit night, when the moon is in its full brilliance, when the stars are shining and the air is pure and a sweet breeze is wafting, at such a time to pray and weep before the Court of God has a delight of its own.

As He left there He encountered some women who were fortune tellers. Some read palms and others interpreted dreams. They all voiced their opinion that 'Abdu'l-Bahá possessed divine spirit and heavenly power. He showered kindness on all of them then returned to the Inn and gave a talk about superstitious beliefs and the severe discipline and asceticism of the Hindus.

He also visited a residence known as the Bahá'í House.[249] He praised it, saying, 'It would have been good if we had stayed here.' The Master then gave instructions for the Nineteen Day Feast to be held the following day, saying: 'Tomorrow I will host the festivity.'

In the afternoon He was invited to a summer school for girls held on the Green Acre common. Mrs Tatum drove Him in her automobile. There He sat on the grass near the bank of the river as the students pitched their tents and began their exercises. The principal and a teacher gave Him information about the school. A group had assembled under the trees to hear the Master's address. With great reverence, the superintendent of the school introduced the Master. He then gave an eloquent talk on both spiritual and material education which drew much admiration from the audience. Afterwards the chairman and school mistress thanked the Master and expressed everyone's appreciation for His talk. The students then stood and sang in praise of 'Abdu'l-Bahá in such sweet tones that everyone was enchanted. When the Master left everyone went to the automobile to shake His hand and to express their gratitude.

In the evening 'Abdu'l-Bahá spoke on the everlasting dominion of God and His Holy Manifestations. After the talk He answered questions.

Tuesday, August 20, 1912
[Green Acre]

Among the friends visiting the Master was Fred Mortensen, a youth who, prior to embracing the Cause, had been a fugitive from justice but was now very humble and tranquil.[250] Despairing of seeing the Master, who had not made known His plans to visit the West, he traveled from Minneapolis to visit Him. Because he could not afford to pay the price of a ticket from Minneapolis to Green Acre, he had ridden the rods under the train and in this way reached Chicago and Green Acre. He explained everything about his journey to the Master, who then told him, 'You are my guest.' Each day the Master bestowed kindness upon him and a few days later He gave him money to pay for his journey home. Unknown to anyone, the Master paid for many such expenses. Twice He sent a speaker from New York to Chicago and adjacent cities and on each occasion, although the person was rich, 'Abdu'l-Bahá gave him more than enough money to defray the expenses of his journey. In addition, He liberally contributed to the poor and to the churches [in which He spoke] in every city.

After speaking with the friends, He went to Miss Farmer's temporary residence [in Portsmouth]. When she saw 'Abdu'l-Bahá, she fell into such a state of rapture that every heart was moved. After comforting her and the others, at Dr Leroy's request He went to see places of historic interest, including a yard where battleships were being built [the Navy Yard in Kittery]. This activity did not please the Master. On His return He said:

> While the Manifestations of God are still alive, the people do not appreciate their value, they curse and execrate them; but after their ascension they worship them. Such is the case with these tent-dwellers who live outside Green Acre. Even Columbus and some ancient philosophers like Socrates were made to suffer but after a time the people took pride in praising them.

This afternoon, under the Persian pines and cypresses of that lovely plain, three hundred people heard 'Abdu'l-Bahá draw a picture of the vista of everlasting life, its spiritual stations and eternal blessings. He then went to the 'Bahá'í House' where we were all His guests. Following His walk after supper, the Master stood at the front hall of the house and spoke. People were even standing in the street to listen to Him. He spoke so beautifully about the relationship of the East and the West that passersby stopped to hear what He had to say.[251]

In the evening there was musical entertainment and dancing in the hall of the Inn. 'Abdu'l-Bahá said, 'Such gatherings and practices are the cause of the corruption of morals.' He also said this evening, 'My thoughts are wholly absorbed by this journey. I can think of nothing else because the outcome of this journey is so great. Up to now in the Cause of the Blessed Beauty a development as great as this has not occurred.'

Wednesday, August 21, 1912
[Green Acre]

During the visit of a group of Bahá'ís with the Master, a young girl came in and said, 'I have come to ask for your assistance. Please tell me what I am fitted to do so that I may occupy myself with it.' The Master asked, 'Do you have trust in me?' She replied, 'Yes.' He then said to her, 'Be a perfect Bahá'í. Associate with Bahá'ís. Study the teachings of Bahá'u'lláh. Then you will be assisted in whatever you undertake to do.' She then said, 'I am a good Jewess.' The Master then said:

> A good Jew can also become a Bahá'í. The truth of the religion of Moses and of Bahá'u'lláh is one. Turn toward Bahá'u'lláh and you will acquire peace and tranquillity, you will hear the melody of the Kingdom, you will stir people's souls and you will attain the highest degree of perfection. Be assured of this.

When she heard the Master's words she was so impressed that she threw herself at His feet and wept.

'Abdu'l-Bahá explained some aspects of the divine philosophy and teachings to the pastor of the Portsmouth church. The pastor said that he had included some of these teachings in his pamphlets and some people had taken offence. The Master said, 'Constancy in all things brings forth fruitful results.'

Mrs Tatum said, 'I feel so dejected today. I am unhappy with myself.' The Master replied:

> This is a sign of progress. The person who is satisfied with himself is the manifestation of Satan and the one who is not satisfied is the manifestation of the Merciful One. An egotist does not progress but the one who thinks himself imperfect will seek perfection for himself and will progress. If a man has a thousand good qualities, he must not look at them. He must search always for his shortcomings. For example, if a man has

a building which is well-constructed and fully decorated but which has a small crack in one of its walls, he will, no doubt, forget the rest and turn his whole attention to repairing that crack. Furthermore, the attainment of absolute perfection for a human being is impossible; thus, however much he may progress he is still imperfect and has above him a point higher than himself. And the instant he sees this point he will not be satisfied with himself. It is for this reason that when someone called Christ 'Good Master', He replied that there is only One who is good and that is God.

Another lady told 'Abdu'l-Bahá that she had lectured in America on universal brotherhood and unity. She was pleased to see the Master in America promulgating these high ideals and that she was going to continue to spread these teachings in the Western states of America. The Master said to her:

> We must endeavor as much as we can to exterminate spite and perversity so that people may be delivered from the shackles of superstition. You must serve in this way and become the cause of the unity of the world of men.

He spoke in the same vein with everyone. There were two people, Dr and Mrs Moore, who had been antagonistic towards the Cause of God from the very beginning. However, they had become so attracted and transformed that they came into the Master's presence with great humility and pledged themselves to the service of the truth. The transformation of such people is a momentous task which will produce great results.

In the afternoon 'Abdu'l-Bahá went by automobile to the home of Mrs [Kate] Ives and sat next to the driver, which is where members of His entourage usually sit. He sat there until the party arrived. When a number of the friends had gathered, He went with them to the hill of Monsalvat.[252] As soon as He arrived about four hundred people sang songs of praise to Him in unison. He addressed this gathering on the necessity of founding the school for the investigation of religions which Miss Farmer wished to establish on that mountain. A moving picture of this gathering was taken.[253]

The gathering was also characterized by a renewed enthusiasm, ardor and love, which seemed to draw all hearts. It was an auspicious day.

He then went to Mrs [Esther Annie] Magee's home where He dined with a group of friends.[254] He spoke to them about the proofs and evidences of the existence of God and the composition of elements according to the will of the Almighty.

Thursday, August 22, 1912
[Green Acre]

So many assembled this morning in the Master's home that there was no room to stand. The Master said that it was not possible to speak to each individually, therefore He stood in front of the group and spoke about the teachings and divine exhortations. At one point He said, 'I hope that harvests will be reaped from the seed-sowing and that it will receive heavenly blessings.'

After the meeting the Master gave permission to some earnest seekers to see Him privately. Afterwards, He went to visit the homes of some of the friends.

Today a lady who had survived the *Titanic* disaster came to see Him. 'I am told,' she said, 'that you advised not to travel by that ship.'

The Master replied in the affirmative. She questioned, 'Did you know that this would happen?' The Master said, 'God inspires man's heart.'

When He returned to the Inn, some prominent people came to see Him. In the course of the conversation they said, 'We have always understood that religion is opposed to science but we are now indebted to your discourses and teachings for throwing a new light on our thinking.'

The Master gave another talk on these issues for their enlightenment. Another group of people came to visit Him, expressing their heartfelt sorrow that He intended to leave Green Acre. They begged Him to write them a few words in His own handwriting and He wrote brief prayers for them in His exquisite script.

In the afternoon He paid farewell visits to some of the friends at their homes. At each gathering He offered life-giving words and in each home He was as the beloved one who steals hearts. He then returned home extremely exhausted, to the point that He could not even sit down. 'Our condition', He said, 'is like that of the exhausted iron worker's apprentice whose master said to him, "Die, but pump."'

After a brief rest He went to the hall at Eirenion and gave a talk on unity among the races, the elimination of prejudice amongst the peoples and nations, and the necessity for the oneness of the world of humanity in this enlightened age. At the end He chanted a prayer in such melodious and sweet tones that every heart was attracted to the divine kingdom and every soul turned to the Beauty of the Beloved.

Friday, August 23, 1912
[Green Acre]

In the morning, while the Master was preparing to leave, He said:

> We have finished our work here. We have sown a seed. Many souls have been attracted and transformed. Every day we have seen gifts such as fruit, flowers, honey and sweets which have been placed here anonymously and without show. This is a proof of the sincerity of their hearts.

'Abdu'l-Bahá was delighted to witness the influence of the Word of God on Green Acre. Indeed, it has become a second paradise on earth and had been transformed into verdancy and freshness.

At His instructions, the suitcases were packed and the carriage readied. The believers and seekers were burning with the fire of love, lamenting and shedding tears. 'Abdu'l-Bahá sat in the carriage while the friends lined both sides of the road. For as long as the carriage remained in sight, they continued to wave their hats and handkerchiefs in farewell. On the way He stopped to visit Miss Farmer, who fell at His feet weeping and received from the Master His infinite favor and utmost kindness.

'Abdu'l-Bahá left Green Acre at 10:00 a.m. and reached Malden, Massachusetts, at 1:00 p.m. He arrived at the home of Miss [Marie P.] Wilson, whose invitation to stay at her house He had accepted.[255] A new spirit was breathed into the bodies and a divine happiness was shed upon the hearts.

As He was tired, 'Abdu'l-Bahá did not eat but instead rested for awhile.

In the afternoon and evening many friends were honored with meeting Him.

Saturday, August 24, 1912
[Malden]

'Abdu'l-Bahá was engaged in writing letters to the new Bahá'ís in Dublin and bestowing His favors on them. He also wrote to the friends in the Western states. Later, several visitors arrived from Malden and Dublin to see Him. One was the president of the New Thought Forum who had come from Boston to invite the Master to speak to his society. Two people from Ṭihrán, Persia, who had come to America on business, also came to see Him. He told them:

> The Persians destroyed their home with their own hands in the hope of building another one; but now they are left in the desert without a home or shelter. We wrote and exhorted them, pointing out that the union of government and the people is like combining milk and honey; otherwise, the neighboring governments will encroach upon the country. In spite of all this they malevolently made false accusations against us.

But God protected us because we were not involved in shedding the blood of even one Persian.

The newspaper '*Fikr*' [Thought] was mentioned, and He continued:

In this newspaper our letter speaks for itself. We are far from taking part in any seditious movement and we hold fast to the will of the Lord.

In the afternoon another group came to visit 'Abdu'l-Bahá. One was a minister from Chicago, who asked about the sins of men and the forgiveness of the Manifestations of the Merciful One. 'Abdu'l-Bahá gave a detailed explanation, which fascinated the minister. The Master stated that forgiveness depends upon our obedience to the admonitions of the Prophets of God and not on the mere verbal statement of belief or on following the words of the ministers of religion.

That evening the friends and seekers of Malden were treated to a talk about the power of the Greatest Name and the unity of nations and peoples. Each day and night witnesses a stream of new inquirers wishing to come into His holy presence.

Sunday, August 25, 1912
[Malden]

The superintendent of a girls' school in Boston came with several people to invite the Master to speak to their students. 'Abdu'l-Bahá invited another group of friends from Boston and Green Acre who had come to visit Him to stay for lunch.

In the afternoon He went to the New Thought Forum. On the way He stopped by the home of one of the friends whose wife was ill with consumption [tuberculosis]. After comforting and consoling her, He proceeded to the meeting of the society mentioned above. When He entered, the entire audience stood in His honor.

After a cordial introduction of welcome, the president of the society announced, without the Master's prior consent, that 'Abdu'l-Bahá would speak on the subject of 'Captivating the Souls'. Not to embarrass the president, 'Abdu'l-Bahá spoke first about the conquest of the cities and towns of the physical world by the kings and then described the conquest of the dominion of the hearts and souls of men by the Manifestations of God. He concluded His talk on the influence and expansion of the Cause of Bahá'u'lláh in this contingent world. He then chanted a prayer in His sweet, melodious voice.[256]

As the Master went to the automobile, crowds of excited and joyful people lined the outside of the hall to express their gratitude, entreating Him to come the next day to speak to them again. The automobile drove through Boston and two other towns and passed several historic landmarks on the way back to Malden.

There was unusual excitement and happiness among the friends who came to 'Abdu'l-Bahá's home that evening. The Master spoke about 21 of the teachings of this Great Manifestation of God which are needed by the people of the world.

Monday, August 26, 1912
[Malden]

At the invitation of Mrs Breed, the Master went for an automobile ride along the coast of the Atlantic Ocean through a wide thoroughfare about nine miles long and guarded on the ocean side with iron rails. It is a recreation spot, very green and clean, and 'Abdu'l-Bahá praised it highly.

Some of the firm believers came to visit the Master. He spoke to them about love and faithfulness:

> This visit is a proof of faithfulness, proof that we have not forgotten one another. In the world of existence nothing is greater than faithfulness, for it allows love to remain unimpaired in spite of the length of time. Behold how faithful were

those blessed souls in Persia who, when under the sword, praised the Blessed Beauty. No affliction or persecution could turn them from faithfulness. On the altar of sacrifice they raised cries of 'Yá Bahá'u'l-Abhá' from their hearts and souls. This is real faithfulness.

In the evening at the girls' school He spoke about the rights and education of women. At the conclusion, everyone came to shake His hand with sincerity and gratitude.[257]

Because 'Abdu'l-Bahá was tired and it was too far to go back to Malden, He stayed at a hotel in Boston and went to sleep without supper.

Tuesday, August 27, 1912
[Malden]

'Abdu'l-Bahá returned to Malden in the morning. He was occupied chiefly in writing letters to the American friends. Believers and seekers came by ones and twos and He lovingly received them.

In the evening there was a well-attended meeting at the Theosophical Society.[258] The gathering became the dawning place of the confirmations of the Abhá Kingdom. The chairman of the meeting introduced the Master to an audience of some five hundred saying:

> Several months ago I attended a convention on the emancipation of religions in this city. Many people of different religions and sects spoke, each one praising the beliefs of his own sect. But a very august personage then stood. By His bearing and by the first few words of His address, everyone felt that this person was spiritual and divinely inspired; that His explanations were heavenly; that He was speaking from God; that He could transform the souls; that He was with God and was the herald of peace and love; that what He said was first practiced by Himself; and that He was a flame from the Kingdom which brightened and

illuminated the minds and hearts of all. That august person was 'Abdu'l-Bahá. I am not worthy to introduce His Holiness to you. You will yourselves know Him better than I.

'Abdu'l-Bahá then stood and gave a stirring address concerning the movement of atoms and the infinite forms that compose this contingent world and gave an explanation of the new teachings of the Cause. During the address, every heart and soul was enthralled. After the meeting everyone spoke of feeling the bounties of the Holy Spirit and of the need for these teachings of love and unity.

Wednesday, August 28, 1912[259]
[Malden]

The president of the Theosophical Society begged the Master that at least one of the friends of the Cause be asked to present these new teachings and principles to his society again. The Master replied, 'I will appoint a person who will talk to you at several meetings.'

When the enthusiasm of the people at yesterday evening's meeting was mentioned to 'Abdu'l-Bahá, He said: 'Yes, it was a good meeting. The souls were stirred. The Blessed Beauty sent His confirmations and strong assistance.'

Today a new group of people came to see the Master and to be refreshed. On seeing the spirit which filled the air, their hearts were exhilarated, their souls grateful and heads bowed in respect.

This evening a meeting filled with joy and enthusiasm was held in the home of Mrs Morey in Malden.[260] 'Abdu'l-Bahá spoke about the divine teachings and kindly admonished the audience, setting aglow a new fire of love in their hearts. When He had finished speaking, a woman asked about the purpose and value of the creation of the world. He spoke first of the virtues of the world of humanity and then about nearness to God, which uplifted the audience. But the questioner was preoccupied, she said that she did not understand His explanation. Therefore the Master spoke in parables, explaining that the greatest result of any perfect creation is the love of the Creator for His creation and that the essential nature of the life-giving God is to create and to spread His bounties and in doing so, God enjoys His creation.

Thursday, August 29, 1912
[Malden]

Today was the last day of the Master's stay in Malden. In addition to receiving visitors every minute to bid them farewell, He was busy correcting letters to be posted.

In the evening a joyful meeting was held at His residence. The friends were encouraged as He exhorted them to exert their utmost to promulgate the Word of God. At the end of the meeting He said to Mrs Wilson, 'Since my arrival in America I have stayed in but two homes, Mrs Parsons's and yours. God be praised that the divine confirmations have descended on you and that you are assisted in serving the Cause of the Blessed Beauty. You must appreciate the value of this blessing.' Then turning to Miss Englehorn, He said: 'I am very pleased with your services. Were you worldly, you would have received your wages but as you are heavenly and divine, your reward is with Bahá'u'lláh.'

Friday, August 30, 1912
[Malden – Montreal]

'Abdu'l-Bahá left today for Montreal. The only servants He took with Him were Mírzá Ahmad Sohrab and myself. Because He had decided to travel to the Western part of America at the pressing invitation of the friends in California, He said, 'We have a long distance to go and must therefore leave as soon as possible.' For this reason, He instructed Mírzá Valíyu'lláh Khán-i-Varqá, Áqá Mírzá 'Alí-Akbar Nakhjávání, Áqá Siyyid Asadu'lláh and Dr Getsinger to remain until His return.

As soon as the friends and a group of Arabs saw 'Abdu'l-Bahá at the railway station in Boston, they surrounded Him, their faces beaming with joy and enthusiasm. At 9:00 a.m. the train left Boston and reached Montreal at 8:00 p.m. On the way, a Canadian was privileged to speak with 'Abdu'l-Bahá. The Master pointed out to him the straight path of truth, and even though this individual had known nothing about 'Abdu'l-Bahá before this encounter, he was attracted to Him.

When we arrived at the station, we saw Mr [Sutherland] Maxwell hurrying forward to greet the Master. He had two carriages to convey the Master and His companions to his home.[261] There a group of friends and a newspaper publisher[262] were waiting to see the Master. At the table, Mrs [May] Maxwell said, 'So many people have telephoned and sent letters about your arrival and I have replied to all. I have become very tired but I consider this fatigue the greatest comfort of my life.' A pastor had telephoned to ask the Master to address his congregation the day after tomorrow. The editor of the newspaper said that he would publish the announcement the next day. When Mrs Maxwell informed 'Abdu'l-Bahá of this, He said, 'Very well. You were tired, having undergone such trouble today. You must rest for the time being.'

Saturday, August 31, 1912
[Montreal]

In the morning, the pastor of the Unitarian Church came with several others to visit 'Abdu'l-Bahá. The Master discussed with them the elimination of religious superstitions and prejudices, which are contrary to science and common sense and which are obstacles to the attainment of the foundation of truth of the divine religions.

A newspaper reporter was then announced. He had come to interview the Master about His life and the history of the Cause. 'Abdu'l-Bahá gave a detailed account, which was recorded by the reporter.

The Master went to the dinner table. Mr Maxwell had come from the customs house and said that when the inspector opened the first suitcase and saw a picture of the Master, he asked, 'Is this the picture of the prophet of Persia?' When he received an affirmative reply, the inspector said, 'There is no need to inspect these goods' and released all the luggage.

Some of the newspapers accounts about the visit of the Master are full of reverence and praise.

In the afternoon, at the invitation of Mr Maxwell, the Master went for ride in the town. While in the carriage He remarked:

> Every city in which the remembrance of God is raised is a divine city. 'Akká was a despised city but when it became the center of the mention of God and the dawning place of His Light, it illumined the world.

When He saw some of the college buildings, 'Abdu'l-Bahá said:

> As only material education is imparted and only natural philosophy is taught, these universities do not produce highly talented scholars. When both the natural and the divine philosophies are expounded, they will bring forth outstanding souls and evince great advancement. The reason for the success of the Greek schools was that they combined both natural and divine philosophies.

As His carriage passed by the Unitarian Church, He said, 'Tomorrow we will raise the Call of God in this place.'

The carriage reached the Roman Catholic Cathedral of Notre Dame. Everything was quiet and no one was in sight. The Master alighted and went in to see the huge building. With rapt attention, He gazed at the vast cathedral, its ornamentation and numerous statues and spoke of its grandeur and embellishments. Standing in an open space at the entrance, He addressed us saying:

> Behold what eleven disciples of Christ have accomplished, how they sacrificed themselves! I exhort you to walk in their footsteps. When a person is detached, he is capable of revolutionizing

the whole world. The disciples of Christ met together in consultation on top of a mountain. They pledged themselves to undergo all manner of hardships, to accept every affliction as a bounty and to consider all difficulties easy to overcome. 'He who is tied to a family, let him arrange to leave it; he who is not should remain single. He should forgo his comfort and his life.' Consulting thus, they descended from the mountain and each one went a different way and never returned. It is for this reason that they were able to leave behind such achievements. After Christ, the disciples truly forgot themselves, and not merely in word. Hence, the Blessed Beauty cited:

> Either be like women and indulge in adornment and pleasure
> Or like men, come out and throw down the gauntlet.[263]

'Abdu'l-Bahá took His seat in the carriage again and told us:

> On our way to Baghdád we had to put up with unbearable hardships. At one time a Turkish soldier of the Ottoman army appeared before us. Mírzá Yaḥyá, on seeing the soldier sitting on the horse with majesty and dignity, cried out with great grief and despair, 'Oh! Where were we? Where are we now going? They say that all heads will bow. When shall it be?' I said to him in reply, 'When the divine bounty attains perfection, persons greater than this soldier will bow their heads under the shadow of the Word of God.' Where is Mírzá Yaḥyá now? Let him come and see how the power of Bahá'u'lláh has so inspired humility in these Americans, who consider the Turks as nothing, that a person like Mr Maxwell, an American, is with deference serving Mírzá Aḥmad,[264] a Persian.

In the evening there was a well-attended meeting at 'Abdu'l-Bahá's residence. He spoke, with good effect, about spiritual progress and the manifestation of divine virtues in human realities. Afterwards many requested private interviews. On receiving satisfactory answers to their questions, they expressed their heartfelt gratitude. Among them was the president of a socialist organization who invited the Master to his group. His request was granted. As it grew late in the evening and other people were waiting for private interviews, we suggested that since the Master might be weary, it would be better if the rest of those waiting came back in the morning. He replied, 'No, this is the time to work. We must not think of our fatigue. Everyone is to be met.'

Sunday, September 1, 1912
[Montreal]

This was a momentous day. From the pulpit of the Unitarian Church, the voice of the Center of the Covenant was broadcast afar. As He prepared to leave for the church, He asked me to sit by Him in the carriage. I said that there was room on the other seat. He replied, 'Come and sit here. When I see someone who is ambitious and selfish, I observe these formalities merely for his correction. Otherwise, everyone may sit wherever he wishes. These things are entirely unimportant.' When the carriage arrived, the pastor, who had been waiting at the entrance, came forward, took the Master's arm with the utmost reverence and courtesy, led him to the pulpit and offered Him his own chair. After the music, the pastor stood and read verses from the Book of Isaiah which allude to the appearance of a promised one from the East. Everyone listened with rapt attention to these verses and felt that they had been specifically written for this day.

In introducing the Master, the pastor said:

> We are honored today with the presence of the Prophet of Peace whose message is the Message of God. God has raised Him to exterminate war and bloodshed. His presence in this church is the cause of eternal honor and the fulfillment of our long-cherished hopes and desires. He is the sign of love among

the people and the promoter of oneness and brotherhood among the sons of men. His object is to free people from the shackles of imitation and to unfurl the banner of the oneness of humanity. He is the temple of kindness, the possessor of the greatest news, the inspirer of the new thoughts and the expounder of the happiness of this great cycle. Although He has suffered violence and affliction for many years and has seen persecutions, His spiritual power is still flowing like the water of life. Although His body has felt the cross, yet His spirit, which is life-giving, has not been crucified. He has journeyed by land and sea to come to these western countries. We extend Him a sincere welcome and offer the incense of gratitude for His teachings which are the cause of the recovery of hearts and are the source of eternal blessings and happiness. Now His Holiness 'Abdu'l-Bahá will speak to you.

The Master rose and, pacing the stage, gave the following address:

God the Almighty has created all humanity from dust, from the same elements. All are descended from one race and all are created to live on the same earth, under the canopy of the same heaven. As members of humanity He created them sharing the same susceptibilities. As created by Him all are one, without discrimination. He provides for all; He trains all; He protects all; He is kind to all. He has left no difference in His bounties and favors to men. He raised prophets and sent divine teachings. These teachings unite all and generate love in human hearts. He has proclaimed the unity of the world of man. He deprecates all obstacles to unity and commends everything that is conducive to harmony and unity. He admonishes all to establish unity at all levels. All the Prophets of God were raised up to deliver the message of love and unity to the sons of men. All the Books of God were revealed to establish fellowship and union. All the Prophets of God were the servants of truth. All their teachings were the essence of truth. Truth is one; it does not accept multiplicity. Therefore, the foundation of truth of all the religions of God is one.

Yet, alas, blind imitations, which have nothing to do with this truth, have crept in. As these vain practices vary, contention, warfare and bloodshed became rampant and strife prevailed. These are the destroyers of the divine foundation. Men kill one another like beasts and bring desolation to one another's families. God has created man for love. He made love the illumination of the world of man. Love is the cause of the unity of creation. All the prophets were promulgators of love. Man, however, arose against the decree of God and acted contrary to the divine will. For this reason, since the beginning of present history, man has never experienced harmony. Bloodshed and massacre have been rampant among them. The hearts have been suspicious of one another. Man has acted against God's good pleasure. All the wars and massacres of the past have been induced either by religious or racial prejudices or by political and patriotic bias which have made this world a place of constant agony for the sons of man.

These prejudices were intense in the Orient, for there was no freedom.

The gloom of blind imitations had darkened the entire Orient and all the nations and religions were on terms of extreme hostility and at war with each other. At such a time Bahá'u'lláh appeared and proclaimed the oneness of the world of man, saying that all men are created by God and all the religions are under the shadow of the mercy of God. God is kind to all; He loves all. All the prophets loved one another. The holy books confirm one another. Why then should there be strife and contention among men? When all are the creatures of one God, and like sheep all are under the protection of one shepherd who helps each one, why should not the sheep live in perfect harmony with one another? If one has gone astray, the others must bring it back and guide it. At the most, if a person is ignorant, he must be informed; if he is imperfect, he must be made perfect; if he is sick, he must be cured; if he is blind, he must be healed and not be made a target of enmity and hatred.

Second, Bahá'u'lláh proclaimed that religion must be the means of love and fellowship. If religion is the cause of hatred, it has no meaning. Irreligion is preferable to such a religion, for it produces enmity and hatred. That which produces enmity is odious to God and that which brings forth love and harmony is acceptable to Him and praised by Him. If religion becomes the cause of bloodshed and rapacity, it is not religion. Irreligion is better than that. Religion is like a remedy. If the remedy produces sickness, it is better not to have it at all. Thus if religion is the cause of warfare and massacre, irreligion is preferable.

Third, religion must be in accord with reason and science. If religion is not consistent with science and reason, it is superstition. God has given us reason so that we may comprehend the realities of things and become lovers of truth. If religion is inconsistent with science and reason, it cannot produce confidence. When confidence is not generated, it is but superstition. Religious issues must therefore conform with reason and science so that hearts may derive assurance, and happiness may prevail.

Fourth, all prejudices – religious, racial, patriotic and political – are destroyers of the human edifice. The religion of God is but one for all. All religions are founded on truth. Abraham summoned the people to reality; Moses proclaimed reality; Christ founded reality; and Muḥammad promoted reality. All the prophets were the servants of reality. All were founders and enforcers of reality. Religious prejudice, therefore, is vain and false, for it negates the truth.

As to racial prejudice: all humanity is one progeny. All are servants of one God. All are of one essence. There is no plurality in race because all are the sons of Adam. Plurality in race is an unfounded belief. Before God there is no England, France, Turkey or Persia. All these people are regarded as one before God. God did not made these divisions. They are made by man; hence, they are false and contrary to reality. Everyone has two eyes, two ears, one head and two feet. There is no racial prejudice among animals, no such prejudice among pigeons. A pigeon of the East will mingle with a pigeon of the West harmoniously. A sheep of the West will not say to a sheep of the East: 'You are of the East and I am of the West.' Instead they mix together. If a pigeon comes from the East, it will mix with the pigeons of the West. It will not say, 'I am of the East while you are of the West.' Is it worthy of man to entertain an attitude which animals do not allow?

Patriotic prejudice prevails although the whole earth is one globe, one country. God has made no divisions in it. He has created all as one. Before Him there are no differences. How can man lay down divisions which God has not created? Europe is one continent. We have created imaginary lines. We fix a boundary and say that on this side of the river is France and on that side Germany, although the river exists for both sides. What idle fancy is this? What ignorance! A thing not purposed by God is made by man, through his own imagination, a cause of bloodshed and strife. Hence, all these prejudices have no valid basis and are odious before God. God has created love, amity and affection which He has desired for His servants. Enmity is reprobated by Him, while love and harmony are accepted in His presence.

Fifth, one of the teachings of Bahá'u'lláh is that every human being must acquire knowledge, so that misunderstandings which are rampant among the people of different nations may be removed. All differences are begotten of misunderstandings. If these are removed, all humanity will become united. Misunderstandings can be removed only when knowledge is universally diffused. It is incumbent on every father to educate his children. If the father is incapable, the community must help so that knowledge may prevail and misunderstandings disappear.

Sixth, Bahá'u'lláh proclaimed the equality of the sexes, because women were not free. Men and women belong to the human race and are the servants of the same God. Before God there is no difference of gender. Whosoever has a purer heart and performs a better deed is nearer to God, irrespective of sex. The differences that exist at the present time are due only to the various degrees of education because women have not had the same opportunity as men. If women were given the same education, they would become equal in all degrees because both are human beings and share the same faculties and in this God has created no differences.

Seventh, a universal language is necessary. A language should be adopted which can be acquired by all. Every person will have to learn two languages – one, his own, and the other, universal, so that all persons will have a means of communication. This will cause the removal of misunderstandings among the various nations. All worship one God and all are the servants of the one God. Differences occur when people cannot understand one another. When they can talk in the same language, differences due to misunderstandings will melt away, while love and harmony will have their sway. The East and the West will then join hands and unite with each other in bonds of union.

Eighth, the world is in sore need of universal peace. As long as universal peace is not established, the world will find no rest. The nations and powers will be forced to form a Supreme Tribunal to which all differences will be referred for decision. As the differences of individuals are settled in the courts of law, so must the differences of nations and peoples be settled, so that they may not lead to wars as at the present time. Fifty years ago Bahá'u'lláh sent epistles to the ruling monarchs of the time. All these teachings were recorded in the Tablets to the Kings and Rulers and to others and were printed and published forty years ago in India, so that prejudices between men might vanish. All those who adopted His teachings have lived in perfect harmony and love. If one goes to their meetings, one sees Christians, Jews, Zoroastrians and Muslims associated together with utmost love and amity. All their talk and effort are concentrated on the removal of misunderstandings among nations.

When I came to America, I found the people noble and high-minded and the government just. I pray to God that this just government and this respected nation may be the cause of proclaiming universal peace and the oneness of humanity. May it become the means of uniting all the nations of the world. May it light a lamp which will give light to the world – the lamp of the oneness of humanity. My hope is that you will all be instrumental in raising aloft the standard of universal peace, that is, that the American nation and government will further the cause of international peace and thus bring security to the whole world. They would win thereby the good-pleasure of God and divine favors would surround the East and the West.

O Thou kind Lord! These people have turned to Thee in prayer. With utmost humility and sincerity they have raised their voices to Thy Kingdom to beg Thy forgiveness. O God! Make this assemblage noble and these persons holy. Enkindle the lights of guidance, illumine the hearts, bring joy to the souls, admit them into Thy Kingdom and enable them to attain felicity in both worlds.

O God! We are abased, glorify us; we are poor, make us rich from the treasury of Thy Kingdom; we are sick, grant us health; we are weak, give us power. O God, guide us to Thy good-pleasure and make us free from self and desire. O God, make us firm in Thy love and assist us to be kind to all creatures. Help us to render service to humanity so that we may serve all Thy servants, love all Thy creatures, be kind to all mankind. O God, verily Thou art the Powerful, the Merciful, the Forgiving and the Omnipotent.[265]

The Master's address on the unity of humanity and the oneness of the Manifestations of God, together with an explanation of the new teachings, was so enthusiastically received by the audience that it is difficult to describe adequately, especially the effect of the prayer He chanted. As well as the local residents, some Turks and Arabs came to the church to pay their respects to the Master.

A wonderful change came over the hearts of the people of the city and a new excitement was felt in the public meetings. One person asserted that the only religion which was worthy to be acknowledged today was the Bahá'í religion while another thanked God that he was granted life to hear the great message.

In the afternoon a number of people of different nationalities, having obtained permission by telephone, came to visit the Master. Some of the Turks became so attracted to Him that they were continually to be found in His presence, both day and night.

This evening a great multitude assembled to hear 'Abdu'l-Bahá. He unfolded the mysteries of the evolution of humanity, the divine civilization and the new birth so impressively and with such majesty that His taj fell from His head and His hair tumbled down. He continued to speak in this state for more than half an hour and at last He passed through the crowd to His room. The longing souls in that meeting did not let the Master rest. Out of respect for the people's wishes, He came out into the crowd and again spoke on spiritual subjects, including the immortality of the spirit, His words diffusing joy and happiness to all.[266]

As He left for His room, some asked for a private interview with Him. Everyone had a request to make and expressed his sincerity and humility and each received His bounties. One of the ladies said that her young son places the Master's picture in front of him and cries out, 'O Thou, my Beloved.' The Master replied, 'It is a proof of your own love.'

Later the Master said to us, 'Tomorrow we should move to a hotel. A traveler should stay in a hotel.' Mr and Mrs Maxwell tried their utmost to dissuade Him but did not succeed.

Monday, September 2, 1912
[Montreal]

After the morning obligatory prayer Mrs Maxwell came to 'Abdu'l-Bahá and said that the people were changing and becoming interested. Her neighbor, who had previously reproached her, was so enchanted after visiting 'Abdu'l-Bahá that she telephoned to request that He visit her home. She also suggested that 'Abdu'l-Bahá use her carriage every day.

After the Master visited and encouraged this neighbor, He went to the hotel [the Hotel Windsor] and rented three rooms. On the way back to the Maxwell home, the Master bought some valuable rings to give as gifts. A large number of people were waiting for Him and attained new spiritual heights and powers through His discourses.

One of His talks concerned the abandonment of blind imitation and the elimination of those customs and dogmas that are contrary to the fundamental truth of the religion of God. He said:

> When educated people see the priests taking bread and wine in their hands, blowing a few breaths over them and saying that the bread and wine are now changed into the flesh and blood of Christ, or hear them saying that by making a confession before a priest their sins are pardoned, they will begin to despair of their religion and become totally irreligious.

At lunch time the Master invited a number of people to the table, saying: 'Come! We are in Montreal, Canada, in this home, eating Persian rice which has been cooked by Mírzá Ahmad. This has a relish all its own; what a tale it makes! Continuing, He said:

> To be grateful for the blessings of God in time of want and trouble is necessary. In the abundance of blessings everyone can be grateful. It is said that Sulṭán Maḥmúd cut a melon and gave a portion of it to Ayáz who ate it cheerfully and expressed

gratitude. When the Sulṭán ate a little of the same melon, he found it bitter. He asked, 'How did you eat such a bitter melon and show no sign of disliking it?' Ayáz answered, 'I had eaten many sweet and palatable things from the hands of the Sulṭán and I thought it very unworthy of me to express dislike on eating a slightly bitter thing today.' Thus man, who is immersed in the blessings of God, should not be grieved if he experiences a little trouble. He should not forget the manifold divine bounties.

In the afternoon, professors, clergy and press representatives came one after another to visit 'Abdu'l-Bahá. The samovar was steaming and fruits and sweets were served to all. That His Persian servants in their Eastern attire served the guests was considered a social novelty and was reported in the press.

One of 'Abdu'l-Bahá talks was this:

> Because of material civilization, industry has progressed and sciences and arts have burgeoned but at the same time weapons of war and bloodshed designed for the destruction of the edifice of humanity have multiplied and political problems have vastly increased. Hence, this material civilization cannot become the means of comfort and ease for all until it acquires spiritual power and the attributes of a divine civilization. Rather, the difficulties will increase and the troubles will multiply.

Continuing, He said:

> The government of the United States of America has recently provided fifteen million dollars toward the cost of building new battleships. Before international peace is established, a great war will in all certainty take place.

'Abdu'l-Bahá made many such important addresses and all who heard Him were eloquent in their praise and adoration of Him.

Today 'Abdu'l-Bahá moved into the Hotel Windsor. As He was leaving for a meeting at Mr and Mrs Maxwell's home, he took the tram. We asked whether we could call for a carriage. He said: 'Oh, it matters little. This saves expense. There is a difference of one dollar in the fare.' He was very careful over this type of personal expense but when He reached the home of Mr and Mrs Maxwell, He gave one pound to each of their servants.

Although two adjoining rooms had been set with chairs in rows, there was still not enough space. We all felt the absence of the Eastern friends. Everyone wished they were present so they too could witness the excitement and joy that was engendered by the talk of the Master, who spoke on the inherent imperfection of the world of nature and its ultimate perfection through divine education.[267] After the Master's talk each guest came to shake His hand and received His blessing yet when He went upstairs, the majority followed Him, especially the new seekers.

Tuesday, September 3, 1912
[Montreal]

The morning was cloudy and rainy. At the hotel the Master was presented with some newspaper articles reporting last night's meeting and giving an account of His talk. Dr Faríd arrived today from Boston to join us. As some professors and clergymen had come by to visit the Master, He spoke to them on the relationship of human souls, universal peace and the harm caused by prejudices. His words were particularly enjoyed by the professors from the university and the ministers showed their humility. After giving a detailed description of the teachings of the Supreme Pen, He said:

> This is the purpose of the people of Bahá. Would you not like to serve such an ideal? I hope you will put forth effort in this direction so that the world of men may find real unity, become released from prejudice and be freed from war and bloodshed. Our efforts are for this. Bahá'u'lláh has opened a broad vista to

humanity. For instance, when the people of different religions, races and nations were reviling each other, He addressed the people of the world saying, 'O people! Ye are the fruits of one tree and the leaves of one branch.'

The minister from the black church extended an invitation to the Master to speak at his church. Because of the lack of time, the Master gave His apologies. Although the Master had intended to stay in Montreal for only two or three days, His visit had lengthened into a week. The fame of the Master had spread throughout the vicinity. Newspapers printed accounts of the meetings and many of the tributes to 'Abdu'l-Bahá. The Master had requested copies of the news stories to be sent to the friends in the East. The response was so generous that one room was completely filled.

During the afternoon, while cheering the friends, He also attended to the mail and read petitions from the friends of the East and the West. At one moment He was answering important questions and the next He was dictating words conducive to the betterment of the social status of women and their confirmation in the Kingdom of God.

When the guests had left and the Master was completely exhausted, He went out alone for a walk to refresh Himself. He then boarded a tram which took Him far out of the city, then another tram which went out of the city by another route and finally took a taxi. The driver asked for the name of the hotel but 'Abdu'l-Bahá did not know. He indicated to the driver to go straight ahead and, suddenly, there was the hotel. With His hair dishevelled and His smiling face, He told us how He had gotten lost. 'Once in the Holy Land,' He said,

> 'Áqá Faraj[268] lost the way to Yirkih. I advised him to loosen the reins of the animal. When the ass was left to itself it went straight to its destination. Today I pointed to the chauffeur to go straight on and by chance I reached my hotel among all these hotels.

That evening He spoke to a meeting of the Socialist Club with majesty and dignity. The audience lined His way and the chairman, who was speaking as the Master arrived, stepped forward, grasped His hand and led Him to the podium. The president introduced the Master in most glowing terms, concluding, 'Now, 'Abdu'l-Bahá will teach us the principles of brotherhood, prosperity and the upliftment of the poor.'

As the Master was delivering His address on economics and the adjustment of society according to the principle of moderation, the audience broke into spontaneous applause, clapping their hands with joy and excitement. At the end, the chairman sought 'Abdu'l-Bahá's permission for those who had questions to ask them. Every answer evoked further applause and admiration to such an extent that the walls of the building seemed to vibrate to their foundations.

The meeting continued to such a late hour that the audience itself began to realize that to continue would not only be impolite but might also be injurious to 'Abdu'l-Bahá's health. As the Master moved towards His carriage, the people surrounded Him, demonstrating their heartfelt reverence and humility. 'Abdu'l-Bahá, often moved to express His thankfulness for the help and assistance of the Blessed Beauty, said, 'Praise be to God that the confirmations of the Kingdom of Abhá are descending continually. Mr Woodcock used to say that Montreal was a city of Catholics and the center of intolerance. Now let him come and see what has transpired here. Not a sound can be heard from the Catholics.'

Wednesday, September 4, 1912
[Montreal]

An account of the Master's talk at the Socialist Club and its influence was published in glowing terms in the newspapers. The force of His explanations and the persuasiveness of His proofs were the talk of the day. Many newcomers came to visit Him. The friends told the Master how happy they were to see the extent to which the

Cause of God had penetrated the hearts. 'Abdu'l-Bahá said in reply:

> The greatness of the teachings of Bahá'u'lláh will be known when they are acted upon and practiced. Not one of a hundred has as yet come into force. All of your thoughts should be turned toward bringing these blessed teachings into practice.

When the translations of some of the newspaper articles were read to 'Abdu'l-Bahá, He said, again, 'This is all through the confirmations of the Blessed Beauty. Otherwise, even if the king of Persia had come here he would not have been able to bring about even one such meeting.'

In the afternoon, for a change of routine, the Master took the elevator down from the seventh floor and went for an automobile ride to the foot of a mountain outside the city limits. It is a fine place where people go for recreation. It has a cable car, which took the Master and His companions up the mountain. The side of the mountain was perpendicular like a wall. The Master said, 'This cable car is like a balloon flying in the air.' It made one nervous to look down. When we reached the top, the Master walked around. It was a magnificent sight, with a view of the whole city stretched before us. The canals, streets and orchards of the town were below. It appeared as if a beautifully painted picture had been spread before one's eyes.

While we were here, translations of other accounts of the meetings that had been published in the evening newspapers were read to Him. Suddenly He cried out:

> O Bahá'u'lláh! May I be a sacrifice for Thee. O Bahá'u'lláh! May my life be offered up for Thee. Thou hast spoken the Word which cannot be refuted. What a wonderful Cause Thou hast founded! It satisfies every assemblage! Each group testifies to its greatness. In the churches it shakes the souls; it excites the Theosophists; it imparts spirituality to the spiritualists; it makes the Unitarians aware of the reality of unity; it makes the

socialists contented and grateful and inspires joy and happiness in the peace meetings. There is no refuge for any denomination except in submission to it. It is a miracle! It is the greatest force in the world of existence. This is all through the assistance of the Blessed Beauty. If healing the lame and crippled is a miracle, it can also be produced by a dose of medicine. This is no great achievement.

From here the Master and His companions went to the home of Mr and Mrs Maxwell where letters from the East were given to Him. He read the petitions of the friends. Among them was a letter from Mírzá Ḥaydar-'Alí, in which he dwelt on the greatness and significance of the journey of the Master. The Master said:

> Yes, the value and greatness of these travels are not known now but will be apparent later on. As we had no other intention except to offer devotion to the Threshold of the One True God, we were assisted and the brightness of divine favor and grace appeared.

Continuing, He said:

> At the time of Muḥammad's migration to Medina under divine protection, Abú Bakr,[269] was with Him. He said to Abú Bakr, 'Be not afraid, God is with us.' These very words became afterwards the cause of his succession to the Caliphate because the word 'with us' included him also. Many proofs and arguments based on these words have been advanced. The value of this bounty, too, is not known now.

At a meeting in the evening at Mrs Maxwell's home, 'Abdu'l-Bahá gave an address on spiritual brotherhood and the economic principles upheld by the teachings of Bahá'u'lláh which will be the cause of the salvation, prosperity and liberation of the nations of the world. This meeting was very special because the Master's talk was so influential. The audience was invited to light refreshments of sweets and beverages. Among the guests were Americans, as well as Turks and Arabs clothed in their splendid robes, all of whom were attracted to 'Abdu'l-Bahá and fascinated by His demeanor and words.

Thursday, September 5, 1912
[Montreal]

The Bishop of Montreal came to visit the Master to express his admiration and gratitude for the Master's address concerning the purpose of the appearance of Christ and the other Manifestations. He was pleased to learn about other meetings and talks. The Master said to him, 'Tonight I shall speak at the Methodist church. You may come if you wish.'

The editor of an illustrated Toronto magazine was announced. He happily recorded a detailed account of the history and teachings of the Cause. Another visitor was a Jewish rabbi who became very enthusiastic when he heard the Master's explanations.

One of 'Abdu'l-Bahá's talks today was this:

> The degree to which these different denominations testify to the greatness of the Cause of God has never been seen in past history. Even socialists say that although so many philosophers have written books on economic questions, the Bahá'í Cause has the solution.

When we arrived at the Methodist Church in the evening, we saw an electric illumined sign reading: 'This evening the Prophet of the East will speak on the principles of the Bahá'í Faith and the salvation of the world of humanity.' When the translation of this announcement was read to the Master, He said, 'So, people are calling me a prophet. Oh, would that they had omitted that word!' In order to correct this impression, in the course of His address He emphasized His devotion to Bahá'u'lláh.

'Abdu'l-Bahá went to the vestry where a number of ministers came to greet Him with such reverence and humility that it was really something to be seen. He then went into the auditorium and took a seat on the platform. The minister welcomed Him by motioning the audience to rise, which they immediately did to show their respect. The minister then made an introductory speech about the world's apathy to the commandments of the Gospel and the urgent need for laws of peace and harmony among the peoples of the West. Finally he urged the audience to listen carefully to the address and the new teachings given by 'Abdu'l-Bahá.

The Master stood before the audience and spoke about the continuity of the Divine Bounties, the power and majesty of the Kingdom of God and these wonderful teachings. The audience was awakened to the Faith to such a degree that a judge named Mr Riger, who had previously heard of the Master and had come for the first time this evening to hear Him speak, stood and said, 'Some have imagined that the succession of the Prophets and the bounties of God were limited. But tonight we have heard with our own ears these divinely ordained teachings from an Eastern prophet who is the successor of the Prophets of God. We will never forget his message. There is no doubt that these teachings of universal peace, the oneness of humanity and the distribution of wealth are in complete accord with the principles of economic law, the equality of rights and the adoption of one universal language. These are the basic principles for the progress of the world of humanity.' The minister then stood and said, 'It is an error to think that the West has attained perfection and that the East has no bounties or teachings to offer to the West. 'Abdu'l-Bahá has said many things which we have not heard before or understood.[270]

The Master then chanted a prayer and publicly thanked the judge. Later, in the vestry, the clergymen were so deferential in His presence, they could not find words to express their gratitude. Of particular note was the judge, who repeatedly expressed his desire to become a Bahá'í.

Friday, September 6, 1912
[Montreal]

In the morning 'Abdu'l-Bahá came into our room. When He saw the pile of newspapers which had been collected to send to the friends in the East, He asked, with surprise, 'What have you done? What are all these newspapers for?' We replied that they were the signs of the power and influence of the Cause of God.

After leaving the church last night, the Master had caught a cold and His voice was hoarse, so even though He had planned to leave Montreal, His departure was delayed for a few days. During this time He went nowhere except to the home of Mr and Mrs Maxwell. However, many came to visit Him at the hotel.

Mrs Maxwell said to Him, 'At the time that I visited 'Akká I despaired of ever having the blessing of children. Praise be to God! My supplications and your prayers at the Holy Shrine of Bahá'u'lláh were accepted and I was blessed with a dear baby.'[271] Bestowing His grace and kindness upon her and the child, the Master said, 'Children are the ornaments of the home. A home which has no children is like one without light.'

Mrs Maxwell said that her husband used to say to her: 'You have become a Bahá'í. Very well, you are responsible for this yourself. I have no hand in it. You must not speak to me about it anymore.' But now, she added, he was so proud of the Master's visit that if kings had come to their home he would not have felt so exalted. The room in which the Master stayed was considered by him to be holy and he would not allow anyone to enter it.

'Abdu'l-Bahá's advice to Mr Maxwell and others was this:

> You must cling to those things which prove to be the cause of happiness for the world of man. You must show kindness to the orphans, give food to the hungry, clothe the naked and offer help to the poor so that you may be accepted in the Court of God.

Here is a quotation from one of the Tablets that was revealed today:

> It is because the friends of California, and particularly those of San Francisco, have so frequently called and pleaded, expressed despair and wept and sent incessant supplications, that I have determined to go to California.

Saturday, September 7, 1912
[Montreal]

Today 'Abdu'l-Bahá spoke to a group of people who came to visit Him at the hotel. Here is some of what He explained:

> As in the physical world there are four seasons, so in the realm of religion there is the season of heavenly and spiritual springtime. When its outpourings gradually diminish, the trees of existence cease to be verdant and creeping torpor spreads, it will become like winter. The souls will become withered and distressed and the soil of the hearts will become full of thorns and thistles. There will be no flowers, no hyacinths, no greenery, no pleasure, no freshness and no cheer. Then, once again, the divine spring will raise its tabernacle. The gardens of the world of humanity will become green and verdant, full of freshness and purity. The flowers of reality will open and the trees of existence will bring forth enduring fruit. This is the law of God and is in accord with the world of creation and this is the cause for the reappearance of holy Manifestations Who effect renewal and change in religious laws and commandments.

In the afternoon the Master spoke about the oneness of the fundamental truths of the religions of God and the vain imaginings and beliefs of various peoples, saying:

The foundation of all religions is one and the aim of all creeds of the world is also one. All are believers in the oneness of God. All believe that a mediator between the Creator and the creatures is needed. The question is that to the Jews Moses is the last, to the Christians it is Christ, to the Muslims it is Muḥammad and to the Parsis it is Zoroaster. But their differences are only those of names. If these names are set aside, it is evident that their aim is one. Every divine religious law was complete for its time. The renewal of the laws of God and the appearance of the Manifestations of the bounties of the Lord in each cycle are necessary. Thus the people who seek truth and inner meanings can discover the divine mysteries and become aware of the secrets of the Books of God. They know God to be the Supreme, His bounties infinite and the doors of His mercy unbarred. They believe in all the Prophets and affirm 'No difference do we make between any of them' [Qur'án 2:130]. But those who adhere to outer meanings only, who worship outer form, cling to imitations and follow their superstitions. They use the allegories set forth in the verses of God to deny the Cause of the Lord of Signs. Therefore, offer thanks to God that you have attained unto reality, have responded affirmatively to the Call of God, have given up dogmatic imitations and have become cognizant of the mystery of oneness. Offer thanks to God. Be grateful to your Lord.

Sunday, September 8, 1912
[Montreal]

'Abdu'l-Bahá's discourses today consisted of divine exhortations, admonitions and expressions of farewell to the friends. 'I have sown the seed,' He said. 'You must water it. You must educate the souls in divine morals, make them spiritual and lead them to the oneness of humanity and to universal peace.'

In the afternoon He gave an account of His imprisonment in the Most Great Prison and of His return to the Holy Land.

Someone suggested that His return to 'Akká might bring trouble to Him and again cause His imprisonment. 'Oh no,' He replied,

> that organization has been rolled up; that system has been rendered null. Those days were so hard that all had believed that when the Commission of Investigation returned to Constantinople 'Abdu'l-Bahá's life and name would be effaced. But God did not will it. As we were imprisoned for the Cause of God and not for political reasons, while in prison we were not perturbed and had no worries. However, the others thought that after I was set free I would raise the banner of independence among the Arabs and unite them with me! See, how ill-informed was such a judgment!

As this was the last day of His stay in Montreal, all the friends, both old and new, expressed their sorrow. 'Abdu'l-Bahá consoled them with the glad tidings of certitude, spiritual nearness, assistance and heavenly grace.

Monday, September 9, 1912
[Montreal – Toronto – Buffalo]

In the morning the bill for $700 for the week's stay at the hotel was paid. As usual, 'Abdu'l-Bahá directed me to take personal charge of His bags and move them myself. I fell short of my duty as the hotel stewards carried His bags with the other luggage. When He saw that His bags were not with me, He said: 'In spite of these repeated reminders, you were neglectful. I would not have asked you to be so careful had it not contained valuable documents and writings which I wish to present to the libraries of London and Paris. Otherwise, material things are not important to me.'

All luggage sent through the railway station had to be examined by the Customs officers; but the chief officer at the Customs and his assistants passed our baggage, indicating that they were perfectly satisfied and had no reason to examine the effects of the

Bahá'ís! When the Master was told this, His face opened up like a rose and He expounded on the stations of truthfulness and trustworthiness, which are the sources of the prosperity and assurance of the people of the world.

The enthusiasm and ardor of the friends knew no bounds. They surrounded 'Abdu'l-Bahá like moths. Until the train pulled out of the station at nine o'clock, the friends continued to sigh and express their sorrow at His departure.

It is astonishing to see that 'Abdu'l-Bahá does not want any comfort and will not take any rest, even while traveling on the train. When translations of the newspaper articles and letters from the friends were read to Him, He immediately answered and bestowed His bounties upon them. To some He wrote in His own hand. When He was tired of writing, the Master spoke about the coming of Christ from the heaven of holiness:

> The Gospel expressly records that in His first coming, although Christ was born to Mary, He Himself said that He came from heaven. Thus, the meaning of 'heaven' is the greatness of the Cause and eminence and might of the Manifestation of God Who spreads this divine Cause by His heavenly power and divine strength and not through material means.

Whenever His eyes fell on the luxuriant beauty of the lakes and rivers along the route He would remember the Blessed Perfection.

At noon He said to us: 'You have lunch. I will not eat anything until I am hungry.'

The air in the coach was stifling and, owing to the speed of the train, even though the windows and doors were closed, the dust was heavy. 'Abdu'l-Bahá felt tired. When the train reached Toronto to change tracks, He walked a little on the platform, saying that He was exhausted. 'We have not gone far,' He said, 'yet we feel tired. How will the great distance to California be traversed? We have no choice, as in the path of God we must regard troubles as blessings and discomforts as greatest bounties.' We reached Buffalo late at night but, in obedience to His request, the friends were not informed.

Tuesday, September 10, 1912
[Buffalo]

The moment the news of the Master's arrival in Buffalo became known, the friends eagerly hastened to meet Him, grateful that their city had been blessed with His presence. Journalists came one after the other and left happy and satisfied, which surprised everyone. Owing to articles about the Cause in the city's newspapers, a great number of people came to visit on the morning of 'Abdu'l-Bahá's arrival. The teachings so touched the hearts of the people that when the Master went out in the afternoon, passersby who saw Him pointed to Him, saying: 'Look! There goes the Messenger of Peace, the Prophet from the East!'

At the request of some of His companions, after a short walk He took the trolley to Niagara Falls. It was far away and the round trip fare cost 50 cents per person. We had never seen or heard such huge, magnificent waterfalls. It was a beautiful sight. The great river feeding the falls is flanked on both sides by lakes, fields, mountains and woods. At some places the river falls from a height of a hundred meters. Because of the height of the falls and the crash of the water, small droplets of water form sprays which appear like a great sand storm. Below is a very large lake where people entertain themselves in barges and sailboats.

'Abdu'l-Bahá went to the edge, admired the great falls and recalled the days of the Blessed Perfection:

> There were small waterfalls in Mázindarán which Bahá'u'lláh liked so much that He used to camp near them for several days.

Continuing, He said:

So much electricity can be generated from this water that it will suffice the whole town and it is also very good for the health.

While sitting on the bank of the river He ate some pears and grapes and then walked for some time in the park. We suggested that He should stay here a few days but He replied, 'Even half a day is not possible. We have no time for amusement. We must keep ourselves engaged in our work.' He sat down on a bench in the center of the park and said, 'I washed my hair with warm water without applying soap. It is much cleaner and takes longer to become dirty. Come and see how clean and soft it is.' We touched His hair, which was like silk, very soft and absolutely clean. On this occasion 'the place of His lovers was noticeably vacant'.[272]

On the trolley ride back to the hotel, newspaper articles about His arrival in Buffalo were read to Him. The headline read: "Abdu'l-Bahá, the Prophet of Peace, has arrived in Buffalo. The Bahá'ís are very happy to see Him among them in their homes. Their great longing for His arrival is fulfilled. Our hearty congratulations to the Bahá'ís.' When the Master reached the hotel He met a number of journalists who were waiting for Him.

This evening 'Abdu'l-Bahá's talk was about unity and amity among the peoples of the East and the West and also about the degrees of love which bring the whole creation into existence. His message breathed a new spirit of love and joy into friends and seekers alike. They all gathered around Him, shook His hand and expressed their humble appreciation. He then went into another room, followed by some journalists who made a note of His words.

Later in the evening He strolled along the store fronts with us. The gas and electric street lamps, as well as the brightly lit theaters and coffee shops, were picturesque. We reached a spot where several poor people had gathered. He gave a sum of money to each. Seeing the grandeur, nobility, generosity and grace of the Master, a huge crowd, with the utmost courtesy, lined up near Him and He showered kindness on all. It was a strange sight for them to see

Him walking in the street accompanied by His Persian servants in Eastern attire. Everyone said, 'This is the same Prophet of Peace who has been acclaimed in the newspapers!'

For dinner 'Abdu'l-Bahá ate a little bread and cheese and went to bed for the night.

Wednesday, September 11, 1912
[Buffalo]

People from all walks of life came to visit Him, including friends from Spokane and Mr Collins from Ottawa, who said that there were two thousand people in his city who believed in this golden age and in 'Abdu'l-Bahá and who wanted to have a glimpse of the Master. The Master entrusted him with a special Tablet and sent him, now ablaze like a ball of fire, back to his home.

Today the newspapers appeared with a new title for the Master, 'The Prince of the East', which 'Abdu'l-Bahá did not welcome. He spoke with the reporters about the beginning and end of creation:

> If we determine a beginning and an end for creation, it is as if we determine a beginning and an end for God. There can be no creator without a creation. The sun without light and a king without subjects and a country are simply inconceivable.

Here are some of His words to the friends:

> I am exceedingly pleased because I see you firm and unwavering in the Cause of God. Some individuals are like rootless plants, they are pulled out by the slightest breeze. But those who are steadfast are like trees that have strong roots and foundations. Storms cannot shake them; rather, they add to their freshness.

The minister of the Church of the Messiah was greatly pleased to hear the Master's teachings. He stated that they could not be contradicted by anyone. After thanking the Master for accepting his invitation to come to his church, the minister left.

In the afternoon the Master went to see two of the friends who were ill. When he arrived at their home, the neighborhood children crowded around Him, gazing at Him with reverence. Some asked about His native country and why He had come here. The friends explained it to them. The Master asked one of the friends to get change for a five dollar bill. He then distributed the coins among the children, who rushed to receive them, causing the Master to drop the rest of the coins. He then went into the home of Mr Mills where a number of friends had assembled. Refreshments had been prepared. The friends enthusiastically listened until the early evening hours as the Master unfolded the divine mysteries and encouraged them. Everyone begged His assistance and blessings and the desire of each for a few words from His own pen was granted. He then said, 'Tomorrow we leave for Chicago.' As soon as these words were uttered, the friends became downcast. Men and women, young and old, surrounded Him, supplicating Him for His blessings and confirmations in His absence.

When 'Abdu'l-Bahá arrived at the Church of the Messiah, the minister received Him at the entrance and led Him to a study where he humbly expressed his gratitude. He presented the Master with the official church newsletter in which he had published an extensive article about the history and teachings of the Cause. It had been written in a scholarly style and concluded with words in praise of the Master. When the article was translated for the Master, He turned to the minister and said, 'You have left nothing for me to say here tonight. You have published everything in this booklet.' We remarked that there could be no miracle greater than this, that clergymen were testifying to the greatness of the Cause of God with their own tongues and pens. The Master replied, 'I have told you repeatedly that the Blessed Perfection is assisting us. All these confirmations which descend continually are from Him.' He then went to the stage, stood before the audience and became the center of attraction for friends and seekers alike.

The minister introduced 'Abdu'l-Bahá in these words:

> It is my great honor to present to you the prophet of peace, the leader of the Bahá'í Cause. A short history and teachings of this Cause were published in today's issue of the church newsletter and distributed this evening. I need not therefore dwell on these subjects. I propose to give as much time as possible to this eminent speaker. This great personage has traveled to many parts of the world and has delivered innumerable talks on the question of international peace. In Washington He gave a unique address in a church of our creed. The essential principles of this religion are the same as ours. I feel it an honor that I have been given the privilege of introducing to you the prophet of peace, His Holiness 'Abdu'l-Bahá.

The Master stood and spoke on the divine teachings and the unity of the diverse nations under the canopy of the Word of God. The audience was so fascinated that although 'Abdu'l-Bahá wished to leave the church early, it was not possible. The people came one after the other to meet Him and to give Him their regards. In return each received illumination from the Branch of the Ancient Root.[273]

An unusual and outstanding feature of this evening's experience was that at the conclusion of the meeting, the minister encouraged the congregation to go to the Bahá'í meetings to investigate and discover truth. This caused 'Abdu'l-Bahá to express gratitude for the assistance of the Blessed Beauty and He continued to speak about the importance of this great journey until about 2:00 a.m. when He finally rested.

Thursday, September 12, 1912
[Buffalo – Chicago]

'Abdu'l-Bahá called us before dawn. He had already packed and readied His bags. We packed our belongings in readiness for our departure. Because the chambermaid for His room was not there, He left a dollar for her with the hotel manager. When He reached the railway station, the driver wanted more money than the usual fare. 'Abdu'l-Bahá paid no heed to him, saying, 'A man may give $1,000 without minding it but he should not yield even a dollar to the person who wishes to take it wrongfully, for such wrongful behavior flouts justice and disrupts the order of the world.'

As articles from the Buffalo newspapers were being translated for 'Abdu'l-Bahá in the train, He again offered thanks for the assistance and protection of the Abhá Kingdom. He said:

> The confirmation and assistance of the Abhá Kingdom are more manifest than the sun. No eye or ear has seen or heard of such confirmations. Christ went into the Temple of the Jews where He spoke on the teachings of the Torah prohibiting buying and selling in the house of God. Up to the present time Christians glory in this and rejoice over it. But today through the assistance of the Abhá Beauty the Cause of God is proclaimed with the utmost openness in the churches and assemblies of the West.

The train passed by Niagara Falls. Beautiful villages and factories nestled in green fields and wooded mountain valleys came into view. As midday approached, and as the number of passengers increased at every station, the heat grew more and more intense, causing 'Abdu'l-Bahá to become tired and weary. He commented that, 'The friends in America expect me to visit each city. How would this be possible? It is impossible to sit in a train every day from morning until afternoon; the body cannot stand it.'

Today the train traveled through several states. At 8:00 p.m. the lights from Chicago appeared in the distance like brilliant stars and the train pulled into the station.

The Master waited until all the passengers had left the train and then He slowly disembarked. The spacious train station was crowded with His friends. As soon as His feet touched the ground their hearts were stirred. One person hurried forward to shake His hand; another ran to kiss the hem of His robe; another held a bouquet of flowers to present to Him; and yet another raised his voice in praise and gratitude on attaining the bounty of meeting Him. It was an impressive sight, a field of yearning lovers canopied by heavens resounding with songs of joy. The friends formed two lines and 'Abdu'l-Bahá walked majestically between them showering His blessings on each one. He then went by automobile to the home of Mrs True, the maidservant of the Mashriqu'l-Adhkár.[274] There one of the Japanese friends bowed at His feet and received His blessings.

After a brief rest, 'Abdu'l-Bahá appeared before the gathering. His eyes fell on Mr [Saichiro] Fujita, the Japanese gentleman. He remarked:

> So, how is our Japanese Effendi? Recently the government of Japan has undergone a change. A new emperor has come to the throne. The sovereignty of the former Mikado has come to an end; all the hue and cry have ceased, a handful of dust was thrown over him and covered all his imperial regalia. Such was the kingdom of the Mikado. The same is true of all the other kings.
>
> But as you are a believer in God, you have a kingdom which will never collapse and will be everlasting. Offer thanks to God, Who has bestowed upon you such a kingdom, greater than that of the Mikado. The first Bonaparte was a famous man and a great general who conquered most of the countries of Europe and became the emperor of France. The whole of Europe trembled before his command. The star of his prosperity set and it shall never rise again. At last a trifling incident obliterated his dominion and he became a prisoner in a state of extreme hardship in St Helena where he lamented until his death. One day as he was talking with his generals, they said that Christ, too, was a wise man like Napoleon. He replied, 'No, you are mistaken. There is a vast difference between Him and me.'

The sovereignty of Napoleon ceased as soon as he died but the Kingdom of Christ is eternal. The former established his mortal kingdom with bloodshed and the sword while Christ established the Kingdom of God with the life-giving breaths of the Holy Spirit. Napoleon established his kingdom through the power of oppression while Christ established His through the power of the love of God. A hundred thousand Napoleons may be effaced but the Kingdom of Christ will remain forever. Such is the Kingdom of God.

Friday, September 13, 1912
[Chicago]

Mrs True prepared tea for us. When some of the Persian friends remarked to 'Abdu'l-Bahá that 'there was better tea' than this, the Master replied, 'This tea is very good because it has been prepared with love.' Referring to His expenses, He said:

> Sometimes I give away as much as $1,000, if I have it, but at another time I do not spend even a single dollar. This is so that affairs are regulated. Thus it is that I say that I want the friends to become divine and godly under the shadow of the favor of the Abhá Beauty. Through the teachings and bestowals of the Blessed Perfection happiness and prosperity can be gained. I swear by God, besides Whom there is no other God, that although we might have traversed America from the east to the west, had not His confirmations and favors been with us, no one would have paid any heed to us. It is all through His aid and assistance that these doors have been opened. It is with the power of faith that we ascend to the highest apex and attain honor in the all-glorious Kingdom. So it is that these honorable souls serve us with such love and sincerity.

Visitors began to arrive. The friends from surrounding communities pleaded with Him to come to their cities. But because of the limited time and His plan to journey to the West, He did not accept their invitations. Reporters also came. He spoke on various subjects relating to the Cause and they took notes for publication in their newspapers.

At the meeting 'Abdu'l-Bahá spoke about the establishment of the divine civilization through the power of Bahá'u'lláh and about the world's need for the divine teachings:

> Without divine civilization the mysteries of the Kingdom are not revealed and the bounties of heaven are not ascertained; supernatural wisdom and power do not manifest themselves; the intelligence of humanity does not reach maturity; the world of humanity does not become the mirror of the world above; spiritual powers fail to overcome animal influences of nature. These perfections are attained through divine civilization of which the world of man is in need.

After the meeting one of the friends who came to see Him was Mr Jackson of Kenosha, Wisconsin.[275] He told 'Abdu'l-Bahá that the believers and seekers were anxiously awaiting His visit and that a minister had asked Him to promise to speak in his church.

Since the friends were allowed to visit en masse, each morning there was such a crowd that there was no way up or down the stairs. When the Master got tired, He would take a walk outside and then return to the house.

Today another group, including some of the black believers, visited 'Abdu'l-Bahá. Here are some of His words to them:

> If a man has spiritual characteristics, be he white or black, he is near to God. Some have protested to me, asking why I seek to cultivate love between the whites and the blacks. Yet what a great error they make. You see people who love their dogs because of their faithfulness and the protection they provide. If but one good trait endears a dog to a human, why shouldn't praiseworthy qualities cause a man to be loved and respected? Why

should fellowship with an upright person be avoided? When people are prepared to fondle an animal day and night, why should they shun association with an intelligent human being?

My hope is that you will rid and purify yourselves of imitations so that your thoughts and minds will be broadened and elevated, that you will be seekers of the truth, the lovers of the servants of God and the cause of the oneness of humanity.

Today an important philosopher together with the president of the Workers' Union, a socialist, visited the Master. They were so moved by the Master's explanations and proofs of the existence of God and His divine laws that the friends' hearts were overjoyed to see their sincerity and humility before Him.

This evening the three large rooms on the ground floor of Mrs True's home were filled with so many visitors that people were standing in the hallways. The Master walked among the crowd and spoke about the assistance of the Blessed Beauty, the spread of the Cause of God and the impact of the Word of God on the churches and meetings. The gist of His talk was this:

> Look at the history of the world and try to find a parallel instance in which a native of the East has come to the countries of the West, particularly America, and called out to them in the churches and meetings there, raised the divine call in many of the large cities and invited everyone to the Abhá Kingdom, with no one taking exception. Nay, on the contrary, those present at the gatherings have heard him with patience and unbounded joy. These things have been achieved solely through the confirmations of the Abhá Kingdom.

Saturday, September 14, 1912
[Chicago]

Among 'Abdu'l-Bahá's words were these:

If the Blessed Perfection had not exerted Himself to raise up the Cause of God, the Cause of the Primal Point [the Báb] would have been completely effaced. Similarly, had it not been for the power of the Covenant after the ascension of the Ancient Beauty, it is evident what the people would have done, how they would have spent their time, like Mírzá Yaḥyá, taking many wives and satisfying their lusts and desires. They would have destroyed the divine standard.

He then gave an account of the fruitless Kheiralla.

When someone remarked that the Tablet of Ishráqát [Splendors][276] had been translated and published in German, the Master said:

All the affairs and conditions of the world serve the Cause of God. If they had driven me out of the United States or had refused me entry, it would have been a good thing. Opposition serves to promote the Cause of God, how much more helping the Cause accomplishes!

Then He said, 'Let us go for a walk before everybody arrives.'

He walked along the shore [of Lake Michigan] and spoke about the sacrifice of a Japanese admiral:

With this type of sacrifice they attained success. But remember, if he had lived, it would have been better for his nation and government. Observe, a general sacrificed himself and his children for the emperor and became renowned for sincerity and faithfulness. From this example it becomes obvious what we should do in the path of the Abhá Beauty. If you view it in the light of justice, you will see that the emperor did not bestow upon his general a thousandth portion of the grace that the Blessed Beauty bestows upon us.

Returning to the house, He found several believers and seekers from Chicago and surrounding communities. All were grateful to hear His divine words and teachings.

In the afternoon 'Abdu'l-Bahá was invited to speak at the Theosophical Society where He ignited a fire of spirituality in the minds of the audience. The president of the society introduced the Master with great respect, saying:

> Gentlemen, today it is a great bounty and high honor for us to be in the presence of a person who is the greatest prophet of peace and harmony. There is no doubt – and I feel and say on behalf of the audience – that to the present time we have not had the honor of hearing the life-giving words from the tongue of a living prophet. Therefore, with unbounded happiness and heartfelt honor I present to you His Holiness 'Abdu'l-Bahá, the prophet of peace and the founder of universal brotherhood.

The Master rose and spoke brilliantly about the distinction between spiritual realities and the animal nature of man, and the appearance of the perfection of man in the image of God. He explained some of the teachings of the new Manifestation. The audience applauded with so much excitement and joy that it felt as though there were an earthquake in the auditorium.

The president thanked the Master and acknowledged the truth and greatness of 'Abdu'l-Bahá. To show their concurrence with the words of their president, the members of the audience rose together in great excitement, a clear proof of the extraordinary powers of the Center of the Covenant. 'Abdu'l-Bahá again arose and spoke:

> I am very happy with your warmth and consideration. God be praised that there exist in America such societies founded on human principles, the appreciation of spiritual values and the investigation of truth. I am most grateful to this society and hope that your inner perception may increase and that the bounties of God will be with you.

When the Master went into another room the people rushed into it. Most of them wished to tell Him, 'We testify to the truth of this Cause.' The degree of excitement in the hearts of such a large gathering cannot be imagined. That such a transformation can occur in such a country is beyond belief.

Sunday, September 15, 1912
[Chicago – Kenosha]

In the morning 'Abdu'l-Bahá spoke to Dr [William Frederick] Nutt about Kheiralla in such majestic and forcible tones that both the hearer and the translator trembled with fear. Finally, He said:

> He wants me to send for him. As a visitor to this country, the great and lowly of this land come to see me. If his intention be good, he also should come with utmost sincerity.[277]

The Blessed Being was very tired after His talk.

The Master had an appointment in Kenosha and was preparing to go there. He was accompanied by Dr Nutt, a Japanese believer and His companions. On the way we had to change trains. Although we hurried, we missed the second train. The friends were saddened but 'Abdu'l-Bahá said, 'Oh, it matters not. There is a wisdom in this.' We left by the next train and found that the train we had missed was wrecked and some of the passengers injured. It was clear that it had collided with another train. 'Abdu'l-Bahá said, 'This, too, was the protection of the Blessed Beauty.' He then narrated the episode of His leaving Alexandria for America:

> Some proposed that we leave via London by the S. S. *Titanic*, which sank on the same voyage. The Blessed Beauty guided us to come direct.

The friends were waiting with their automobiles at the railway station to take the Beloved to the hall of the Mashriqu'l-Adhkár.[278]

The Master went onto the stage of the auditorium and sat on a chair. It was a divine and joyous festival, the people like heavenly angels of the utmost spirituality, prayerfulness and gratitude. 'Abdu'l-Bahá spoke briefly but effectively about the victorious power and penetrating influence of the Cause of the Blessed Beauty. He then went to a long table that extended the length of the hall which was covered with a variety of multicolored flowers.

As lunch was being served, the young friends, having received 'Abdu'l-Bahá's permission, sang songs of praise to Him, accompanied by a piano. The Master then gave an account of the persecutions and hardships of Bahá'u'lláh, the time spent in the Most Great Prison, the Turkish revolution and the changes that took place after the establishment of a constitutional form of government in Turkey. 'God removed all obstacles', He said, 'and provided all the necessities, thus enabling 'Abdu'l-Bahá to reach this place and have the pleasure of seeing you.'

The friends then brought their children to Him to be blessed. He took the children onto His lap one by one and gave them flowers, fruits and sweets. Mr Jackson said:

> Every time we have held a public entertainment for the friends we have left two seats vacant at each end of the table, one in the name of Bahá'u'lláh and the other in that of 'Abdu'l-Bahá. We constantly longed to witness a day such as this. We have now attained our highest hopes and our eyes have seen the light of the Master.

Another person said, 'When the clergymen were informed of your arrival, they announced in the churches that this evening the prophet of the East will speak at the Kenosha Congregational Church.'

After lunch 'Abdu'l-Bahá left the hall of the 'Mashriqu'l-Adhkár' and went to Mrs [Henry] Goodale's home, where the friends were overjoyed and uplifted to hear Him speak. He said to them, in part:

The Cause of God has always appeared from the East but it has been more effective in the West. Once Badrí Páshá[279] said in an address, 'Gentlemen, Westerners have taken everything from us: the sciences, the arts and the laws they took from the East. Now we fear that they may wrest from us the Cause of Bahá'u'lláh, as well.' Those were his words. But Bahá'u'lláh is neither of the East nor of the West, neither of the South nor of the North. He is holy above all these directions. He is heavenly and godly.

'Abdu'l-Bahá's address in the evening at the Congregational Church was on the unity of the Manifestations of God, that they are one in essence and that the differences among their followers is due to obsolete imitations. His explanation of the divine teachings gave new life and insights to the audience. After His talk, everyone came to Him to pay Him their respects.

Monday, September 16, 1912
[Kenosha – Chicago]

In the morning 'Abdu'l-Bahá prepared to leave for Chicago. The believers, 'like iguanas', gazed at Him with eyes like those of parting lovers. He remarked:

> See what the power and influence of Bahá'u'lláh have wrought. Consider how He has brought the Japanese, the Americans and the Persians all under the shadow of one word and caused them to love one another.

Along the way He spoke of the steadfastness of the believers of the East. He arrived in Chicago in the evening and a continuous stream of friends came to see Him. Some of them wanted to give Him some money but, despite their pleading and entreaties, He would not accept it and instead requested that the money be distributed among the poor. Some reporters had published their articles in the newspapers, which the Master appreciated.

At a gathering of the believers in the afternoon, some of the friends had arranged a musical program at which poems written by Mrs [Louise] Waite (who had been given the Persian name S͟háhnaz K͟hánum by the Master) were sung to piano accompaniment as the Master descended the stairs. The Master walked among the friends in such a manner that everyone was moved, overcame their reserve and shed tears of joy and love. A clergyman came forward and supplicated 'Abdu'l-Bahá: 'O Thou Prophet of God, 'Abdu'l-Bahá, pray thou for me.' The Master bestowed His blessings upon him.

The Master spoke to the friends about the bonds of love which unite the hearts.[280] At the conclusion of the meeting, He called to Mrs True, saying, 'Because of your desire and insistence we came to this house but now we must go to a hotel.'

In the evening He exhorted the friends in sweet and expressive words to spread the fragrances of God, to proclaim the Words of their Lord and to show kindness to His friends. Afterwards, some were privileged to have private interviews with Him. After dinner He told us to pack our things to move to the hotel. In the automobile, He seemed to be depressed. He said:

> I am bearing the discomforts of this journey with stop-overs so that the Cause of God may be protected from any breach. For I am still not sure about what is going to happen after me. If I could be sure, then I would sit comfortably in some corner, I would not leave the Holy Land and travel far away from the Most Holy Tomb. Once, after the martyrdom of the Báb, the Cause of God was dealt a hard blow through Yaḥyá. Again, after the ascension of the Blessed Beauty, it received another blow. And I fear that self-seeking persons may again disrupt the love and unity of the friends. If the time were right and the House of Justice were established, the House of Justice would protect the friends.

He then spoke about how disunity began in the Islamic cycle, saying, 'Because of certain people who sought to fulfill their personal desires and who yet counted themselves among the supporters of the religion, the foundation of Islam was completely uprooted.' He continued in this vein until the automobile arrived at the hotel.

Tuesday, September 17, 1912
[Chicago – Minneapolis]

The Master bade farewell to the friends and promised to come back to Chicago on His return from California. Here are a few of His remarks to the friends:

> I ask the Blessed Beauty to assist you and confirm you. Wherever I go, you will be in my thoughts. I shall not forget any one of you. I beg of God that you may become more enlightened, more severed, more spiritual, more aflame and that you may be humble and submissive, for as long as man does not consider himself to be good but regards himself as weak and deficient, he progresses; but the moment he considers himself good and says, 'I am perfect', he falls into pride and retrogresses.

To another gathering, He spoke about socialism:

> The principles of socialism are outstripped in the religions of God. For instance, God commands, 'But [they] prefer them [the poor] before themselves, although there be indigence among them' [Qur'án 59:9]. That is, the believers spend of their substance and share their possessions and prefer others to themselves willingly and with utmost spirituality. Socialists, however, desire to enforce equality and association by compulsion. Although the preference for others which is the exhortation of God is more difficult because the rich are enjoined to prefer others to themselves, this will become common and will be the cause of tranquillity and an aid to the order of the world, because it depends upon the inclination and willingness of the giver. But socialism and egalitarianism, although easier, as

those who have are made equal with others, yet such a system will not become widespread and is the cause of disturbance and tumult because it rests on compulsion and coercion.

In the Tablets of Bahá'u'lláh it is mentioned that if a rich man neglects the duty of educating his children, the House of Justice is authorized to compel him to assist financially and to educate them. But this is a matter for the family of that wealthy man and comes under the jurisdiction of the House of Justice. The point is that there are matters greater than equality and socialism in divine religions. In the Cause of God there were persons like the King of Martyrs [Mírzá Muḥammad-Ḥasan][281] who, in the days of tribulation, expended all their wealth and property to relieve the sufferings of the poor and the weak. In Persia the Bahá'ís were willing to sacrifice themselves for one another to such a degree that once when one of the Bahá'ís was a guest in the home of another believer, and the authorities demanded the arrest of the guest, the host gave the guest's name as his own and surrendered himself to them, was martyred in his place, thus sacrificing his life for his guest and brother.

Turning to the editor of the Police Journal, 'Abdu'l-Bahá said,

> A newspaper must in the first instance be the means of creating harmony among the people. This is the prime duty of the proprietors of newspapers, to eradicate misunderstandings between religions and races and nationalities and promote the oneness of mankind.

Mírzá 'Alí-Akbar Nakhjavání, who had been granted permission to accompany 'Abdu'l-Bahá on His journey to California, arrived from Malden, joining Mr Fujita, the Japanese, and the other servants. The train left Chicago at 10:00 a.m. Many of the friends had gathered at the railway station and surrounded the Master, begging for divine confirmations, blessings and assistance to render services to the Cause of God.

Although the air was cool and the train was clean and free of dust, still 'Abdu'l-Bahá was tired and weak. In the afternoon we observed a strange phenomenon. We heard moaning from the seat on which the Master was reclining. When we came close to Him we saw that His eyes, like beautiful tulips, were open and that He was chanting a prayer in mournful tones. As we drew even closer, He paid no attention nor looked at us. Although He was awake, He appeared to be sleeping. We tried to understand what He was saying but it was impossible. Meanwhile the train stopped and one of us had the audacity to ask the Master whether He would like to step outside and take a little walk. He came out of His state of reverie and said, 'No, we won't go out.'

During this time 'Abdu'l-Bahá appeared to be sad and depressed. At one time He said, 'I did not sleep at all last night. The ark of the Cause is beset by tempests and storms on all sides. But the confirmations of the Ancient Beauty are with us.'

At 9:00 in the evening, when the train was but a few stations away from Minneapolis, we were joined by Mr [Albert Heath] Hall and some friends. When we reached Minneapolis another group of friends and journalists received the bounty of seeing the Master. He told them that He was very tired and would see them the following morning to answer their questions and to give them material for their newspaper articles.

He went to the Hotel Plaza which faces a lovely park with a beautiful lake. The friends said that many ministers and other prominent people of the city had tendered invitations to the Master. He said:

> We cannot stay more than two days. We come and in each city we create a stir, scatter some seeds, awaken the people, inform them of the Most Great Call and then leave. In this short space of time our work is to proclaim the Cause of God and, praise be to God, the results are evident day by day and accompanied by great confirmations.

Wednesday, September 18, 1912
[Minneapolis]

The assembly hall of the hotel became a joyous meeting place for the friends. With great happiness and excitement the friends eagerly listened to the Master's words.

> Praise be to God that He has given you a prosperous country. Towns are flourishing, commerce is progressing and the outward evidences of prosperity are displayed with utmost beauty and perfection. But all these things are as nothing when compared to the bounties of God. The whole globe is nothing before one ray of the Sun of Truth. Thus it is said in the Gospel that Satan took Christ to the top of a high mountain, showed Him the world outspread and told Him that he would give Him all these things if he would follow him. But Christ refused.

He then answered questions from the audience about socialism and gave interviews to some newspaper reporters about various subjects, such as the necessity for a spiritual civilization, spiritual guidance and the principles and life history of Bahá'u'lláh.

Later, a Jewish rabbi visited the Master and requested that He speak in his synagogue. 'Abdu'l-Bahá spoke with him, saying, 'I have come from your original homeland, Jerusalem. I passed forty-five years in Palestine, but I was in prison.' The rabbi said, 'We are all prisoners in this world.' The Master added, 'But I was imprisoned in two prisons. Even then I was contented and was completely happy and grateful.' The rabbi then said, 'The Prophets of God have always been imprisoned and now His Holiness 'Abdu'l-Bahá, the chosen one of God, is imprisoned.' The Master stated, 'I am but the servant of God; but the practice of people has always been to persecute all the Prophets and the holy ones and then later to prostrate themselves at the mention of their names.' When they finished their conversation, the rabbi expressed his sincere thanks and requested permission to leave. The Master embraced Him and said, 'We desire that all religions unite in bonds of brotherhood, to love one another. May they join hands and embrace each other, and honor and respect one another's masters.'

The Master was invited to the Commercial Club this morning. As He drove through the city's parks and boulevards on the way, He remarked:

> Tonight when we speak in the Jewish synagogue we shall bring proofs and arguments in support of the Spirit [Christ]. This is the wish and confirmation of the Blessed Beauty. It is as if the Abhá Beauty were present in the Mansion at 'Akká and I went into His presence and said that I wished to speak in a Jewish synagogue. It is clear that His wish would be that the truth of Jesus should be demonstrated.

Several newspaper reporters asked Him questions about the principles of the Faith. He told them:

> The laws and commandments of God are of two kinds: one set is composed of those essential spiritual principles which are the basis for human prosperity, praiseworthy morals and the acquisition of the virtues and perfections of man. These never change. The other kind are subsidiary laws related to our material life. These are revealed to regulate transactions and to meet the exigencies of the time. These change in keeping with the requirements of the age.

While He was giving a detailed explanation of the laws of God, prominent members of the Club gathered around Him. They listened with rapt attention to His words concerning the failure of the four criteria [for establishing reality] – namely, the senses, the intellect, tradition and inspiration – to arrive at the correct conclusions and the efficacy of the all-encompassing power of the command of God. They expressed their sincere admiration for His blessings and kindness, particularly for His talk.

Today a billboard outside a building announced: "Abdu'l-Bahá, the venerable Prophet of the East and the Leader of the Bahá'ís, will speak here at noon today.'

In the evening the Master delivered a brilliant address at the Jewish synagogue, providing decisive proofs of the validity and truth of Christ and the Cause of Muḥammad. It was so persuasive that men and women came to 'Abdu'l-Bahá with the utmost humility and admiration. One of them said openly that he would no longer be a Jew.

Thursday, September 19, 1912
[Minneapolis – St Paul]

It was reported to 'Abdu'l-Bahá that the proceedings of the Bahá'í meeting the night before had been published in today's newspapers. He said:

> Notwithstanding this, the Muslims and the Christians alike are not satisfied with us. They are engaged in pleasurable diversions and enjoyable pastimes in their homes while we are laboring to prove the truths of the divine Manifestations in these great temples. So it is with the mischief-makers and Covenant-breakers. Behold how they are preoccupied with themselves and with the satisfaction of their selfish desires, while I am so wholly occupied with spreading the Cause of God in America that I have not had a moment's rest.

After a visit with friends and seekers, the Master went to a museum.[282] Among its many antiques objects were some small tear vials from ancient Phoenicia in which people had preserved their tears at the time of the death of their loved ones and then buried with the dead bodies. 'Abdu'l-Bahá said, 'See how these bottles have outlasted the bodies of men under the earth.' He continued:

When people of the West become wealthy, they begin to collect antique objects in order to render a service to the world of art. But when Persians become wealthy, they keep one hundred horses in their stables, give themselves up to pomp and show, engage themselves in satiating their selfish desires. But in comparison with service to the Cause, both attitudes are barren, producing no result. For example, if the effort these people put into gathering these objects, and the millions of dollars spent acquiring them, were employed for the Cause of God, their stars of happiness and prosperity would shine evermore from the horizon of both worlds. If in this city they brought ten persons into the Cause of God, it would gain momentum and would become the cause of eternal honor and happiness as well as the source of everlasting life.

After returning to the hotel, telegrams reporting the good news were prepared and dispatched to the Assemblies of the East.

Among the friends assembled to meet 'Abdu'l-Bahá were several philosophers and clergymen. The Master spoke about the oneness of mankind, universal brotherhood and the teachings of God. Everyone expressed their admiration and sincere appreciation. The friends were delighted to see 'Abdu'l-Bahá's influence and power and pleaded with Him to prolong His stay. He replied, 'We have little time. We must go everywhere to announce the Cause of God. We have called the people here and now we must hasten to other places until we reach California.'

There was a splendid meeting in the afternoon at the home of Mr Hall. Several people were there, including some philosophers, professors, clergymen and women, all of whom listened to the Master's words with great pleasure. The Master spoke about the oneness and unity of mankind and the increased capacity of this enlightened century. After He spoke, a number of the guests requested the privilege of having a private interview with Him.

Dr [Clement] Woolson brought his automobile to take the Master to a meeting in St Paul, some 15 miles from Minneapolis.

'Abdu'l-Bahá at Green Acre. The Inn is in the background

'Abdu'l-Bahá speaking to Sarah Farmer through His interpreters

*'Abdu'l-Bahá holds
Gertrude Hammond at
Green Acre*

*'Abdu'l-Bahá at
Green Acre*

Charles Mason Remey, seated second from left, *who offered 'Abdu'l-Bahá a cup of water at Green Acre, with Howard Struven,* second from right, *who entertained 'Abdu'l-Bahá in Baltimore*

Fred Mortensen, who rode the rods to see 'Abdu'l-Bahá at Green Acre

*May and Sutherland Maxwell,
in whose home 'Abdu'l-Bahá stayed in Montreal*

Mary Maxwell (Rúḥíyyih Khánum), as a young child

Corinne True, known as the 'Mother of the Temple' for her tireless work to raise the House of Worship in Wilmette

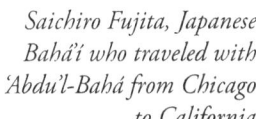

Saichiro Fujita, Japanese Bahá'í who traveled with 'Abdu'l-Bahá from Chicago to California

'Abdu'l-Bahá in Kenosha, Wisconsin, taken September 15, 1912

Louise Waite, who was given the name 'Shahnaz' by 'Abdu'l-Bahá

Albert Heath Hall in 1902. 'Abdu'l-Bahá spoke at his home in Minneapolis

'Abdu'l-Bahá in St Paul, Minneapolis

In St Paul, Minneapolis. Albert Heath Hall is standing on the far right, with Fred Mortensen next to him

'Abdu'l-Bahá with children in Chicago, Sunday, May 5, 1912, following the children's meeting at the Plaza Hotel. Note the Coca-Cola sign in the background

'Abdu'l-Bahá with Musette 'Rouhieh' Jones and Joseph Ioas, taken by Muriel Jones at the Plaza Hotel, Chicago, May 1, 1912

'Abdu'l-Bahá with children in Chicago

'Abdu'l-Bahá at Lincoln Park Zoo, Chicago

Viewing the animals at Lincoln Park Zoo

Descending stairway to a wooded dell, Lincoln Park

'Abdu'l-Bahá at Lincoln Park, Chicago

At Lincoln Park, Chicago

At Lincoln Park, Chicago

Taken at the Revell home, Philadelphia

The distance was covered in comfort and at a good speed. The Master praised the cleanliness and beauty of the Mississippi River and the greenness of the hills, plains and gardens along the way. He arrived at Dr Woolson's home and there addressed the assembled friends who were very taken with His words. His explanation of nature's lack of perfection and its recreation through divine education gave the audience a new perspective.[283]

The Master took a walk in the garden. Several children approached Him and politely asked Him about His country and the purpose of His visit. He spoke with them kindly. They then followed Him in respectful silence and when He approached the house, they asked permission to come inside. To each He gave some coins and showered them with kindness. One tiny child slipped off his father's lap and ran to the Master, saying, 'I love you first and then my father.'

When it was time to leave two automobiles were at the door. One belonged to some enthusiastic women who were new to the Cause. The Master sat in their automobile. Then Dr Woolson came out to say that the automobile meant for the Master was the other one. The Master then went to that automobile and they drove to Minneapolis at full speed to attend the meeting being held in the evening at Mr Hall's home.[284] The other automobile did not reach its destination and it was later learned than it had broken down on the way and that the women had had to make other arrangements. Because they arrived late, they had the honor of having dinner with the Master.

Friday, September 20, 1912
[Minneapolis – Denver]

Today we departed from Minneapolis. In the morning friends and seekers surrounded 'Abdu'l-Bahá like moths. He spoke to them in these words:

You must have deep love for one another. Go to see each other and be consoling friends to all. If a friend lives a little distance from the town, go to see him. Do not content yourselves with words only but act according to the commandments of God. Hold weekly meetings and give feasts. Put forth your efforts to acquire spiritual perfections and to spread the knowledge of God. These are the attributes of the Bahá'ís. Otherwise, what use is there in being a Bahá'í in word alone.

At 8:00 a.m., after packing the parcels to be sent to the East, the Master left the hotel for the train station. The assembled friends were sad and dejected owing to His departure from their midst. He consoled them until the train left the station, saying:

> I shall never forget you. You are always in my mind. Convey to all the friends my kind regards. I love all. I exhort you to be kind to the poor and love them. Help them, for the poor are broken-hearted. If you sacrifice yourself for the rich, they think you do it because you are obliged to. But if you love the poor, they feel joy and are sincerely grateful. To help the poor is essential. May you be under the protection of God.

When the train reached St Paul station, Dr Woolson came to say goodbye and received the Master's blessing. He was showered with bounty.

On the way 'Abdu'l-Bahá spoke about teaching the Cause of God in America and remarked:

> In this country it is essential to have teachers who are attracted, wholly severed and learned like some of the self-sacrificing Persian teachers. The Cause of God must become firmly established in these regions. The teachers must move continually, one after another, from one place to another to raise the divine call. Then will the confirmations of the Abhá Kingdom envelop these nations and wonders will be achieved. This desire of mine has not yet come about. It depends on

the confirmations of the all-glorious Kingdom and on the sanctified breaths of the friends. The one true God is my witness! If a person draws only one pure breath in a state of severance, it will be effective for a thousand years.

Later He related many stores about the days in Baghdád. In the afternoon He spoke about Mr [Edward Granville] Browne and said:

I wrote to him, saying, 'You are the first European teacher and author to have attained His Blessed Presence. Do not lose this distinction.' He did not understand me and his loss will be known when the lights of guidance shine in England with supreme brilliancy.

Two hours after midnight the train reached Omaha. As the Master was extremely tired, as soon as He arrived at the hotel He retired immediately, without eating.

Saturday, September 21, 1912
[Omaha – Lincoln]

In the morning, as we were having tea served by 'Abdu'l-Bahá, the latest news from the Balkan war was relayed to Him. He commented, in part:

Our own 'war' is good because it conquers all. When a crown of thorns was placed on the head of Christ, He saw with His own eyes the crowns of kings under His feet. Now, when I look, I see all the powers and nations defeated, scattered and lost in the wilderness while the Cause of God is victorious over all and subdues all. All future events are evident and visible to the eyes of the holy Manifestations.

He illustrated this by narrating the historical events from the digging of ditches[285] to the victory of Islam over the treasuries of

Anushírván and Khusraw.[286] The hypocrites, who disbelieved in the promises of Muḥammad in their hearts, saw these victories and cried out: 'This is that which God and His Messenger have promised us.'

The translation of an article regarding universal peace was read to the Master. He said:

> If the republics of the Americas assembled and agreed on the question of peace, and if all of them would turn to the [Peace] Assembly[287] at the Hague, most of the powers of Europe would follow suit. But looking at it from another point of view, if an international war breaks out in Europe, international peace will be established more quickly. Also, if these ideas regarding peace spread among the public, the financiers will refuse to give loans for wars and the manufacture of armaments, the railway companies will abstain from transporting instruments of destruction and the armed forces will not engage in carnage and the spilling of blood. Also the boundaries should be established.

Later the Master was interviewed by two journalists and spoke to them about the pernicious attitudes of politicians, the destructiveness of war, the validity of the divine teachings regarding universal peace, the unity of religions and the oneness of mankind.

In one of the Tablets revealed by 'Abdu'l-Bahá in honor of a friend in Mázindarán, these words were recorded:

> The light of Bahá'u'lláh has shone to such a degree on the continent of America that in every city where a number of believers reside, the call of 'Yá Bahá'u'l-Abhá' has been raised. In great churches and meetings 'Abdu'l-Bahá cries out and proves the truth of the Prophet of God [Muḥammad] and of the Báb and of the rising sun of Bahá'u'lláh. Most of the newspapers express praise in glowing articles. Where are the Persians, that they may behold the splendors of the Luminary

of the World [Bahá'u'lláh] Whose light has shone forth from the horizon of Mount Awrang[288] and now illumines the mountains and plains of America? In spite of all this, the people of Núr are still asleep and do not know what an honor has been showered upon that region.

For lunch 'Abdu'l-Bahá had soup prepared especially for Him. The Master instructed us to have lunch at the hotel. In the afternoon after tea, the Master left for Lincoln to visit Mr [William Jennings] Bryan, the [future] Secretary of State of the United States, and said:

> During Mr and Mrs Bryan's last visit to Haifa, we were, while in 'Akká, in great danger, and the enemies were rebellious and increasingly perverse in those last days, thus he was unable to see us. So now we are going to see him.

The train had left just as the Master reached the station. He decided to wait for the next train. A few minutes later, a man who had seen our Persian dress and *kuláhs* came to us and said, 'We received a telegram from the friends in Minneapolis and have been looking for 'Abdu'l-Bahá.' He immediately ran to give the news to the other friends and brought them to Him. They were extremely grateful that He had not left by the first train. The Master spoke to them about the major calamities that had befallen the Cause of God, saying:

> Up to now, whatever has occurred has had the effect of spreading the Cause of God. When the Blessed Beauty left Ṭihrán and when He departed from Baghdád for the Holy Land, it was so devastating that the friends shed tears of blood. Now it has become evident what mysteries were concealed in that event and what victories lay in store; even the prophecies of the holy books regarding the Holy Land and the promised Manifestation were fulfilled through that banishment.

A professor who had heard of some of the principles of the Bahá'í Cause was very happy and grateful to have visited the Master. At midnight the Master left Omaha and three hours later arrived in Lincoln.

Sunday, September 22, 1912
[Lincoln]

In the morning the Master spoke about the animosity of the enemies and their evil intentions towards the Blessed Beauty. Then the conversation turned to the corruption and iniquity of the Covenant-breakers. He said:

> Shu'á of darkness[289] wrote to his father quite openly that his purpose was to amass wealth and worldly property. With reference to me he stated that he was waiting for the fulfillment of the promise in the verse, 'God will assuredly send down one who will deal mercilessly with him.'[290]

Two newspaper reporters came to interview Him and recorded the interview with the utmost courtesy and respect. The Master instructed us to telephone and inquire about Mr Bryan and his wife. Expressing regret that Mr Bryan was not at home, Mrs Bryan said she and her daughter would be pleased to receive 'Abdu'l-Bahá in their home. The Master and His entourage hired a large automobile and drove a long distance outside of the city until they reached a large estate which is located in one of the finest places in the region. Mrs Bryan hurried towards the automobile to greet 'Abdu'l-Bahá. She and her daughter expressed their joy and happiness for His blessings. After they had had tea and listened to Him, they begged Him to visit some of the rooms of the house, particularly the library and Mr Bryan's study. They showed Him a book compiled by Mr Bryan and asked Him to pray for the success of his endeavors. Mr Bryan was currently on a campaign tour on behalf of [the future] President Wilson and was to lecture in many cities. In honor of the occasion, 'Abdu'l-Bahá took a notebook and in His own hand wrote a prayer for assistance. He then said a few words which increased their happiness, devotion, assurance and honor. With that He departed.

Among those visiting the Master at the hotel in the afternoon were some Arabs. They had read about His arrival and His speeches in the newspapers and wished to see Him. The newspaper articles about His arrival and the Manifestations of God were translated and read to Him. It made Him happy to know that a stay in the city of only 12 hours had become the cause of spreading the teachings of God.

At 8:00 p.m., just before leaving the city, the Master came and sat in the lobby of the hotel. A number of people who had read about the new teachings in the newspapers approached and were introduced to Him. They all listened carefully to His explanations and expressed their pleasure. At 11:00 p.m. the train left Lincoln. His companions tried to persuade Him to take Pullman accommodation for Himself but He would not allow it, saying:

> We must all be together. The only purpose of this journey is to serve the Cause of God. We have no other aim. We will all sleep in our coach seats.

He spent the night resting in the chair, sometimes sleeping, and sometimes awake. And in this way His time passed.

Monday, September 23, 1912
[Denver]

The Master reached Denver around two o'clock in the afternoon. Mr and Mrs Ashton and some friends came to the station to meet Him. The moment they saw Him they became excited and full of joy. They took Him to the Hotel Shirley where we had made reservations on the third floor of this lovely building. He said to some newspaper reporters who had come for an interview: 'I had no rest last night and am very tired. Give me a little time.' They returned at 5:00 p.m. and were permitted to take His photograph and to ask questions. At eight in the evening He went to the home of Mrs [Sidney] Roberts where friends both old and new had gathered.[291] There were so many people that they were seen standing as far as the front entrance. He spoke to them about the power of the Abhá Kingdom which had enabled Him to travel far in spite of His weak constitution and which had gathered the friends in the assemblies of the love of God. After His talk He bestowed His special blessing on each person. As the Master was leaving the meeting, the pastor of the Church of Divine Science approached Him with the utmost humility and invited Him to speak at his church. 'Abdu'l-Bahá accepted. Since so many people wished to have an interview with Him, He announced that during the few days He would be in Denver, He would see anyone who would call upon Him at the hotel between nine and twelve in the morning.

Regarding His health, He said:

> In the early stages of our long journey to California my health was affected. But as the journey was made for God and to diffuse the divine fragrances, my longstanding indisposition has been cured without any medicine. The confirmations of Abhá are descending from all sides.

He added:

> It is written in the Ḥadíth [Islamic traditions] that cities shall draw nearer to each other. Besides spiritual nearness and communications between the cities of the hearts and friendships between diverse people in the promised Day, how physically close have the cities and countries also become. Truly, if not for railroads and the power of steam, how could these long distances be traversed with such ease? This is one of the miracles of this promised century of our current age.

Tuesday, September 24, 1912
[Denver]

There was a rush of people from early morning until noon. Friends, seekers, professors, clergymen and philosophers all came to see Him. They each raised questions and were filled with joy on hearing the Master's words.

He was invited by some clergymen to speak in their churches. He tendered His regrets, saying, 'My stay here is brief.'

Today the newspapers published 'Abdu'l-Bahá's picture along with those of His companions, as well as articles describing His talks.

After the meeting He went for a walk and strolled through parks and boulevards. As the Master passed by the government buildings, monuments and statutes of American heroes, He remarked: 'Their victories are trifling in comparison with the first victories of Islam, yet they are famous and a source of honor to all who know them. But these great victories have been completely forgotten.' All eyes were attracted to 'Abdu'l-Bahá, to His glory, dignity and grandeur, as He walked with His companions dressed in their *kuláhs* and Persian clothes. One of the Master's companions remarked that the people viewed this picturesque sight as an amusing comedy. He replied, 'Yes, it is a heavenly act, a performance of the Kingdom, a wonderful pageant.'

Those who had read the newspapers about the arrival of the Master were heard saying to each other, 'He is the Prophet of the East, the Messenger of Peace.' Those who had cameras took the Master's photograph as He walked by.

In the afternoon He was invited to the suburban home of Mrs Clark. As we rode on the train some passengers were seen to be whispering about us. He said, 'Tell them we are neither Turks nor Arabs, neither of the East nor of the West, rather we are of heaven and of God.' One of the companions said, 'Being of that is good but being of God is better.'

When the Master arrived at Mrs Clark's home, several of the

friends had already gathered to see Him. He spoke to them about the confirmations of the Abhá Beauty and the power and influence of the Word of God. 'See how He has made the Easterner and the Westerner friends', He said, 'and has bestowed sincere love and true friendship. Otherwise, what connection would there be between us and Americans, between this Japanese youth[292] and Mírzá Maḥmúd-i-Zarqání? Mrs Clark said: 'I have frequently dreamt that my home would become honored with the footsteps of the Beloved Master. I am extremely thankful and grateful that my dreams have come true. My heart is now freed from ego, whereas before I used to consider myself better than anyone else.' The Master said:

> Thank God, because the first self-conceited one was Satan. A man must never consider himself greater than others. Rather, he must always be humble and self-effacing. The bird, as long as it sees itself at a low level, is given impetus to soar and progress; but the moment it fancies itself high in the air, it begins to descend.

Someone in the audience asked, 'What shall I do to become a true servant?' He replied:

> Act in accordance with the teachings of Bahá'u'lláh. Do not only read His teachings but put into practice in your lives the Hidden Words and the other holy writings. Whatever I say is not even a drop from the ocean of the Supreme Pen and the treasure-filled sea of the bounty and favor of the Abhá Beauty.
>
> I have brought the message of Bahá'u'lláh to this country in order to teach people to investigate truth, to render service to humanity, to endeavor to bring about international peace, to exert every effort to guide humanity, to show kindness to all creatures and to raise the Call of the Kingdom. Man must be endowed with divine attributes and must enter the concourse of the exalted ones. These teachings are only a drop from the

sea concealed in the Hidden Words. We must pray for each other. If we act according to the divine teachings, by God besides Whom there is none other God, we shall shine like lamps. But woe betide those people who are aware of the teachings of Bahá'u'lláh and know them to be the cause of eternal salvation and divine nearness but still do not bring their actions into conformity with them. Such is a source of great distress. Thus it is incumbent upon us to endeavor day and night to follow the teachings of God. This is the cause of eternal esteem, this is divine favor, this is the honor of mankind and this is everlasting life.

Another person asked about telepathy or communication from mind to mind. He replied:

It is evident. If a lover holds the hand of a beloved, it is obvious what feelings ensue. They communicate face to face and speak heart to heart, as this light is communicating now with human eyes, the sun with the earth, the cloud with the land and the breeze with the tree. This process is found in all things.

The Master was asked about His health and comfort, to which He replied:

I have not come for rest and diversion. I have come to raise the call of the Abhá Kingdom in order to diffuse the divine fragrances. Had I desired rest, I would have secured it more easily in the East. Now I must journey to various cities and countries and call people to the divine Kingdom. Suppose I had rested for a few years, what results would it have had?

Early in the evening when He returned to the hotel the Master discovered that the editor of *The Post* had placed an automobile at His disposal. On the way to the Church of Divine Science, He remarked:

Behold the power and confirmation of the Blessed Beauty: The pastor comes in person with all humility to invite us and the proprietor of a leading journal sends his automobile for our use, so that we may raise the call of God in the church. Truly, such confirmations have never been seen in other dispensations and in no age have the Manifestations of the Cause of God met with such reverence and honor. But these things should be the cause of humility and self-effacement. We must not consider that they are due to our addresses or our eloquence. These shining lights which you see will instantly darken if the origin of their bounty is severed from them.

When the Master's automobile reached the church, a crowd of people was seen standing outside. Immediately the pastor came forward, and taking the Master's arm, led Him to the pulpit. The pastor reverently introduced the Master to the audience. Then 'Abdu'l-Bahá stood and delivered an address on the reality and condition of the Manifestations of God.[293] After His talk, the people came to the pulpit to see Him and shake His hand, surrounding Him like moths. Another clergyman, with the utmost humility, asked the Master to speak at his church. He was so persuasive that every tongue was forced to say, 'All heads are bowed before Him.' With great courtesy, the Master tendered His apologies because of His limited time but promised to return.

As the Master left the church He was perspiring so much that His companions were concerned about His health and tried to keep Him warm with His *'abá*, shawl and blanket. Indeed, the guidance and protection of the Abhá Beauty prevailed and His assistance bestowed. Everything relating to this journey has been the cause of joy and a sign of the power of the King of Manifestations.

Wednesday, September 25, 1912
[Denver]

Most of the people coming today to see the Master were prominent and well-known. Because they so were attracted and transformed by His talks on the divine teachings of the oneness of humanity, universal peace and the principles of the religions, today I wrote to the friends in the East inviting them to come and see how people who had previously had no appreciation for those from the East, especially the Persians, now come in groups to the threshold of the Master and stand waiting their turn to become the recipients of His favor. They consider an interview with Him a source of pride and glory. Many philosophers, professors, clergymen and lecturers come with bowed heads to show their sincere humility. The people from churches and other organizations are also attracted and fascinated, happy to see His life-giving countenance. The Center of the Covenant has caused the Persians to be renowned for their respectability and has crowned the peoples of the East with eternal honor and glory. And how the newspapers of this region praise the Master and the learned and literary people of the West emphasize the importance of these teachings! Notwithstanding this, most of the Persians are asleep and do not understand the cause of their greatness and honor. They are asleep on the bed of negligence and resting in the lap of pride.

After the meeting the Master took a walk. His heart was filled with joy as He said:

> Did you see what a fire was set aglow in the hearts? A person must first be happy and attracted himself to be in a position to transform others. He himself must be impressed in order to impress others. You must act in a way that will make me happy, then you will see what will happen.

To one who visited Him at the hotel, He remarked:

> I have come to your city and found tall buildings and advancement in material civilization. Now I will lead you to my own city which is the world above. Its administration is the oneness of humanity, its law is international peace, its palaces are ever shining with the lights of the Kingdom, its season is always spring, its trees are ever green, its fruits are fresh and sweet, its sun is ever ascending, its moon is always full, its stars are ever brilliant and its planets are ever circling. That is our city and the Founder is Bahá'u'lláh. We have enjoyed the pleasures of this city and now I invite you to that city. I hope that you will accept this invitation.

To another He said:

> Man must take flight from the cage of the body and become pure spirit, for the body is a cage which causes difficulties for man and makes him the captive of nature and involves him in all types of misfortunes. But when a person discards all his physical habits, he is freed from all fetters. As physical powers attract the world of nature, so spiritual powers must break these chains. This condition is not realized by thought alone. The powers of nature are ever alert to allure man. The eye is fascinated by beautiful scenery; the ear is entranced by music; the heart is attracted by delights and human passions. A man may be rich but still he wants more because he is attracted by the world of nature; he has means of livelihood yet he desires more. Therefore, the spiritual powers must dominate so that he may be freed from these fetters and attain salvation. Man is like a bird in a cage. A bird cannot attain freedom merely by knowing that in the free world there are pure breezes, spacious skies, beautiful gardens, pleasant parks and fountains; rather, the bird must find a power to break the cage and soar into the wide firmament.

He then narrated a story about detachment:

The Persian friends travel mostly on foot. They sleep whenever they get tired. They rest wherever they see a shady tree. Once a person came to an Amír. The Amír wished to present him with a gift and with insistence gave him a robe. Later, when he became tired, he lay down under a tree in the forest with the robe folded under his head. But he could not sleep as he repeatedly imagined that a thief was crouching nearby to take away the robe. At last he rose, threw the robe away and said, 'As long as this robe is with me, I shall not find rest. To find rest I must give it up.' How long will you desire a robe for your body? Release your body that you may have no need for a robe.[294]

A public meeting was held in the afternoon at the home of Mrs Roberts. 'Abdu'l-Bahá walked awhile in the garden outside the house. Although most of the friends watched Him respectfully from a distance, when several ladies from Washington DC saw Him, they ran towards Him, expressing their faith and happiness in the divine teachings which they had heard from His own lips in Washington.

In brief, the Master's talk that afternoon was to say farewell to the friends, to encourage them in their endeavors to diffuse the fragrances of God and to explain issues related to teaching. They were all set ablaze by His words.

In the evening the proprietor of the Hotel Shirley and the publisher of a newspaper announced that there would be a public meeting in the large hall of the hotel. The spacious room was filled to capacity. I will never forget the joy and excitement of the audience. At times the audience was plunged into a state of sadness and wonder and then into a state of such happiness and joy that peals of laughter could be heard outside the building. It is not possible to describe the excitement and attraction of the people. They all expressed their sadness that the Master was leaving the city. Those men and women staying at the hotel who because of their wealth and pride had previously not deigned to look at us, now sought us out. Everyone was fascinated by the majesty and grandeur of 'Abdu'l-Bahá and gave their hearts to Him.

Thursday, September 26, 1912
[Denver]

As He intended to leave Denver, His talks with the believers became exhortations. He said:

> I hope that you will be under the protection of God, will succeed in rendering service to humanity and will always be a source of happiness to every heart. The best person is he who wins all hearts and is not the cause of grief to anyone. The worst of souls is he who causes hearts to be agitated and who becomes the cause of sadness. Always endeavor to make people happy and their hearts joyful so that you may become the cause of guidance to mankind. Proclaim the Word of God and diffuse the divine fragrances.

Someone asked Him about eating meat. He replied:

> God has appointed provision for every living creature. To birds He has given beaks so that they may pick up seeds. To animals such as cows and goats He has given teeth like scythes in order that they may eat grass. To carnivores He has given claws like forks and canine teeth so that they may prey because they cannot eat grass. Their food is meat. But man's food is not meat for he has not been created with means to eat flesh. God has given him beauty of form and has created him blessed and not rapacious and bloodthirsty.

The Master's train left Denver at 9:00 a.m. Some of the articles that had been published in the Denver newspapers were translated for Him. They made His heart very happy as they described the spread of the teachings of God in that city and contained translations of 'Abdu'l-Bahá's words. Among them was the translation of these words:

> The contingent world is like the human body that has grown from the embryonic state and reached maturity and perfection. It may be said that the development of the human being from the beginning of life to the age of maturity is but a preparation for the appearance of the power of reason. This is the age of maturity and the time of the manifestation of the Most Great Intellect and the Most Ancient Bounty so that divine and material civilizations may be joined and the perfection of the human world may dawn.

Around midnight 'Abdu'l-Bahá became fatigued owing to the speed and motion of the train. We proposed that because California was still some distance away, if He would consent, it might be a good idea to stop for two or three days. At 2:00 a.m. the train reached Glenwood Springs, beautifully situated near many hot springs. We stayed at the Hotel Colorado, which is a fine hotel overlooking the river, nestled among green parks and wooded mountains.

Friday, September 27, 1912
[Glenwood Springs]

After morning tea, the Master left the hotel for a walk. Three magnificent mountains stood in the distance on three sides, each crowned with trees and adorned with flowers of many hues. They were like peacock feathers and had a unique beauty from every viewpoint. 'Abdu'l-Bahá strolled in the spacious garden and boulevard adjacent to the hotel until He reached the river where there were bath houses and hot springs. On the other side of the river, spanned by a two-story bridge, the tall buildings of the city could be seen rising high on the horizon.

At the insistence of His companions the Master went to the

baths with the entire party, thus bestowing upon us everlasting honor. The rooms and bathing facilities were magnificent. In a special room hot water gushed from a natural cave. It was so hot that a person could not stay more than 15 minutes. Coming out of the bath, the Master said:

> Today I am relieved of fatigue. We have been to many lovely places during this journey but because of our work we had no time to look at the scenery. We did not even think of a moment's rest. Today, however, we have had a little respite.

As the Master viewed the clear, transparent waters of the river shining like pure pearls and the majestic mountains and parks, He said, 'May God not have mercy on the tyrants who kept the Blessed Beauty imprisoned between four walls in 'Akká. How such scenes were loved by Him! Once He said that He had not seen greenery for several years.'

When He returned to the hotel He stood outside in the garden and said, 'It would be good to eat here.' The garden was adjacent to a large pond with fish of various colors and was enclosed on three sides by the hotel structure. Having seen the Denver newspapers, the hotel manager recognized the Master and us from photographs. Without waiting for the Master's request, the manager instructed the waiters to serve lunch in the garden. A large table was erected and beautiful chairs set out. The Master sat down and instructed His companions to do the same. Both before and after lunch the Master generously tipped the waiters. When the residents of the hotel saw the majesty and glory of the Master they told others. Groups of people approached Him. Others watched from their rooms and balconies. Many were heard to say, 'How nice to dine this way. It is evident that this is a very prominent person.' Gradually the purpose of 'Abdu'l-Bahá's mission dawned upon the hotel guests as they were informed of the Cause of God.

In the afternoon 'Abdu'l-Bahá took a walk in the garden and to some shops. While we were crossing a bridge, a messenger approached with some telegrams for us. One of them informed the Master that Mr [Thornton] Chase was seriously ill in a Los Angeles hospital. This made the Master and us very sad. He repeatedly mentioned the faithfulness of Mr Chase. Later He said:

> To turn to the Covenant is to obey the Blessed Beauty which is a cause of gathering together the people of Bahá. Let me explain clearly. The command to the people of Islam to prostrate before the black stone[295] was simply a command to obey the Prophet of God and to prove the influence of the Cause of God. Now, were it not for the Word of the Blessed Beauty, we would be like everyone else and not different in the least.

The Master and His party left Glenwood Springs at about midnight.

Saturday, September 28, 1912
[En route to Salt Lake City]

The train passed through the Rocky Mountains of Colorado. Some of these rose precipitously like walls from the railway bed, formidable and immense. Gazing at their summits one felt as if the mountains would fall down. There were some special roofless observation cars on the train so that passengers might have a full view of the majestic mountains. In these observation cars the passengers could see the mountains on the right and the serene river on the left. As the train passed through these beautiful scenes, the Master said:

> Dear friends, the waves of the bounties of the Blessed Beauty are surging. As I look I see the ocean of His favor swelling and saying, 'I am with you.' Truly, were it not for these glad tidings and His assistance, what could I have done? Just one person alone in the east and west of America, in the mountains and wilderness – it is no light matter. It is easy to say these things

but it was unimaginable that they would let us into these churches. See how His aid and favor descend upon us. This trip fills us with wonder! Offer thanks to the Blessed Beauty that He has bestowed such confirmations upon us.

Later, the Master told stories about the time of Muḥammad, the Messenger of God, and mentioned the cave and His words, 'God is indeed with us'.[296]

The train reached Salt Lake City in the afternoon. The Master decided to stay in the city for one night. By chance, even as the city was being blessed by His footsteps, a large national agricultural convention was being held and the entire city was festively decorated.

Sunday, September 29, 1912
[Salt Lake City]

In the morning several newspaper reporters who had heard of His arrival came to see the Master. They were fascinated with 'Abdu'l-Bahá's words concerning the history and teachings of the Cause of God. To one of them He said:

> When I entered this city, I saw there was quite a stir. I asked the reason and was told that an agricultural convention was being held. I remarked that Bahá'u'lláh, too, organized a convention in Persia. The difference is that your congress is of this world but Bahá'u'lláh's is divine. Great persons have come to the congress but their motive is earthly as they have assembled to consider questions concerning agriculture. But in that other congress holy ones have gathered who irrigate the field of hearts with the water of eternal life, as their motive is heavenly. This congress is decorated with earthly lamps while that is embellished with heavenly lights. The music of this is terrestrial while the strains of that are celestial. This convention meets in a private hall while that gathering is held under the

tent of the unity of mankind and international peace. The queen of this congress is a lady bedecked with ornaments and embellishments of this mortal world but the king of that congress is the King of the Throne of Eternity, Whose sovereignty is divine. When I compared these two congresses I became extremely glad and prayed that God may bless your farming and bestow upon you spiritual strength and capacity for life everlasting.

Today many were attracted by the Master's visit with us to the State Fair.[297] He had been invited to the hotel by some delegates while others pleaded with Him to prolong His stay. Because of the shortness of time, He could not accept their invitation. 'If we had time,' He said, 'some seeds would have been sown in this city, too. But the people are enjoying the celebration and we have no time at our disposal.'

This city is called the City of the Mormons because the majority of its inhabitants are of the Mormon denomination which allows polygamy and divorce.

In the afternoon the Master went to the place specifically set out and decorated for the agricultural exhibition. Alighting from the tram, He went to the exhibit of agricultural machines for plowing, planting and harvesting. He asked about their usage and cost. He then went to the vegetable and grain section and the fruit section. The Master praised the agricultural progress of America. The fruits and vegetables exhibited were among the finest specimens of grapes, apples, pears, pomegranates, cabbages and very large pumpkins, all of many colors and of varieties that we had not seen before.

The section manager saw the Master among the visitors and came towards us and the interpreter, asking to be introduced to Him. He accompanied the Master, offering Him samples of many fruits (even though the purchase, sale and consumption of these items was strictly prohibited). He described to 'Abdu'l-Bahá the various methods of agriculture and then concluded the tour at the grain and mineral display. The Master told us to purchase seeds of some of the fruits and flowers so they could be sent to the Holy Land to be planted at the Most Holy Shrine.

As He was returning to the hotel, the Master saw a Cardinal walking proudly with people on his way to dedicate a church. This Cardinal had heard about the Master and had spoken about the false Christ, thus he was often mentioned by the Master in His meetings.

Monday, September 30, 1912
[Salt Lake City, en route to California]

The Master left the Keynon Hotel in Salt Lake City to continue His journey to California. He spoke on various subjects. The following are some of His words:

> The Cause of God is penetrating. It will encompass the whole world. Now as I observe the wilderness of America, I see it full of Bahá'ís. Formerly, when we asserted in the East that international peace and unity of nations was a necessity, the people laughed at us. Now behold the congresses of peace that have come into existence. The law of God is the panacea for all ills because it is in accordance with the needs of the realities of creation. Legislators have devoted considerable discussion to this point. The most distinguished of them concluded that the laws must be derived from the necessary relations inherent in the reality of things. But the divine Manifestation asserted that to institute such laws is beyond human capacity, for human intelligence cannot encompass the realities of things, nor can it comprehend the essential relationships of such realities. Therefore, divine law is necessary, as it embraces the realities and penetrates all things.

Today the Master was in the best of health and happiness. In spite of all the hardships of the long journey, He was as charmingly fresh as a flower. With unmitigated joy He mentioned the Ancient Beauty, Bahá'u'lláh.

In the afternoon He spoke about spiritual education and intellectual training:

> Peter was devoid of all schooling and so untrained that he could not remember the days of the week. He would tie up seven loaves of bread and open one each day. When he opened the seventh parcel he would know that it was the seventh day and that he had to go to the synagogue. However, under Christ his spiritual education was such that he became the cause of the enlightenment of the world. Indeed, what holy beings are raised up under the shadow of the Word of God!
>
> I remember once in Ṭihrán when I was a child, I was sitting by Áqá Siyyid Yaḥyá Vaḥíd[298] when Mírzá 'Alíy-i-Sayyáḥ[299] came in wearing the táj and carrying the rod of a dervish and with his bare feet covered with mud. Someone asked him where he was coming from. He replied that he had come from the fortress of Máh-Kú, from the august presence of the Báb. Vaḥíd arose immediately and threw himself at the feet of Sayyáḥ, and with tears streaming down his face he rubbed his beard on Sayyáḥ's feet saying, 'He has come from the court of the Beloved.' Although Vaḥíd was a renowned and illustrious person, still he was humble before the servants of the Threshold of God.[300]

Among the interesting things we saw along the way were the wooden covers over the railroad tracks. For a distance of some 50 miles deep passes are snow bound during the entire winter and become almost impassable for trains. Now, owing to these over, the difficulties are removed and the train can pass easily through the area. In English, these covers are called snow sheds. The history of California records that in olden times many people became snowbound and perished in these parts. One example is the Donner party, the story of whose demise is very sad.

Monday night, eve of October 1 1912[301]
[San Francisco]

Tonight the train carrying the beloved Master reached the shores of the Pacific Ocean. Dr [Frederick] D'Evelyn, a devoted Bahá'í, came running as soon as he saw the Master and prostrated himself at His feet. On the way to the city Dr D'Evelyn described for about 15 minutes the yearning of the friends and how they longed to see the Center of the Covenant. When we reached the house especially prepared for 'Abdu'l-Bahá the waiting friends came out to welcome Him. Mr and Mrs Ralston, Mrs Goodall, Mrs Cooper and the other friends were ecstatically happy to have the honor and bounty of being in His presence and to have supper with Him.

Tuesday, October 1, 1912
[San Francisco]

From early morning the enthusiasm, eagerness, excitement, joy and singing of the believers surrounded 'Abdu'l-Bahá, just as in the stories of the iguana and the sun and the moth and the candle. It was the ultimate example of a joyful reunion among the lovers of God. These ecstatic friends offered thanks for the bounty of attaining His presence and being near to Him.

'Abdu'l-Bahá continuously gave thanks for the confirmations of the Abhá Kingdom and for the power and influence of the Cause of God and encouraged the believers to proclaim the Cause of God. At noon He went for a walk and then took a little rest.

I will describe 'Abdu'l-Bahá's residence, as He saw it, because it is unique among all the homes in America which have been graced by Him. It is situated on an elevated plot of land on a wide street surrounded by a spacious garden. 'Abdu'l-Bahá would approach the house, climb a few steps and stand on the porch where He would see fragrant flowers and plants set in pots around the veranda and porch. When the Master entered the house, He would see on his right three large rooms, decorated with fine furniture and many varieties of flowers. Each room opens on the other by means of wide doors covered with velvet curtains, which when drawn, create one large hall.

Every morning and afternoon the hall is filled with so many friends and seekers that there is standing room only. Many who seek private interviews meet Him on the second floor. On this second floor, accessible by a carpeted staircase, there is a large room occupied by some of His servants and to the left a small tea room. Across the hall is another room occupied by the Master. Attached to this room is a tea room and a bathroom. Situated in a corner of the house the room commands a view of a large part of the city. At night the lights of the city appear like twinkling stars. Here many Americans, Japanese and Indians come into 'Abdu'l-Bahá's presence one after another. Each one has a question or statement to make. Many of the friends bring their children, supplicating His blessings and requesting Persian names for them. One of the Japanese friends at Mrs Goodall's home in Oakland asked the Master for Persian names for his two sons and 'Abdu'l-Bahá gave them the names Ḥasan and Ḥusayn.[302]

The third floor, where we have our rooms, is identical to the second floor. We each have our own room and are able to be close to the Master. The kitchen and dining room are on the first floor where some of the friends have the honor of dining with the Master at His table.

At each dawn, after offering prayers of gratitude, the Master calls His servants and serves us tea with His own hands. Using stories and narratives, He explains issues relating to the blessings of God and expresses gratitude for His divine confirmations. Later the friends arrive to experience the bounty of being with Him and to give praise. Whenever a group assembles, the Master comes downstairs to speak to them about great and lofty matters.

Before both lunch and dinner the Master takes a walk or goes for a ride. Mrs Goodall, Mrs Cooper and Mr and Mrs Ralston send two automobiles every day for His use. Whenever He goes out, the friends watch Him from the doors and windows of their houses. Even among the seekers there is much excitement.

'Abdu'l-Bahá is reverently received at the churches by the clergymen. Each respectfully accompanies Him to the pulpit and introduces Him to their congregations with glowing praise. They speak of Him as the Prophet of the East, the messenger of peace and tranquillity and attest to His great station and the importance of the teachings. Following His addresses at the meetings, crowds of people continually surround Him, begging for blessings and confirmations. When He returns to His home afterwards He offers praise and gratitude for the confirmations of the Abhá Beauty.

Wednesday, October 2, 1912
[San Francisco – Oakland]

Among some of the prominent people visiting 'Abdu'l-Bahá was the president of Stanford University at Palo Alto.[303] He was so attracted to the teachings that he begged the Master to come to his university and speak. Some newspaper reporters also visited the Master and were permitted to record His words about the teachings and history of the Cause. They too were showered with His special bestowals.

The Master gave a short address at a public meeting on the subject of spiritual life:

> We aspire to find true human beings in this world. Man becomes human only through spiritual life, and the foundation of such a life is made up of heavenly perfections, divine attributes, service to humanity, eagerness to receive eternal bounties, praiseworthy morals, unity, love of God, wisdom and knowledge of God. If the aim were this physical life only, then this creation would be in vain and men would not have more honor or be nobler than other creatures. The greatest of sensual pleasures, beauty of appearance and freedom are found among the animals. Birds excel all in sensual pleasures, for they build nests on the loftiest branches and breathe the purest air. All seeds and fruit are their property. Limpid streams, charming

plains, beautiful fields, verdant hills, green valleys, exquisite gardens and lovely flowers are all for their pleasure and happiness. They have no grief, regrets, aspirations, ambitions, quarrels, contentions, wars or massacres. If the purpose of existence is sensual life and pleasures, then animal and man are equal. Happiness and pleasure are rather the possession of the bird and not those of distressed and sorrowful men.

There was a gathering in the afternoon at the home of Mrs Goodall and Mrs Cooper in Oakland. The friends of Oakland and San Francisco rejoiced at meeting Him and the seekers were grateful and appreciative of His guidance. A large crowd filled the spacious house. Both before and after the meeting, those who had not had the honor of meeting 'Abdu'l-Bahá came in groups to the second floor and were honored to receive His bounty. The Oakland friends brought their children to be blessed by 'Abdu'l-Bahá. His talk to the gathering was on the power of the Word of God, the influence of the Supreme Cause and the union of the people of the East and the West. The audience became increasingly humble as the people listened to the Master.

There is a bay between San Francisco and Oakland which can be crossed in 15 minutes by boat. The Master's automobile was being ferried across the channel at night. When it reached midway, we saw a magnificent sight: lighted boats traveling back and forth against the shimmering lights of San Francisco. The splendid buildings and towers adorned with brilliant lights seemed to be golden palaces set with colored jewels. Lights from the homes crowning the high hills appeared like a string of pearls. The Master enjoyed the scene and whenever He went that way He praised it highly.

Thursday, October 3, 1912
[San Francisco]

Many friends, both old and new, had the honor of visiting 'Abdu'l-Bahá and receiving enlightenment from Him. Some of

His words to the gathering of the friends were these:

> As there are four seasons in this material world, so it is in the spiritual world. When the divine spring is over and the heavenly bounty ceases, the trees of being lie dormant. Lifelessness and stillness prevail over the world of man. People become spiritless and withered. Autumn and winter set in. There exists no flower or greenery, no cheerfulness or mirth, no happiness or joy. Then the spiritual spring spreads its tent once more. The gardens of the hearts regain their freshness, charm and verdure. The buds of knowledge open and the anemones of reality appear. The world of man becomes another world. This is the divine law and is a requirement of the world of creation. This is the cause of the appearance of the many Manifestations of God.[304]

In the afternoon, after seeing many visitors and answering questions from some reporters,[305] at the invitation of Mrs Goodall the Master went to see the beautiful and tranquil Golden Gate Park located outside of the city. In the automobile on the way to the park the Master spoke about the grandeur of the Revelation of the Blessed Beauty:

> No one was a denier of His virtues. All the wise men of the East considered Him the greatest person in the world. But they said, 'Alas, that He has claimed divinity for Himself.' Many of the people of the East said and wrote about me, too, 'all agree that he excels in knowledge, learning, speech and explanation, but, alas! he is the propagator of a new law'. They expected us to be servants and propagators of their old dogmas and customs, not knowing that we are obliged to serve humanity and spread universal love and harmony.

He concluded, 'If all others have a few daughters and sons, I have thousands of spiritual offspring and heavenly children like you.'

When He returned, and after seeing the friends and bestowing His favors upon them, He sent telegrams to the Assemblies in the East. Among them was this: 'Rejoicing among friends of God in San Francisco. Truly confirmations are overwhelming and happiness complete. 'Abbás.'

Friday, October 4, 1912
[San Francisco]

After morning prayers, two Japanese Bahá'ís came to see 'Abdu'l-Bahá. The Master expressed His happiness on seeing their faith and sincerity in the Cause, saying:

> This is an historic event. It is out of the ordinary that an Iranian should meet Japanese people in San Francisco with such love and harmony. This is through the power of Bahá'u'lláh and calls for our thankfulness and happiness. If it be said that Bahá'u'lláh brought a man from heaven and another from earth and caused them to meet midway between the earth and heaven, do not be surprised. The power of Bahá'u'lláh makes all difficulties simple. I like the Japanese greatly because they are audacious and intelligent. Whatever they turn their attention to, it becomes a success.

The visitors invited the Master to come to Japan to realize the potential of the Japanese people and asked His permission to contribute articles on the Faith to the Japanese newspapers. He readily granted their request and showed them great kindness.

In the afternoon a representative from the [San Francisco] *Post* came to interview the Master, who said to him:

> In this enlightened age everything has been renewed – sciences have been renewed, new arts have come into being, new skills have appeared, new thoughts have been expressed, new inventions have come to light and new discoveries have been made.

In reality, the world of being has become a new world. Thus, the principles of religion also must be renewed.

To a journalist from the [San Francisco] *Bulletin* He said:

> God created man after His own image and likeness . . . but now, behaving contrarily, man has become more merciless and fearless than rapacious beasts. A beast kills only one animal each day for his food, while merciless man tears apart a hundred thousand people in a day merely for fame and dominion. Should a wolf tear a sheep apart, they would kill it; but if a man massacres a hundred thousand men in blood and dust, he is given an ovation and is pronounced a marshall or a general. If a man kills another or sets fire to a house, he is condemned as a murderer; but if he annihilates an army and overturns a country, he is called a conqueror and is admired. If a man steals a dollar he is thrown into prison but if he plunders the homes of people and lays waste a city he is called a commander and is praised.

Saturday, October 5, 1912
[San Francisco]

Some clergymen and professors came to visit 'Abdu'l-Bahá in the morning in His second-floor room. Some of the Master's words to the pastor of the First Congregational Church in Oakland were these: 'If a man is not a clergyman and is unprejudiced, it is not a cause for wonder. But if a man is a clergyman and is not prejudiced, he certainly deserves praise and glory.'

At the public meeting 'Abdu'l-Bahá spoke about the material progress of the world:

> These countries have reached the apex of material progress. They are like bodies in the utmost health and form which are, however, devoid of spirit. A spiritless body is a dead one. Indeed, its perfection depends on the acquisition of spiritual capacity and divine civilization.

The Master remarked repeatedly:

> The people of America have a great capacity for the acquisition of spiritual qualities but they are immersed in material affairs. They are like machines which move uncontrollably; they move but are devoid of spirit. They will attain perfection when the spirit of divine civilization is breathed into them and this material civilization becomes infused with spiritual refinement.

The Master went to the public park in the afternoon, which He appreciated very much, especially when He went near the lake and saw the remnants of a few marble pillars left over from the destruction caused by the great earthquake of 1906. He remarked, 'The world and its condition will change to such a degree and the Bahá'í Cause will prevail to such an extent that nothing but a remnant – like these pillars – will remain of the previous order.' Sitting on a bench, the Master spoke about the sensitivity of the vegetable kingdom:

> Although sensitivity in plants is slight as compared with that manifested in animals, within their own kingdom they have sensitivity and vegetable spirit. Cut across a conical shape, sprinkle a little sulphate of copper on it, add a little water and then observe it with a magnifier. You will find its components rushing toward the center. Their sensitivity is apparent in their effort to reach the center until they form a cylinder.

In the evening the Master spoke to the assembled friends at His residence about the ascendancy of spiritual power and the divine life of humanity. The friends, both new and old, were deeply impressed and attracted to Him. At the end of each meeting the friends, one by one, came into His presence to beg His assistance and blessings. Their state was such that it cannot be described.

Sunday, October 6, 1912
[San Francisco]

The Master was invited to deliver an address at the First Unitarian Church of San Francisco. The moment He entered the church the audience stood respectfully. When the music ended, the Master was introduced by the pastor of the church, who dwelt on His 40 years of imprisonment, the martyrdom of the Eastern Bahá'ís, 'Abdu'l-Bahá's release from prison and His journey to spread the teachings of the Ancient Beauty. He also mentioned the teachings of universal peace and the unity of nations and peoples under the shadow of the Greatest Name. The pastor then read a translated passage from the *Hidden Words*.

The Master stood and delivered a comprehensive talk on the degrees of love, amity, peace and the oneness of mankind; the universality of the Manifestations of God; the truth of Islam; and the news of the appearance of Bahá'u'lláh. He concluded by chanting an inspiring prayer in Persian. Again the pastor stood, praised the Master's talk and thanked Him for His address. At the conclusion of the meeting, a crowd of people came to the Master to shake His hand, expressing their sincerity and heartfelt appreciation. Those who had not yet had the honor of visiting Him took His address so they might meet Him at His home.

In the afternoon a number of Bahá'ís and non-Bahá'ís gathered to meet Him. In answer to a question from an Indian regarding Sufism and the Trinity, He stated:

> The reality of divinity is holy beyond descent and incarnation but the divine Manifestations are expressive of the attributes and perfections of God, the All-Praised, the Exalted. They are like mirrors placed before the Sun of Truth, so if they claim that the Sun of Truth is in them, they speak the truth. However, they mean that the signs and light of the Sun of Truth are in them, and not the Sun itself.

In the evening 'Abdu'l-Bahá went to the First Congregational Church in Oakland. The influence of the Cause and the majesty of the Covenant made such an impression and was so widespread that during his introduction the pastor of the church said: 'Tonight the messenger of God will speak in the church of God and you will hear with your own ears.'

The Master spoke magnificently on the fundamental oneness of the principles of religions and the truth of Islam. His words moved and deeply affected everyone, increasing their joy and eagerness and raising the status of the Cause of God.

Monday, October 7, 1912
[San Francisco]

While tea was being served in the morning, the Master recalled the events of last night, saying:

> The pastor said: 'The messenger of God will speak in the church of God.' No one will believe it unless they see it themselves. No matter to whom you may write these words, they will think it an exaggeration and will not believe it to be true.

Among those visiting the Master today was the Mayor of Berkeley. He questioned the Master about economic issues and received useful answers. In conclusion 'Abdu'l-Bahá said:

> We must strive until mankind achieves everlasting felicity. Laws are needed which can both preserve the ranks of individuals and secure peace and stability for them because society is like an army, which needs a general, captains, lieutenants and privates. Not all can be captains nor can all be soldiers. The grades of responsibility are essential and the differences of rank a necessity. Just as a family needs old and young, master and mistress, servants and attendants, likewise society needs organization and structure. However, all must be part of an

order which will ensure that each lives in complete comfort within his own station. It should not be that the master lives in comfort while the servant is in pain; that is injustice. Similarly, it is impossible that all be either servants or masters; then there would be no order.

The mayor asked, 'Will these things be realized soon?' The Master replied:

As these laws are in conformity with the demands of the time, they will unfailingly prevail, although they will be implemented gradually. Everything can be prevented or resisted except the demands of the time. The time is ripe for the governments to remedy these ills. Relief must be brought to the toiling masses. Otherwise, if these ills are allowed to become chronic, their cure will be difficult and they will precipitate a great revolution.

The Master then gave an account of the unity and self-sacrifice of the friends of the East and expounded on various aspects of the true economic laws, which He had written while in Dublin. The mayor was so impressed that he could not help expressing his sincere admiration. He then invited the Master to an important meeting to be held in the city that evening. Because this meeting had political aims as its objective, the Master tendered His apologies.

This evening the Master spoke to a Bahá'í gathering at a hall on the subjects of divine civilization, spiritual capacity and heavenly power.[306] The fragrances of the bounties of God subdued every heart, particularly those of the friends visiting from Honolulu and those from the vicinity. After the meeting 'Abdu'l-Bahá remarked: 'I love the friends of Honolulu very much. I wish that I could go to that area and to Japan to see how much capacity for the Cause of God they possess.'

At the request of a Jewish friend, the Master spoke to some Jews who had come, saying:

> The day and age promised by the divine Prophets has appeared. This is the day in which Zion dances with joy. The day has come in which Carmel is revived and is rejoicing. That day has come for you to return to Palestine and see how it is flourishing.

Tuesday, October 8, 1912
[San Francisco – Palo Alto]

Today was one of the most significant days. At the invitation of Dr David Starr Jordan, 'Abdu'l-Bahá went to Leland Stanford Junior University in Palo Alto. The teachings of the Cause of God were given to a large, illustrious audience at this important educational center. Apart from some 1,800 students and 180 professors from the university, many civic leaders and prominent people from the area were also assembled in the auditorium; its satellite rooms and hallways were full and many people were standing outside the entrance as well.

The president stood and made his introductory remarks:[307]

> It is our privilege to have with us, through the kindness and courtesy of our Persian friends, one of the great religious teachers of the world, one of the natural successors of the old Hebrew prophets. He is said sometimes to be the founder of a new religion. He has upward of three millions of people following along the lines in which He leads. It is not exactly a new religion, however. The religion of brotherhood, of good will, of friendship between men and nations is as old as good thinking and good living may be. It may be said in some sense to be the oldest of religions . . . I have now the pleasure, the great honor of presenting to you 'Abdu'l-Bahá.

The Master then spoke about the unity of all phenomena, man's predominance over nature, universal peace and divine civilization in such a way that the entire audience was overcome with admiration.[308] The applause shook the building to its very foundation. The president closed this memorable occasion with these remarks:

> We are all under very great obligation to 'Abdu'l-Bahá for this illuminating expression of the brotherhood of man and the value of international peace. I think we can best show our appreciation by simply a rising vote of thanks.

The audience immediately rose and showed their respect by clapping and stomping their feet.

The Master had lunch with Dr Jordan at his home. Later that evening the Master spoke at the Unitarian Church of Palo Alto. His theme was the reality of divinity. The people were told the mysteries of the Kingdom and learned of spiritual matters. 'Abdu'l-Bahá then went to the home of Mrs Isabel Merriman for dinner. The group present at the table was honored to be in His presence and were enchanted by His words.

Wednesday, October 9, 1912
[Palo Alto – San Francisco]

Before He left Palo Alto several people gathered around 'Abdu'l-Bahá. He spoke of the differences in various religions, with special reference to Christianity, saying:

> Some called Christ God, some the Word of God, some others the Prophet of God, and through these differences disputes arose so that instead of spirituality there was hatred and amity was replaced by enmity. But Bahá'u'lláh has closed all the doors to such differences by appointing the interpreter of the Book and by establishing the Universal House of Justice – that is, the People's Parliament. And by commanding an end to

interference in people's beliefs and consciences, He has barred the way to these divisions. He has even said that if two persons differ in a matter and that difference ends in discord, then both are wrong and their position unacceptable.

After many similar talks, the Master returned to San Francisco. A meeting was especially called in the evening at the Japanese Club to hear Him speak.[309] As the meeting began, a Japanese scholar stood up, and after obtaining permission from the Master, recited in English an ode about the attributes of the Cause of God and praising 'Abdu'l-Bahá. The chairman then introduced the Master with great respect.

The Master then gave a fascinating talk on the dangers of prejudice, the validity and proofs of the Prophets and the truth of Islam and Christianity. He also spoke on the spread of the Cause of God, the influence of the divine teachings and spiritual education, as well as explaining the teachings and writings of Bahá'u'lláh. Even though the talk was first translated from Persian into English and then from English into Japanese, the audience was awed and excited to hear His powerful reasoning and was anxious to hear the translation of the talk.

From this day forward multitudes came every day in great humility to see 'Abdu'l-Bahá and to offer praise and thanks for the teachings.

Thursday, October 10, 1912
[San Francisco]

In addition to the gatherings of the friends at the Master's residence, there were also meetings outside, which demonstrates the grandeur and power of the Centre of the Covenant. One took place at a high school in Berkeley where the Master spoke on the reality of God and the proofs of the revelation of the Manifestations and their teachings. Many from the area were enthused with His talk and came afterwards to receive illumination from Him.

Another meeting was held at the Open Forum in San Francisco.³¹⁰ Although the audience was composed mostly of philosophers and professors, they were all humbled by the talk. The Master's profound words contrasted the philosophy of the East with that of the West, elucidated the power beyond nature and explained the inherent distinction between mankind and other creatures. He concluded with the assertion that if philosophers believed that the highest perfection was not to believe in intellectual and spiritual truth, it would be preferable to go to the cow, who, without any formal training, already had this attribute.³¹¹ When the Master uttered these words, everyone burst into laughter. This kind of humor, delivered in such a light-hearted manner, is popular and accepted by the Americans and so brought smiles and joy to the audience. At the conclusion of the Master's talk, when a philosopher stood up, several were heard to say to one another that the cow takes the lead in not believing in intellectual thought. The result was that everyone, even the philosophers, bore witness to the might of the divine teachings and influence of the words of 'Abdu'l-Bahá. Indeed, the Master's address provided a perfect and decision proof for such people.³¹²

Friday, October 11, 1912
[San Francisco]

Some physicians were in His presence today. The Master spoke with them about the use of diet to heal diseases. He then dealt with the spiritual remedy for the intellectual diseases of the people and nations:

> Today, the greatest and speediest remedy and the sole effective antidote that the Divine Physician has prescribed for the world's ills is the oneness of humanity, universal peace, the explanation of the principles of the divine religions and the removal of dogmatic imitations and customs which are contrary to science and reason. Indeed, one of the chief reasons for

irreligion among people is that the leaders of religion, such as the Catholic priests, take a little bread and wine, blow a breath over it and then say that the bread is the flesh of Christ and the wine is the blood of Christ. Of course, a man of understanding would not accept these dogmas and would say that if this bread and wine is turned into the flesh and blood of Christ by the breath of a priest, then the priest must be superior to Christ. Thus Bahá'u'lláh has said, 'Every matter that is contrary to sound reason and science and is opposed to the fundamental principles of the divine religions is an obstacle to progress and a cause of people avoiding and rejecting the laws of God.'

A Bahá'í children's meeting was held in the afternoon at the home of Mrs Goodall and Mrs Cooper. When the Master saw the children, He remarked: 'Praise be to God! What radiant children they are!' He spoke briefly, encouraging and praising them for their courtesy and upbringing. Kissing them one by one, He greeted each child in short English sentences and each received from Him some flowers and sweets.

He then went upstairs to meet with some Indians who had come to visit Him. His conversation with them was this:

> Man must irrigate the Blessed Tree which has eternal fruits and is the cause of life for all on earth. This goodly Tree, though hidden at first, will erelong envelop the whole world, and its leaves and branches will reach the heavens. It is like the Tree which Buddha planted: although at first it was a small sapling, it eventually enveloped the countries of Asia.

The Master left Mrs Goodall's home to go for a walk. He stopped at a neighbor's door. The lady of the house brought a chair for Him. He sat for a while, pleased with the woman's reverence and thoughtfulness, and bestowed His loving kindness upon her.

In the evening the Master spoke before a joyful gathering of the Theosophical Society. The president of the society introduced

'Abdu'l-Bahá in glowing terms, referring to the appearance of perfect souls and divine manifestations, saying:

> Each of those teachers was an educator of the world of humanity and each brought a Book for the training of the souls. This evening we have the exalted honor to have one of these educators among us. He has brought a new Message for the evolution of humanity and will speak to us this evening. I have the utmost honor to introduce to you His Holiness 'Abdu'l-Bahá, whom you know well.

The Master then spoke about the rising of the Sun of Reality from different signs of the zodiac, the immortality of the spirit and the universality of the new Revelation. The audience was very interested and requested His permission to ask questions. Their enthusiasm and admiration was heightened when they heard His persuasive answers.

Saturday, October 12, 1912
[San Francisco]

The Master's address at the Jewish Temple was unique and magnificent.[313] His talk, which was delivered to some two thousand Jews, concerned the truth of Christ, the reality of Islam, the oneness of humanity and universal peace. This gathering was clear evidence of the power and majesty of the Center of the Covenant. Indeed, it can be counted as a miracle. The proofs supporting the truth of the reality of Christ and Muḥammad, the Messengers of God, flowed from 'Abdu'l-Bahá's lips with such majesty and authority that all were dumbfounded. After His talk, many humbly came to see Him to express their gratitude, except for a few narrow-minded ones who turned their heads away and left in scorn. The chairman of the meeting, considered to be an eminent and learned Jew, introduced the Master:

It is our privilege to welcome in our midst 'Abdu'l-Bahá, a great teacher of our age and generation. The heart of the Orient seems to be essentially religious, and now and then, out of the heart of the Orient, the fundamental religious message for the world is stated and restated. This century is very great and this age is the age of the maturity of the world. 'Abdu'l-Bahá is the representative of one of the religious systems which appeals to us Jews, because we feel that we have fathered that idea throughout the centuries. This morning He will speak to us, the followers and the children of Israel, in His native tongue through an interpreter, on 'The Fundamental Unity of Religious Thought'. I am certain that whatever He says will be of great significance to us.

Address by 'Abdu'l-Bahá[314]

The first bestowal of God to the world of humanity is religion because religion consists of divine teachings. Certainly divine teachings are preferable to all other sources of instructions.

Religion confers upon man life everlasting. Religion is a service to the world of morality. Religion guides humanity to eternal happiness. Religion is the cause of everlasting honor to the world of man. Religion has ever helped humanity towards progress.

But the proof must be established. To achieve this end, we should investigate religion as seekers of truth. When we do so, we find that religion is the cause of progress and development. Let us see, then, whether or not religion is the cause of illumination; whether or not religion is the impetus which enables man to make extraordinary strides.

Let us investigate in search of truth, without being bound by blind imitations or dogmas. If we are bound by blind imitations, some will believe that religion is the cause of happiness and others will say that religion has been the cause of degradation. Hence, we must investigate whether religion is the cause of human advancement or of retrogression, so that no doubt shall linger in our minds.

We shall therefore investigate the Prophets and review the episodes of their lives. We shall avoid traditions that some will find it possible to repudiate and shall cite historical facts provable to all and which are irrefutable. They are these:

Among the Prophets was Abraham, who prohibited idolatry and was a herald of the oneness of God, consequently He was banished by the people from His native land.

Let us observe how religion became an impetus towards progress. Abraham founded a family which God did bless. Owing to its religious basis the Abrahamic house progressed. Through divine benediction, Prophets issued forth from His lineage. There appeared Isaac, Ishmael, Jacob, Joseph, Moses, Aaron, David and Solomon. The Holy Land was ruled by them and a glorious civilization was established. All this was due to the religion which was founded.

Hence, religion is the cause of honor and the happiness of mankind. Unto the present time Abraham's household is spread over the whole world.

Let us consider even a greater reality. The children of Israel were in captivity in the land of Egypt. Being subject to the tyranny and oppression of the Egyptians, they were in the utmost state of degradation and slavery. The Egyptians were so antagonistic towards the Israelites that they were assigned the most arduous and servile tasks.

The children of Israel were in abject poverty, abasement, ignorance and barbarism when Moses appeared among them. Outwardly Moses was no other than a shepherd but through the power of religion He exhibited extraordinary grandeur and efficacy. His prophethood was spread throughout the land and His law became renowned throughout all regions.

Although Moses was single and alone, through the power of religion He rescued all the children of Israel from bondage. He conducted them to the Holy Land and founded a civilization for the world of humanity. He educated the children of Israel and enabled them to attain to the highest degree of honor and glory. Releasing them from their bondage, He caused them to reach the zenith of freedom. They progressed in the acquisition of human perfections and advanced in culture, in the arts and sciences, in philosophy and in craftsmanship. In brief, their growth and progress reached such an exalted state that even the Greek philosophers took journeys to the Holy Land in order to study philosophy with the children of Israel. It is an established historical fact that even Socrates, the Greek philosopher, came to the Holy Land and consorted with Jewish leaders, studying wisdom with them. When he returned to Greece, he formulated his basis for divine unity and advanced his belief regarding the immortality of the spirit after the dissolution of the body. These verities Socrates learned from the children of Israel.

Likewise Hippocrates and many other philosophers went to the Holy Land and acquired lessons from the Jewish prophets about the basis of philosophy and returned to their country to spread such verities.

A Cause which changed such a weak people into a powerful nation, rescued them from captivity, caused them to attain to sovereignty, transformed their ignorance into knowledge and philosophy, granted them prosperity and endowed them with an impetus to advance along all paths of attainment, such a Cause makes it evident that religion is a source of honor and progress for humanity, a foundation for eternal happiness.

But blind imitations and dogmas which crept in later, those are ever a destructive force and the cause of the retrogression of nations. It is written in the Torah and in historical records that when the Jews were fettered by forms and imitations the wrath of God became manifest.

When the foundation of the law of God was ignored, God sent Nebuchadnezzar. He killed the men, enslaved the children, laid waste the Holy Temple, took seventy thousand Jews into captivity to Babylon and caused the Torah to be burned.

We see that the foundation of the divine religions has been the cause of progress and blind imitations have led to abasement and humiliation. Thus, the Greeks and the Romans conquered the Jews and were able to oppress them. Under Titus, the Roman emperor and commander of the army, the Holy Land was attacked. The Israelites were scattered and became fugitives. He killed their men, pillaged their possessions and destroyed Jerusalem. The dispersion of the Jews has continued ever since.

Hence, the foundation of the religion of God which was laid by Moses was the cause of eternal honor, the advancement and development of the nation and the life of the Hebrew people. The dogmas and blind imitations which crept in later debased the Israelites and caused them to be expelled from the Holy Land and to be scattered throughout the earth.

In short, the mission of the Prophets is no other than the advancement and education of the world of humanity. The Prophets are universal Educators.

Should we desire to determine whether these messengers were Prophets, we should investigate the truth. If they have been Educators of the people, enabled them to attain knowledge after having been in the abyss of ignorance, then we are sure that they were Prophets. Such evidence is irrefutable. We do not need to cite other matters which may be denied by some.

The deeds of Moses are conclusive proofs. No other proof is needed. If a man be unbiased and fair in investigating reality, he will undoubtedly bear testimony to the fact that Moses was verily a great Educator.

Let us not digress from the subject. But I ask you to be fair in your judgment, setting aside all prejudice.

We should all be seekers of truth. We should be aware that the purpose of the religion of God has been to promote amity and fellowship among men. Therefore, the foundation of the religions of God is one. Reality does not accept multiplicity. Every religion is divided into two parts. One part is concerned with the world of morality, the upliftment and advancement of the world of humanity, the knowledge of God and the discovery of the realities of things. This part of religion is spiritual and is its essential and fundamental part. It is the foundation of all the religions of God. Therefore, all religions are one and the same.

The second part has to do with social relationships. This part is not essential; it is subject to change according to the requirements of the time. In the time of Noah certain conditions required that all sea foods be made lawful. Because of certain exigencies at the time of Abraham, it was lawful for a man to marry his sister, even as Abel and Cain had done, but in the Torah this practice was prohibited.

Moses lived in the wilderness. There were no prisons for the punishment of criminals. Hence, according to the exigency of the time, the law was an eye for an eye and a tooth for a tooth. Is it possible to follow such a law now? In the Torah there are ten commandments concerning murder. These ten ordinances, concerning the treatment of murderers, cannot be enforced now.

Even regarding capital punishment, wise men are studying this question, as they maintain that capital punishment should be abolished.

The laws of the Torah were from God but they were suited for that time. If a man committed theft to the extent of a dollar, the exigency of that time demanded that they cut off his hand but now you cannot cut off a man's hand for stealing one thousand dollars. Such laws were laid down in every Dispensation in accordance with the needs of the age and are subject to change; they are non-essential. The essentials are spiritual in character and have to do with morality. They are the one foundation of religions and are subject to neither change or multiplicity.

The basis of the law was promulgated by Christ. That same foundation of religion was promulgated by Muḥammad. Since all the Prophets called on the people to accept this reality, the purpose of all the Prophets has been the same. They upheld the honor and advancement of humanity and instituted the divine civilization of man. The proofs of the validity of a Prophet and the signs of the divine revelation received by Him are in the deeds of that Prophet. If His deeds have led to the advancement of humanity, beyond any doubt He is of God.

Be fair in your judgment! At the time when the Israelites had been taken into captivity, when the Roman Empire had effected the dispersion of the Hebrew nation and when the law of God had passed from among them and the foundation of the religion of God had been destroyed, at such a time Christ appeared. The first thing He did was to proclaim the validity of the Mosaic mission. He declared that the Torah was the book of God and all the prophets of Israel were valid and true. He promulgated the prophethood of Moses and proclaimed His name throughout the world.

In Persia, India and Europe the name of Moses had not been heard of before the appearance of Christ. Throughout these regions there was not a copy of the Torah. It was through the instrumentality of Christ that the Torah was translated into six hundred languages. It was Christ who raised aloft the standard of the Prophets of Israel, so that most nations of the world believed that the children of Israel were verily the chosen people of God, that that nation was a holy nation, blessed by God, and that all the prophets of Israel were dawning points of divine inspiration, day springs of divine revelation and shining stars from the eternal Realm.

Hence, Christ promulgated Judaism. He did not deny the prophetic validity of Moses but rather promoted it. He did not efface the Torah but rather published it. The portion of that Dispensation which concerned social transactions underwent changes in accordance with the conditions of the time. This is of no significance. The essential teaching of Moses was promulgated by Christ.

With the superlative power and efficacy of the Word of God, He gathered most of the nations of the East and the

West. This achievement was effected at a time when these nations were in the utmost contention and strife. He ushered them into the overshadowing tent of the oneness of humanity. He educated them to become united so that the Roman, the Greek, the Assyrian, the Chaldean and other foreign nations were united and blended into a heavenly civilization. This efficacy of the Word and divine power, which are extraordinary, prove conclusively the validity of the revelation of Christ. Observe how His heavenly sovereignty has endured. This is indeed conclusive proof and manifest evidence.

Now, consider again! When Muḥammad appeared, in His first address to His people He said that Moses was a Prophet of God and the Torah was the Book of God. He called on His people to believe in Moses, in the Torah and the Prophets; and also to accept Christ and the Gospel. In His Book the story of Moses is described seven times and in all these passages Moses is praised. Muḥammad states that Moses was one of the Prophets endowed with constancy and established a new Law; that He heard God's voice in the wilderness of Mount Sinai; that He was the Interlocutor of God; that He was the bearer of divine Tablets. Although the Arabian tribes opposed Muḥammad, eventually He conquered all of them, because falsehood is defeated by truth.

You should consider that Muḥammad was born among the barbarous tribes of Arabia and He lived among them. Outwardly He was illiterate and uninformed of the holy books of God. The Arabian nations were in ignorance and barbarism, to the extent that they buried their daughters alive. This act was considered to be the expression of valor and sublimity of nature. They lived under the yoke of the Persian and Roman governments, were scattered throughout the Arabian desert and were subjected to continuous internecine strife and bloodshed.

When the light of Muḥammad dawned, the darkness of ignorance was dispelled from the Arabian desert. In a short space of time those barbarous tribes reached a degree of civilization which extended to Spain and was established in Baghdád and influenced the people of Europe. What proof is there concerning His prophethood greater than this? The evidence is clear, unless one ignores impartiality and adheres to unwarranted discrimination.

The Christians believe in Moses as a Prophet of God. The Muslims are believers in Moses and praise Him highly. Has any harm come to Christians and Muslims because they have admitted the validity of Moses? No, on the contrary, their acceptance of Moses and confirmation of the Torah prove that they have been fair-minded.

Why should not the children of Israel praise now Christ and Muḥammad? This will do away forever with enmity and hatred which have lasted for two thousand years, so that differences and animosities may pass away forever.

The Muslims admit that Moses was the Interlocutor of God. What harm is there if the Jews would say that Christ was the Spirit of God and Muḥammad was the Messenger of God? Thus there will be no hatred, no disputation, no warfare and no bloodshed.

I now declare to you that Moses was the Interlocutor of God; that Moses was the Prophet of God; that Moses brought the fundamental law of God; that Moses was the founder of a basis for the happiness of humanity.

What harm is there is this declaration? Do I lose by saying this to you and believing it as a Bahá'í? No! By God! On the contrary, as a Bahá'í it benefits me. Bahá'u'lláh becomes well-pleased with me and will confirm me. He says, 'Well done; you have been fair in your judgment; you have impartially investigated the truth; you have believed in a Prophet of God and you have accepted the Book of God.'

As it is possible to do away with warfare and massacre with a small measure of liberalism in the world, why not do it? Thus bonds are established which can unite the hearts of men. What harm is there in this? Inasmuch as the other nations praise

Moses, why should the Jews not also praise the other Prophets?

The followers of each religion should praise the Founders of the other religions so that the welfare of mankind, the happiness of the world of humanity, the eternal honor of man and universal fellowship may ensue.

God is One and He has created all of us. He provides for all; He protects all; He is kind to all. Why should we be so unkind? Why should we engage in strife?

This century is the century of science, it is the century of the discovery of the mysteries of nature; it is the century of service to the world of humanity. It is the century of the manifestation of the reality of things, the century for the oneness of mankind. Does it behoove us in this century to linger in our fanaticism and tarry in our prejudice? Does it behoove us to still be bound by old superstitions and be handicapped by superannuated and empty beliefs and regard these as grounds for waging war, shedding blood and shunning and anathematizing one another?

Is it not better for us to be loving to one another? Is it not preferable for us to enjoy fellowship, raise our voices to the heavens in tune with the melody of the Concourse on High and in glorification of the oneness of mankind? Is it not more praiseworthy to celebrate the unity of God and laud His Prophets in glorious assemblages and public meetings? On such a day, the world will become the paradise of the All-Glorious.

What does this mean?

It means that contending nations which have been characterized by these qualities and religions which have been formerly as wolves and sheep, with divergent creeds, will associate with each other in the utmost affection and amity and unite with each other in fellowship and love.

This is the meaning of the prophecy of Isaiah. Otherwise it will never come to pass literally, for the wolf will never live peacefully with the sheep, and the lion and the deer will never associate together, inasmuch as the deer is food for the lion and the sheep will ever be the prey of the wolf. As you know, the teeth of the lion are carnivorous. It has no molars to eat grass; hence it must eat flesh.

Therefore, this prophecy is symbolic of the state of affairs when nations and races, symbolized by wolves and sheep, among whom there is a bond of fellowship and association, will be unified and will treat each other kindly and liberally in that promised day.

In a word, the century is upon us when fellowship is to be established!

The century has come when all the religions are to be at peace with each other!

The century has come when all the nations shall become one nation!

The century has come when all mankind shall live under the tabernacle of the oneness of mankind.

'Abdu'l-Bahá gave this address in the afternoon at the home of Mrs Goodall and Mrs Cooper:

> Today we spoke in the Jewish temple. You saw how it was proven that Christ was the Word of God and Muḥammad the Messenger of God. From the beginning of Christianity and Islam up to the present day, no one has spoken thus, proving the validity of Christ and Muḥammad in a Jewish temple and in a manner to which no one took exception. Rather, most were appreciative and content. This is none other than the assistance of Bahá'u'lláh.

The effect and influence of the address were such that from then on there was evidence of unity and communication between the Christians and Jews. They even made plans to visit each other's places of worship to give talks about the unity of peoples and religions. Whenever they met 'Abdu'l-Bahá or attended Bahá'í gatherings, they expressed their gratitude from the depths of their hearts for this great Cause and its new teachings.

Sunday, October 13, 1912
[San Francisco – Pleasanton]

In the morning one of the Japanese friends came with a group of people to visit the Master. This Japanese friend said that he had studied most religions but found none as useful and effective in bringing tranquillity to the people as this Faith. The Master replied:

> I hope that you will become heavenly and not just be a Japanese, an Arab, an Englishman or a Persian, Turk or American; that you will become divine and bring your life into accord with the teachings of Bahá'u'lláh. Observe: I am one of the servants of Bahá'u'lláh, helpless and weak but as I am under the shadow of His teachings you see what confirmations descend upon me.

The fame, grandeur and beauty of the Master were such that many civic, educational and social leaders of the area visited Him, considering it an honor to be in His presence. His noble mission and talks about the Cause of God, together with the enthusiasm of the people, seemed to fulfill the verse from the Qur'án: 'The day when the people shall stand before the Lord of creation.' Mrs [Phoebe] Hearst, a wealthy and prominent person who had visited the Master a few years ago in the Holy Land[315] but who had become disaffected through the influence of unspiritual people, suddenly requested permission to visit Him. Realizing the privilege of His presence, she invited Him and His companions to her home. Because her invitation was sincere, it was accepted. In the afternoon, the Master and His servants went with Mrs Hearst to her home. After traveling inland, through the streets of Oakland and Berkeley, the automobile passed through verdant hills, green valleys and lovely towns and villages until it reached Mrs Hearst's large, regal mansion. It is situated on a beautiful hillside on the outskirts of Pleasanton, surrounded by luxuriant gardens, green lawns and pathways overflowing with flowers. Some of Mrs Hearst's relatives were also present among her guests.

In keeping with the circumstances of the occasion, for there were people of different backgrounds present, the Master's talks were brief yet full of wisdom. Many important ideas were couched in short sentences, giving the maximum effect with a minimum of words. The guests asked questions of each other about the Cause.

After dinner, the Master went into the outer hall and spoke briefly:

> Every universal matter is from God; and limitations are from man. Therefore, if people's services and efforts are undertaken for the benefit of all, they are acceptable to God and leave lasting traces. Otherwise, every other effort is limited and transitory.

After obtaining the Master's permission to have music, the guests sang songs accompanied by the piano. The meeting ended with great joy and happiness.

Monday, October 14, 1912
[Pleasanton]

In the morning 'Abdu'l-Bahá spoke about the election of the president of the republic. He said:

> The president must be a man who does not insistently seek the presidency. He should be a person free from all thoughts of name and rank; rather, he should say, 'I am unworthy and incapable of this position and cannot bear this great burden.' Such persons deserve the presidency. If the object is to promote the public good, then the president must be a well-wisher of all and not a self-seeking person. If the object, however, is to

promote personal interests, then such a position will be injurious to humanity and not beneficial to the public.

He then went to lunch. At the request of those present at the table the Master chanted the following prayer:

> He is God! Thou seest us, O my God, gathered around this table, praising Thy bounty, with our gaze set upon Thy Kingdom. O Lord! Send down upon us Thy heavenly food and confer upon us Thy blessing. Thou art verily the Bestower, the Merciful, the Compassionate.

The Master then spoke extensively on the history of some famous people.

In the afternoon He went for an automobile ride through valleys, hills and meadows as far as the breakwater. When He returned to the house, the Master rested in the garden on special chairs brought for Him and the others and gave a detailed history of the life and teachings of the Blessed Beauty.

At the dinner table He spoke of His gratitude for the blessings of God and the importance of assisting the weak and poor. He was asked, 'How is it that the desires of some people are achieved while others are not?' The gist of the Master's response was:

> What conforms with divine decree will be realized. In addition, good intentions and sound thoughts attract confirmations. The desires of human beings are endless. No matter what level a human being reaches, he can still attain higher ones, so he is always making effort and desiring more. He can never find peace but through effort and resignation, so that, notwithstanding all efforts in worldly affairs, the human heart remains free and happy. He neither becomes proud on attaining wealth and position nor becomes dejected on losing them. This station can be attained only through the power of faith.

Such explanations and exhortations repeated at every meeting were warnings and reminders for these prominent people. Day by day their humility and sincerity increased owing to His presence.

Tuesday, October 15, 1912
[Pleasanton]

Early in the morning Mrs Phoebe Hearst presented the Master with flowers of various hues and perfumes. She suggested that, if He wished, He could stroll through the surrounding gardens and nursery. He first toured the house and then went to the nursery which had many beautiful flowers. A few rare specimens attracted His particular attention. He said that the seeds of those flowers should be sent to the Holy Land for cultivation in the gardens adjoining the Shrines of the Báb and Bahá'u'lláh. Continuing, He said: 'The real flowers are those in the garden of the hearts. The flowers of the love of God which are grown with the warmth of the Sun of Truth perfume the peoples of the world and never wither.'

At the table during lunch His discourse concerned the greatness of this time, the dignity of the world of humanity and the importance of acquiring eternal virtues and perfections. Turning to the grandchildren of Mrs Hearst He said:

> In reality, children are the ornaments at the table, especially these children, who are very sweet! The hearts of children are extremely pure and simple. A person's heart must be like a child's, pure and free from all contamination.

His prayer at the dinner table was this:

> He is God! How can we render Thee thanks, O Lord? Thy bounties are endless and our gratitude cannot equal them. How can the finite utter praise of the Infinite? Unable are we to voice our thanks for Thy favors and in utter powerlessness we turn wholly to Thy Kingdom beseeching the increase of

Thy bestowals and bounties. Thou are the Giver, the Bestower, the Almighty.

He then gave an account of the history of the kings of the world and concluded with remarks about the death of Alexander.

When in the city of Zor[316] the lamp of his life was extinguished and the last morn had dawned upon him, the wise men assembled by his corpse. One of them said, 'Gracious God! The whole world could not contain this ambitious man yesterday but today a small plot of earth is sufficient to hold him.' Another remarked, 'With all his greatness, glory and eloquence of speech, Alexander never advised us in such a manner as he is instructing us today with this silence.' Another said, 'A few hours ago this man considered himself the sovereign of the whole world but now it has become evident that he was a servant and a subject.'

After dinner, He went into the salon. Mrs Hearst and her guests were so attracted by His words and actions that although she had not spoken openly to her relatives about the Faith and had been cautious about it, without hesitation she invited the Master to speak about the teachings of the Cause of God. He spoke of devotion to the Cause, the appearance of the lights of the Kingdom, universal peace and the oneness of humanity. After an exposition of the teachings, He spoke briefly on the variety and diversity in human capacities, adding: 'Christ likened divine words to seeds, and the hearts and capacities of his listeners to soil of different kinds.' Mrs Hearst related her experiences of her days in 'Akká and told of her joy on hearing a prayer chanted in the Holy Land. At her request the Master, in a melodious voice, read a prayer in eloquent Arabic. Although the listeners did not understand Arabic, most of them said that the beauty of the Tablet and 'Abdu'l-Bahá's voice caused them to draw nearer to God. Some of those present this evening expressed their desire to accept the Faith. They said that although they had been aware of the Cause and had associated with the believers, by listening to the Master they now understood more.

Wednesday, October 16, 1912
[Pleasanton – San Francisco – Oakland]

Although some of Mrs Hearst's relatives had previously been narrow-minded and aloof, they were now humbled and transformed. This was most notable when it came time for the Master to depart and He was bidding them farewell. The Master called all of the servants and attendants of the house and the maids, orderlies, cooks and butler stood in a line before Him. He encouraged them to be truthful, honest and devoted to their work. Thanking them for their services, He said: 'As I am like a father to you, I wish to leave a memento with you.' He gave each two guineas[317] and left. The grand and illustrious guests stood by humbly, astonished and impressed with 'Abdu'l-Bahá's generosity, grandeur and majesty.

Mrs Hearst begged 'Abdu'l-Bahá to allow her to accompany Him to San Francisco. Her wish was granted and she traveled with the Master. Some of His words to her were these:

> The Cause of God is sanctified from all political power and worldly affairs. Among the divine teachings are trustworthiness, detachment and sanctity. So if you should see a man coveting property and evincing greed toward the wealth of others, know that he is not of the people of Bahá. The people of Bahá are they who, should they happen to come upon a valley of gold and silver, would pass by it like lightning in utter disregard.

The Master encouraged her especially to protect and train her youngest grandchild. 'This child', He said, 'has a well-proportioned forehead and an open, pleasant face and if given heavenly instruction will be the cause of the eternal happiness of this family.'

When the eminent men of America and the liberal-minded

people of its cities see such behavior, wisdom, majesty and power exemplified by the Master, even though they are prominent themselves, they are fascinated by His unique character and fall in love with Him.

This afternoon the Master gave an address at the Century Club in San Francisco on the rights and education of women before an audience of women and their husbands. They were captivated and so overcome with joy that they begged to be introduced to Him and to attain His presence. This was a gathering of wealthy people and there was an abundance of food and refreshments. The Master had some tea and sweets and then left. When He was outside the building, crowds of people surrounded Him, demonstrating their joy, love and respect.

After the meeting, the Master remarked:

> I speak according to the demands of the time and the capacity of my listeners. 'The father makes gurgling sounds for the newborn infant, although his wisdom be capable of measuring the universe.'[318]

Later in the evening the Master and some of the friends and His servants went to Oakland to attend the Nineteen Day Feast. On the way He spoke of the sadness of the friends in Seattle, saying:

> They are upset that I am not going there. However, in spite of the great distance, they have come to see us, notwithstanding the effort involved. Had it been but a one- or two-day trip, I would have gone to Portland and Seattle but the distance is great. I would not visit Los Angeles were it not for the purpose of visiting the tomb of Mr Chase.[319] The friends all have expectations but if I should want to go to all these places, the journey would become too long and that is impossible. However, in my heart there is such love for the heavenly friends that I do not wish even a speck of dust to touch them. God forbid! If I see harm coming to one of you, I will throw myself in its path to shield you.

When the Master reached the home of Mrs Goodall and Mrs Cooper He took a walk before the Feast on the shores of the lake.[320] He returned for the meeting and spoke to the friends and seekers, saying:

> On the way here we were saying that it never occurred to us that we would come to California and meet with the friends in this manner or that we would proclaim the Cause of God in great assemblies. How Bahá'u'lláh suffered, what persecutions and hardships He endured! He saw His property plundered and carried off. He was chained and imprisoned so that hearts would be connected, that the East and the West would find harmony, that the oneness of humanity would come about and that universal peace may reign.

The friends had gathered to play the piano and sing songs of praise while awaiting the arrival of the Master. When their melodious voices reached His ears from the lower hall, He wrote a letter to Ḥájí Mírzá Ḥaydar-'Alí (the 'Angel of Carmel'), beginning:

> O thou who art partner and co-sharer with 'Abdu'l-Bahá in servitude to the Threshold of Bahá! It is evening and these wandering birds are nestled in the home of the maidservant of God, Mrs Helen Goodall, in Oakland, California. It is the Nineteen Day Feast. A number of the faithful friends and the pure and illumined leaves of God are supplicating the all-glorious Kingdom. All the delicacies are spread and ready and the table is exquisitely arranged. Oh, how thou art missed! Severed from all else, they sing a new song and with a new voice repeat spiritual notes. They are in a state of absolute love and supplication. Oh, how thou art missed! Oh, how thou art missed!

'Abdu'l-Bahá joined the gathering, invited the friends to sit at the table and began to serve them, anointing each with perfume and serving delicacies while circulating amongst them, saying:

Praise be to God! We are assembled in the home of Mrs Goodall and Mrs Cooper in utmost love and affection. Every delicacy is provided. All hearts are in utmost love and serenity. All eyes are turned to the Abhá Kingdom. It is a good gathering, it cannot be surpassed. The Supreme Concourse is now beholding this assemblage and crying out, 'Blessed are ye! Blessed are ye! O ye servants of the Blessed Beauty! Blessed are ye; blessed are ye with your radiant countenances! Blessed are ye; blessed are ye with hearts like unto rose gardens! Observe, what a favor is conferred upon you, what a bounty is bestowed upon you that 'Abdu'l-Bahá is in your midst, makes mention of you and congratulates and compliments you.'

He then said, 'Go on with your supper. I shall go upstairs and then come back.'

After supper 'Abdu'l-Bahá returned and spoke engagingly about spiritual susceptibilities, spiritual relationships, brotherhood and the heavenly supper of the friends. The meeting concluded after a prayer in Persian chanted by the Master. The friends, full of enthusiasm and joy, came one by one to shake His hand and to beg His blessings and assistance.[321]

There was such heavenly joy and happiness among the friends that this meeting shall never be forgotten and shall bring forth wonderful results. The Master stayed there for the night.[322]

Thursday, October 17, 1912
[Oakland – San Francisco]

The Master left for San Francisco early in the morning. He had lost His seal, so all of His Tablets and writings made during this time were signed by Him with His own pen.

Mail from the Eastern friends was brought to Him. I read a letter from Ḥájí Mírzá Ḥaydar-'Alí and, on his behalf, prostrated myself at the feet of the Master. He raised me up with His hands and said, 'I embrace you on behalf of Ḥájí.' He did this with a smile and such kindness that it will never be forgotten.

In today's gathering 'Abdu'l-Bahá gave an account of the martyrs of Jahrum,[323] testifying to the firmness and steadfastness of the friends in the East. The services and sincerity of Mírzá Abu'l-Faḍl were highly praised by the Master. He also gave accounts of the last days of His imprisonment in 'Akká, the oppression of Sulṭán 'Abdu'l-Ḥamíd and the conduct of the Commission of Investigation.

> This commission of investigation and oppression was on its way back to Istanbul from 'Akká when the majesty of the justice of God revolutionized all matters. Sulṭán 'Abdu'l-Ḥamíd was deposed and one member of the commission was murdered, another died and two of them absconded. One of these two begged for his daily expenses from the friends in Egypt.

Some philosophers, religionists and civic leaders of the town came one by one to see the Master. They were attracted by His words on spiritual matters and left with the utmost sincerity. One questioned Him about spirit and matter. The Master replied:

> This question may be answered in two ways, philosophically as well as spiritually. Philosophically, the answer is easy because in philosophy the spirit is energy and all matter is endowed with energy; and this power is inseparable from matter, as in electricity. In other words, matter is a vehicle for spirit but the transformation of matter does not involve the extinction of that power because transformation and transference are in the properties of matter.
>
> Immaterial beings or realities, however, are protected and preserved and their essential power remains unaltered. The manifestation or appearance of the spirit varies due to changes in matter and bodies. This, however, does not mean that spirit itself is subject to extinction.

The listeners were pleased to hear 'Abdu'l-Bahá explain this subject in detail and testified to His divine knowledge and to the cogency of His explanation and argument.

Today the Master spoke twice at public gatherings at His residence. In the first of His addresses He exhorted the audience to keep the soil of their hearts pure and holy so that the flowers of the virtues of humanity might grow and that the blessings of God might descend upon them. In His other address (given after He had taken a short walk), He explained that heat and motion are essential for the contingent world.

Friday, October 18, 1912
[San Francisco – Los Angeles]

At the time of His departure for Los Angeles, He said to the friends from Portland and Seattle who had begged Him to come to their cities:

> Send my love and good wishes to all the friends in Portland and Seattle and tell them that I am always with them. Meeting physically is as nothing compared with spiritual bonds. What is important is spiritual nearness.

When the message of the Master reached those eager friends, they telegraphed their acquiescence and instead requested permission to visit Him. They arrived during the last days of His stay in San Francisco and attained the blessing of His presence, their eyes ever filled with tears and their hearts burning with the fire of love at their nearness to the Master.

At the railway station several believers asked to be permitted to accompany 'Abdu'l-Bahá to Los Angeles. Among them was Mrs Goodall. The Master had a very pleasant journey on the train. When various newspaper accounts were read to Him, He said, 'These revolutions in Turkey are the preliminary stages for my return.' In the afternoon a resident of Los Angeles received permission to visit the Master in the train and entered His presence with the utmost sincerity and reverence.

Early in the evening 'Abdu'l-Bahá arrived at the Hotel Lankershim and the friends from that city, in transports of joy and happiness, gathered around Him. Several church and society leaders invited Him to speak at their meetings but He replied: 'I have absolutely no time. I have come here to visit Mr Chase's grave and to meet the friends. I will stay here one or two days and then I must leave.'

Saturday, October 19, 1912
[Los Angeles]

After prayer and meditation, the beloved Master, accompanied by several of the friends, went to Mr Chase's grave.[324] The tram stopped near the cemetery, which is located a few miles from the city. The Master alighted and walked towards the grave with dignified solemnity and serenity. He went directly to the grave site without asking directions from anyone. He praised the site and the lushness of the trees and grass. He stood there for a few minutes leaning against a nearby tree. He then stood near the grave of that distinguished man and spread over it bouquets of flowers, adorning that sanctified soil with such love and affection that bystanders were astonished. Facing in the direction of the Holy Land, the Master chanted Bahá'u'lláh's Tablet of Visitation. All stood in solemn reverence behind Him. After chanting the Tablet of Visitation, He recited a prayer in Arabic for the forgiveness of the departed soul. He then gave a short account of this faithful believer's services, steadfastness and forbearance. Before He left, He placed His forehead on the grave and kissed it. Tears flowed from the eyes of the believers as they bowed before that sacred spot, each one longing to attain to that sublime and exalted station. The spot became an abode of lovers.

When we returned to the hotel, we found a multitude of people waiting for the Master. Some representatives of the press were also present and 'Abdu'l-Bahá spoke to them on various subjects. One of His statements to a newspaper reporter was this:

> In the world of existence, civilization is found to be of two kinds: material civilization and spiritual civilization. Philosophers founded the former while the divine Prophets established the latter. For instance, the philosophers of Greece established a material civilization whereas Christ established a spiritual civilization. Material civilization is the cause of worldly prosperity but divine civilization is the means of eternal prosperity. If divine civilization, which is all-encompassing, is established, then material civilization will also attain perfection. When spiritual perfection is attained, then physical perfection is a certainty. Material civilization alone does not suffice and does not become the means of acquiring spiritual virtues. Rather, it leads to an increase in wars and disputes and becomes the cause of bloodshed and ruin. Despite all this, it is surprising that divine civilization has been completely forgotten and the people are constantly submerged in a sea of materialism. This is why night and day they have no peace and are engaged in war and killing. Every day there is bloodshed and ruin, suffering and distress, preparation for a universal war and the destruction of mankind.

In the afternoon He spoke to a larger crowd about the teachings of the Supreme Pen and the greatness of the Bahá'í Cause. In the course of His talk, He said:

> If you desire the nearness of God, you must sever yourself from everything and become purified and sanctified from the dross of this transitory world. You must become submerged in the sea of the love of God. You must occupy your time with His mention and praise. Bahá'u'lláh alone must be the Beloved of the world. Observe: until the disciples of Christ renounced themselves they did not resuscitate the world. Thus, you must

always be occupied with the mention of God and in spreading the teachings of Bahá'u'lláh.

Later some of the elite and wealthy came to see Him. They were fascinated and attracted to Him and immensely pleased to be in His presence.

At the evening meeting He spoke on the eternal benefits resulting from the gatherings of the friends, encouraged them to render service to the Cause of God and to turn themselves to the Kingdom of the Almighty Lord. At the conclusion of the meeting the Master was so exhausted that He could not even take supper. We left a little cheese and bread in His room so that He could have it if He got hungry during the night. (Often His food was as simple as this.) He usually took His meals in the dining room of the hotel but it would sometimes be brought to His room.

Sunday, October 20, 1912
[Los Angeles]

Today more than the usual number of friends and seekers, from all strata of society, came to see Him. There were so many that it was impossible to see them individually, except for a very few who were granted private interviews. Therefore, a public meeting was arranged and one of the many topics, which was a warning to people of insight, was the disgrace and ignominy of the son of the arch Covenant-breaker, the lightless Shu'á'u'lláh.[325]

This man, who is wholly severed from God, is engaged in pursuing worldly desires and deception. When the fame of the Center of the Covenant spread through the city, Shu'á'u'lláh spoke about Bahá'u'lláh and his blood relationship with Him. He persuaded a newspaper editor to write two misleading articles in which he tried to show that because of his biological relationship, he was bound to inherit the station of the Prophets. The Master paid no attention to such nonsensical writings and attached no importance to Shu'á's pretensions. When a newspaper editor asked the Master about this man's relationship, He said:

> I will tell you one thing and it will suffice once and for all. Beyond this neither question me nor will I reply. And that is the words of Christ when told that 'your brothers have come to see you'. He said, 'They are not my brethren but you are my brethren and kindred.'[326] Christ attached no importance to the original relationship with His brethren. Notwithstanding this, my house is open to all. He who wishes may enter and he who wishes to go out may leave.

The editor published the Master's exact words in his newspaper.

The son of the arch Covenant-breaker, who had boasted that he would speak out 'in the court of the King of the Covenant' and make his wishes known, was from that time on not heard from again. He had wanted to introduce himself around and to raise himself in the estimation of those who did not know the story but he failed like Kheiralla, who, in Chicago, had sent a message asking to be summoned to see 'Abdu'l-Bahá. The Master had answered him in similar terms: 'Since my arrival in this city,' He said, 'I have not requested to see anybody. But should anyone come to me, I will meet him with utmost kindness and regard.'

Despite this, these unjust people have spread various false rumors. They have gone so far in their careers of untruth to say that although the Master had given His word that He would see them, He had broken His promise. God protect us from the wickedness of the envious! All their impostures and connivings have been shattered, for their only hope was to create doubt and disbelief in the hearts of the people; instead they have become the means of warning them.

The Master repeatedly said: 'These two persons have disgraced themselves once again. Otherwise, I would not have mentioned their names but it is not good for the Cause nor are they worthy of mention or attention.' He also said:

If they have good intentions for the Cause of God, they must render some service and they must go out to teach the Cause. If they are able, they should raise the cry of 'Yá Bahá'u'l-Abhá' in churches and gatherings. What will they reap by sowing doubt and disbelief? They will get nothing but manifest loss in this world and the next. The Blessed Beauty has promised explicitly that the servants and sincere ones who devote themselves to the Cause of God after His ascension shall achieve success and be made victorious. Now see which of the servants are firm and serving and which ones hinder and damage the Cause. One of their misgivings is that the true One has always been oppressed and wronged. What has this to do with the matter? Yes, initially the Cause of God has always been denied but with utmost divine aid and assistance the Lord has ever been the protector and savior of the righteous. The reward of eternity will belong to the God-fearing and honor will belong to the sincere servants of God. Thus He says in the Kitáb-i-Aqdas, 'Let not your hearts be perturbed, O people, when the glory of My presence is withdrawn, and the ocean of My utterance is stilled. In My presence amongst you there is a wisdom, and in My absence there is yet another, inscrutable to all but God, the Incomparable, the All-Knowing. Verily, We behold you from Our realm of glory, and shall aid whosoever will arise for the triumph of Our Cause with the hosts of the Concourse on high and a company of our favored angels.'[327]

This evening in a large auditorium the Master gave a detailed address to a group of the friends about many issues pertaining to the Cause. He spoke about the tribulations and afflictions of the Blessed Beauty and encouraged the friends to be obedient to the verses of the Supreme Pen, to be firm in the Covenant of God and to live in harmony with one another. He spoke in such explicit terms that those present were made firmly aware of their duties. He also told them about those things which are the means of preserving unity and harmony among the Bahá'ís.

Monday, October 21, 1912
[Los Angeles]

From morning until noon all the rooms in the Master's suite were filled with people. Even the corridor was filled. The Master moved among the crowd, sometimes in the rooms and sometimes in the corridor, instructing the assemblage in the divine teachings, persuading them to serve the cause of universal peace and encouraging them to develop divine virtues and heavenly perfections in themselves.

When the people were told the Master was leaving, they became saddened and expressed their deep sorrow. Some churches and clubs sent messages inviting the Master to prolong His stay and to speak before their audiences. He was unable to accept their invitations and responded: 'I have no time, as I must return soon to the East. Nonetheless, I have great love and attachment for each one of you.'

With great eagerness, friends both old and new brought their children to meet 'Abdu'l-Bahá and to receive His blessings and protection.

As the time of departure grew near, the friends in Los Angeles were in a spiritual and prayerful mood. The Master spoke to them:

> Thank the Lord that you have attained His eternal favors and have been blessed with seeing eyes. All are blind but you are endowed with sight. All are earthly but you are heavenly. Although you live on earth, you soar high in heaven. It is my hope that day by day you will seek assistance and will rise to promote the Word of God. Go every year to visit the grave of Mr Chase on my behalf, for he was a sanctified soul; his station will be known later.
>
> I have come a long distance to see you; I have traveled 12,000 miles. Praise be to God that I have found you in spiritual joy and happiness. I pray that you may live under the care and protection of God and be assisted by Him in rendering greater service to His mighty Cause, so that each of you may

become a fruit-bearing tree in the garden of His favor, full of freshness and life. May you acquire more bounties of the Kingdom and engage yourselves in guiding souls, so that Los Angeles may become a divine city and a center of the lights of the Kingdom. If the friends of God act according to the teachings of Bahá'u'lláh, they will succeed in guiding the people, will promote the unity of mankind and will strive for universal peace. Heavenly confirmations will descend upon them and they shall attain that station which is the desire of the holy ones and near ones.

When the Master reached the railway station, it was learned that Mrs Goodall, without telling us, had secured pullman reservations for everyone. Although the Master had a comfortable berth in the train, He was so tired He could not sleep.

Tuesday, October 22, 1912
[San Francisco]

In the morning the Master remarked, 'I did not sleep at all last night but was deep in thought.' When the train arrived at the station a group of friends greeted the Master with joy and happiness. The Master spoke repeatedly today about the steadfastness and enthusiasm of the friends in Los Angeles. His had been elated to witness their constancy in the Cause.

The believers from San Francisco and surrounding areas gathered group by group at the Master's residence, where He received them in His room. He strongly encouraged them to spread the divine fragrances and teach the Cause of God. To the seekers He gave the glad tidings of the dawning of the Morn of Guidance and the coming of the era of peace, tranquillity, amity and unity among the nations of the world.

His address in the morning at the public meeting centered around the days of the Blessed Beauty, the exaltation of the Word of the God and the vain imaginings of the followers of Yaḥyá. In the afternoon He spoke particularly on the duty of teaching the Cause of God and gave a detailed account of the Tablets of Bahá'u'lláh revealed to the kings and rulers of the world.

After an evening stroll, 'Abdu'l-Bahá showed special kindness to the friends from Portland and Seattle, who had arrived today to visit their beloved Master. He spoke with them on several subjects, saying, among other things:

> Until now it never happened that someone from the East, impelled by the promptings of his conscience, should come to the West to see the friends of God and to associate with respected individuals with such sincere love and friendship and without any political or commercial motive or the desire of sightseeing. It is without precedent and is not recorded in any history. If others have come, it has been to sightsee or for commercial or other reasons.

In response to some questions, He said:

> A great war and commotion shall inevitably take place in the world. Things will come to such a pass that the generality of mankind will rise against the statesmen of the world and say, 'You sit in your palaces in perfect comfort; you eat and drink sumptuously; you sleep blissfully; you eat delicious food and relax in gardens with beautiful views. But for the sake of your name and worldly fame, you throw us, your subjects, into war, shed our blood and tear our bodies to pieces. But no thorn ever pricks your hands and not for a moment do you leave your rest and comfort.'[328]

Wednesday, October 23, 1912
[San Francisco – Oakland]

Today there was a public meeting in Oakland at the home of Mrs Cooper and Mrs Goodall. The Master spoke kindly about the devotion and steadfastness of His hostesses and praised the firmness and enthusiasm of the California Bahá'ís.[329] As these were the last days of His stay, the friends' hearts were moved and their enthusiasm and affection increased. He had lunch and dinner there.

In the evening the Master spoke of the retirement of the Blessed Beauty[330] and the distress of the believers, speaking at length of Áqá Abu'l-Qásim-i-Hamadání.[331] 'From the circumstances, as reported,' 'Abdu'l-Bahá continued,

> we surmised that because Áqá Abu'l-Qásim-i-Hamadání had previously been with Bahá'u'lláh and had also set out on a journey when the Blessed Beauty disappeared, then Darvish Muḥammad was really the Blessed Beauty and must be in the vicinity of Sulaymáníyyih. Thus it was that we sent the friends to petition Him, implore and supplicate Him to return to Baghdád.

After the meeting the Master went to His room but the friends implored His presence among them. He then returned to the gathering, saying, among other things:

> I have now been for some time in these regions. In any city I have entered I have met with the friends and other people. In all the gatherings and most of the churches I have called out to the Abhá Kingdom and invited people to the Cause of the Blessed Beauty. At night I have implored and supplicated and prayed and asked for assistance, so that the rays of the Sun of Reality may shine on this country, illumine all the regions of America, bestow everlasting life; that its citizens may acquire heavenly civilization and that they may be bountifully favored through the teachings of the Blessed Beauty.
>
> Praise be to God! This has come to pass through the grace of the Blessed Beauty and the assistance of the Abhá Kingdom. The call of God has been raised in all the cities of America.

Accounts of the greatness of the Cause have been published even in the newspapers.

He also spoke with joy and happiness about the establishment of the Cause in the countries of the East and the firmness and steadfastness of the Persian friends.

One day, as He was strolling, He called to remembrance the days of the Blessed Beauty, referring with sadness to His sojourn in Sulaymáníyyih, to His loneliness and to the wrongs inflicted upon Him. Though He had often recounted that episode, that day He was so overcome with emotion that He sobbed aloud in His grief... All His attendants wept with Him, and were plunged into sorrow as they heard the tale of the woeful trials endured by the Ancient Beauty, and witnessed the tenderness of heart manifested by His Son.[332]

The Master remained in Oakland for the night.

Thursday, October 24, 1912
[San Francisco]

A group of believers from Oakland and the vicinity arrived. Some brought their children, supplicating the Master to give them His blessings and protection and requesting Persian names for them. All were honored and delighted to have seen the One around whom all names revolve and their eyes overflowed with tears of joy. He encouraged them to make every effort to bring about universal peace and the unity of mankind. He also spoke about His address at the Jewish temple.

On the way back to San Francisco He spoke to a group of young Bahá'ís who were teaching the Cause of God and were dedicated to diffusing the divine fragrances:

> Thank God that the divine bounty has reached you, that the Sun of Truth is shining upon you and that the water of everlasting life has been provided for you. If a man drinks from a

sweet spring, he ought to guide others to the same sweet water.

You have asked me to speak about how to teach the Cause of God. I have spoken at length on this but I repeat that the teacher himself must be detached and devoted so that his breath may affect others. Whoever has taken a step in this field has succeeded. The doors of knowledge are opened before him, his eyes become seeing and he is assisted with the breaths of the Holy Spirit. He is guided himself and becomes the cause of guidance of others. Of course, a person sings a joyous song only when he himself is delighted and rapturous. Thus when one begins to guide others and adduces proofs, then his taste becomes sweeter and his heart more joyful.

Moreover, everything is limited except the bounty of God and this bounty descends upon man through teaching the Cause of God; then divine inspiration will assist him. It is for this reason that Christ said that whenever you wish to talk do not think about it, the Holy Spirit will inspire you. If you desire eternal honor, everlasting life and heavenly exaltation, then teach the Cause. Divine confirmations shall attend you; this has been experienced. But it calls for firmness and steadfastness. Consider the disciples of Christ and observe with what firmness they arose until the Cause of God advanced. They even sacrificed their lives for this.

In response to a question about purchasing land for a Mashriqu'l-Adhkár, He said: 'It is very good but for the present it is better to help with the Mashriqu'l-Adhkár in Chicago.'

The Master went to visit some schools and interesting places. Among them was a technical school, whose students stood respectfully in His presence. He was pleased with them and bestowed kindness upon them. He then went to see a purpose-built auditorium constructed in a circular shape with stairs and seating on three sides. Looking towards the stage, one could see the entire audience. At the other end was a large podium with a platform designed in such a way that when a lecturer spoke, his voice could reach the audience without an echo. The building was very large and had been built for special occasions and public events; it had no roof. It was much admired by the Master.

In the afternoon 'Abdu'l-Bahá spoke at a gathering of the believers on the importance of teaching the Cause:

> Every day confirmations surround some specific pursuit and every hour has a purpose decreed for it. Today, teaching the Cause of God and spreading the divine teachings are what attract heavenly assistance. It is the season of seed-sowing and of propagating the Word of God.

In the evening He spoke about the imprisonment and persecution of the Blessed Beauty and of the power and influence of the Greatest Name. As He bade farewell to the friends, His words were powerful and impressive. The hearts of the believers were in turmoil and their eyes brimming over with tears. They were saddened because it was the end of the Master's stay among them and His lovers were feeling the pain of separation from Him.[333]

Friday, October 25, 1912
[San Francisco – Sacramento]

Today we were to depart from San Francisco. The Master's residence was full to capacity with a multitude of friends. The power of the Cause, the influence of the Covenant of God and the ardor of the friends were overwhelming. What warmth and affection this gathering of true lovers generated in the early hours of the morning! When they heard the Master coming downstairs, everyone rose reverently. When they saw His feet on the stairs they raised the cry of 'Alláh-u-Abhá', their eyes fixed intently on His face, like sun-loving iguanas. Seeing the ardor and attraction of the friends, the Master was deeply moved, His face transformed. He anointed all with attar of rose and said to them:

Here I want to bid you farewell. This meeting and assemblage are very moving. This is the last draught in the goblet! How thankful we must be to the Blessed Perfection that He has brought the hearts so near to each other. This attar that I give you is but a token of the fragrance of the Abhá Paradise – the best of all fragrances. I am very sad to be separated from you and I do not know how to express it. It is not possible to give tongue to the feelings of the heart. I am greatly moved because I saw the love of Bahá'u'lláh in you, I witnessed the light of Bahá'u'lláh in your beings. I am so moved that I cannot speak. I leave it to your hearts to feel what I feel. Although I am going away from you, you have your place in my heart. I will never forget you. When I reach the Shrine of Bahá'u'lláh, I shall lay my head on the Sacred Threshold and beseech confirmation for every one of the friends. These days of our meeting were blissful days. They cannot be bettered. I met you every day and I always found the hearts attracted, the eyes turned unto the Abhá Kingdom. There cannot be better days. Do you not forget them and I shall not. I beg of God that the results of this amity shall become evident, that it shall lead to spirituality in the world, to impart guidance to all who dwell on this earth. I hope for such results from this gathering that it will not be like other gatherings of people who forget each other as soon as they disperse. It is certain that because this gathering has been a divine assemblage, it will never be forgotten and whenever recollected it will produce fresh delight. This is my wish.

He was sad as He left the house. Some of the friends begged His permission to accompany Him to Sacramento, the capital of California. Among them were Mrs Goodall, Mrs Cooper and other wonderful handmaidens of God such as Mrs Ralston, who are serving the Cause with heart and soul.

As the train passed two or three stations beyond San Francisco, it reached a bay where there are ferries on whose decks are two railroad tracks that can be joined to the tracks on the banks.

'Abdu'l-Bahá spent His time visiting with the friends and completing an article about the history of Bahá'u'lláh's time and His teachings. The train arrived in Sacramento at noon.

An elegant woman, who had previously received a promise from the Master, was at the station.³³⁴ She begged Him to grace her home with His presence. He accepted and we rode in her automobile to her home. Mrs Goodall and Mrs Cooper enthusiastically assisted the other friends accompanying the Master. En route the Master remarked to us, 'Let us consult together about staying at this lady's house.' When we arrived at her home, the Master requested that Mrs Goodall and Mrs Cooper be telephoned and asked to come. When they arrived we could see that they too did not wish Him to stay at the house. The Master then said, 'We must act according to the consultation with the friends.'

After the Master bestowed His kindness on the hostess, He said:

> You desired greatly that we should come to your house. We have come. We shall also take luncheon here. But at night we will stay in the hotel, for in each city we have stayed at hotels. Notwithstanding the supplications of the friends to stay in their homes, we have not accepted these invitations. But today we have come to your house.

The Master spoke in this vein until the woman finally agreed. He then went to the Hotel Sacramento. On the way He spoke and said, 'I desire to act always according to the counsel and wishes of the friends unless it is a very important matter which is not good for the Cause of God, then I do hold tenaciously to whatever is advantageous to the Cause.' Continuing, He said: 'The value of my conduct and fellowship is not known yet, but it shall be known later.'

A meeting was held in the evening in the salon of the hotel.³³⁵ A large number of friends and seekers were attracted to the teachings and discourses of the Master. Since it was evident that there were much interest among the audience, the friends announced there would be a public meeting the following morning in the same hall.³³⁶

Saturday, October 26, 1912
[Sacramento]

'Abdu'l-Bahá's address this morning³³⁷ concerned the influence of the Divine Manifestations, together with a brief history of the Cause and its teachings, which clearly had a powerful effect on the audience. After the talk the people came to Him in groups to express their sincere interest. Journalists wrote several complimentary articles about His exposition and the divine teachings.

The friends arranged a farewell luncheon in His honor in the hotel's dining room. The table was exquisitely decorated. More than 50 friends were there, each grateful to be present. This glorious meeting of the friends from the East and the West in the presence of 'Abdu'l-Bahá, so full of love and harmony, astonished all who witnessed it and hastened the spread of the Word of God. The manager of the hotel came with the utmost respect and courtesy to see 'Abdu'l-Bahá and was given a seat. Later he said, 'What I have seen of the majesty of this holy being is that although no one knew him in this city, yet in the course of one day and one night he has created a stir in the city and a spiritual yearning in the hearts of its people.'

Thus did the power of the Covenant of God and the grandeur of the Cause shine resplendently in the eyes of the people.

After lunch 'Abdu'l-Bahá bestowed kindness upon each of the friends, exhorting and admonishing them. Every soul offered praise and glory to the Lord of the Kingdom until after midday, when the train left for Denver. When it was time for Him to leave Sacramento, 'Abdu'l-Bahá was heard to say: 'A spiritual commotion has for the time being been created in this city. Let us see what God desires.'

The Master passed the afternoon with His companions in the train in a delightful manner. At times He told humorous stories and at others praised the scenery of the countryside, the pleasant air and the beauty and verdancy of the surroundings. Some railway employees came to Him saying that the Master had been on the same train with them when they had traveled to California earlier. The Master replied, 'Yes, it was so destined that I should see you once more on this trip. On this train there are many Greek passengers. Do you know where they are going?' They informed the Master that they were going to their country in response to a call to fight against Turkey. The Master said:

> God does not want war. These wars are against the divine will. He desires peace and love for His servants. I pray that this darkness may be dispelled and the light of the Kingdom may envelop the world. God is kind to all. We, too, should be kind to one another. We should not fight for a handful of dust. The earth is our endless tomb. Is it worthy of us to wage war and shed blood for this tomb while God has destined that we win the cities of men's hearts and bestowed upon us an eternal Kingdom? Is it worthy of us to shut our eyes to such an everlasting honor and instead make war over dust?

A salesman was selling pennants from different schools. The Master said, 'Tell him to bring the banner of universal peace if he has it. We want such a flag under which the whole world may find rest and peace.'

Several passengers who heard His discourses left their seats and drew near Him. Among those who were moved and impressed was a Jewish lady, who was very enthusiastic and interested. The Master said to her:

> It is obvious that you have a pure character, so I want you to become aware of the truth of divine matters. At the time of each Manifestation of God the people were heedless and ignorant of the truth except for a few who investigated and understood the divine words. The same is true today. So thank

God that you have been endowed with capacity and desire to investigate the truth. Know this much: that the treasury of God is replete; He will shower the same bounties and gifts on those of this day as He showered on those of previous generations. We must endeavor to gain heavenly enlightenment, to understand the mysteries of the holy books, to become the cause of guidance to others and to illumine hearts. I pray that you may strive until you are blessed with these favors.

During this conversation people were surrounding the Master, eagerly and attentively listening to His words, which they considered to be both weighty and the truth.

The same woman came to Him again in the evening, saying that she wished to be educated so as to be able to convey the teachings to others. As her words and spiritual capacity were accepted by the Master, He gave her an account of Bahá'u'lláh, explaining the reasons for the opposition to His teachings and unfolding before her the teachings of the Supreme Pen. Meanwhile, two people with socialist views requested permission to be admitted into His presence. He spoke with them on matters concerning economics, universal peace, the unity of religions and the common weal. Their happiness was boundless. As they approached the railway station they asked 'Abdu'l-Bahá to give them His address and those of the Bahá'ís so they could write to them. Their request was granted.

Sunday, October 27, 1912
[En route to Salt Lake City]

When the Master emerged from the Pullman section of the train to take tea, the Jewish lady returned, saying that she was convinced of the truth of this Cause and that she had accepted the teachings of Bahá'u'lláh.

Today the Master spoke beautifully about the existence of God and other subjects. During a conversation, an individual questioned Him about His purpose in traveling to America. The Master replied:

> I have come to America to raise the standard of universal peace and to promote the unity of mankind. My aim is to create love and harmony among the religions. But some people ask me, 'Is your country developed? Is it prosperous and has it good trees, sweet fruits, beautiful animals and swift Arabian horses?' But I speak to them of the trees of the world of existence, of the fruits of human virtues and of heavenly morals and traits and call people to the Kingdom of God.

Such explanations transformed the minds of the hearers and created love and sincerity in their hearts.

In the afternoon we changed trains for Salt Lake City. The Jewish lady was so attracted to the Cause that she tried to change her ticket so that she could accompany the Master from Denver to Chicago. However, she was unable to do so, which made her unhappy as she was to be separated from the Master. The Master then gave her the addresses of some Bahá'ís she could contact.

The Master occupied Himself for about an hour reading many letters from the friends. He later spoke about the days of Baghdád and the apathy and ignorance of the populace. He said:

> How they reproached us, but they were ignorant of the future of the Cause. They did not know that the Cause of God can make an atom a brilliant sun, bestow the magnificence of Solomon on an ant, give eternal honor to debased ones and endow the ignorant ones with divine knowledge.

We suggested that He obtain a Pullman berth but He would not permit this, saying, 'The seats are comfortable. We can lean back and sleep.'

Monday, October 28, 1912
[en route to Denver]

'Abdu'l-Bahá took tea in the dining car. Áqá 'Alí-Akbar Nakhjavání remarked that it seemed the Master was happier because He was going towards the East. The Master replied, 'Yes, my greatest happiness is to be near the Holy Shrine.' Looking out of the window, He continued: 'I love this plain because it is so much like the plain of 'Akká.'

The Master then dictated replies to His letters. In the afternoon, a vendor came by with various items for sale. The Master was looking at some ore specimens from the mines when a few children drew close and looked at Him with curiosity. He beckoned to them and asked, 'What shall I buy you?' He spoke to them with more love and kindness than the most benevolent father and bought each child various items costing about a dollar. More children ran to Him. He said, 'They, too, look poor' and also bought them a dollar's worth of items.

When they saw this, the people were interested, curious to know who this great personage was. When someone asked the Master about His aims, He gave a detailed explanation of the divine teachings. For a long period of time the passengers gathered around His seat, some standing and some sitting, listening to His sweet voice and sublime words. We had never before seen or heard the Cause taught in such a manner. It was characteristic of this journey that the Master raised the call of Yá Bahá'u'l-Abhá as the train passed through the mountains, valleys, plains and rivers.

Some Turks came to see Him in the afternoon. They said that there were more than 50 of them on their way to Constantinople in response to a call to assist their government and people. They were impressed to hear the Master's explanation of universal peace and the unity of mankind. The Master asked that tea and water be brought from the train's kitchen to another compartment where He served them tea. They thanked Him for His kindness and became attracted to His noble qualities and conduct.

'Abdu'l-Bahá reached Denver at about midnight. As the Master was very tired, He went to a hotel near the station to rest.

Tuesday, October 29, 1912
[Denver]

When the friends were informed of the Master's arrival, they eagerly hastened to Him to gaze once more on His face. He spoke to several newspaper reporters who had come to interview Him about the Cause and who recorded His statements for publication.

At a meeting He again spoke about the cardinal in California, saying:

> One day in California I saw a cardinal walking with pomp and ceremony in front of a procession. Inquiring about the occasion, I was told that a new church had been built and the cardinal was to officially open its doors to the public. I said, 'This show and ceremony of the cardinal is like that of Christ. However, there is a slight difference. Christ opened the gate of heaven; this cardinal is going to open that of a church. Christ had a crowd following Him but they were there to hurl contempt and abuse at Him. This cardinal had a crowd with him but they are there to help. Christ had a crown but it was made of thorns, while this cardinal wears a crown set with lustrous jewels. Christ had clothes but they were made of old, coarse cloth, while this man's robe is made of the finest brocade of the day. Christ spent His days in sorrow, while this cardinal's days are spent in security and comfort. Christ's home was a desert, while this cardinal's home is a splendid building, like that of a king. Christ's throne was upon a cross, while this man's place of rest is a throne of ease and comfort. The adornment of Christ's banquet was the blood of that beloved countenance, while the ornament of this man's court is the goblet of colored wine. So, this cardinal's display is similar to that of Christ, with only the slightest differences.'

Although the Master told this story humorously in several gatherings in different words, it was always a warning to the people and the cause of their awakening.

Despite the Master's exhaustion, He gave two public talks: one in the afternoon at the home of Mrs Roberts and the other in the evening at the Church of the Messiah. In both gatherings He spoke of the similarity of the principles of all religions as well as the revision of certain social laws to meet the needs of the time. His explanations were delivered so impressively that the audience was enlightened as well as extremely interested.

As He was leaving the church, 'Abdu'l-Bahá said farewell to all those who had gathered around Him. They pleaded with Him to stay a little longer but He said, 'I must return soon to the East.'

Returning to the hotel, He instructed us to pack. We hastened to obey His orders and caught the first train. With a happy face, the Master said: 'Now we are going again toward the East. We have no more work to do in America.' He did not take a sleeper on the train this evening, saying:

> It is not a matter of our reluctance to pay one dollar but of our unwillingness to be dependent on bodily comfort. We must be equal to the hardships of traveling like a soldier in the path of truth and not be slaves to bodily ease and comfort. American trains especially are very clean and comfortable and there isn't great distinction between the trains except for having sleepers.

Wednesday, October 30, 1912
[En route from Denver to Chicago]

While having tea in the morning, the Master said:

> This journey has passed pleasantly. The three days from California to Denver were comfortable and delightful. I did not believe that my weak constitution could bear the hardships and length of this journey.

At my request, 'Abdu'l-Bahá wrote an account of His travels in America to the friends in the East. This piece of writing and another article about the history and teachings of the Blessed Beauty are still among the papers of His personal belongings and have not as yet been circulated.

In the afternoon 'Abdu'l-Bahá conversed with passengers seated near Him, and after a few introductory remarks, spoke to them about the teachings. As the call was raised in the train, others clustered around Him and were delighted to hear His discourse on the unity of mankind, universal peace and divine civilization. Most of the passengers were interested and wanted to know more.

A man of Sufi inclinations saw the others listening with rapt attention, and spellbound by the words of the Master, asked to come near. The Master had him sit close by. After a few words, the man said, 'All are from God.' The Master replied:

> Yes, this is true, but one man is so exalted that others bow down before Him and He is adored by them like Christ or Moses, who called people to the oneness of divinity and who became the cause of the education of a nation, while another is so degraded that he bows down before dust and worships ants and serpents. Are these two one and the same? No, certainly not! Divine Manifestations are a different creation. All humanity is created by God but how they differ in intelligence. One is the wisest of the wise and the founder of the laws of happiness and prosperity, while the other is the most ignorant of the ignorant and a destroyer of the edifice of peace and honor.
>
> Prophets, therefore, have a station of their own. Many people crossed the desert of Sinai but it was Moses who heard the voice of God because the divine Manifestations have a spiritual power peculiar to themselves. Mighty nations existed at the time of the appearance of the divine Manifestations but they were degraded and became obliterated. But observe what a banner of unique being Christ unfurled without friend or

helper. All are from God but all have different stations. Both men and animals are from God but what a difference there is between them.

A minister visited Him. The Master advised him to abstain from dogmatic imitation and described to him the real meaning of baptism. Everyone was impressed by the Master's explanations and asked for addresses of the friends from whom they could learn more about the Bahá'í teachings.

In the evening He said, 'Let us reserve sleepers for all of us. We slept in our seats last night and that is enough. Let us not suffer any more hardship.' We suggested that we would just get a sleeper for Him but He replied, 'No, we must share equally.' Therefore, six sleepers were reserved for the night.

Thursday, October 31, 1912
[En route from Denver to Chicago]

At daybreak the train was only one station from Chicago. Here, one of the most sincere Bahá'ís, Mr [Albert] Windust, who is the editor of the *Star of the West*, boarded the train to welcome the Master and became the recipient of His kindness and favors.

The Master remarked this morning:

> It is now more than two years that I have been far from the Holy Shrine of Bahá'u'lláh. Now I must return. If God wills it, I shall make another journey in another direction according to a special program which I have already thought out, so that I can proclaim the Word of God in another way. Let us see what is the will of God. Now we are traveling from California to Chicago. Praise be to God that this journey has passed most pleasantly. At the time of leaving Haifa, I had several ailments and did not expect to cross oceans and plains with such ease and comfort and to make such a long journey.

When the train reached the station in Chicago, the friends were transported with joy on seeing the Master's face. The Master went to the Hotel Plaza where He had stayed during His first visit. People came in groups to see Him and remained in His presence until late in the afternoon. Many ministers invited Him to speak in their churches. He accepted some invitations but had to send regrets to others because of the lack of time. Some journalists were given detailed interviews about the history and teachings of this great Cause, which they took down for publication.

Some of 'Abdu'l-Bahá's comments to the friends were these:

> We went to California and a great commotion was set up in the souls. A new spirit was breathed into people. In universities, churches and gatherings people were stirred and the blessed Cause was proclaimed. Decisive proofs were advanced and the teachings of the Blessed Beauty were explained. No one took exception; rather, all offered praise and glory, even the clergymen.

Some engineers came to Him and He said to them:

> This Cause has spread all over the world. It has brought peace and tranquillity to different nations and religions, has united diverse peoples and has laid the foundation for the prosperity of mankind. Among its principles are the establishment of universal peace among nations and governments, the oneness of the world of humanity and the uniting of sects and religions under the tabernacle of unity.

Then turning towards some new inquirers, He said:

> Behold the creative power of Bahá'u'lláh! He brought us from the most remote countries of the East and acquainted us with you. How He has connected our hearts and attracted our spirits to each other and has drawn all under the banner of

peace and tranquillity! See how He has delivered us from religious, political, national and racial prejudices and saved us from the gloom of superstitions. Behold what a power this is! Had all the powers of the earth combined they could not have joined the hearts in such a manner but Bahá'u'lláh has joined all with a single word. Such is the power of Bahá'u'lláh! We must all turn toward the Abhá Kingdom and pray for confirmation and help so that His aid and assistance can support us from all sides and that we may become the cause of proclaiming the Word of God and of bringing peace and salvation to the people of the world. We must render service to the Kingdom of God so that divine grace may surround all and the favors of Bahá'u'lláh may attain full expression.

To another group of the friends He said:

This is the third time that I am in Chicago. It is now your turn to come and visit the Holy Shrine. Praise be to God that divine grace has encircled you! He has chosen you from among His creation and made you favorites of His court. How many are the divines who have called on God in their churches saying, 'O our Lord! O our Lord!' Yet when their Lord appeared they remained veiled. You were neither ministers nor monks and you have attained this grace. This is what Christ meant when He said, 'Many are called but few are chosen' [Matt. 20:16; 22:14]. Similarly, He said, 'The people are entering the Kingdom from all directions but the sons of the Kingdom are leaving it.'[338] Although from distant lands, you have become enlightened whereas most of the countrymen and neighbors of Bahá'u'lláh have remained veiled. Be thankful unto God!

'Abdu'l-Bahá delivered a public address in the hotel's salon, giving decisive proofs of the greatness and power of the Cause.[339] As a result, many people learned of the divine teachings and were attracted to the fragrances of God. After dinner Mrs Waite sat at the piano and sang a song she had written in praise of the Beauty of the Covenant.

Friday, November 1, 1912
[Chicago]

Among those visiting 'Abdu'l-Bahá for the first time was a man from Russia. When he was admitted into the Master's room he began to complain about Russia. The Master said to him:

> Do not speak ill of Russia. Render good to friend and foe alike. Say that you are one with all. Be a true well-wisher of people. Give up your evil thoughts and pray for all. Be at peace and make peace with all. Do not express hatred or resentment toward anyone. Be a proclaimer of peace and say, 'Now I feel no enmity toward anyone.' Praise all and be mindful of the story of Christ. When everyone expressed disgust on seeing the body of a dead dog, Christ said, 'What white teeth it has!'

The visitor was so overwhelmed that he cried out, 'Today I have found the way to salvation and safety.' The Master replied, 'If you follow these teachings you will see things greater than this.'

A minister came to see 'Abdu'l-Bahá. The Master spoke with him about the sanctity of God. When a crowd had gathered, the Master went into the hall of the hotel and continued His conversation with the minister on the same subject, explaining that God's holiness is beyond imagination or likeness. Afterwards, after repeated invitations from a prominent man, the Master went to a private museum. This man had collected in a magnificent building specimens of antique art, pictures, drawings and other relics of past craftsmanship. When the Master returned to the hotel, He said: 'This man took us to his house to show pictures and other objects. I was greatly surprised to find that people go to view things which are nothing more than children's toys but they fail to examine this divine system.'

Dr Milburn, the minister of the Congregational Church, with his wife and others came to see the Master with the utmost humility. 'Abdu'l-Bahá said: 'I have not forgotten our previous meeting or your talk in the church. There is not a shadow of a doubt that it was inspired by the Holy Spirit. It will remain for eternity in the history of this Cause.' He then told them about the zeal and enthusiasm of the friends in California. Mrs Milburn begged Him to come to their summer home. He replied, 'It is impossible because we must soon return to the East.'

On seeing their sincerity and interest, the Master said:

> Chicago has great capacity. I hope that the banner of the unity of mankind will be unfurled in this city and that the believers here will be united and be as the different flowers of one divine garden and become the adornment of the world of humanity, so that the dormant pulse of this country will beat vigorously.

'Abdu'l-Bahá spoke about receiving assistance in the Cause of God:

> My health was absolutely not up to traveling but the assistance of the Blessed Beauty helped me. All affairs advance with His aid. Without His aid, all would come to naught. When I left Syria I was ill and weak and also was not used to traveling. All were astonished. But now I am in Chicago and have other journeys ahead of me. You must continue to follow these teachings and promote universal peace and the unity of mankind so that misfortunes and calamities such as the Balkan disaster may cease and wars and massacres disappear completely. Observe: it is the children who are orphaned and families which are destroyed. The flames of the fire of war are day by day becoming more intense. You must become the cause of quenching this fire so that the light of love may enlighten the world.

The Master addressed some socialists, saying:

Bahá'u'lláh delivered us from all prejudices. It is prejudice that destroys the world. Every enmity, war, misunderstanding and suffering that has ever occurred in this world has been from either religious, patriotic, racial or political prejudice. Prejudice is contemptible and injurious in whatever form it may be. When these prejudices are removed from the world then will the world of humanity find salvation. We are striving for this mighty purpose. Twenty thousand persons have been sacrificed for this great Cause. With the utmost meekness they were martyred in order that these prejudices be eliminated and so that brotherhood and unity would be established. Our endeavors and self-sacrifice have been in order to unite diverse nationalities and to bring the various denominations under the shade of the one Word. Some may speak while others may even labor for good causes but they do so to obtain personal benefits and to gain a name for themselves. Even these works are of a limited nature. But Bahá'ís strive day and night for the public weal and in order to render service to humanity and to gain eternal honor.

With a merry twinkle in His eyes, He continued:

If the socialists succeed they would seize the world's wealth and then divide it. But the Bahá'ís sacrifice their lives and properties. Socialist principles would annul class differences and distinctions and thus cause disorder in the system. But Bahá'u'lláh has laid down a great foundation for a system which, although it advocates the oneness of humanity and upholds the common weal, will preserve the various ranks. Every rank should perform its duties. Rights should be equal and all are the servants of one kind God. He who performs righteous acts is nearer to God and he whose efforts are more virtuous is more bountifully confirmed.

Turning towards the ladies He said with a smile:

I have said in America and Europe that there is only the question of votes in which women have been held back and claim equality with men. In California they even have this right. In all other respects it is men who must demand equality of rights. How many men in Europe and America work from morning until evening and whatever they save is spent on adornments and jewelry and colorful clothes and the latest fashions for their wives who spend their time in pleasure and enjoyment? In reality, these poor men are servants of their wives.

Once a respectable gentleman came with his wife to see me. A little dust had settled on the wife's shoes. She instantly asked her husband to clean them. As the poor man was cleaning her shoes he glanced at me. I said, 'Madam! Do you also clean your husband's shoes?' She replied that she cleaned his clothes. I said, 'No, that is not equality. You, too, must clean his shoes.' Now then, it would be better if you occasionally stand up for the rights of men.[340]

One time an American woman had gone on a long trip to Europe, all in great comfort, while her poor husband was back in America, working hard and sending his earnings to her. This is the case with most of the wealthy and middle classes of the West, whereas there must be equality. A condition must be realized in which the man and woman sacrifice their rights for each other, serve each other with heart and soul and not through force and violence. This condition cannot be realized except through the power of faith. Hearts must be attracted to the divine fragrances so that each one prefers the other to himself and does not consider himself above the other.

A Parsi Bahá'í came to 'Akká to ask me to make honorable mention of his deceased wife. He was lamenting piteously saying, 'That woman worked hard for forty years in my home but as I had no wealth she never had any comfort.' To put it briefly, spiritual susceptibilities must reach this stage, they must become heavenly. Physical susceptibilities are of an animal nature and it is heavenly enlightenment which is worthy of man.

Such detailed explanations were given daily. They were so numerous that if collected in a book, it would be a volume of immense size.

A public meeting was held in the evening at the home of Mrs True.[341] The Master delivered an impressive address concerning the majesty of the Manifestations of the Pre-Existent Beauty, the opposition of the people of the world and the final victory and influence of the Cause and the Covenant of God.

Saturday, November 2, 1912
[Chicago]

Great numbers of people came to see the Master and each in turn was ushered into His private room. Most of the friends, both old and new, brought their children to be blessed by Him. He embraced each of them with the utmost kindness, anointed them with some attar of rose and gave them fruit, sweets and flowers.

When the crowd became too large He went to the floor below His in the hotel and spoke to the guests about the aims and intentions of the Manifestations of God:

> The divine religions were revealed for love and amity and have brought about harmony among the different peoples and nations. But as time passed dogmas and imitations crept in and caused differences and enmity. Praise be to God that now the doors of the Kingdom are open, the sun of truth is resplendent and casting its rays upon all, the cloud of mercy is bestowing the utmost favors and the sea of bounty is surging. Know then the value of this bestowal and the worth of these days.

He was invited to have lunch at the home of Mrs Russell. Among the guests were some of Dr [Susan] Moody's relatives. Addressing them 'Abdu'l-Bahá said:

> Behold how the power of Bahá'u'lláh has connected the hearts and has joined the East and the West. When Dr Moody first went to Ṭihrán she did not know the Persians and they, too, did not know her at all. But the moment they heard of her intended journey from America to Persia, hundreds prepared to receive her with utmost love. With great esteem they welcomed her in Ṭihrán. All the friends are now like brothers and sisters to her – even more than that and kinder. She is well-known as a Bahá'í in Ṭihrán and is respected and loved within and without the community.

In the evening the Master gave an impressive talk at a gathering of blacks. Many white people were also present. He spoke on love and brotherhood among the different races and nationalities. He talked about Isfandíyár, the black servant of the Blessed Beauty, referring to his faithfulness, obedience and goodness of heart, saying: 'If a believer in God prays for piety, it does not matter whether he is robed in black or white.' Both black and white were affected by His words and came one after the other to shake His hand and express their gratitude for His blessings.

He then went to Mrs True's home where the friends had gathered for consultation. They asked Him about the duties of a board of consultation. He said:

> The first duty of the members is to be in harmony and unity among themselves, for this will bear good results. If there is no unity or – God forbid! – if it becomes the cause of differences, then of course its non-existence is better than its existence. If Assemblies of consultation or the general meetings of the friends become the cause of ill feelings, they must be abandoned.
>
> How pleased I was with the believers in California who said, 'We do not want any board of consultation because it would lead to striving for leadership and power and will become the cause of differences. Now, praise be to God!, we are

serving as much as we can, having no other thought than the diffusion of the divine fragrances.'

Then, when the unity of the members has been achieved, their second duty is to recite verses and prayers in a state of contriteness and spiritual awareness so that they will feel themselves to be in the presence of God.

Third, their thoughts and discussions must be directed to the teaching of the Cause of God in all areas and regions. They must arise with all their strength for this great matter and make the necessary arrangements and prepare for the teaching of the Cause.

Fourth, they must be occupied and concerned with rendering help to the poor, the needy and the sick.

Fifth, they must improve and administer the affairs of the believers and other matters.

The Master spoke on similar topics and the meeting concluded in an extraordinary spirit of happiness among the friends.

Sunday, November 3, 1912
[Chicago]

Today was the last day of 'Abdu'l-Bahá's stay in Chicago. He was invited to speak at four gatherings. In each meeting the power of His utterances and His explanations produced great interest and enthusiasm in the audience.

In the morning, in the hotel's main hall, the Master encouraged the friends and others to be united and to create within themselves the utmost love and harmony. He ended His talk with praise and gratitude for the assistance of the Abhá Kingdom and left for one of the churches.

The pastor of the church introduced the Master in glowing terms and was full of praise and admiration. He referred to Him as the Persian apostle and Prophet of the East and described His 40 years of imprisonment and hardship, His freedom, His travels to Europe and America, His addresses in churches and large gatherings in both continents and lastly his own conviction of the value of 'Abdu'l-Bahá's explanations and talks.

'Abdu'l-Bahá stood and put forward decisive proofs and arguments, describing the appearance of the Manifestations of God, the veils and opposition of the people, the Tablets of Bahá'u'lláh to the kings and the influence of the Cause of God among the people. His words were so penetrating that every soul was stirred and informed of the circumstances prevailing in this day of the Manifestation.

There was a meeting in the afternoon at the Congregational Church. Its pastor, Dr Milburn, expressed his great joy to the Master for blessing and honoring the church with a second visit. 'Abdu'l-Bahá delivered a magnificent address on the greatness of this age, the necessity of achieving the oneness of humanity, universal peace, the oneness of creation, and concluding with explanations of the teachings of Bahá'u'lláh. His address was delivered with such majesty and power that all hearts were quickened with the love of humanity and became lovers of peace and harmony, abandoning prejudice and disunity. After the talk, people rushed to the stage and surrounded the Master as He left the pulpit for His automobile, supplicating His spiritual blessings and assistance.

From there He went to Dr Milburn's home where a number of people met Him. Among them was an editor who asked that a message from the Master be given through his journal to the whole of humanity. The Master's message was this:

> Praise be to God that the centuries of darkness have passed and the age of enlightenment has arrived!
>
> Praise be to God that all traces of superstition and imitation have vanished and the minds and thoughts of men have broadened, inventions have gained new life, the arts and sciences have been revived, new plans have been evolved, discoveries have increased, all things have been revitalized, the rulings that

regulate the world have been renewed! Thus it was necessary that the laws of God also be changed and the reality of divine religions be renewed, for divine teachings had been forgotten and there was nothing left but dogmatic imitation. The foundation of the divine religions is one and that is the truth which generates love and affection and is the cause of the unity of mankind. But imitations vary and they are the cause of disagreements and are the destroyers of spiritual foundations.

Glad tidings, glad tidings, that the Sun of Truth has shed its radiance!

Glad tidings, glad tidings, that the heavenly light has encompassed all regions!

Glad tidings, glad tidings, that the gates of the Kingdom have been opened!

Glad tidings, glad tidings, that the melody of the Supreme Concourse has been raised.

Glad tidings, glad tidings, that the breaths of the Holy Spirit are giving life and the world of humanity is reborn!

Awake, O people of the world, awake! Give heed, O peoples and nations, give heed! Destroy the root of conflict and strife; abandon imitations and prejudices which lead to cruelty, so that you may acknowledge the Truth and the light of the oneness of humanity may shine brilliant and manifest as the sun; the standard of universal peace be hoisted; perfect love and harmony may reign among the races, religions and nations; and the world of man may find peace and acquire a divine image and likeness. This is my message.

That night he went from there to the home of Mrs Davies where, through the generosity of whose daughter a splendid banquet had been arranged for the Nineteen Day Feast. Several people visited the Master on the second floor of the house, among them some engineers who wanted His comments about the House of Worship. The Master answered:

The Mashriqu'l-Adhkár is circular in shape. It has nine paths, nine gardens, nine pools with fountains and nine gates. Each path will lead to a center such as an orphanage, a hospital, a school, a university and other buildings that are dependencies of the Mashriqu'l-Adhkár. In the building there will be an organ, balconies and a rostrum especially for prayers and devotional programs but addresses may be given there as well.[342]

Later the Master spoke of the importance of the House of Justice and the significance of the laws of this Dispensation, stating that each is a complete and powerful proof for the unity of the peoples of the world.

He then went downstairs for a public meeting and gave a farewell address to the believers in which He described the harmfulness of imitations and superstitions.

'Imitations', He said, 'destroy the edifice of human prosperity and conflict with the religion of God. Beware lest you occupy yourselves with such superstitions.'

It is not possible to describe the impact on the minds, the exhilaration of the spirits and delight of the souls. When His automobile left, everyone wept and expressed their sorrow at their separation from their beloved.

Monday, November 4, 1912
[Chicago – Cincinnati]

The Master left for Cincinnati in the morning. At the request of the friends there who longed for a glimpse of His face, the Master sent a telegram informing them that He would stay with them one night in order to visit the believers. At the Chicago train station the friends of God, both men and women, wept as they saw their Master depart. It was a grand occasion and a testimony to the greatness of the Cause of God and the influence of His Covenant. Well-respected people of the West have been attracted to the Beloved of the East. They hovered like moths around the divine lamp and wept at their friend's departure. Among those who accompanied 'Abdu'l-Bahá to the next station was Mrs True with whom the Master spoke about the Tarbíyat Schools in Ṭihrán.[343]

In the evening Cincinnati was blessed by the arrival of the Master. With eagerness and excitement, the believers anxiously awaited a glimpse of His face. Mrs Farmer and other believers had arranged a public meeting at the Grand Hotel after which a beautiful banquet was given. Arriving at the hotel, 'Abdu'l-Bahá first went to the hall where some five hundred had assembled to hear Him. He spoke about the sovereignty and endless bounties of God and concluded with explanations of the teachings of Bahá'u'lláh from the holy writings. His words captivated the hearts of His listeners.

The Master then went into the dining room of the hotel where He was delighted to see the beaming faces of the friends, the brightness of the electric lights, the table decorated with colorful flowers and the hearts immersed in the love of God. More than 50 people were seated around the table. The Master sat at the head of the table while the Persian friends sat nearby. In great happiness 'Abdu'l-Bahá spoke these heavenly words:

> It is an excellent table for we have assembled here through the love of Bahá'u'lláh. Tonight I am exceedingly happy to be with you. You must be very happy and in a prayerful attitude for no better meeting could be held. The holding of meetings at which people from the East come to the far West and sit together with you with such love and affection was impossible but through His penetrative power Bahá'u'lláh has made this easy and has joined the East and the West. Would that the friends of Persia were here now and could see this!

When the conversation turned to Los Angeles, the Master spoke about Mr Chase and the nobility of his spirit. He chanted a prayer in life-giving strains:

O Thou kind Lord, we render thanks unto Thee that Thou has brought us from the farthest lands of the East to the most distant lands of the West and gathered us at this table arrayed with the finest, most diverse, sweetest and most delicious material foods. We thank Thee especially for the presence of those who have turned toward the Kingdom of Thy favor and have fixed their eyes upon the horizon of Thy kindness.

O Lord! These souls have turned toward Thee, they desire Thy pleasure and are grateful for Thy blessings. They walk in the ways of Thy will.

O Lord! Grant them heavenly food; enable them to partake of the Lord's supper. Exalt this noble lady in Thy Kingdom, bestow everlasting life upon her and grant her Thine eternal favor.[344] As Thou hast given us these earthly blessings so, too, give us heavenly food. Bestow upon us Thine everlasting grace. Strengthen us to arise in praise and gratitude to Thee that we may be aided and assisted to do that which beseems Thy glorification.

Thou art the Mighty, the Generous, the Compassionate.

About 40 of the friends stayed at the hotel rather than return to their homes that night.

Tuesday, November 5, 1912
[Cincinnati – Washington DC]

Early in the morning 'Abdu'l-Bahá called His ardent lovers to Him and bestowed kindness on everyone. Several representatives of the press came to see Him and recorded His words about the history of the Cause and the teachings of the Abhá Beauty. Their reports appeared in various newspapers and publications.

Although the Master had planned to leave in the morning, the crowd of seekers and the attraction of the friends caused Him to prolong His stay until noon. Today He spoke about the Universal House of Justice and the International Parliament of man, where representatives from all the parliaments of the world will resolve conflicts between nations, such as that in the Balkans. This organization will cure the chronic diseases of the nations.[345]

He then gave an account of how Constantine embraced Christianity and came under the shelter of Christ. He said, 'Although he wore a crown as a monarch, yet he had to offer his all to the Son of Mary.' He spoke at length on such topics until He was tired. Then the friends invited Him for a drive through the public parks.

At noon the Master left for Washington DC. At the time of departure, the friends were happy as they recalled their visit and reunion with Him but wept because of His departure from their midst. These opposites, happiness and sorrow, like heat and cold, were both felt and seen.

A few stations beyond Cincinnati, a doctor sitting near the Master asked permission to speak with Him and inquired about the object of His journey. The Master said to the doctor:

> My aim is to create harmony and concord among the different groups and to eradicate prejudice, hatred and enmity so that the peoples and nations of the world may become brothers and well-wishers of mankind and not engage in wars and massacres, and that catastrophes such as that in the Balkans with their bloodshed and annihilation of families may not occur again. Until such events cease, humanity will find no rest, the tabernacle of universal peace will not be raised and the oneness of the world of man will not be realized. We are all the flock of God, members of the same human race and the creatures of one Creator. God is kind to all and His bounties are equally bestowed upon all.
>
> Sixty years ago Bahá'u'lláh instituted the foundations of such teachings in Persia. He advocated the establishment of universal peace and the oneness of humanity. The Sháh of Persia and the Sultán of Turkey threw us into prison. They killed twenty thousand of us hoping that this Cause would be annihilated and that these teachings of Bahá'u'lláh would be

forgotten. But in spite of these obstacles the religion of Bahá'u'lláh progressed day by day. Then there was a revolution and the constitution was established and I was set free.[346] Leaving the prison of 'Akká, I traveled to countries in Africa, Europe and America, called people to these blessed teachings and invited nations and religions to the oneness of the foundation of all religions and the abandonment of prejudices, wars, dogmatic imitations and superstitions.

The doctor was delighted and very impressed by the Master's words and thanked Him sincerely. The Master replied:

> I, too, am very pleased to make your acquaintance. I, a Persian, am delighted to meet an eminent Westerner like you in utmost harmony and fellowship. This meeting of ours is an example of the joining of the East and the West.

In the afternoon Washington was again blessed by the arrival of the Master. The friends eagerly hastened to meet Him and accompanied Him to a house rented especially for Him. In the evening great numbers of friends gathered around Him like moths around a brilliant candle. The Master spoke about His journey to California, the influence of the Word of God and the devotion of the friends to the Abhá Beauty.

Wednesday, November 6, 1912
[Washington DC]

In the morning 'Abdu'l-Bahá addressed an assemblage of friends concerning the spread of the Cause of God in both the East and the West and the union of the various sects and denominations under the shadow of the Word of God. He stated:

> Soon after the ascension of the Blessed Beauty I wrote:

> Erelong ye shall see the banner of the Covenant
> Hoisted over the world.

And again:

> Shed splendors on the East,
> In the West scatter perfumes,
> Invest the Slav with life.
> Carry light unto the world.[347]

Some of the ignorant scorned us, saying, 'How can the East and the West be illumined with the light of the Cause and the whole world be perfumed by the sweet fragrance of the Word of God?' Now behold how this great union has come about and how the hearts of the people of the East and the West have been enlightened with this manifest light. The Blessed Tree has taken firm root in the earth and the signs of its greatness have encompassed all regions.

He then gave an account of the appearance of the Manifestations of God. 'Outwardly', He said,

> the holy Manifestations of God were completely humiliated and despised. They were mocked by all. But in a short space of time the penetrative influence of their words filled the hearts and the sun of their greatness and majesty illumined the world.

As news of the situation in the Balkans reached us, the tenor of the Master's speech inclined towards explanations of the verses of the Manifest Book.[348] At a public meeting at Mrs Parsons's home, He held the book in His hands and explained Bahá'u'lláh's admonition to Sulṭán 'Abdu'l-'Azíz[349] and the prophecies about the change of circumstances in Adrianople, asserting that these prophecies were certain to be fulfilled. He also explained the prophecies about the change of circumstances in Ṭihrán and the uprising of its inhabitants, saying that the fulfillment of those prophecies was a clear proof of the vastness of knowledge and the penetrating influence of the Word of God.[350]

In the evening He spoke on the spread of the Cause of God despite imprisonment by the enemies and the supremacy of the divine Word notwithstanding endless afflictions and troubles. He said:

> Bahá'u'lláh, without earthly power and worldly means, laid the foundations for eternal glory and promoted divine teachings. Notwithstanding that all earthly powers and antagonistic peoples and religions arose against Him in order to thwart His efforts and executed twenty thousand of His followers, yet with divine power and heavenly majesty He made His Cause to be all-conquering and His blessed Word to have pervasive influence. And today we see diverse groups from different countries and of various nationalities have found sincere love and true unity within the refuge of His laws and teachings.[351]

Thursday, November 7, 1912
[Washington DC]

Each hour people came to receive bounties from 'Abdu'l-Bahá's presence. The Master answered many important questions.[352]

He had lunch at Mrs Parsons's home. At the table, He joyfully offered thanks for the confirmations and assistance of the Abhá Kingdom. As well giving interviews at Mrs Parsons's home, He also spoke to a large gathering at the Universalist Church[353]. On behalf of the congregation the pastor thanked the Master for coming and then reminded the audience about the importance of knowing something about all religions and abandoning prejudice, which would broaden their horizons. He then gave an account of the Cause, how it had become the target for the persecution and sacrifice of so many souls in its path and concluded by reading a few passages from the Book of Isaiah. The audience was thus prepared to hear the Master's discourse.

The Master rose and delivered an impressive address, at the beginning of which He said:

> In truth, I have found much love and justice in the people of America. I have observed that they have complete freedom of thought in all matters, which is deserving of praise. So I am greatly pleased with the pastor and thank him for his expression of love for us. The leaders of religions must be like this so that people may become broad-minded. They must be kind to all nationalities for God is kind to all and His love is infinite. Therefore, the love of His servants must also be universal and without limitation.

In His address He dealt with brotherhood and the oneness of humanity, explaining some of the teachings and principles of Bahá'u'lláh. The audience was so impressed and moved that the pastor again came to the pulpit to express thanks and praise on their behalf. He was honored that this was the second occasion on which the Master had given an address in the church. He said that the Master's words would become the cause of honor and happiness to humanity, especially since we are all sheep of God's flock, each other's brothers, and that God is our real shepherd and protector. The pastor then requested a prayer which the Beloved recited in Persian.

One by one members of the audience came to shake the Master's hand, begging for His assistance and blessings.

Such meetings in the churches of Washington and the influence and impact of the Master's talks have excited envy in the hearts of certain ministers who have neither interviewed nor heard Him and they distributed leaflets full of calumny and criticism to the people coming out of the churches.

Friday, November 8, 1912
[Washington DC]

'Abdu'l-Bahá spoke in the morning to a gathering of the friends:³⁵⁴

> I am very happy to have met you. I hope that through the favors of the Blessed Beauty you shall become the instruments for the glorification of the divine Cause and the spread of the Word of God so that this city may take precedence over all the other cities of America. As this city is the capital of America, so shall it, God willing, become the center of divine signs. When you arise to teach the Cause of God it will soon be firmly established and will spread because this city has capacity, as there is resistance and some ministers are opposing the Cause. It has been established by experience that when the cry of opposition is raised by leaders of religion the Cause of God gains strength. I always beg assistance for you and my heart is ever with you. You must trust in the favors of the Blessed Beauty which can change a gnat into a phoenix, a drop into an ocean, a stone into a diamond and an atom into a world-illuminating sun. You must not look to your own capacities but to the bounties of the Abhá Kingdom.

In the afternoon 'Abdu'l-Bahá took a stroll along the boulevard and remarked that 'The city of Washington is better planned and laid out than the other cities of America.' In His view the plan of this city was very pleasing because in other cities the buildings were too high and the population too congested. The buildings in Washington were mostly of four to five stories and its boulevards straight, well-proportioned and exquisitely landscaped. Each house has a front yard with flowers and bushes so that in the springtime the entire city becomes like a beautiful garden. All of the squares there have beautiful parks and gardens. In contrast, some of the streets and boulevards of New York and Chicago, with their tall buildings looming like steep mountain peaks, seem like narrow gorges or deep mountain passes and the crowd of humanity like the files of an army. It is difficult to pass through some of those streets either on foot or in a vehicle.

To resume. The Master's address at the Jewish synagogue in Washington created a commotion among the listeners and the force of His argument caused the hearts of many to throb. On His arrival He said:

> I shall repeat the same subjects I spoke on in the Jewish synagogue of San Francisco, and I shall illustrate more clearly the evidences to prove the reality of Christ and the strength and truth of Islam. It is therefore not necessary to repeat them here.[355]

Such was the force of His explanations that both friends and seekers felt that some might take exception and object. 'If the Jews will not speak,' they said, 'the Christians, at least, will not remain silent.' Some of the Jews sitting near the pulpit actually made signs to the interpreter that the time was over. But the Master ignored this and went on to give detailed, decisive proofs and plain arguments to prove the truth of Christianity and Islam.

After the address, the chairman of the meeting, a person of much integrity and one of the fair-minded rabbis, came to the pulpit to thank the Master for His admonitions and exhortations. He then asked the audience not to become agitated or excited. 'We must not', he said, 'be perplexed at what goes against our own convictions and beliefs. Rather, we must, with perfect composure and sincerity, investigate the truth so that we may discover the reality of everything.'

In brief, the firmness and courage of 'Abdu'l-Bahá and the force of His argument were noted by everyone both inside and outside the synagogue.

Saturday, November 9, 1912
[Washington DC]

The Master called on the Jewish rabbi, showered him with kindness and countless blessings, and spoke to him regarding peace and harmony among the Jews, Christians and Muslims as well as the need for respect for the leaders of each other's religions. The Master said:

> Whenever these people mention each other's leaders with due reverence then all sufferings and contentions shall cease and instead of hatred there will be love and instead of enmity and disunity there will be harmony and affection. This is my purpose.

The Master continued to speak in this vein with the rabbi, who left His presence with humility and respect.

Several distinguished persons visited the Master on the second floor of Mrs Parsons's home, to whom He spoke about various spiritual and important issues. The eternal bounties poured forth like refreshing rain, beautifying the gardens of the hearts and causing the world of the spirit to triumph and to overflow with glad tidings.[356]

In the evening the band of lovers observed the Feast of the Covenant with a magnificent banquet in one of the city's largest halls. The sounds of their congratulations and praises created a festive and beautiful celebration. Large tables were arranged in the center of the hall in the shape of the figure nine. At the head of the tables was the Master's chair, on two sides were the chairs of His companions, while the remaining chairs were occupied by the friends. The tables were decorated with flowers and other ornaments and the doors and walls were decorated with screens, flags, festoons, lanterns and banners. Above all of these was the symbol of the Greatest Name. More than three hundred guests were present, apart from those serving as hosts. Almost everyone at the banquet was in formal attire and their attention focused on the Master.

As soon as the Master arrived they all sang with one voice a song in praise of 'Abdu'l-Bahá. When He had taken His seat, Mr Remey stood in the center of the hall facing the Master and devoutly read a paper, afterwards congratulating the Master on behalf of the friends and assuring Him of their obedience and renunciation of the world. Before eating 'Abdu'l-Bahá rose and recited the following prayer:

> He is God! O Lord! We are assembled here in the utmost love and are turned toward Thy Kingdom. We seek none other but Thee and desire not but Thy good pleasure.
>
> O Lord! Make this food heavenly and make those assembled here of the hosts of Thy Supreme Concourse so that they may become life-giving and the cause of the enlightenment of the world of man, that they may arise to guide all the peoples of the world.
>
> Thou art the All-Powerful, the Almighty, the Forgiving and the Kind.

He then invited everyone to begin their dinner, saying, 'Tonight I myself wish to serve the friends of God.' He therefore made several rounds, distributing sweets and flowers and anointing each person with attar of rose. When the Master completed one round, the friends sang songs of praise to the accompaniment of the piano. After supper, the Master rose and spoke about the preeminence and distinction of the gatherings of the friends of God, saying that the actions and services of the people of Bahá would be everlasting.[357] This gave further encouragement to the friends to burst enthusiastically into wonderful songs and melodies, giving renewed joy to the hearts and to the souls a new delight. This was one of those great gatherings that demonstrate the majesty and power of the Center of the Covenant.

The Master then went into another room where a number of

people were granted private interviews. Among them was a gentleman who had lost both legs in a railway collision and wore artificial limbs. To him the Master said:

> Mutilation of the body brings no harm to the soul. This is one of the proofs of the immortality of the soul, for death consists of the change and dispersion of the members and elements of the body. As a bodily change does not bring about change in the soul, it is evident that the soul is unchanging and imperishable.

When the Consul General of Turkey and others came to see Him, 'Abdu'l-Bahá spoke to them about the Universal House of Justice.[358]

Sunday, November 10, 1912
[Washington DC]

This was the last day of the Master's stay in Washington. An enthusiastic crowd assembled early at His residence. His talk covered various subjects. He encouraged the friends by assuring them that divine assistance and confirmations would descend upon them; then He counseled them to show firmness in the Cause of God. He also mentioned the book written by Mírzá Abu'l-Faḍl in answer to the objections of a Christian minister.[359]

The friends and seekers continued to come to see Him until noon, at which time Mrs Parsons invited a number of them to dine with Him. Private interviews were granted in the afternoon on the second floor. He responded to questions about the interpretation of dreams, firmness and steadfastness in the Cause of God, the futility of opposition, the teachings of the Abhá Beauty, economic issues and so on.

The Master then came downstairs to a public meeting where He spoke on the oneness of the Divine Essence.[360] At the close of His address, He bade everyone farewell.

A spirit of longing spread over the audience and with the utmost humility and reverence they begged His assistance and blessings. The fire of love blazed within them. After the meeting several people pleaded with Him to grant them private interviews. They were overjoyed when permission to ask a few questions was given. Some brought their children to receive His blessings.

In the evening a meeting attended by both blacks and whites was held at the home of Mr and Mrs Hannen.[361] As this was the last night of His stay, the meeting had a significance of its own and more than ever the hearts were filled with enthusiasm. When the Master arrived He was so tired that He went upstairs to rest for a brief time. When He heard the audience's restlessness and impatience, He allowed them to come to Him group by group. They came, kissed His hand and requested His assistance and blessings. Even though He was tired, each person received His kindness and blessings. He counseled them to be firm in the Cause of God and to hold fast to the mantle of love and union.

When all these people concluded their visit, grateful for His bestowals, the Master came downstairs and spoke about unity and amity between the blacks and whites, expressing His happiness at seeing both races present in the meeting. During His talk He mentioned the sincerity, honesty and services of Isfandíyár, the black servant of Bahá'u'lláh.

He took supper with a number of the friends. The host and hostess, Mr and Mrs Hannen, were overjoyed beyond measure because their services were accepted by 'Abdu'l-Bahá and He bestowed upon them His special favors.[362]

Monday, November 11, 1912
[Washington DC – Baltimore]

The believers were so eager to see 'Abdu'l-Bahá that they began to arrive at His residence from early morning. Their hearts were burning with the fire of separation and each craved His assistance and bestowals.

The believers had already assembled when 'Abdu'l-Bahá arrived at the railway station at 9:00 a.m. To the amazement of onlookers, they gathered around Him, their hearts filled with sorrow and anguish. This happened in every city of America when 'Abdu'l-Bahá arrived and departed. Onlookers were at a loss to understand how a person from the East in Iranian dress had won the veneration and respect of the men and women of America.[363]

Some of the friends accompanied the Master to Baltimore where He stayed at a hotel. Among the many visitors who came to see Him was a newspaper reporter who was given a detailed discourse on universal peace and the ability of the American people and government to enforce it. The Master's words were noted down for publication.

Later, 'Abdu'l-Bahá spoke at the Unitarian Church of Baltimore regarding the oneness of the world of man, the immutability of the principles of the divine religions and the changing of the social laws according to the demands of the time.

When 'Abdu'l-Bahá left the church He went to lunch at the home of Mr [Howard] and Mrs [Hebe] Struven.[364] The Baltimore believers were overjoyed to see their Master. In one of His talks to the friends He said:

> Praise be to God! I have spent time with you in utmost happiness. I am very pleased with you and will not forget you. I pray that you may daily become more illumined and more spiritual. When I reach the Holy Land, I shall lay my head on the threshold of the Blessed Shrine and, weeping, I shall supplicate on your behalf for assistance and heavenly favors, eternal honor and everlasting joy.

The Master and the friends then left for the station in two automobiles. On the way 'Abdu'l-Bahá embraced Mr Struven as a kind father embraces a son and with the utmost kindness thanked him for his many services to the Cause in such glowing terms that the others were astonished.[365]

A message from the friends in Philadelphia was relayed to 'Abdu'l-Bahá expressing their hope and expectation that since it was on His way, He might be able stop in their city. He replied, 'We have been there once. Now we have neither time nor possibility. Send them a telegram saying that they may come to the station so that we can meet for a few minutes.'

At 6:00 p.m. when the train reached the station, the friends, both men and women, were on the platform. When the train stopped, they immediately rushed towards the Master's seat and fell upon His feet, fulfilling their hearts' desire. With great eagerness and enthusiasm, many of them accompanied the Master to the next station, honored to be in His presence. They begged His assistance that they might render service to the Cause of God and then, weeping, left Him. When the other passengers saw these 30 or so friends from Philadelphia hovering near the Master with such heartfelt emotions, their curiosity to know more was aroused. Fascinated by His majesty and grandeur, they surrounded the Master to hear explanations of the divine teachings. They were transformed and attracted to the teachings and asked for the addresses of the friends and assemblies. Teaching the Cause of the God and guiding the people along the road gives so much joy and excitement that there are no words to describe it.

At about 1:00 a.m. the city of New York was once more graced with the presence of 'Abdu'l-Bahá. He stayed at the same house which had previously been rented at His instruction. Thus for the second time this house became the court of the Center of the Covenant and the threshold of bounty and favor. The owners of the house and their relatives had joined the group of sincere and devoted believers and were counted among the lovers of 'Abdu'l-Bahá.[366]

Tuesday, November 12, 1912
[New York]

Early in the morning, Mrs Champney, the owner of the house, and her relatives came to see 'Abdu'l-Bahá and to receive His blessings. They were at a loss to know in what language they could express their gratitude for the fact that their home had become the residence of the Master and the point of adoration for His lovers. The house is located on Riverside Drive near the Hudson River. Each morning and evening the Master walks in the gardens on the banks of the river.

As there is a war raging between the Balkan states and Turkey, it is the main topic in all the newspapers and people look upon these visitors in their Persian garments with eyes full of prejudice. We have even been refused accommodation in some of the large hotels because they thought we were Turks. The Master remarked, 'Observe how much enmity and hatred prejudices have produced among various parties and peoples and what suffering and hardship have been caused by them.' But whenever those who feel enmity towards us have been informed of the Cause of God and entered 'Abdu'l-Bahá's presence, they become humble and are honored to meet Him.

'Abdu'l-Bahá had been repeatedly asked by some of the New York Bahá'ís to see some of the wealthy people who wanted Him to visit them in their homes, but each time He said:

> I deal with the poor and visit them, not the rich. I love all, especially the poor. All sorts of people come here and I meet them all with sincere love, with heart and soul. Yet I have no intention of visiting the homes of the rich.

On another occasion, a famous man, Mr Andrew Carnegie, humbly requested an interview with the Master. Although he was one of the America's millionaires, his request was granted and is recorded in one of His writings.[367]

In the afternoon was the usual weekly meeting of the Baháʾí women at the home of Mrs Krug. When the Master arrived, Mrs Krug was reciting a prayer. When she finished, ʿAbduʾl-Bahá spoke:

He is God!

This is the assemblage of my daughters in the home of my daughter, Mrs Krug. Therefore I am very happy with this gathering. It is a good gathering, very illumined. It is a spiritual assembly, a heavenly assemblage, the glances of favor surround this meeting and the Supreme Concourse looks down upon it. They heard the prayer that you read and it made them joyous. They thank Baháʾuʾlláh saying, 'We thank Thee, O Baháʾuʾlláh, that these maidservants are attracted to Thee and are turned to Thy Kingdom. They have no purpose but Thy Will; they wish for no station but that of service to Thy Cause.'

O Baháʾuʾlláh! Assist these noble maidservants; make these worldly daughters heavenly; inspire their hearts and gladden their souls.

O Baháʾuʾlláh! Make these bodies as light-giving candles, these beings the envy of flower gardens and fill their souls with a melody which will enrapture the Supreme Concourse and make them dance for joy. Make each of them a brilliant star so that the world of existence may be illumined with their light.

O Baháʾuʾlláh! Give them heavenly power, bestow on them the inspiration of the Kingdom and vouchsafe to them divine assistance so that they may be enabled to render service unto Thee.

Thou are the Compassionate, the Merciful and the Lord of Bounty and Favor.

There was a gathering in the evening at the home of Mr Kinney which was attended mostly by black people. At the meeting the Master likened the faith of Mr [Arthur] Dodge to that of Peter and expressed His admiration for that sincere and true servant who was so firm in the Covenant. The Master showed similar kindness to Mr [Hooper] Harris who was permitted to speak to the public gathering before the Master's address. The Master's talk was a confirmation of Mr Harris's speech, an explanation of the prophecies of the Book of Daniel concerning the Most Great Manifestation and the statement in the New Testament about the Promised One.[368]

Wednesday, November 13, 1912
[New York]

The Master described for the friends His journey to California and His talks at the university and at gatherings in San Francisco. He said:

> As they were delivered in scientific terms and with rational arguments, none could deny them and not a single voice was raised in opposition. In fact, in the gatherings like that at the university where one hundred and eighty professors and teachers and eighteen hundred students were present together with other notable people, if one had spoken using religious terminology and expressing religious opinions and imitations which are wholly contrary to science and reason, none would have paid any attention; rather, they would have scorned and mocked us.
>
> One reason that people despair of the world of religion is this very matter of superstitions and imitations practiced by religious leaders. When intelligent and learned people see these imitations and customs as being contrary to reason and knowledge they forsake the divine religion and are not aware that these are idle fancies of the leaders and have nothing to do with divine principles. The foundations of divine religion do not negate sound reason and true science. The principles of divine religion do not contradict knowledge and insight, except for

some principles and minutiae of the law which were given according to the exigencies of the time and age. Of course, the second or social laws suited to the Mosaic dispensation and useful for the Jewish people at that time are now purposeless and ineffective and seem futile, but they were pertinent and useful at the time.

Now, praise be to God, Bahá'u'lláh has solved these difficulties. All His teachings and laws are in keeping with the spirit of this age and the needs of the people. And greatest of all is the abandonment of religious superstitions and dogmas and the conformity of spiritual matters with scientific and rational arguments.

'Abdu'l-Bahá spent the afternoon at the home of Mr Kinney. As was His daily custom, the Master went for a walk in the morning and afternoon in the gardens along the bank of the river on Riverside Drive.

His public talk at Mr Kinney's home concerned the immersion of the friends in the sea of bounty and favor. 'Abdu'l-Bahá encouraged them to remain firm and constant in the Covenant of God. After the meeting another group came to visit. He also encouraged them to arise, teach and spread the fragrances of God and inspired them to render service to the world of humanity so that others might arise from among the friends, girding their loins to bring about unity and harmony among the nations.

When some of the friends requested that the verses of the holy writings and divine Tablets be translated into English, He said: 'A committee consisting of experts in several languages is essential for the translation of the Sacred Writings.'

Several friends brought their children to Him. He took the little children in His arms and showered them with His kindness and affection. Among them was the little daughter of Mr Jones, who ran to the Master in all the meetings and did not wish to leave His side. She was always sad when she had to leave Him.

The Master spoke this evening on the importance of the

friends striving to detach themselves from earthly passions and worldly desires and to remain aloof from the doubts of selfish persons who outwardly appear faithful but who are inwardly the cause of confusion to others. He gave a lengthy discourse on firmness in the Covenant of God, obedience to the Center of His Covenant, the unity of the believers, the afflictions and tribulations of the Abhá Beauty and the martyrdom of the Manifestations in order that unity and harmony might be brought to the nations of the world.

During this talk two large rooms at Mr Kinney's were filled to capacity. At first the Master sat on a chair between the two rooms but He later arose in a majestic and dignified manner, speaking with such forceful tones that everyone was delighted and full of admiration.

Thursday, November 14, 1912
[New York]

After granting private interviews to some of the friends, the Master came downstairs to the gathering. Among His statements were these words:

> The most blessed moments of my life are those which I spend in the company of the friends of God. These are the best times. Therefore, I am extremely happy to be with you now. Praise be to God that your faces are illumined, your hearts and souls are rejoicing and all are turned toward the Abhá Kingdom. This is the utmost happiness for me.
>
> I pray to the threshold of Bahá'u'lláh that He may grant all of you eternal happiness, honor you in His Kingdom and bestow upon you everlasting life. Thus, the friends of New York may be freed from all limitations and become the cause of the enlightenment of the world of man. This is my greatest wish and Bahá'u'lláh will assuredly assist you.

Most of the evening meetings were at the home of Mrs Kinney and the daytime meetings were at Mrs Krug's home. There was always a crowd of visitors at His residence and, whether He was in or out, a multitude was always there waiting.

At the meeting this afternoon at Mrs Krug's home, He spoke of the exalted station of the people of Bahá given them through the bounties and confirmations of the Abhá Kingdom, which can turn black dust into a brilliant ruby, a grain into a harvest, a fisherman into a Peter and a village woman into a Mary Magdalene, the pride of the people.

As they passed before Him one by one, they received His bestowals and blessings. He returned to His residence on foot. Near Central Park a gentleman approached Him and said, 'I have heard much about you and have been waiting for the moment to see you. I am thankful that now I have attained the honor of meeting your Excellency.' He followed the Master to His residence, greatly interested in His explanations and the wonderful Bahá'í teachings.

This evening friends and seekers immensely enjoyed and benefited from hearing the Master's explanations of the mysteries of the Books of God and other important issues. He was asked about music and singing in the Mashriqu'l-Adhkár. He replied, 'Singing and chanting of scripture and prayers in verse or in prose should be used but I do not interfere in matters not expressly stated in the Text. Whenever and whatever the Universal House of Justice ordains, that will be the criterion.'

Later in the evening He spoke at length to a woman Christian Scientist who was quite fanatical in her beliefs. The Master explained to her the meaning of the assertion that there is no evil in existence. He said:

> By saying there is no evil in existence is meant that what has come from the Origin of existence and being is good and useful. It is good in its time and place and not evil. For example, I can say that there is no darkness in the sun because

darkness is the absence of light and has no existence in itself. Oppression is the absence of justice and ignorance is the lack of knowledge. Hence, the imperfections and defects of the world of creation, the contingent world, are merely the absence of virtues and the lack of perfections. These defects have not come from the Source; rather, the essential properties of the world of matter which are change and transformation cause the training of all things and the manifestation of perfections of realities and spirits.

Saturday, November 15, 1912
[New York]

Mr Wilhelm and other friends heard these words from 'Abdu'l-Bahá:

Education and training are the most important issues in the world of existence. Without an educator, little progress can be made in material affairs, still less in spiritual affairs and divine morals. How can humanity find composure and eternal happiness without an educator? Apart from the human world observe the rest of creation, how each and every created things is in need of training by an educator. Without education they will not attain perfection. For instance, this flower cannot by itself reach this perfection and attain this charm, color and loveliness. Thus, there are two great blessings in the world of existence: one is innate capacity which is bestowed by the Creator; and the other, acquired perfections which depend upon training by a teacher and educator.

The Master went downstairs to join the assembled friends. Among His words were these: 'The whole world is like a physical body and the power of Bahá'u'lláh may be regarded as the main artery in the body of existence.'

Today He called on Mr MacNutt and spoke to him in strong terms about his relationship with the Covenant-breakers and showed him a letter Mr MacNutt had written to Chicago offering help to and praising Dr Nutt, a friend of Kheiralla. The Master asked, 'Is this your writing?' Mr MacNutt replied, 'Yes, but my intention was something else.' He tried to give a different angle to his purpose but could not. The Master was saddened about Mr MacNutt but His purpose was to admonish and warn him against his own conduct.

In the afternoon, after seeing Mr Topakyan, the Persian Consul General, and other prominent people, the Master went to a meeting of the Divine Knowledge Club, whose members are mostly women. The president of the club is an educated woman who claims divine knowledge and heavenly inspiration through Bahá'u'lláh. Spiritualists, astrologers and Christian Scientists frequent her club meetings. She spoke with closed eyes, as if she were sleeping and receiving inspiration. She appeared to be in a trance and in a state of total absorption. Because she is known among the Bahá'ís for her sincerity and is a supporter of the Cause of God, the Master was very kind to her.

Today, at this lady's request, the Master went to a meeting of her club and delivered an address concerning the circumstances of the time and the different seasons in the contingent world. He said:

> The day of the Manifestation of God is the divine and spiritual springtime when the trees of human souls become green and flourishing, new beauty and freshness are brought to the gardens of the hearts and new inspiration and fresh bounties are bestowed.

His talk commanded their complete attention and all bowed their heads in humility and respect. On the way home, He remarked, 'Observe what idle fancies and vain imaginings are still prevalent in America!' The Master's guidance on removing the superstitions and vain imaginings of these people is as follows:

Man explains things in two ways. One explanation originates from his personal feelings, thoughts and understanding. This cannot stand as proof or criterion for all and does not satisfy the hearts. The other is a statement supported by proofs. It produces significant results and promulgates momentous matters which are necessary to the world of man. It is like the explanations and proofs of the Bahá'ís, who invite all to the oneness of humanity and to universal peace. This explanation has proofs and is effective.

The Master continued with a story of the Jewish rabbis:

In Jerusalem every now and then they broadcast a promise giving a specific time based on the holy scriptures and say that on such a date the Promised One will appear to deliver the Jews. They say, 'We have derived these from the holy texts.' But when that time and day approach they cast a doubt over their promise and give another. Thus they keep the Jews under the influence of their wish and desires and deprive them of the truth. Now they refer to the time of Daniel [Dan. 12:12] and hold out a promise that the Promised One will appear in the year 1335 [AH, i. e. 1963].

There was a public meeting in the evening at the home of Miss Juliet Thompson. The Master spoke about the greatness of this cycle, the victory of the Cause and the influence and importance of the teachings and laws of Bahá'u'lláh. His talk was delivered in such awe-inspiring tones that the minds were dazzled and the hearts captivated by the grandeur and majesty of the Center of the Covenant. Both before and after the meeting many people were honored to visit with Him in a separate room.[369]

Saturday, November 16, 1912
[New York]

After morning prayers and meditation, the Master spoke of the afflictions and persecutions of the believers in the East and their perseverance and steadfastness in the Cause of God. He spoke graciously of the family of Ḥaḍrát Samandarí[370] and other old Persian friends. Later, at a gathering of the friends, He spoke these words:

> The holy Manifestations endured great afflictions and persecutions and at every moment accepted torment and oppression. Christ suffered violent persecutions, accepting the suffering of the Cross and the most glorious martyrdom. The results of these persecutions were eleven disciples who were truly blessed souls. They became luminous and heavenly; they became the cause of the enlightenment of the people of the world.
>
> I hope that you, too, may reach such a station, that it will be said that you are the fruit of the revelation of Bahá'u'lláh; that it will be said, 'It is these people who are the aim of this new revelation; they are the jewels of existence; they are illumined, divine, spiritual and heavenly.' If someone asks what Bahá'u'lláh has done, they will be told, 'He has educated these people.'[371]

'Abdu'l-Bahá then spoke about the divine laws and religions:

> Divine religions consist of two parts. One aspect is that of spiritual laws which constitute the foundation of all divine religions. They are immutable and unalterable. The second aspect consists of social laws and relates to material affairs, and changes according to the exigencies of the time.

To a new group He said:

> Gracious God! Although people see with their own eyes that in the dispensation of Christ the eleven disciples were ordinary men who, because of their faith in Him, found eternal life and shone from the horizon of perpetual honor; and that the Jews, with all their worldly honor, became contemptible; and that Caiaphas, the greatest enemy of Christ, was, together with his whole family, obliterated from the face of the earth while a simple fisherman, because of his belief in Christ, became the great Peter, yet, despite all this, still they take no heed.

In the afternoon meeting His address on the reality of God and the victory of the Manifestations of God threw the entire audience into an extraordinary state of excitement and attraction, especially the friends from New Jersey, who with Mr Hoar, after the meeting went to the Master's room and became the recipients of His grace and special bestowals.

Sunday, November 17, 1912
[New York]

Early in the morning 'Abdu'l-Bahá voiced His thankfulness to the Abhá Kingdom, saying:

> Praise be to God! His divine help and assistance have enveloped us and the confirmations of the Abhá Kingdom have surrounded us. The Cause of God has reached every ear and the divine fragrances have spread throughout all regions. The East and the West are illumined with the light of the most great guidance. The foundation of the Cause of God is firmly and securely established. The friends of the Blessed Beauty have risen in faithfulness and occupied themselves in proclaiming the Word of God. The foundation of the Mashriqu'l-Adhkár is laid. I have no further desire. I wish to reach Haifa and to settle again in the Holy Land. It is now your turn to serve, to render your servitude to the holy threshold.

Occupy yourselves day and night in the diffusion of the divine fragrances. All confirmations encircle those who are engaged in rendering services to the court of oneness. Nothing avails except servitude to the Blessed Beauty. If, after the ascension of the Blessed Beauty, I had not risen in servitude to Him, these confirmations would not have descended.

After a short pause, He continued:

Had there not been this servitude, constancy and confirmation the affairs would have fallen into the hands of the ambitious and the standard of the Cause would have fallen forever. Unseemly matters would have ensued. The story of Yaḥyá would have been repeated. Had it not been for the firmness and power of the Ancient Beauty, the mainstay of the Cause would have fallen apart. Nothing would have been witnessed but the propagation of selfish desires and, apart from these, nothing would have remained but some words and phrases.

Today He mentioned the passing of Áqá Riḍá Ghánad Muhájir[372] and spoke about the greatness of his station, saying, 'I must go myself to the Holy Land to build his effulgent tomb with my own hands and read there a prayer of visitation.'

From morning until the afternoon every room of the Master's residence was full of people. All were recipients of His everlasting bounties and bathed in the surging waves of the love of God.

This evening the Master spoke to a gathering of the friends regarding the maturity and perfection of the world and gave an account of Bahá'u'lláh. He concluded His address with the chanting of a prayer in a melodious voice, immersing the hearts in a sea of ecstasy and rapture. Many new people attended the meeting and were impressed and moved by the blessings of 'Abdu'l-Bahá. They remained in His presence until He left, expressing their sincerity and reverence.[373]

Monday, November 18, 1912
[New York]

In the morning the Master was occupied revealing Tablets in answer to letters from the believers. He permitted some friends and newcomers to interview Him in His own room. When the visitors grew too numerous, He appeared in the gathering and showered love and kindness upon all.

Whenever the Master became tired, He would go alone to the nearby gardens along the bank of the river to rest. He said, 'When I am alone, I do not talk, my mind is not busy and I can rest a little. But when I am not alone I must speak; I perspire and feel exhausted.'

These were the final days of His stay in America and there was a great rush of visitors. There was not one moment when people were not present.

In the afternoon, while talking to a group of the friends, 'Abdu'l-Bahá suddenly said: 'We wish to build a House of Worship on that side of the water.' Later He said: 'This city shall become good when the call of "Yá Bahá'u'l-Abhá" shall reach the highest heaven from it. If the believers arise as they should erelong the word of God will envelop all these regions.' He also added, 'As the United States of America is far and free from the arena of the prevailing political turmoil, this government and country can prevent war between the nations and bring about peace and harmony among them.'

The Master was invited by the poet Mr Moxey and Mrs Moxey for supper. The hosts were among the devoted friends of 'Abdu'l-Bahá and they were eloquent in their praise of Him. During the Master's previous visit to New York Mr Moxey had written a book of poetry, describing the demeanor, majesty and power of the Master. Mrs Moxey, who was a famous musician, opened the gathering by playing the piano and singing a melodious song of praise in His honor. The Master began His address with these words:

Thornton Chase, the first American Baha'i, who passed away in California before 'Abdu'l-Bahá arrived there

William Ralston, an early Californian Baha'i

Ella Goodall Cooper, left, and her mother Helen Goodall. 'Abdu'l-Bahá stayed in Mrs Goodall's spacious home while in Oakland, California.

'Abdu'l-Bahá walking in front of Helen Goodall's home in Oakland, California, October 12, 1912

'Abdu'l-Bahá leaving the First Unitarian Church, San Francisco, Sunday, October 6, 1912

'Abdu'l-Bahá and His entourage on the main drive, Leland Stanford Junior University, Palo Alto, California, following His address on October 8, 1912

'Abdu'l-Bahá at the children's meeting at Mrs Goodall's home in Oakland

'Abdu'l-Bahá with Indian students from the University of California at Berkeley, taken at Oakland, October 12, 1912

Phoebe Hearst, who had arranged the first pilgrimage of Western Bahá'ís to 'Akká. 'Abdu'l-Bahá visited her Pleasanton home while in California.

'Abdu'l-Bahá meeting Bahá'ís in the grounds of Mrs Goodall's home, Oakland, California

Albert Windust, editor of Star of the West

'Abdu'l-Bahá, taken in Washington DC by Mariam Haney in November 1912 with, left to right, *Lorraine Hopper, Laila Bowman, Mary Aldrich and Katherine Doyle*

The family of Joseph and Pauline Hannen, Washington DC.
Left to right: *Amelia Knobloch, Alma Knobloch, Carl A. Hannen, Pauline Hannen and Joseph Hannen*

Howard and Hebe Struven. 'Abdu'l-Bahá had lunch at their home in Baltimore, Maryland

Dr Florian Krug, who initially opposed the Faith but became a Bahá'í after meeting 'Abdu'l-Bahá in 1912

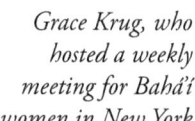

Grace Krug, who hosted a weekly meeting for Bahá'í women in New York

Hooper Harris, New York Baháʼí lawyer, seated with Mírzá Maḥmúd Zarqání, Harlan Ober and Hand of the Cause Ibn-i-Akbar

'Abdu'l-Bahá in Chicago with entourage, including, left, Ghodsieh Khánum Ashraf, the first Persian woman to travel in the United States

Bahá'í banquet at the Great Northern Hotel, New York, November 23, 1912, held in commemoration of the Day of the Covenant. More than 300 guests attended

‘Abdu'l-Bahá prepares to leave the United States

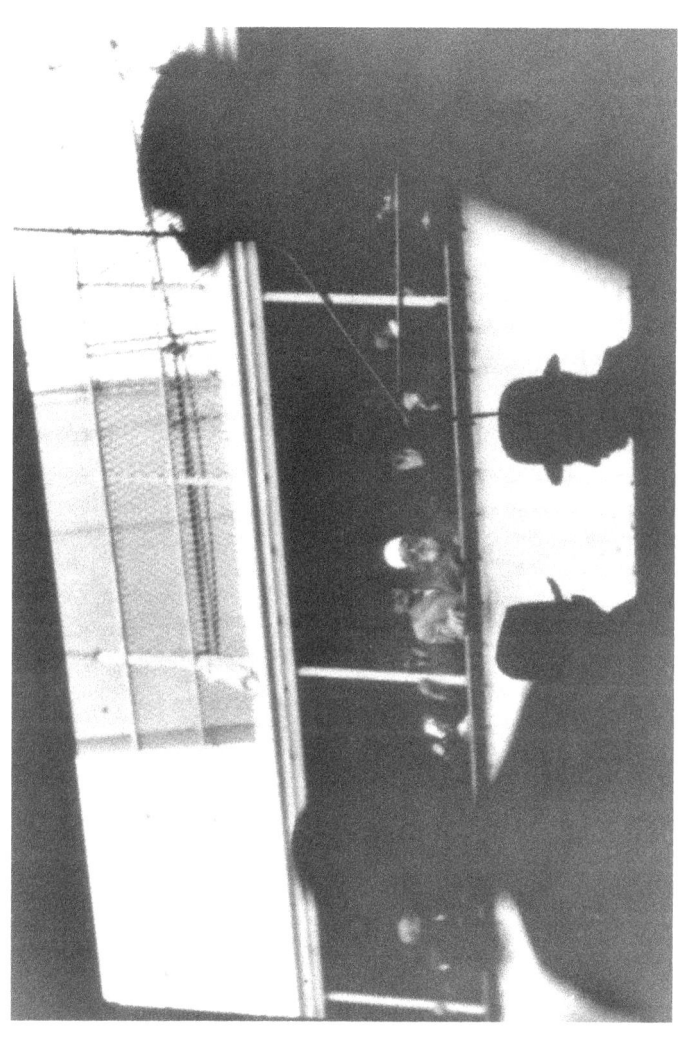

One of the last pictures of 'Abdu'l-Bahá taken in the United States, as He departs on the S.S. Celtic, December 5, 1912

The S.S Celtic, the ship on which 'Abdu'l-Bahá returned from America to Europe (Picture courtesy of the Ulster Folk and Transport Museum)

I praise God that I am with you. Such an assembly would be utterly impossible to hold through worldly power and outward means because you are Westerners and we are Easterners. There was nothing to connect us. We had neither patriotic, racial, commercial nor political connections with you. But Bahá'u'lláh removed all these estrangements and prejudices and invited all to divine love. He joined all under the shade of the blessed Word. Hence, we are united and assembled here in such love. This love is the greatest of all means, as all other means and ties are limited; but harmony that comes about through the love of God is infinite and everlasting.

These impressive words transformed the hearts. After the meeting several of the friends and His companions were honored to have supper with Him. Everyone was grateful and showed great devotion in that home.[374]

Tuesday, November 19, 1912
[New York]

The Master spent the day at the home of Mrs Krug in the utmost happiness. A number of the believers and His companions were also very happy to witness the Master's joy, the influence of the Cause of God and the power of the Covenant of God.

In the afternoon, at a public meeting attended chiefly by women, 'Abdu'l-Bahá spoke on the equality of the rights of women and their education and progress through the Manifestation of this supreme age. He encouraged them to acquire the perfections and virtues of the world of humanity.

Later, at the home of Mr and Mrs Kinney, He asked Mr Harris to speak at the meeting of the friends.

As Mr MacNutt's apparent equivocation and lack of firmness seemed to be causing his degradation in the eyes of the friends, he came to the Master and implored Him to recommend him to them. The Master replied, 'The remedy depends upon your sincere repentance and your open denouncement of the violators in the meetings of the friends.' In compliance, Mr MacNutt rose and gave an account of his journey to Chicago and his meeting with Kheiralla. Some felt that he spoke ambiguously. The Master asked him to explain his actions in plain words so that the friends might be satisfied and this blemish on his character be removed. Again he testified in clear terms of his faith in the Covenant and his rejection of the Covenant-breakers. The Master went to the podium and expressed His pleasure at Mr Harris's talk and for Mr MacNutt's words of repentance. The Master then went upstairs and called Mr Hoar, Mr Harris, Mr Dodge and other friends to Him and asked them to embrace Mr MacNutt and exhorted them to have the utmost love and unity among themselves. He encouraged and inspired them to spread the divine word and to diffuse the fragrances of God. He told them that they must sacrifice all other affairs for the accomplishment of this great affair.[375]

Despite this, the Master and the friends, in their inmost hearts, were saddened by Mr MacNutt's earlier actions. Some felt that he was not trying hard enough to show his humility and firmness in the Covenant. After the Master's departure from America, Mr MacNutt went to California and other regions of America. The believers stayed away from him. He wrote many letters of repentance to 'Abdu'l-Bahá, who sent him many encouraging and kind words.

Wednesday, November 20, 1912
[New York]

The Master again called some of the friends and asked them to show kindness and love to Mr MacNutt and to be patient with him. Some of His words were these:

> You must all arise in unison to serve the Cause of God. You must work hand in hand to teach the Cause and know that the confirmations of Bahá'u'lláh will descend upon you. My hope

is that New York will excel all other cities because at the beginning it had precedence over them. God willing, it shall be so again. The favors of the Kingdom of God are great, the attention and bounties of the Blessed Beauty are fixed upon you and His hidden hosts are assisting you. Arise in this arena and you shall see what will transpire.

I am but one of His servants. After the ascension of the Blessed Beauty, the Ottoman people and government arose against me as did enemies of the area from different nations and religions. In such a state everyone was attacking me from outside and even my brothers from inside opposed me. But in a short time the enemies were frustrated and brought low so that some of them cried, 'Would to God that Bahá'u'lláh had not ascended because this Cause has become even greater, its fame has spread to more places, and its support has become stronger.' Therefore, we must arise in servitude so that His confirmations may surround us from all sides. Undoubtedly whenever you arise to serve and proclaim the Cause you shall be assisted and shall attain success. Rest assured.

In the afternoon the friends gathered at the home of Mr Harris, each one eager and delighted to see the Master and to listen to His words. While He was leaving His residence, some school children saw the Master and rushed towards Him. They asked, 'Who is this man who looks like Christ?' Miss Juliet Thompson spoke to them outside the house about the Cause and the life of 'Abdu'l-Bahá. They asked to meet Him and they were invited to come to Mr Kinney's home, where 'Abdu'l-Bahá spent most of His days, the following Sunday.

Both private and public meetings were held in that home. The first to third floors were filled with people, some even standing on the stairs. From this day forward a spirit of steadfastness in the Covenant of God, unity and faithfulness appeared among the friends as the Master burnt away the veils and the hearts of the believers attained the highest degree of love and union. This was the Master's purpose in staying so long in New York. Furthermore, many wonderful friends became humble and sincere in His presence.

He spoke this evening to a large gathering about the influence of the Cause and the victory of the Supreme Word over the nations and powers of the world.

Thursday, November 21, 1912
[New York]

The Master was occupied revealing Tablets to the friends until about noon when the crowd downstairs became too large. He appeared in this gathering of eager souls, greeting and extending His kindness to all, saying: 'I have been busy since early morning and am tired. I do not feel like speaking at all and wish to go out for a walk.' After a short talk in which He encouraged the friends to establish love and harmony among themselves and to make every effort in the Cause of God, He walked to Broadway and then to Central Park. He was not pleased with the dense population and the height of the buildings, saying: 'These are injurious to the public's health. This population should be in two cities, the buildings should be lower and the streets should be tree-lined as they are in Washington. How can these two places compare?'

Indeed, the condition of New York City is strange and its population so large that in addition to surface streets, there are three railway lines running the entire length of the city; one underground, another on the surface and a third above the streets on bridges about two stories high. These railway lines are continuously filled with people and are their mode of transportation. On some of the streets, automobiles and carriages have to stop for some 10 to 15 minutes because of the congestion until the traffic officers give them permission to continue.

Most buildings are from 17 to 18 stories high and each floor has some 20 to 30 apartments, most of which have bedrooms, a living room, a dining room, bathrooms with hot and cold running water and many comforts.

There was a large gathering this evening at Mr and Mrs Kinney's attended by both old and new friends. The Master's talk was mainly admonitions to the friends about love and unity among themselves and the propagation of the divine Cause. The hearts and souls were ignited by the fire of the love of God and their tongues praised the Beloved.

Friday, November 22, 1912
[New York]

The Master spent the morning until noon at His residence. In the afternoon He went to a gathering at the home of Mrs Krug. The meeting with such eager friends was very enjoyable. A feature of the afternoon was the visit from a Christian minister. He was a just and fair-minded man who visited with the Master before the meeting in a separate room. His first question to the Master was, 'What are the new teachings in this Cause?' The Master replied, 'The fundamental principles of all religions are one. They are unchangeable and do not differ. This is what Christ meant when He said, "I am not come to destroy the law of the Torah but to promote it."'[376]

The minister: 'Yes, I understand. Do you mean that at the beginning the followers of all the religions were pure and undefiled but grew polluted and negligent?'

The Master: 'If there is no change or alteration, then there is no renewal. Not until night falls will a new day dawn. If the religion of Moses had not changed, Christ would not have appeared.'

The minister: 'Thank you, I understand this well. Now tell me, will there be another cycle after this Bahá'í cycle?'

The Master: 'The sovereignty of God has no beginning and no end and the outpouring of His bounties is endless.'

The minister said, with relief, 'Now my doubts are wholly removed with nothing left but certainty.'

He was so sincere and humble that the Master was pleased with him and said, 'I wanted to give detailed answers to each of your questions but you quickly realized the outcome of each answer right from the beginning. Thus must a person have aptitude and a pure motive.'

Appearing at the meeting, the Master held the minister's hand and praised him very highly as an example of justice. To the friends He said: 'Beware, beware lest you follow your prejudices and selfish interests. You must always be just in all matters and investigate the truth.'

This evening in similar language the Master vividly described the harmfulness of prejudice, alienation and disunity and the advantages of love and friendship, concluding with strong appeals to the friends to propagate the guidance given by God and to associate in a spirit of love and kindness with all denominations and the servants of God.

Saturday, November 23, 1912
[New York]

The friends arranged a banquet in commemoration of the Day of the Covenant and the journey of the beloved of all hearts. Today many came to the Master with bouquets of flowers in their hands. The banquet was held in the ballroom of New York's Grand Northern Hotel. The hall was decorated similarly to that in Washington with festoons, banners, ornaments and exquisite screens, with the Greatest Name suspended above all on the stage in its customary calligraphy.

In the center of the ballroom were two rectangular tables, between which was another large table exquisitely set. Around these tables on both sides were placed small circular tables bedecked with colorful flowers, a variety of sweets and crystal glassware. The electric lighting reflected the glassware and caused the whole room to shine brilliantly. More than three hundred guests, formally attired, attended. Several friends and specifically Miss Lali Lloyd served at the banquet.

When the Master appeared, all rose from their seats and with smiling faces cried out, 'Alláh-u-Abhá!' Many of the hotel guests saw the banquet and were astonished to see the grandeur of the Master and the sincerity and enthusiasm of the friends. After the Master took His seat, Mr Hoar, on behalf of the Baháʼís, read an address of welcome expressing obedience and firmness in the Covenant. The Master rose and responded with an address about the divine teachings and the oneness of humanity. He then walked around the tables and perfumed the heads and faces of the friends with attar of rose. When He returned to His chair, the friends, accompanied by the piano, sang songs of praise to Him.

Later the Master spoke about the wars and massacres of the nations and the need for the teachings of the Greatest Name. He encouraged all towards peace, harmony and sincere love for all the people of the world.[377] After His talk, the Consul General, Mr Topakyan, and others gave short speeches praising ʻAbduʼl-Bahá.

This evening's banquet was so grand that the hotel staff were curious to know about the Cause. They came to see the Master to ask about the banquet and why so many distinguished Americans were praising and glorifying a person from the East. Indeed, it was a banquet for a king and a source of awakening to every person of insight.

Two photographs were taken with a good quality glass and special lighting. Although the photographs do not show the entire group, they tell much about the banquet.[378]

Sunday, November 24, 1912
[New York]

A gathering of black Baháʼís was held at the home of Mrs Kinney. They had been invited by the New York Baháʼís to attend the banquet of the Covenant but when the proprietor of the hotel heard about it, he was not pleased. The more the friends endeavored to persuade him, the more vehement was his refusal. He said, 'If the people see that one colored person has entered my hotel, no respectable person will ever set foot in it and my business will go to the winds.' Such is the depth of prejudice between blacks and whites. Since it was impossible to invite the black Bahá'ís to the banquet, the friends arranged today's feast for their black brothers. Many white women came forward to serve their black guests, showering them with love. The Master approved of this meeting very much and He said:

> Today you have carried out the laws of the Blessed Beauty and have truly acted according to the teachings of the Supreme Pen. Behold what an influence and effect the words of Bahá'u'lláh have had upon the hearts, that hating and shunning have been forgotten and that prejudices have been obliterated to such an extent that you arose to serve one another with great sincerity.

The Master's words made a great impression. The meeting embodied the grandeur of the Covenant and demonstrated the power and influence of the Cause in uniting, in sincerity and love, two races of humanity.

In the afternoon the children who had earlier seen the Master on the way from school, had been so attracted and had asked to see Him, came to visit Him. He spoke to them with deep affection and kindness, asking about their health and welfare. To each He gave candies and flowers and then sprinkled them with attar of rose. He then gave them kindly counsels and encouraged them to acquire knowledge, science, good morals and sincerity, saying:

> I hope that you will be educated as you ought to be and that each of you will become the pride of your family. May God assist you to acquire divine knowledge in the school of the world of humanity. I shall pray for you and beg assistance for you. Truly, the hearts of the children are very pure. This was why Christ said, 'Be ye like children.'[379] Praise be to God who created you illumined children. Praise be to the Lord who hath created His creatures perfectly. God has created you as human beings so that you may daily acquire better morals and human

virtues. You must obey your parents so that they may be pleased with you, and so that God will be pleased with you, and that you may become the children of the Kingdom and mirror forth the words of Christ.

Although these young visitors were children, they took their leave in an attitude of sincerity, reverence and attraction that astonished all.

This evening 'Abdu'l-Bahá spoke at a public meeting of the friends on the underlying unity of creation and the oneness of humanity. His sweet words and explanations attracted the hearts and souls, as in other meetings, leaving them much attached to the Center of the Covenant.

Monday, November 25, 1912
[New York]

Some of the friends came to 'Abdu'l-Bahá's residence early this morning, asking that they be admitted into His presence during His prayers so they could be blessed and their souls cleansed. As soon as they reached Him they fell into transports of joy, awe-struck at the august spirit of that moment.

Later a Christian minister came into His presence in the utmost humility and, weeping, held the Master's 'abá in his hands and begged that his wife and children be healed. The Master showered him with kindness, consoled him and prayed for him. Although the minister was not a Bahá'í, he showed the reverence and respect to 'Abdu'l-Bahá that is usually reserved for Christ.

The Master's fame, grandeur and holiness has spread so far that in every city of the United States of America prominent people become in His presence like humble servants, while knowledgeable and well-known scholars refer to Him as the Prophet of the East and the Messenger of Peace, even though He has always forbidden the use of such terms for Himself in writing or speech. He always explains to them His servitude to the Threshold of the Abhá Beauty.

As the multitude grew, and the Master could not easily see everyone individually, He went downstairs to apologize for not being able to see them owing to the volume of His work, His preoccupation with other matters and His fatigue and frailty. He prayed for all and inspired and encouraged the friends to put all their energy into propagating and spreading the fragrances of God.

In the afternoon, the Master was invited to two meetings. The first was at the Women's Club of New York where He spoke on the education of women, their acquisition of good morals and the equality of their rights. The audience was interested and excited and everyone came to shake His hand, begging confirmation that they might better serve and acquire human perfections.

The Master then went to Mrs Cochran's home where most of the visitors were newcomers who had not previously been in 'Abdu'l-Bahá's presence. He appealed to them to abandon harmful prejudices and to acquire heavenly virtues and eternal perfections through spiritual power. The address appeared to breathe a new spirit into all those present.[380]

Tuesday, November 26, 1912
[New York]

In the morning, after revealing Tablets and granting interviews, the Master joined the gathering of the friends with these words:

> I always derive great pleasure from being with you. I shall always remember these gatherings. I shall never forget them. If I cannot see each one of you individually every day that should not undermine our real love. See how much work I have to do! It is more than a week since I received this letter from my sister, the Greatest Holy Leaf [Bahíyyih Khánum], and other members of the household, but I have not had the opportunity to open it yet. I was looking for another letter when I came upon this unopened letter. Then I heard that you were waiting here and I came downstairs to see you because I have no time to see

you individually. In spite of this, if anyone has an urgent matter I will see them privately, even if only for a few minutes. Had I time I would always be with you. My happiness lies in seeing you, for in your faces are apparent the glad tidings of the Abhá Kingdom and in your hearts heavenly love and attraction. If outwardly we fail to meet, it does not weaken our real love. God willing, you shall all be assisted and immersed in the sea of bounty and the favor of Bahá'u'lláh.

In the afternoon at a meeting of the friends, the Master turned towards Mrs Krug and said:

A believer in Bahá'u'lláh is he who is firm in the Covenant. He who is firm in the divine Covenant is a believer, a servant of the believers, a seeker of Bahá'í harmony and unity and a promoter of fellowship and amity among the friends of God. Is it possible that one can accept a book and refuse to accept him who teaches it? Is it possible to accept the sun and to reject its rays? He who rejects the rays is a rejector of the sun, too.

Furthermore, many say, 'We have no need of divine Manifestations; we ourselves have direct communication with God.' They do not know that the divine Manifestations are the bright rays of the Sun of Truth and a means of educating the realities of man. Therefore, he who rejects the bounty of the Sun of Truth and thinks himself not in need of it is like the one who says he is not in need of God and rejects both God and reality, in spite of the fact that all creation is receiving incessant bounty from God and is dependent on Him, as the body is dependent upon the soul.

In the evening the Master spoke to the gathering on man's ability to understand the reality of certain things using his intelligence because man's intelligence is the discoverer of reality. For instance, through the process of reasoning, intelligence can comprehend the existence of God and understand that this magnificent universe cannot exist without a Creator. These works are not without a Maker and this garden of creation cannot exist without a Gardener.

Wednesday, November 27, 1912
[New York]

In the morning the Master gave several talks to the Bahá'ís, one of which was the following:

> The purpose of the divine Manifestations has been the education of holy souls. Some have imagined that their purpose was to found temples and churches or to establish a new nation or to gain personal fame and that for these considerations they accepted severe degradation and became targets for the arrow of fate. These are idle fancies because those holy Beings knew well that the dominion of God existed when there was no trace of them and that it shall continue to exist when no trace of them remains. Thus fame or oblivion, honor or degradation are one and the same to those Gems of existence. Indeed, their ultimate desire is selfless devotion to the one true God and absolute nothingness in His court. Their only motive has been the education of blessed souls and sanctified beings who are the foundation of divine education and promoters of the most great guidance and the supreme favor.
>
> The people of Bahá must endeavor day and night to promulgate this lofty purpose. They must endeavor and strive strenuously to educate themselves and other sanctified souls. They must awaken the peoples and nations of the world and free them from dogmas and imitations. They must pass beyond the world of names and fix their gaze on realities and inner meanings.

At the end of the meeting some friends gave Him written petitions asking for spiritual assistance. He said, 'We have received so many letters that there is no time to read them; how, then, is it possible to answer them?'

In the afternoon again the friends and seekers arrived in groups. The Master's talk mainly concerned the need for both a spiritual and a material civilization. 'The coming of age and maturity of man', He said, 'will appear when these two civilizations become entwined.'

The Master spoke to a leader of the socialists on economic issues, the brotherhood of humanity and the Bahá'í teachings. The man was overwhelmed to hear such solutions to questions upon which the well-being of the world depends.

The Master spoke to a group of women about education, training, virtues and the rights of women. In brief, every day and night, to a greater and greater extent, the faces shone with the fire of the love of God and the souls beamed with the radiance of the beauty of the Beloved.

Thursday, November 28, 1912
[New York]

Several friends came at dawn to the Master's residence, begging admission into His presence and saying that watching Him at prayer would be its own spiritual lesson. We were astounded to see how eager they were, proof that the power of the Word of God has dispelled old habits and opened the gates of bounty such that at so early an hour these souls had taken leave of their comfortable beds and sought refuge at the majestic gate of the Center of the Covenant.

These were the last few remaining days of the Master's sojourn in America as He planned to leave for England soon. At dawn and in the evening a stream of believers and prominent people, in a spiritual and prayerful attitude, came into His presence. They came to offer supplications, to turn to the Eternal Face, to look upon the Dawning Place of the Divine Covenant and to cling to the mantle of His grace and favor. At every moment the cries and ardor of His lovers increased and the fire of love in their breasts glowed more fiercely. There was not a moment's rest day or night for the Master. He was either delivering addresses at various public and private gatherings or talking to a friend in His private room. He gave joy to every sad one, hope to the hopeless and was a flame of fire to the heedless while guiding those who strive onto the right path.

Today the Master's public address concerned the spiritual capacity of the Americans. He said:

> Although they are engrossed in material civilization and physical pursuits, still, unlike people in some European countries, they are not wholly devoid of spiritual susceptibilities. They are seekers and desire to investigate reality. They wish for peace and tranquillity and they desire fellowship and love among humanity.

In the evening He expressed His happiness at the spirituality and services of the friends in their efforts to diffuse the fragrances of God.

Friday, November 29, 1912
[New York]

At the request of Mrs Emery, the Master moved to her home. The time of His departure was drawing near. On reaching the house, He said, 'Today I must rest for I am extremely tired.' Nevertheless, the friends and seekers continued to come to visit Him at the homes of Mrs Emery and Mrs Kinney. One of His discourses today was this:

> One of the bounties of religion and faith is the attainment of peace of the heart and soul and the joy of spirit and conscience. This station can only be gained through faith and understanding. Peace of mind is the soul's delight, as it is the means of acquiring that extraordinary state in which man finds

happiness in times of affliction and tranquillity in trouble. In spite of poverty he acquires a sense of affluence and in a state of riches and power he offers help and protection to the weak because the well-assured soul is like a tree which has strong roots and is not shaken by any event. This cannot be attained except through complete faith and understanding. How many are the people who have all means of comfort, luxury, security and wealth and every means of enjoyment and good living, yet they have no peace of mind and are ever anxious and uneasy! If outwardly they are happy one day, they become depressed and anxious the next. If they find physical rest at one moment, they face suffering and misfortune the next, until the time comes to leave this world, then they will do so with utmost regret and distress.

But those who have faith in God act according to the divine teachings; even though they need a little food to survive, they will pass their lives in the utmost happiness and joy. This is one of the bounties of religion; this is eternal happiness, life everlasting and real affluence. Without this all riches lead to woe and all power and strength are the cause of hardship and affliction. Therefore, offer praise unto God that you are endowed with this imperishable wealth and have attained this supreme blessing.[381]

Today some of the friends offered money to the Master but He would not accept it despite their pleading. Instead He told them, 'Distribute it among the poor on my behalf. It will be as though I have given it to them. But the most acceptable gift to me is the unity of the believers, service to the Cause of God, diffusion of the divine fragrances and adherence to the counsels of the Abhá Beauty.'

The believers were saddened because He did not accept their gifts. However, since these were the last days of His visit and He was about to leave, the New York Bahá'ís collected several gifts for the women of the holy household and for the Greatest Holy Leaf.

Saturday, November 30, 1912
[New York]

Some of the believers agreed among themselves to go to 'Abdu'l-Bahá and cling to His robe until He accepted their gifts. They came and begged He accept their offerings. The Master called them, saying:

> I am most grateful for your services; in truth you have served me. You have extended hospitality. Night and day you have been ready to serve and to diffuse the divine fragrances. I shall never forget your services, for you have no purpose but the will of God and you desire no station but entry into the Kingdom of God. Now you have brought presents for the members of my family. They are most acceptable and excellent but better than all these are the gifts of the love of God which remain preserved in the treasuries of the heart. These gifts are evanescent but those are eternal; these jewels must be kept in boxes and vaults and they will eventually perish but those jewels remain in the treasuries of the heart and will remain throughout the world of God for eternity. Thus I will take to them your love, which is the greatest of all gifts. In our house they do not wear diamond rings nor do they keep rubies. That house is sanctified above such adornments.
>
> I, however, have accepted your gifts; but I entrust them to you for you sell and send the proceeds to the fund for the Mashriqu'l-Adhkár in Chicago.

When the friends continued to plead with Him, He said: 'I want to take from you a present which will endure in the eternal world and a jewel which belongs to the treasuries of the heart. This is better.'

No matter how much the friends supplicated and pleaded, He would not accept their gifts and instead asked them all to contribute towards the Mashriqu'l-Adhkár fund. He did this everywhere He traveled.

Mrs Goodall and Mrs Cooper asked the Master, as He had not accepted their gifts – which would have drawn blessings and confirmations upon them – to give them permission to render Him some service on His travels. They even wrote letters to some of His companions, asking them to intercede on their behalf that they might render a service and share the Master's travel expenses. However, He would not accept their offer and refused all entreaties.

There was a public meeting at the home of Mrs Kinney. 'Abdu'l-Bahá spoke about love, loyalty, unity, the amity of the believers, spreading the Word of God, the promotion of universal peace and the brotherhood of humanity. The excitement and joy of the believers were beyond description.

Sunday, December 1, 1912
[New York]

Some of the friends came to see 'Abdu'l-Bahá very early in the morning. They saw Him at prayer and heard from His lips the prayers and verses of the Supreme Pen.

At the Master's residence, streams of visitors were honored to attain His presence and grateful for His blessings and favors. Aflame with the love of God, they showed reverence towards His Cause.

The Master's talk concerned the capacity of the Americans to bring about universal peace. He said:

> As Americans are removed from most political difficulties they live at ease in isolation and, compared to most other regions, are more desirous of peace and harmony, so they can succeed in bringing about universal peace provided they arise as they should and the nation and government put forth strenuous efforts and, through spiritual power, carry out the divine teachings and principles. The matter of peace, in the religion of Bahá'u'lláh, is a firm command and a religious obligation.

It is not the resolution of a congress or the edict of a committee of some nation or country influenced by selfish desires and subject to amendments. Because it is a fundamental principle, it will inevitably come to pass. As the denial of Christ and opposition to Him are considered infidelity in religious terminology, the rejection of peace has the same status in the religion of Bahá'u'lláh.

No affair in the world succeeds without sacrifice. Up to now twenty thousand persons have been sacrificed for this Cause. The Bahá'ís have accepted every affliction and persecution. For forty years I was in a prison for promulgating universal peace and the oneness of humanity. Because these teachings were contrary to the interests and the despotism of the S͟háh of Persia and the Sulṭán of Turkey, they arose in opposition and oppression. With all their power they girded their loins to uproot and efface the Cause of God. But the Cause of Bahá'u'lláh was victorious and the fame of His Revelation spread worldwide. Every opponent was overthrown and humiliated because this Cause was supported by the All-Powerful and because His teachings answer the need of the age to promote human happiness and provide supreme guidance.

In the afternoon 'Abdu'l-Bahá spoke to a group of Christian ministers, saying:

> The teachings of Christ are forgotten. Consider that Christ commanded Peter to sheathe his sword. He also said, 'Whosoever shall smite thee on thy right cheek, turn to him the other also' [Matt. 5:39]. But now, contrary to these teachings, see how Christians are killing one another. Christian leaders considered the shedding of the blood of each other a lawful act. What blood has been shed over the conflict between Protestants and Catholics!

This evening the Master spoke at a public meeting at Mrs Kinney's home about superstitions, dogmas and the blind imitation of the various religions, concluding with an explanation of the teachings of the Abhá Beauty. As supper was served, and as He had at other times, the Master invited some of the friends to His table to enjoy the Persian dishes. They were overjoyed to see their Master's smile and to hear His stories.

Monday, December 2, 1912
[New York]

After the Master had finished His morning prayers, the friends began to come to visit Him such that by midday the Master's residence was filled with people. He went downstairs and spoke to them:

> I have stayed a long time with you in New York. My stay in other towns has not been a tenth as long. I have met with you day and night, individually and collectively; conveyed to you the admonitions of Bahá'u'lláh; delivered to you the heavenly glad tidings; and explained the means of human progress. I have elucidated the harmful effects of prejudices and imitations and the impurity of selfish desires, expounded the teachings of Bahá'u'lláh and clarified the meanings of the divine proofs and questions.
>
> The time for my departure is near and I am making arrangements for the voyage. Therefore I shall not be able to attend every meeting, so I shall bid you farewell. I am pleased with you and grateful for your services. Truly, you have shown great kindness and extended to me the utmost hospitality. I supplicate to the Kingdom of Bahá'u'lláh to shower upon you His assistance and confirmations so that day by day you may be more assisted to defend the rights of Bahá'u'lláh, that your hearts may become more enlightened, your morals heavenly, your souls transported with joy and your conduct proof of

your faith and certitude. May you be in the utmost sanctity, be completely attracted and turned to the Abhá Kingdom and become like brilliant lights. May you become evident signs of the Blessed Beauty and proofs of the reality of Bahá'u'lláh so that you may illuminate the world. And when people look at your deeds and conduct they will see the traces of holiness and severance and will behold heavenly brightness in you and all will testify that 'these people are truly proofs of the reality of Bahá'u'lláh', and that 'Bahá'u'lláh is undoubtedly the Sun of Truth who has educated these people through His power'. May they see divine lights in your behavior, find the signs of the love of God, observe praiseworthy conduct in you and seek the virtues of the world of man within you. You must each become the proclaimer of truth and shine from the horizon of the world of humanity like brilliant stars. This is what is meant by defending the rights of Bahá'u'lláh; this is the purpose of the Blessed Beauty in suffering afflictions and accepting confinement in the Most Great Prison. He bore all afflictions and difficulties and ascended to the Kingdom of God a prisoner so that we would act according to His teachings and arise and carry out that which is consistent with faithfulness; that we may act upon His exhortation and raise the call of the Abhá Kingdom and proclaim the light of the bounties of truth, so that the waves of the Most Great Ocean may surge high, this world may become the mirror of the world above, this bed of thorns may turn into a flower garden and this region of dust may reflect the All-Glorious Paradise.

In the afternoon He said:

> We have sown some seeds and hope that the sun of favor will shine upon them, the rain of mercy will pour down, and the breezes of generosity will waft over them, because America has receptivity.

In the evening, He spoke to a gathering of the friends and said:

> I supplicate and implore that the clouds of mercy may shower upon you and the Sun of Truth may shine upon you so that you may attain to the purpose of the holy Manifestations of God. This is my supplication because you are the beloved ones of the Blessed Beauty and the servants of the Greatest Name. I undertook this voyage in order to see you and, God willing, you will come to the Holy Land and we shall meet there in that land which was trodden by the sacred feet of the Prophets of God.[382]

Tuesday, December 3, 1912
[New York]

Group after group of older and newer believers sadly and tearfully came to see the Master, encircling Him and weeping at His imminent departure. Their hearts were sad and overcome with anguish. They confessed to Him their negligence and shortcomings in serving the Cause and their failure to obey His instructions and begged His assistance and blessings, confirmations and favor.

Today the believers were so overcome by emotion that even a stone would be affected. Their anguish would melt any heart. Indeed, in His presence they bowed and knelt so deeply that one could not distinguish between their heads and their feet.

There were two large meetings this afternoon and evening. One was at the home of Mrs Krug, which was filled with many people who had come just to be in 'Abdu'l-Bahá's presence. The Master's talk was this:

> He is God! Praise be to God that Mrs Krug has been the cause of your gathering in this meeting where you are engaged in mentioning God and in adducing proofs. I hope that day by day you will become more attracted, become more enlightened and make extraordinary spiritual progress. You should learn

from one another so that you may know how to teach the Cause and guide the souls. Your hearts must be so attracted that when a question is heard you will be able to give a conclusive answer and the Holy Spirit may speak through your tongue. You must be assured and confident that the favors and confirmations of the Blessed Beauty will make a drop into an ocean, a seed into a fruitful tree, an atom into a luminous sun and a stone into a brilliant jewel. His favors are great, His treasuries inexhaustible and His bounties infinite. God, Who has bestowed favors upon others, shall surely bestow His favors upon you. I supplicate at the Court of the Almighty and beg that mighty confirmations may surround you, that from your tongues may flow irrefutable proofs and that your hearts become recipients for the splendors of the Sun of Reality. May your thoughts expand and your stations be exalted, so that you may be able to diffuse the fragrances of God and to make prodigious progress in the world of man. Unless a man acquires perfection for himself, he cannot teach others how to attain such perfection; and unless he gets life for himself, he cannot give life to others. We must therefore try first to acquire the bounties of the Kingdom for ourselves and attain life everlasting, and then endeavor to quicken the nations and give life to the world. Thus, we must constantly pray to His Holy Court and seek His eternal bounties. We must acquire pure hearts like unto mirrors, so that the lights of the Sun of Reality may shine. Every night and day we must supplicate to Him and beg for His assistance, saying: 'O Lord, we are weak, make us strong; we are ignorant, make us wise. O Lord, we are poor, give us the wealth of the Kingdom. O God, we are dead, bestow upon us everlasting life; we are in utter lowliness, exalt us in Thy Kingdom. Should Thy heavenly confirmations surround us, each one of us can be a luminous star, otherwise we become lower than dust. O God, help us; make us victorious; assist us to overcome self and desire; and deliver us from the world of nature. O God! Quicken us through the breaths of the Holy Spirit so that we may arise to serve Thee, engage ourselves in worshipping Thee and broadcast the signs of Thy Kingdom with utmost truthfulness and sincerity. Thou art the Powerful, the Mighty, the Generous and the Compassionate.[383]

From this meeting the Master went to Mrs Kinney's home.[384] The rush of friends and seekers was greater than ever before and all hearts were aflame. The Master exhorted them to exert their utmost to propagate the divine principles and to diffuse the fragrances of God. He explained the new teachings and the Cause of Bahá'u'lláh. After the meeting, the believers gathered around Him. He bade farewell to each, bestowed His favor upon all and then went upstairs.[385]

Wednesday, December 4, 1912
[New York]

Among the new seekers who met the Master today was a rabbi to whom the Master spoke extensively about the Torah, saying:

> The verse 'God created heaven and earth in six days' has reference to the Day of God and the spiritual creation, for there was no day or night before the creation of this heaven and earth. And the meaning of 'the water' in the verse of the Torah 'The spirit of God moved upon the face of the water like a bird' is the water of knowledge which is the source of heavenly life. It is written that God said, 'Let us make man in our image'; this means in the image of divine names and attributes, for God is holy above all physical images and is pure and sanctified above all forms or likenesses.

Elucidating further the nature of biblical language and the mysteries of the holy books, He explained the signs and prophecies regarding the promised Manifestation. The rabbi was impressed and acknowledged the Master's insight.

Later some prominent people, including professors, came to meet 'Abdu'l-Bahá. They told him about Professor Colombo who had written an article about the Mashriqu'l-Adhkár near Chicago in which he referred to the contributions of the Eastern Bahá'ís towards its construction as one of the indications of the greatness of the Cause. The Master spoke with them about the dogmas and blind imitations of the priests and the superstitions of the religious leaders.

At the Kinney's home in the afternoon, a number of Mr Kinney's students met the Master. Some came during the meeting and others after it. The Master spoke to them about understanding the holy Book:

> The object of reading and reciting is to understand the inner significance of the verses and mysteries of the Book. Had reading sufficed, all the Jewish people should have acknowledged Christ but as they lacked understanding of the mysteries and the inner meanings, they were deprived of the bounty of believing in Him. They interpreted the book in a literal or outward manner and did not find the appearance of Christ to conform to their traditions, imitations and the prevailing customs of their people, so they denied and rejected Him. Hence, they remained heedless and ignorant of divine realities and mysteries.

This evening there was a large gathering at the Theosophical Society of New York. The subject of the Master's address was 'The Eternity of God's Kingdom': material existence, the betterment of the world through the divine favors, the guidance provided by the Manifestations of God and their reflection upon the world of creation. 'This is the law of God, and thou shalt not find any change in it.'[386] This is a translation of the Master's address:

> He is God! Those who are uninformed of the world of reality, and do not study created things, cannot investigate and

discover hidden truths. They only have a superficial idea of things, are embodiments of ignorance and blind imitators. They believe that which they have heard from their fathers and do not have any knowledge or understanding of their own and are bereft of hearing and insight. They rely on traditions and tales and follow the path of their ancestors. They imagine that God's dominion is accidental, that this world has existed for but six thousand or eight thousand years and that before that time God had neither creation nor sovereignty.

Should this notion be accepted, then, the Lord forbid, the Divine Reality is to be regarded as accidental, not eternal, whereas as long as there was God, He must have had a creation; as long as there was light, there must have been recipients of that light, because light cannot become manifest without illumining its recipients. So likewise without a creation, the existence of the Creator cannot be proven.

The Divine Reality presupposes a creation, the All-Provider presupposes a recipient of His bounty. To imagine a God without His creatures is like imagining a king without a country and a people. A king must have a kingdom. Could there be a king without a country and subjects? It is an impossibility. If there had been a time when there were no country and no army, how could we say there was a king at that time? Thus he must have had his people. Thus, as the Divine Eternity is infinite, His creation is also without beginning and without end. From everlasting God was the Creator, the All-Provider, the Quickener and the Bestower. There was no time when His attributes did not express themselves. Cessation is wholly inconceivable. The sun is the sun because of its light and heat. If we conceive the cessation of heat and light, we predicate the non-existence of the sun. If it had no light and no heat, it was not the sun. Likewise, when we say that at one time God had no creation and no recipient of His grace, we assert that there was no Creator. This is denying the eternity of the Divine Entity and regarding Him as an accidental being. It is obvious that this endless universe, this mighty handiwork of God, this vast firmament, these gigantic globes are not merely six or seven thousand years old. They are ancient. The reference in the Torah to six thousand years has an inner meaning and should not be taken literally. It is stated that God created the heavens and the earth in six days. If before such a creation there was no sun, no east and no west, how was it possible to determine the length of each day without the existence of a sun? Thus the statement has a different meaning.

The sovereignty of God is eternal and not accidental. His creation, His Kingdom, His Army are coexistent and will continue as such. The bestowals and bounties of God are constant and are uninterrupted. Like the light and heat of the sun, they have no cessation. The holy Manifestations of God, Who are the dawning places of divine bounties, have ever been and shall ever be. The wisdom and purpose of their appearance is to cause the image and likeness of God to appear in the world of man.

The reality of man possesses two aspects: one being the image and likeness of God and the other is the material and satanic aspect. Besides the physical body, man has a reality which is called the spiritual body, or the heavenly creation or form. When man says, 'I saw', who is it that says 'I saw'? Clearly it is something besides the physical body. When one thinks, it is like consulting with oneself. It is clear that there is a second entity which is being consulted. It is not the physical body that advises man 'to do' or 'not to do' a thing and informs him whether it is profitable or harmful.

Frequently a person firmly decides on a course of action, but later, upon some reflection, changes his mind. The reason is that he has consulted a reality, has become aware of the harm involved and has changed his former decision.

In addition to this, man journeys in the world of dreams. Though the body is here, the soul wanders in the East and West of the world. Who is it that makes these journeys? It is the second entity. Although a man has died and his body is under the earth, one's soul can, in a dream, ask him questions and receive answers. What is it that is talked to? It is the second reality. Hence, it is clear that besides the physical body man possesses another reality. Though the body grows weak, becomes fat or defective, still that reality remains unaltered. In sleep the body of man appears dead but that reality moves, understands, talks and discovers. This reality is the spiritual form and the heavenly temple, not the physical body. It reveals hidden realities, comprehends things, discovers arts and sciences, subdues electricity and other forces and communicates simultaneously with the East and the West. Plainly it is not the body. If it had been the body, similar powers and perfections should have existed in animals, for they share our physical powers. Hence, it is the second reality that reveals hidden realities, permeates the universe, becomes informed of mysteries, leads to the Kingdom and is a guide to the people of the world. It is this reality that distinguishes man from the animal. But this reality is in a state between the divine world and that of the animal. If spiritual forces prevail, this human reality becomes the noblest of all creatures and the possessor of the image and likeness of God; but if the animal aspect predominates, man becomes lower than animals because in man, animal desires and passions are even stronger and more harmful. For instance, anger, lust, struggle for existence, war, contention, fraud, deception, greed and avarice are among the imperfections of man but the necessary qualities in animals. A crafty man without spiritual education is as the fox. In the animal we find covetousness, aggression and passion. These qualities are also in man. Since the reality of man is comprehensive, his expression of these animal qualities is more vehement. They are among the exigencies of the world of nature and lead to the gloom of imperfections. They are the cause of utter degradation and misfortune.

On the other hand, man is the repository of divine

perfections and heavenly favors that bring him eternal happiness and everlasting honor. Such perfections as justice, fidelity, truthfulness, purity, wisdom, piety, mercy, bounty, love, amity, nobility and sagacity enable man to comprehend the realities of things and unfold hidden mysteries. Human reality is therefore between light and darkness and has a threefold nature: the heavenly, the human and the physical. The physical condition is darkness upon darkness and the source of trouble, disgrace, discord, bloodshed and war. The heavenly condition, however, which is the zenith of the human aspect of man's nature, is light upon light and the means of acquiring everlasting prosperity, peace and tranquillity, honor and glory.

The holy divine Manifestations have appeared to make it easy to replace the gloom of animality with the lights of heavenly qualities and to change the imperfections of the world of nature to the perfections of the spirit so that the heavenly aspect may prevail, the image and likeness of God may appear in the world of man and the divine illumination and spiritual virtues may become manifest. These holy dawning places are the Educators of the world of existence and the Teachers of man. They deliver human beings from the darkness of error and heedlessness and the defects and vices of nature and lead them to the realm of spiritual virtues and heavenly perfections. Those who are ignorant become wise, those who are like animals attain human perfections, the rapacious become angelic, the tyrannical and proud become just and humble, so that earthly man becomes heavenly, the human is changed into the divine, the suckling child attains its maturity and the poor and abased attain wealth and glory. If the holy Manifestations had not appeared, all humanity would have remained in a state of animality, if not worse. If the children are not educated and are not trained in schools, they will remain ignorant. If plains and hills are left to their natural state, they will turn into jungles and forests which will not bear sweet and luscious fruit, but when the gardener takes control, flowers bloom, fruits appear and prosperity sheds its blessings. Creation is a dreary forest full of thorns under the yoke of nature and the holy Manifestations are the divine gardeners and the supreme educators of the world of man who come to promote the progress of the world of existence in order that the trees of beings may continue to be verdant, may burst into fresh foliage, may yield good fruits and may adorn the gardens of the human realities. This divine bestowal of this heavenly education is continuous.

It is impossible that this great bounty should cease, that this divine bestowal should end and that the Sun of Reality should sink forever into a setting not followed by a sunrise, a death not followed by a revival. How can the Sun of Reality, shining from the divine world, remain set forever and be precluded from educating the world of existence? No, by God! The function of the sun is to give illumination. How can it set forever and its effulgence brought to an end? Its bounty is eternal, its luster is ever manifest, its rays are perpetually radiant, its breezes are continually wafting and its bestowals are ever apparent. We must be expectant and hopeful, turning our gaze in the direction of His bountiful Kingdom that through the appearance of these holy Manifestations humanity may attain the blessings of the All-Glorious, that the earth be changed and the contingent world may become a garden and a paradise of delight. But the appearance of the divine Manifestation must take place in the most perfect form and invested with unparalleled powers and virtues. With a divine influence and heavenly might He must be exalted above all else and peerless in all His attributes, just as the sun is exalted above other stars. Though every star and planet shines in its place and gives light in the night, the sun has another splendor and its radiance is greater. The Manifestation of the bounty of God must also be like the physical sun so that the world may be convinced that He is a divine Teacher, an Educator of the world of man, a sun of reality and the brightest Light shining from the realm on high. His effulgence and influence must be inherent and not acquired from other human beings, otherwise we would say that others imparted such powers to Him. How can a man, who is educated by other human beings, become the educator of humanity at large? The Manifestations of the bounty of God must be self-subsistent, not under the shadow of others. He must be an educator, not educated by others. He must be perfect, not deficient. He must be independent of all, not dependent on training by others. He must combine in Himself all perfections, unrestricted by human limitations, so that He may be able to educate humanity, dispel the gloom of ignorance, through divine power change the world, bring about universal peace, establish the oneness of humanity and unite the diverse religions. I hope that the divine bounties and blessings may shine brightly so that the lights of the Sun of Reality may give luster to our eyes, illumination to our hearts and joy to our souls and may ennoble our thoughts and grant us eternal life. Then we may attain to the apex of the world of man.

For nine months I have been touring America, calling the people to the oneness of humanity. I have delivered addresses in churches and large assemblies in many cities, inviting the people to the oneness of mankind and to love and unity. The people of America extended a cordial welcome to me. In fact, Americans are a noble nation, with capacity to acquire every virtue and investigate every truth.

Since I shall leave your shores tomorrow, I bid you farewell. I pray that divine confirmations, heavenly glory and eternal life may be granted to you, so that you may reach the highest pinnacles of the world of man. I am most grateful to you and shall never forget you. I shall ever supplicate at the court of the Almighty and beg divine assistance and heavenly bounty for you.[387]

The Master's talk enthused the audience and one by one they came to Him to express their sincere thanks and admiration. When they were told of His imminent departure, they became downcast. It was astonishing to witness the deep sorrow of the friends and the lamentation of their hearts as they contemplated their separation from Him.

Thursday, December 5, 1912
[New York]

A great number of believers from New York and other cities came to the S. S. *Celtic* to bid farewell to their beloved. The tears in their eyes bespoke of their great sorrow. The sobs and lamentations of both the young and the old could be heard from afar. Although the first class lounge was quite large, it could not contain the crowd of believers. Some were sitting and others standing outside the lounge. As He moved among the friends, the Master spoke to them words of exhortation and admonition, consoling their hearts as He bade them farewell. He guided the sorrowing ones onto the path of everlasting happiness and reminded them of the glad tidings of the Abhá Kingdom until the time came for the friends to depart. He then spoke His parting words:

> He is God! This is our last day and my last meeting with you. In a few minutes our steamer will leave these shores and this is my last exhortation to you. I have repeatedly spoken to you and invited you to realize the oneness of humanity. I have impressed upon you that all human beings are the servants of the same God and God is kind to all; He provides for all and gives life to all. In the presence of God all are His servants and His bounties are equally distributed among all. We must also be kind to the people of the world and forget all religious, racial, patriotic and political prejudices. The whole earth is one globe. All nations are one family. All are the servants of one God. Therefore he who causes grief to another's heart has sinned against the Lord. God desired the joy of all hearts. He wishes that every individual may pass his life in utmost happiness and felicity and should abandon religious, racial, patriotic

and political prejudices. Praise be to God! Your eyes are illumined, your ears are opened and your hearts are informed. You must not entertain these prejudices and differences. You must look to the bounty of God. He is the real Shepherd who is kind to the whole flock. When God is kind to all, is it befitting that we, who are His servants, should engage in war and conflict with one another? No, by God! We must be grateful to God and the way to express gratitude for His bounty is to love each other, show amity and affection and evince friendship and kindness toward all.

In brief, beware, lest you offend any heart or engage in backbiting. You must be friends to all and regard all as your own kith and kin. Your supreme object must always be to bring pleasure to a heart, to give food to the hungry, clothes to the naked, honor to the degraded, help to the helpless and comfort to the distressed. This is the way to win the good pleasure of God. This is that which is conducive to eternal happiness. This is the light of the world of man. As I wish eternal honor for you, so I exhort you with these words.

Behold what is happening in the Balkans! Human blood is being spilt! How many children are rendered orphans! How ruthlessly properties are looted! What a fire is aflame! God has created them to love one another but they are shedding one another's blood. God created them to help and assist one another but they are engaged in plunder and destruction. Instead of being a cause of comfort to their kind, they persecute one another. Make your motives lofty and exert with heart and soul every effort; perchance, the light of universal peace may shine forth and this gloom of estrangement be dispelled. May all human beings become one family and every individual seek the welfare of all. May the East help the West and the West assist the East, for the whole earth is one country and all its people are under the favor and protection of one Shepherd.

Behold! What persecutions have the Prophets of God suffered so that human beings may love one another and cling to the cord of love and unity. These sanctified souls ever sacrificed themselves for this aim. But behold! How ignorant is man! In spite of all these sufferings, people are warring against one another. Notwithstanding all the exhortations, they are massacring one another. What ignorance! What heedlessness! What gloom! They have a God who deals kindly and equally with all yet they move and act against His good pleasure. He is benevolent and merciful to all but they are in utmost hatred and war. He gives life to all but they bring death. He brings prosperity to the countries but they destroy one another's households. How heedless they are! Your duties are different because you have been informed of the divine mysteries and your eyes and ears are opened. You are to deal kindly with all the people of the world. You have no excuse before God. You know that the pleasure of God lies in the welfare and prosperity of all. You have hearkened unto His words of advice, His exhortations and His teachings. You must love all, even your enemies. To those who show you ill-will show them your good-will. To those who oppose you be a faithful friend. You should act according to these teachings. Perchance, the abysmal gloom of war and bloodshed may vanish; the light of God may shine forth; the East may be enlightened; the West may be filled with fragrance; the North and the South may embrace each other; and the nations of the world may associate with one another in utmost love and amity! Unless the world reaches this station, it can find no rest, no enduring happiness.

But if men act according to these holy teachings, the world of dust shall reflect the lights of the Kingdom and the earth shall become the Abhá paradise, a garden of blissful joy. I hope that each one of you will be assisted to act according to these teachings so that, like a brilliant star, you may give light to humanity and like a spirit move the body of the contingent world. This is eternal glory! This is everlasting happiness! This is the image and likeness of God and unto this I call you! I pray God that you may attain it.[388]

When the passengers and officers of the steamer heard this address and saw the devotion of the friends, they were overwhelmed and asked themselves, 'What is it? Who is this personage in whose presence the Americans stand with such reverence and humility?' Young and old alike were like moths to a candle, circling about the light of the Covenant.

One by one the friends came to 'Abdu'l-Bahá to shake His hand, to take hold of the mantle of His grace and favor and to supplicate His assistance and confirmation. Then, in great sorrow, they left the ship. They stood on the wharf, weeping and overcome by emotion, their heads bowed with grief and their hands lifted towards the heavens in prayer as they gazed their last at the Center of the Covenant. As the steamer moved out to sea, their grief and sadness and the fire of their devotion knew no bounds. The throng of believers, stretching as far as the eye could see, waved farewell to the Master, now far in the distance. And He said:

> Observe how the power of the Cause of God has created a tumult in the hearts and what a revolution it has produced. See how the aid and assistance of the Abhá Beauty have reached us constantly and invariably the lights of victory have shone from the supreme horizon. These have been from the promised confirmations of the Kingdom of God and the assistance of the invisible sovereignty of the Abhá Beauty, which He has promised clearly in the verse, 'Verily, We behold you from Our realm of Glory, and shall aid whosoever will arise for the triumph of Our Cause with the hosts of the Concourse on high and a company of Our favored angels.'[389]

The events that took place during 'Abdu'l-Bahá's travels in Europe and His return to the East are recorded in the second volume of this book.

* * *

A hundred thousand thanks and praises for the confirmations of the Abhá Beauty and the bestowals of that essence of faithfulness, the Center of the Covenant, that this lowly servant was able to complete this first volume of the Kitáb-i-Badáyi'u'l-Áthár in the year 1332 AH [at the end of 1913 AD]. With his own hand he wrote it and submitted it to 'Abdu'l-Bahá (may the lives of His followers be a ransom for His Covenant of faithfulness). In the year 1914 I was commissioned to go to India to obtain permission to publish and distribute it. With the assistance of the friends Mr Javan Mard Goshtasp and Mr Mehtar Isfandíyár Bahrám,[390] I was able to publish it in 1914 in Bombay.

[Signed] Maḥmúd Ibn-i-Ismael Zarqání

BIOGRAPHICAL NOTES

'Abdu'l-Bahá (1844–1921) Eldest surviving son of Bahá'u'lláh; the Center of the Covenant; the Mystery of God; the Master. 'Abdu'l-Bahá accompanied His father on His exiles, spending more than 40 years as a prisoner. After the passing of Bahá'u'lláh in 1892, 'Abdu'l-Bahá became the head of the Bahá'í Faith and worked to maintain the unity of its followers. Freed by the Young Turks' Rebellion in 1908, 'Abdu'l-Bahá began to travel outside the Holy Land, making His first visit to Europe in 1911. See Balyuzi, *'Abdu'l-Bahá*.

'Abdu'l-Ḥamíd II (ruled 1876–1909) Sultan of the Ottoman Turkish Empire, known as 'the Great Assassin'. As the result of the plotting of Mírzá Muḥammad-'Alí, in 1901 he restricted 'Abdu'l-Bahá's freedom, confining Him and His family within the city walls of 'Akká. He later sent two commissions of inquiry to investigate false charges made against 'Abdu'l-Bahá by the Covenant-breakers. He was deposed in 1909 following the Young Turks' revolution of 1908. See *God Passes By*, pp. 269–72.

Abu'l-Faḍl Gulpáygání, Mírzá (1844–1914) Preeminent Persian Bahá'í scholar and author, noted for his learned treatises on the Bahá'í Faith, who was sent to the United States by 'Abdu'l-Bahá in 1901 to deepen the American Bahá'ís and to counter the attempts of Kheiralla to create a division within the American Bahá'í community. He was named an Apostle of Bahá'u'lláh by Shoghi Effendi.

Abu'l-Qásim-i-Hamadání, Áqá (d. 1856) Sole companion of Bahá'u'lláh during His retirement to Sulaymáníyyih. He was set upon by highwaymen or frontier patrols and was mortally wounded. When found near death, he gave his name and bequeathed all his possessions to Darvísh Muḥammad-i-Írání, the name Bahá'u'lláh had assumed. See Balyuzi, *King of Glory*, pp. 116–117.

Afnán-i-Yazdí (1830–1911) Also known as Ḥájí Muḥammad-Taqí, the Afnán, a cousin of the Báb and the chief builder of the first Bahá'í House of Worship in 'Ishqábád, in Russian Turkistán, which had been initiated by 'Abdu'l-Bahá in or about 1902. Taqí's state title was Vakíl'ud-Dawlih. He was named an Apostle of Bahá'u'lláh by Shoghi Effendi. See 'Abdu'l-Bahá, *Memorials of the Faithful*, pp. 126–9.

Asadu'lláh-i-Qumí, Siyyid A member of 'Abdu'l-Bahá's entourage.

Ashraf, Qudsíyyih First Persian woman to travel to the United States. She represented Bahá'í women of the Orient at the laying of the corner-stone of the Wilmette Mashriqu'l-Adhkár.

Bagdadi, Dr Zia (d. 1937) Medical doctor from Iraq who settled in the United States in 1909 and was a prominent member of the Chicago Bahá'í community. He represented the Arab Bahá'ís at the laying of the corner-stone of the Wilmette Mashriqu'l-Adhkár. See *Bahá'í World*, vol. 7, pp. 535–9.

Bell, Alexander Graham (1847–1922) 'Scottish inventor and teacher of elocution and speech correction. He went to live in Canada in 1870. He developed a method of teaching speech to the deaf and in 1873 became professor of vocal physiology at Boston University. In 1876 he obtained a patent for the telephone, which he developed during long evening sessions with the mechanic

Thomas Watson. His other inventions included the photophone, a device that transmitted sound on a beam of light, and the graphophone, which recorded sound on wax discs.' At the time of 'Abdu'l-Bahá's visit he lived in Washington DC. Law, *Giant Book of 1000 Great Lives*, pp. 32–3.

Bosch, John (1855–1946) California vintner who became a Bahá'í in 1905 and subsequently changed his profession. His property at Geyserville, California, was used as a permanent Bahá'í summer school from 1927 and was deeded to the American National Spiritual Assembly in 1936. See *Bahá'í World*, vol. 11, pp. 488–94.

Bourgeois, Louis (d. 1930) French-Canadian architect who became a Bahá'í in the winter of 1906–7 and moved to West Englewood, New Jersey, to assist in the development of the Bahá'í community. His design was chosen for the Mashriqu'l-Adhkár in Wilmette. See Whitmore, *Dawning Place*, pp. 76–86.

Breed, Alice Ives (b. 1853) Well-known society and club woman of Boston and one of the early Bahá'ís in the United States. She was the wife of Francis W. Breed and the mother of Florence Breed, who married Ali Kuli Khan. See Gail, *Summon Up Remembrance*.

Browne, Professor Edward Granville (1862–1926) Distinguished British orientalist from Cambridge University who published many books and articles on the Bábí and Bahá'í religions and who had four interviews with Bahá'u'lláh in 'Akká in 1890. He is best known to Bahá'ís for his pen-portrait of Bahá'u'lláh. See Balyuzi, *Edward Granville Browne and the Bahá'í Faith*.

Bryan, William Jennings American politician who became Secretary of State under President Woodrow Wilson. He had tried to visit 'Abdu'l-Bahá while on his travels near 'Akká but had been unable to do so. 'Although he was defeated three times for the presidency of the United States, William Jennings Bryan was for many years a leader of the Democratic Party and it was his influence that won the Democratic presidential nomination for Woodrow Wilson in 1912. He . . . negotiated treaties with 30 countries, representing three-fourths of the world's population, for investigation of disputes before resorting to war. He published a paper called The Commoner and gave lectures advancing the cause of prohibition, of religion and of morality. Because of his opposition to war, he resigned from office in 1915 in protest against the sinking of the Lusitania. After the war he moved to Florida and worked to advance moral and religious causes.' *Compton's Encyclopedia*, America Online edition, January 1, 1993.

Carnegie, Andrew (1835–1919) Industrialist and philanthropist born in Scotland who migrated to the United States as a young man. He 'started at the bottom in a railway company but rose rapidly and made shrewd investments. During the American Civil War he founded iron and steel firms and established trusts to use his money for the good of the community. He endowed over 1,000 libraries and founded universities and colleges, giving away 300 million dollars in his lifetime.' Law, *Giant Book of 1000 Great Lives*, p. 72.

Chase, Thornton (1847–1912) Called by 'Abdu'l-Bahá 'the first American believer', Chase became a Bahá'í in 1894 in Chicago and was the principal organizer of the Chicago Bahá'í community. He founded the Behais Supply and Publishing Board in 1900, which was incorporated as the Bahai Publishing Society in 1902. He wrote a number of pamphlets about the Bahá'í Faith, an introductory book, *The Bahai Revelation*, and an account of his pilgrimage in 1907, *In Galilee*. He was given the name T͟hábit (Steadfast) by 'Abdu'l-Bahá and was named a Disciple of 'Abdu'l-Bahá by Shoghi Effendi. His grave site in Inglewood, California, is visited annually by the Bahá'ís. See Whitehead, *Some Early Bahá'ís of the West*, pp. 1–12.

BIOGRAPHICAL NOTES 433

Cooper, Ella (1870–1951) Prominent American Bahá'í teacher who accepted the Faith in 1898 and, with her mother Helen Goodall, helped establish the first Bahá'í community on the American West coast, in Oakland. She was among the third group of Western pilgrims to visit 'Akká, in March 1899. After her second pilgrimage in 1908 she and her mother published a small book, *Daily Lessons Received at Acca*. See Whitehead, *Some Early Bahá'ís of the West*, pp. 21–34 and *Bahá'í World*, vol. 12, pp. 681–4.

Dayyán, Mírzá Asadu'lláh-i-Khuy A Bábí on whom the Báb conferred the designation 'Dayyán' (lit. 'conqueror' or 'judge'). After the martyrdom of the Báb, a number of His followers turned to Dayyán for guidance. He claimed to be 'He Whom God shall make manifest' but after meeting Bahá'u'lláh in Iraq he retracted the claim. Mírzá Yaḥyá instigated the murder of Dayyán, 'whom he feared and envied'. See Shoghi Effendi, *God Passes By*, p. 165.

D'Evelyn, Dr Frederick Learned and staunch San Francisco Bahá'í, elected chairman of the local community in 1911. He was encouraged by 'Abdu'l-Bahá to plan the first International Bahá'í conference, in 1915.

Ḍíyá Páshá, Yúsuf Turkish Ambassador to the United States at the time of 'Abdu'l-Bahá's visit.

Dodge, Arthur Pillsbury (1849–1915) Lawyer, publisher, inventor and self-made man who became a Bahá'í in 1897. He was named a Disciple of 'Abdu'l-Bahá by Shoghi Effendi. See Stockman, *Bahá'í Faith in America*, vol. 1, pp. 116–17 and *Star of the West*, vol. 6, no. 13, pp. 100–1.

Dreyfus, Hippolyte (1873–1928) Prominent French lawyer and the first Frenchman to become a Bahá'í, in 1901. He wrote a number of works on the Bahá'í Faith and translated several of Bahá'u'lláh's writings into French. In 1911 he married Laura

Clifford Barney with whom he had worked on a French translation of *Some Answered Questions*. He was named a Disciple of 'Abdu'l-Bahá by Shoghi Effendi. See Shoghi Effendi's appreciation of him in *Bahá'í World*, vol. 3, pp. 210–14.

Dreyfus-Barney, Laura (1879–1974) Prominent American Bahá'í who accepted the Faith in Paris around 1900. She made a number of extended visits to 'Akká, asking questions of 'Abdu'l-Bahá, the answers to which she later compiled as *Some Answered Questions*. She was twice decorated by the French government for her services to humanity. See *Bahá'í World*, vol. 16, pp. 535–8.

Faríd (Fareed), Dr Amínu'lláh Nephew of 'Abdu'l-Bahá's wife and a member of 'Abdu'l-Bahá's entourage, serving as translator for many of His talks. He began to solicit funds clandestinely from the American Bahá'ís, using a seal of 'Abdu'l-Bahá's which he had stolen. He was later declared a Covenant-breaker for his disobedience to 'Abdu'l-Bahá. See Taherzadeh, *Covenant of Bahá'u'lláh*, p. 341.

Farmer, Sarah Jane (1847–1916) American philanthropist who became a Bahá'í upon meeting 'Abdu'l-Bahá in 'Akká in 1900. She gave Green Acre, her property at Eliot, Maine, to the Faith for use as a permanent Bahá'í summer school. She was named a Disciple of 'Abdu'l-Bahá by Shoghi Effendi. See *Green Acre on the Piscataqua*.

Fujita, Saichiro (1886–1976) Young Japanese man who became a Bahá'í in Oakland, California, in 1905, the second Japanese in the world to accept the Faith. He was invited by 'Abdu'l-Bahá to travel with His entourage to California from Chicago. For a time he lived with the family of Corinne True and in 1919 was invited to serve 'Abdu'l-Bahá in the Holy Land. He served the Master and afterwards Shoghi Effendi until 1938, when he went to Japan for the duration of the second world war. In 1955 he returned to the

Holy Land where he served Shoghi Effendi and then the Hands of the Cause and the Universal House of Justice. See *Bahá'í World*, vol. 17, pp. 406–8.

Getsinger, Dr Edward (1866–1935) Early American believer who had become a Bahá'í by 1897. He and his wife Lua were the first American-born Bahá'ís to visit 'Abdu'l-Bahá, remaining in the Holy Land from November 1898 to March 1899. See Metelmann, *Lua Getsinger*.

Getsinger, Lua (1871–1916) Outstanding American Bahá'í traveling teacher who accepted the Faith in Chicago in April 1897. She and her husband, Edward, played a central role in opposing Kheiralla when he began to question the authority of 'Abdu'l-Bahá. Lua devoted nearly all her time to teaching the Faith, spending much time away from home. In 1914–15 'Abdu'l-Bahá sent the Getsingers on a teaching trip to India. Lua went on to 'Akká and then Egypt, where she died of an illness she had contracted in India. She was given the title 'Herald of the Covenant' by 'Abdu'l-Bahá and was named a Disciple of 'Abdu'l-Bahá and 'Mother Teacher of the West' by Shoghi Effendi. See *Bahá'í World*, vol. 8, pp. 642–3 and Metelmann, *Lua Getsinger*.

Goodale, Mr and Mrs Henry L. Bahá'ís from Kenosha, Wisconsin in whose home 'Abdu'l-Bahá stayed for one night on September 15, 1912.

Goodall, Helen (1847–1922) Prominent American Bahá'í teacher who accepted the Faith in 1898 and, with her daughter Ella Cooper, helped establish the first Bahá'í community on the American West coast, in Oakland. After her first pilgrimage in 1908 she and her daughter published a small book, *Daily Lessons Received at Acca*. She was named a Disciple of 'Abdu'l-Bahá by Shoghi Effendi. See Whitehead, *Some Early Bahá'ís of the West*, pp. 21–34.

Grant, Rev Dr Percy Stickney Rector of the Church of the Ascension, New York, and a friend of Juliet Thompson. See *Diary of Juliet Thompson*.

Greatest Holy Leaf, Bahíyyih Khánum (1846–1932) Daughter of Bahá'u'lláh and Navváb, and sister of 'Abdu'l-Bahá.

Gregory, Louis (1874–1951) Prominent American Bahá'í traveling teacher and advocate of racial unity. The son of Georgia slaves, Gregory was admitted to the bar in 1907 and became a Bahá'í in June 1909. His marriage to Louisa Mathew, a white English Bahá'í, in September 1912 was the first Bahá'í interracial marriage in America. Gregory traveled extensively throughout the American states teaching the Bahá'í Faith, particularly among blacks in the South. He was elected to the Executive Board of the Bahá'í Temple Unity in 1912 and to the National Spiritual Assembly of the Bahá'ís of the United States in 1922. He was the only black to serve on either body until 1946. He was posthumously appointed a Hand of the Cause of God by Shoghi Effendi. See Morrison, *To Move the World*; Harper, *Lights of Fortitude*, pp. 85–98 and *Bahá'í World*, vol. 12, pp. 666–70.

Hall, Albert Heath (1958–1920) Lawyer, the son of a minister, who became a Bahá'í between 1900 and 1903. While he was handling the case for the defense of Fred Mortensen, he taught the young man the Faith. Hall was president of the Executive Board of the Bahá'í Temple Unity from 1911 to 1914. See Whitehead, *Some Early Bahá'ís of the West*, pp. 111–14.

Hannen, Joseph (1872–1920) Leading Washington Bahá'í and active teacher of the Faith who became a Bahá'í shortly after his wife, Pauline. Along with his wife, he pioneered teaching the Faith to blacks in the United States. Among those they taught was Louis Gregory. In 1916 'Abdu'l-Bahá sent the first Tablet of the Divine Plan to the southern states in care of Joseph. He was named a

Disciple of 'Abdu'l-Bahá by Shoghi Effendi. See Hannen Moe *Aflame with Devotion, The Hannen and Knobloch Families and the Early Days of the Bahá'í Faith in America*, Stockman, *Bahá'í Faith in America*, vol. 2, pp. 137, 224–6.

Hannen, Pauline (1874–1939) American Bahá'í teacher and advocate of racial unity who accepted the Faith in Washington DC in November 1902. She taught several members of her family the Faith, including her husband Joseph and her sisters Fanny Knobloch and Alma Knobloch. Overcoming her own racial prejudice, she began to teach blacks in Washington, opening her home for Bahá'í meetings. She also organized the Bahá'í children's classes in the city. See Hannen Moe *Aflame with Devotion, The Hannen and Knobloch Families and the Early Days of the Bahá'í Faith in America*, *Bahá'í World*, vol. 8, pp. 660–1 and Stockman, *Bahá'í Faith in America*, vol. 2, pp. 137, 224–6.

Harmon, W.W. Boston metaphysician and Theosophist who 'revered 'Abdu'l-Bahá, supported the Bahá'í teachings and associated with the Bahá'í community' (Smith, 'The American Bahá'í Community', in Momen, *Studies in Bábí and Bahá'í History*, vol. 1, p. 169). His controversial explanation of the Bahá'í writings caused a rift in the American Bahá'í community.

Harris, Hooper (1866–1934) American lawyer who became a Bahá'í in New York City in 1899. He answered the call of 'Abdu'l-Bahá in 1906 for an American to go to India to teach the Cause, leaving New York that year with Harlan Ober. They first went to 'Akká to receive instructions from the Master. 'Abdu'l-Bahá sent with them two Iranian teachers, neither of whom could speak English: the elderly Hand of the Cause Ibn-i-Abhar and Mírzá Maḥmúd. See *Bahá'í World*, vol. 6, pp. 486–8.

Ḥaydar 'Alí, Ḥájí Mírzá (c. 1830–1920) Prominent Persian Bahá'í known by Western Bahá'ís as the 'Angel of Carmel'. He became a

Bábí and later met Bahá'u'lláh in Adrianople. He suffered many years of persecution and imprisonment in Egypt and the Sudan because of his fidelity to the Cause of Bahá'u'lláh. In his later years He served the Master in Haifa. See Ḥaydar 'Alí, *Delight of Hearts* and Balyuzi, *Eminent Bahá'ís*, pp. 235–50.

Hearst, Phoebe Apperson (1842–1919) American philanthropist and mother of the newspaper tycoon William Randolph Hearst. She was a supporter of Green Acre and met Sarah Farmer in 1897. In 1898 the Getsingers called on her and she became interested in the Faith. She organized and financed the first pilgrimage of Western Bahá'ís to 'Akká in 1898–9. She financed a number of Bahá'í teachers and some Bahá'í publications, including the first English translation of the Arabic *Hidden Words*. She began to distance herself from the Faith after some adverse newspaper publicity. See Whitehead, *Some Early Bahá'ís of the West*, pp. 13–19 and *Bahá'í World*, vol. 7, pp. 801–2.

Hemmick, Alice Barney- Mother of Laura Dreyfus-Barney. She was closely associated with the Bahá'í community, although 'It is not clear to what extent she may have considered herself a Bahá'í.' Hollinger, *Agnes Parsons' Diary*, p. 144, biographical notes.

Hoar, William H. (1856–1922) Early American Bahá'í, named a Disciple of 'Abdu'l-Bahá by Shoghi Effendi. Hoar heard of the Faith at the World Parliament of Religions in Chicago in 1893 and became a Bahá'í in January 1896. He was instrumental in forming the first Bahá'í consultative body in New York, the New York Bahá'í Board of Counsel, elected on December 7, 1900. He was elected to the Executive Board of the in 1909, serving for three years.

Ḥusayn Khán, Mírzá (Mushíru'd-Dawlih) Persian ambassador to Constantinople in the time of Bahá'u'lláh. Although involved in the banishment of Bahá'u'lláh from Baghdád, he testified at the court of Náṣiri'd-Dín S͟háh to the dignity, majesty and high-mindedness of Bahá'u'lláh. See Shoghi Effendi, *God Passes By*, p. 159 and Balyuzi, *King of Glory*.

Isfandíyár Loyal servant of the household of Bahá'u'lláh, a member of the family entrusted with marketing and other family affairs. Despite the great danger to his own life when Bahá'u'lláh was imprisoned in the Síyáh-C͟hál, he remained in the household to serve the holy family. Bahá'u'lláh's wife sent Isfandíyár to Mázandarán in northern Iran to be safe but he returned one week later to pay the household's debts. See Afnán, *Black Pearls*, pp. 27–32.

Ives, Rev Howard Colby (c. 1876–1941) Unitarian minister, pastor of the Brotherhood Church, Jersey City, New Jersey who became a Bahá'í after meeting 'Abdu'l-Bahá. His autobiography, *Portals to Freedom*, is an account of his conversion to the Bahá'í Faith. See *Bahá'í World*, vol. 9, pp. 608–13 and Ives, *Portals to Freedom*.

Jání, Ḥájí Mírzá Merchant who was the first to become a Bábí in Kás͟hán. He was an early historian of the Bábí Cause and was later martyred.

Khan, Ali Kuli (1879–1966) Distinguished Bahá'í and diplomat who came to the United States in 1901 as a translator for Mírzá Abu'l-Faḍl. His marriage to Florence Breed in 1904 was the first marriage between a Persian and an American Bahá'í. He was an early translator of some of the most important works of Bahá'u'lláh into English. See the two-volume biography written by his daughter Marzieh Gail, *Summon Up Remembrance* and *Arches of the Years*.

Kheiralla, Ibrahim George (1849–1929) Syrian Christian who became a Bahá'í around 1888. He migrated to the United States in

1892 and began to teach the Faith in New York. In 1894 the Faith began to establish itself in North America through his classes. He began to question the authority of 'Abdu'l-Bahá after February 1900 and eventually broke with the Bahá'í Faith, creating a crisis in the Bahá'í community. See Stockman, *Bahá'í Faith in America*, vol. 1, pp. 158–84; Smith, 'The American Bahá'í Community, 1894–1917' in Momen, *Studies in Bábí and Bahá'í History*, vol. 1, pp. 88–99; and Hollinger, 'Ibrahim George Kheiralla and the Bahá'í Faith in America' in Cole and Momen, *From Iran East and West* (Studies in Bábí and Bahá'í History, vol. 2), pp. 95–133.

Killius, Mr and Mrs Albert C. Bahá'ís who represented Spokane, Washington at the Fourth Annual Convention of the in Chicago, April 27 to May 1, 1912.

Kinney, Edward (1863–1950) and **Carrie** (1878–1959) Wealthy New York Bahá'ís. Edward, a musician, was introduced to the Bahá'í Faith by Howard MacNutt in the winter of 1895 and wrote to 'Abdu'l-Bahá confirming his belief the same night. Carrie became a Bahá'í shortly afterwards. In 1907 'Abdu'l-Bahá asked the Kinneys to go to Egypt to help Zia Bagdadi establish the first tuberculosis hospital in Alexandria. On their return to New York their large home at 780 West End Avenue became a meeting place for Bahá'ís. 'Abdu'l-Bahá gave His first talk in America here on April 11, 1912. 'Abdu'l-Bahá named Edward 'Saffa' (serenity) and Carrie 'Vaffa' (certitude). See Whitehead, *Some Early Bahá'ís of the West*, pp. 43–53; *Bahá'í World*, vol. 12, pp. 677–9 and *Bahá'í World*, vol. 13, pp. 864–5.

Knobloch, Fanny (1859–1949) One of three sisters (the others are Alma Knobloch and Pauline Hannen) born in Germany who migrated to the United States. She became a Bahá'í in Washington DC in 1904. She was the guest of 'Abdu'l-Bahá while He was in Dublin, New Hampshire, and was invited to Paris as His guest in 1913. In 1923 she pioneered to South Africa. See Hannen Moe

Aflame with Devotion, The Hannen and Knobloch Families and the Early Days of the Bahá'í Faith in America, Bahá'í World, vol. 11, pp. 473–6.

Krug, Dr Florian (b. 1859) New York surgeon who was initially opposed to the Faith but became a Bahá'í after meeting 'Abdu'l-Bahá in 1912. It was he who closed the lids of the Master's eyes after He passed away. See *Bahá'í World*, vol. 8, pp. 675–6; Gail, *Arches of the Years*, pp. 106–7; and Rutstein, *He Loved and Served*, p. 93.

Krug, Grace (d. 1939) American Bahá'í teacher who heard of the Faith around 1904, accepting it a few years later, despite initial opposition from her husband. She was in Haifa with her husband when 'Abdu'l-Bahá passed away in November 1921. See *Bahá'í World*, vol. 8 and Gail, *Arches of the Years*, pp. 106–7.

Lunt, Alfred E. (d. 1937) Prominent Boston Bahá'í lawyer who became a Bahá'í shortly after hearing a lecture by Ali Kuli Khan in the winter of 1905. He was engaged by Sarah Farmer as her lawyer in her struggle to keep Green Acre in the hands of the Bahá'ís. He was a member of the Executive Board of the and later of the National Spiritual Assembly of the United States. See *Bahá'í World*, vol. 7, pp. 531–4 and Whitehead, *Some Early Bahá'ís of the West*, pp. 121–9.

Lynch, Rev. Frederick Author of the book *International Peace* and an active member of the peace movement.

MacNutt, Howard (d. 1926) Lawyer, company executive and early New York Bahá'í. Howard learned of the Faith from Kheiralla in January 1898 and he and his wife, Mary, became Bahá'ís shortly afterwards. They moved to Brooklyn in 1902 and became the nucleus of Bahá'í activity there. After observing a Nineteen Day Feast in 'Akká in 1905, he and his wife helped to establish the Feast in North America, hosting what was perhaps the first Feast to be held in the country in May 1905. His ideas about the station of 'Abdu'l-Bahá differed from those held by other Bahá'ís and he fell out with some, particularly Arthur Dodge. He also failed to break off his relationship with Covenant-breakers when 'Abdu'l-Bahá requested him to do so. He publicly repented of this in November 1912. He collected and edited 'Abdu'l-Bahá's talks given in America, publishing them as *The Promulgation of Universal Peace*. See Whitehead, *Some Early Bahá'ís of the West*, pp. 35–42.

Mathew, Louisa (1866–1956) British Bahá'í who accepted the Faith in Paris. She traveled with 'Abdu'l-Bahá on the S.S. *Cedric*. 'Abdu'l-Bahá intimated to her that He would be pleased if she would marry Louis Gregory, whom she had met on pilgrimage. Their marriage in September 1912 was the first marriage between a black and a white Bahá'í. From the 1920s Louisa spent most of the year teaching the Faith in Eastern Europe, returning to the United States in the summers to be with her husband. See Morrison, *To Move the World*.

Maxwell, Mary (1910–2000) Hand of the Cause of God and prominent Bahá'í lecturer and traveler. The daughter of Sutherland and May Maxwell, she married Shoghi Effendi, the Guardian of the Bahá'í Faith, in 1937. Shoghi Effendi gave her the title Amatu'l-Bahá Rúḥíyyih Khánum. She was appointed a Hand of the Cause in 1952. See Rabbani, *Priceless Pearl* and Harper, *Lights of Fortitude*, pp. 168–82.

Maxwell, May Ellis Bolles (1870–1940) Prominent early American Bahá'í and teacher of the Faith. She learned of the Faith in Paris when Phoebe Hearst brought her group of pilgrims through on the way to 'Akká. May joined the party, arriving in the Holy Land in February 1899. This marked her acceptance of the Faith. When she returned to Paris she formed the first Bahá'í group in Europe. In 1902 she married William Sutherland Maxwell and moved with him to Montreal, where their home became a focus of teaching. Their daughter, Mary, was born in 1910. May traveled widely for the Faith and was named a martyr by Shoghi Effendi when she passed away in Buenos Aires. See Nakhjavani, *The Maxwells of Montreal* vols. 1 and 2, *Bahá'í World*, vol. 8, pp. 631–42.

Maxwell, William Sutherland (1875–1952) Hand of the Cause of God and outstanding Canadian architect. In 1902 he married May Ellis Bolles and their home in Montreal became a center of Bahá'í activity. He became a Bahá'í after meeting 'Abdu'l-Bahá in 'Akká in 1909. After the passing of his wife in 1940, he moved to the Holy Land at the suggestion of Shoghi Effendi, who had married Sutherland's daughter Mary in 1937. He designed the superstructure for the Shrine of the Báb and supervised its construction. He was appointed a Hand of the Cause in 1951. See Nakhjavani, *The Maxwells of Montreal* vols. 1 and 2, *Bahá'í World*, vol. 12, pp. 657–62 and Harper, *Lights of Fortitude*, pp. 276–86.

Mills, Mountfort (d. 1949) Eminent lawyer who became a Bahá'í in 1906. He was the first chairman of the National Spiritual Assembly of the United States and Canada and prepared the final draft of the Declaration of Trust and By-Laws of the National Spiritual Assembly in 1927. He successfully appealed the case of the House of Bahá'u'lláh in Ba<u>gh</u>dád to the League of Nations. See *Bahá'í World*, vol. 11, pp. 509–11.

Moody, Dr Susan I. (1851–1934) American physician who became a Bahá'í in 1903 in Chicago. At 'Abdu'l-Bahá's invitation she went to Persia in 1909 to provide medical care for the Bahá'í women. She founded the Tarbíyat Girls' School in Ṭihrán in 1910. She lived in Persia for 15 years. See *Bahá'í World*, vol. 6, pp. 483–6.

Mortensen, Fred (1887–1946) Juvenile delinquent who became a Bahá'í through his lawyer, Albert Hall, and who 'rode the rods' to see 'Abdu'l-Bahá in Green Acre. He spent many years teaching the

Faith across the United States and was a member of the Chicago community for 21 years. See *Baháʼí World*, vol. 11, pp. 483–6.

Muḥammad ʻAlí, Mírzá (1853–1937) ʻAbduʼl-Baháʼs half-brother, the arch-breaker of Baháʼuʼlláhʼs Covenant. See *God Passes By*, pp. 246, 249 and Taherzadeh, *Covenant of Baháʼuʼlláh*, pp. 125–34.

Muḥammad ʻAlí Mírzá Shah of Iran following the death of Muẓaffaruʼd-Dín S͟háh in 1907. He abdicated in 1909.

Muḥammad-Taqí Mans͟hádí, Siyyid Persian Baháʼí living in Haifa, and later Port Said, through whom Tablets and letters were sent and received. The Covenant-breakers attempted to win him to their cause but he remained loyal to ʻAbduʼl-Bahá. See ʻAbduʼl-Bahá, *Memorials of the Faithful*, pp. 54–7.

Nabíl-i-Zarandí, Nabíl-i-Aʻẓam (d. 1892) Title of Muḥammad-i-Zarandí, the author of *The Dawn-Breakers*. He learned about the Bábí Faith at the age of 16 and met Baháʼuʼlláh in 1851. He made several journeys on behalf of Baháʼuʼlláh, was imprisoned in Egypt and is the only person known to have made the two pilgrimages to the House of the Báb in S͟hírázʼ and the House of Baháʼuʼlláh in Bag͟hdád in accordance with the rites set out by Baháʼuʼlláh. After the passing of Baháʼuʼlláh, and at the request of ʻAbduʼl-Bahá, he arranged a Tablet of Visitation from Baháʼuʼlláhʼs writings which is now used in the Holy Shrines. Shortly afterwards, overcome with grief, he walked into the sea and drowned. See Balyuzi, *Eminent Baháʼís*, pp. 268–70.

Nak͟hjavání, Mírzá ʻAlí-Akbar Member of ʻAbduʼl-Baháʼs entourage. His son ʻAlí Nak͟hjavání was elected to the Universal House of Justice in 1963.

Náṣiriʼd-Dín S͟háh Shah of Iran from 1848 to 96. See Momen, *Bábí and Baháʼí Religions*, pp. 156–60.

BIOGRAPHICAL NOTES 445

Nutt, Dr William Frederick Early American Bahá'í active in Chicago who later broke the Covenant.

Ober, Harlan (1881–1962) Early American Bahá'í traveling teacher. He learned of the Faith in 1905 and became a Bahá'í in 1906. Shortly afterwards he traveled to India with Hooper Harris in answer to 'Abdu'l-Bahá's call for American Bahá'ís to visit the country. He served on the Executive Board of the for a number of years. In 1912, at the suggestion of 'Abdu'l-Bahá, he married Grace Robarts; 'Abdu'l-Bahá Himself presided at the ceremony. His friendship with Louis Gregory took him on many teaching trips to the Southern states and he was much in demand as a public speaker. After the passing of his wife in 1938 he remarried and, in 1956, pioneered in Pretoria, South Africa. In 1957 he was a appointed a member of the Auxiliary Board for Protection in Africa. See *Bahá'í World*, vol. 13, pp. 866–71 and Whitehead, *Some Bahá'ís to Remember*, pp. 118–44.

Parsons, Agnes (1861–1934) Washington DC society matron and early Bahá'í. She heard about the Bahá'í Faith in 1908 and became a confirmed believer during her pilgrimage to 'Akká in 1910. She was 'Abdu'l-Bahá's hostess during His stay in Washington and arranged for Him to visit Dublin, New Hampshire, her summer residence. On her second pilgrimage, in 1920, 'Abdu'l-Bahá instructed her to organize the first race amity conference, which she did in 1921, working closely with Louis Gregory. See Hollinger, *Agnes Parsons' Diary*; *Bahá'í World*, vol. 5, pp. 410–15; Morrison, *To Move the World*, pp. 134–43 and Whitehead, *Some Bahá'ís to Remember*, pp. 76–96.

Parsons, Arthur Jeffrey (1856–1915) Husband of Agnes Parsons and a librarian at the Library of Congress.

Peary, Admiral Robert Edwin (1856–1920) American Polar explorer. At his seventh attempt he became the first person to reach the North Pole, on April 6, 1909. He accomplished this by sailing to Cape Sheridan in the *Roosevelt* then traveling by sled to the Pole.

Ralston, William and Georgia Early California Bahá'ís. Georgia was a childhood friend of Ella Goodall Cooper and learned of the Faith from her and Helen Goodall around 1910. She traveled with Helen and Ella to New York to see 'Abdu'l-Bahá. See Brown, *Memories of 'Abdu'l-Bahá*, pp. 24–5.

Remey, Charles Mason (1874–1974) Prominent early Bahá'í and traveling teacher, appointed a Hand of the Cause in 1951 but declared a Covenant-breaker in 1960. Remey became a Bahá'í in Paris in December 1899 and served the Faith devotedly for many years in various capacities. He was a member of the Executive Board of the . In 1909 he and Howard Struven set out on the first round the world Bahá'í teaching trip, one of his many journeys to teach the Faith. He was appointed president of the International Bahá'í Council in 1951. After the passing of Shoghi Effendi in 1957, he broke the Covenant. See Harper, *Lights of Fortitude*, pp. 287–306.

Ridáy-i-Shírází, Áqá Believer exiled with Bahá'u'lláh to 'Akká. Between Baghdád and Constantinople he and Áqá Mírzá Mahmúd traveled ahead of the party to prepare the food and make arrangements for the comfort of the believers. See 'Abdu'l-Bahá, *Memorials of the Faithful*, pp. 39–41.

Robarts, Grace (d. 1938) Early American Bahá'í teacher whose marriage to Harlan Ober in 1912 was at the suggestion of 'Abdu'l-Bahá. She secured and made ready the various apartments in which 'Abdu'l-Bahá stayed during His journey in America. Her nephew, John Robarts, was appointed a Hand of the Cause. See *Bahá'í World*, vol. 8, pp. 656–60 and Whitehead, *Some Bahá'ís to Remember*, pp. 118–44.

BIOGRAPHICAL NOTES 447

Roosevelt, President Theodore (1858–1919) 26th President of the United States, 1901–9.

Rúḥá Khánum Third of 'Abdu'l-Bahá's four surviving daughters. She married Mírzá Jalál, the son of the King of Martyrs. She broke the Covenant in the 1940s.

Salmán, Shaykh Early believer who carried many Tablets from Bahá'u'lláh for distribution among the friends in Persia. He also conducted Munírih Khánum to 'Akká before her marriage to 'Abdu'l-Bahá. See Taherzadeh, *Revelation of Bahá'u'lláh*, vol. 1, p. 113 and Balyuzi, *King of Glory*, pp. 344–7, 441–4.

Shoghi Effendi (1897–1957) Eldest grandson of 'Abdu'l-Bahá and appointed in His Will and Testament the Guardian of the Bahá'í Faith. Brought up in the Master's household in 'Akká, in his youth he became his grandfather's secretary for a time before leaving the Holy Land to study at the University of Oxford. When 'Abdu'l-Bahá passed away Shoghi Effendi became head of the Bahá'í Faith. Under his guidance the Bahá'í administration was developed and the Faith taken to virtually every country in the world. In 1937 he married Mary Maxwell. He passed away in London, where he is buried. See Rabbani, *Priceless Pearl* and Rabbani, *Guardian of the Bahá'í Faith*.

Shu'á'u'lláh, Mírzá Son of Mírzá Muḥammad-'Alí, arch-breaker of the Covenant. He arrived in the United States in 1905 and remained until the 1930s or 1940s. He attempted to win converts to his father's cause from among the Bahá'ís but was unsuccessful.

Sohrab, Mírzá Ahmad (d. 1958) Persian Bahá'í and a major translator of 'Abdu'l-Bahá's Tablets into English. He had been sent by 'Abdu'l-Bahá to the United States in 1903 to translate for Mírzá Abu'l-Faḍl. He settled in Washington DC and became well-known in the American Bahá'í community. After the passing of 'Abdu'l-Bahá he opposed the establishment of the Bahá'í administrative order decreed in the Will and Testament of 'Abdu'l-Bahá and was declared a Covenant-breaker. See Taherzadeh, *Covenant of Bahá'u'lláh*, pp. 343–7.

Struven, Howard and Hebe Early Baltimore Bahá'ís. Howard's brother, Edward, learned of the Bahá'í Faith from Lua Getsinger and became a Bahá'í immediately. Howard became a Bahá'í in 1899. In 1909 'Abdu'l-Bahá asked him to travel around the world with Mason Remey, the first round the world Bahá'í teaching trip. He married Hebe (Ruby) Moore, Lua Getsinger's sister, in 1912. See Clark, 'The Bahá'ís of Baltimore, 1898–1990' in Hollinger, *Community Histories*, pp. 111–45.

Ṭáhirih (1817–52) Outstanding heroine of the Bábí Dispensation, the only woman among the Letters of the Living. See Shoghi Effendi, *God Passes By*, pp. 7, 33, 75 and Nabíl, *Dawn-Breakers*, p. 628.

Thompson, Juliet (1873–1956) Prominent early American Bahá'í and artist. She learned about the Faith from May Bolles in Paris and became a Bahá'í in 1901. After a few years she settled in New York. In 1909 she went to 'Akká on pilgrimage and met 'Abdu'l-Bahá, to whom she became devoted. When He arrived in New York in 1912, she followed Him everywhere and He agreed to allow her to paint His portrait. Juliet wrote a moving story about Mary Magdalen, *I, Mary Magdalen*, published in 1940. See *Diary of Juliet Thompson*; *Bahá'í World*, vol. 13, pp. 862–4; and Whitehead, *Some Early Bahá'ís of the West*, pp. 73–85.

True, Corinne (1861–1961) Prominent early Chicago Bahá'í teacher and Hand of the Cause of God. Corinne learned of the Bahá'í Faith in 1899. The deaths of five of her eight children between 1899 and 1909 drew her closer to the Faith. 'Abdu'l-Bahá asked her to spearhead the building of the Mashriqu'l-Adhkár in Wilmette, a task she undertook energetically over a number of years and for which she was known as the 'Mother of the Temple'. She was elected to the National Spiritual Assembly of the United States and Canada in 1922. She was appointed a Hand of the Cause in 1952. See Rutstein, *Corinne True*; Whitmore, *Dawning Place*, pp. 18–35; and Harper, *Lights of Fortitude*, pp. 391–407.

Valíyu'lláh Khán-i-Varqá, Mírzá (1884–1955) Prominent Persian Bahá'í and Hand of the Cause of God. The son of the martyr-poet Mírzá 'Alí-Muḥammad-i-Varqá, Valíyu'lláh Khán-i-Varqá joined 'Abdu'l-Bahá's entourage in America. He was appointed Trustee of the Ḥuqúqu'lláh in 1940 and a Hand of the Cause of God in 1951. See *Bahá'í World*, vol. 13, pp. 831–4 and Harper, *Lights of Fortitude*, pp. 329–32.

Varqá, Mírzá 'Alí-Muḥammad Persian Bahá'í martyred, together with his twelve-year-old son, Rúḥu'lláh, by the brutal Ḥájibu'd-Dawlih. See Shoghi Effendi, *God Passes By*, p. 296 and Harper, *Lights of Fortitude*, pp. 42–9.

Waite, Louise R. (d. 1939) Poet-composer who became a Bahá'í sometime before 1902 in Chicago. She was given the Persian name Shánaz Khánum by the Master. See *Bahá'í World*, vol. 8, pp. 661–4.

Wilhelm, Roy C. (1875–1951) Prominent New Jersey Bahá'í and wealthy entrepreneur posthumously named a Hand of the Cause of God. Roy learned of the Bahá'í Faith through his mother but did not become a Bahá'í himself until he accompanied his mother on her pilgrimage to 'Akká in 1907. In 1908 he met Martha Root and introduced her to the Faith. In 1909 he was elected to the Executive Board of the , serving on this and its successor, the American National Spiritual Assembly, almost continuously until 1946. At 'Abdu'l-Bahá's behest, a unity feast was held in the grounds of his home in West Englewood, New Jersey, in June 1912, an event which is commemorated every year. He was posthumously appointed a Hand of the Cause of God by Shoghi Effendi on December 23, 1951. See *Bahá'í World*, vol. 12, pp. 662–4 and Harper, *Lights of Fortitude*, pp. 129–41.

Wilson, President Woodrow (1856–1924) 28th President of the United States (1913–21). His '14 points', upholding democracy and self-determination of states, was intended to form the basis for a peace treaty after World War I. He was largely responsible for the establishment of the League of Nations. His presidency ended in failure when the Versailles treaty was not ratified by the American Senate.

Windust, Albert R. (1874–1956) Early Chicago Bahá'í and publisher. He became a Bahá'í in 1897 and was a member of the first Spiritual Assembly of Chicago. He became the first publisher of Bahá'í literature in the West, including the *Hidden Words*. In 1910 he founded and printed the Bahá'í magazine *Star of the West* and later collected and published three volumes of 'Abdu'l-Bahá's Tablets to American believers. He also helped Howard MacNutt to publish *The Promulgation of Universal Peace*. See *Bahá'í World*, vol. 13, pp. 873–4.

Yaḥyá, Mírzá (c. 1832–1912) Younger half-brother of Bahá'u'lláh who turned against Him and caused division and enmity among the Bábís. See Shoghi Effendi, *God Passes By*, pp. 112–27, 163–70 and Taherzadeh, *Covenant of Bahá'u'lláh*, pp. 60–96.

Yamamoto, Kanichi (1879–1961) First Japanese Bahá'í. Kanichi learned of the Faith in Hawaii after leaving Japan. He became a Bahá'í in 1902. In 1903 he left Hawaii to become a butler to Helen Goodall's family in Oakland, California. He arranged the meeting at the Japanese YMCA at which 'Abdu'l-Bahá spoke on October 7, 1912. See *Bahá'í World*, vol. 13, pp. 831–3 and Whitehead, *Some Bahá'ís to Remember*, pp. 176–86.

Zarqání, Mírzá Maḥmúd-i- (c. 1875–1924) Persian Baháʾí travel teacher and chronicler of ʿAbduʾl-Baháʾs travels in the West. In his youth Maḥmúd made travel teaching trips around Iran. From 1903 he began to go to India, where he traveled for several years and learned Urdu. During this period he went on pilgrimage to Haifa, where he was responsible for transcribing Tablets, and from there he accompanied ʿAbduʾl-Bahá on His journey to Europe and America.

BIBLIOGRAPHY

'Abdu'l-Bahá. *Memorials of the Faith.* Wilmette, IL: Bahá'í Publishing Trust, 1971.
—*The Promulgation of Universal Peace.* Wilmette, IL: Bahá'í Publishing Trust, 1982.

Afnan, Abu'l-Qasim. *Black Pearls: Servants in the Households of the Báb and Bahá'u'lláh.* Los Angeles: Kalimát Press, 1988.

Bahá'í World, The. vols. 1–12, 1925–54. rpt. Wilmette, IL: Bahá'í Publishing Trust, 1980.

Bahá'í World, The, vol. 13. Haifa: The Universal House of Justice, 1970.

Balyuzi, H. M. *'Abdu'l-Bahá.* Oxford: George Ronald, 1971.
—*Bahá'u'lláh, The King of Glory.* Oxford: George Ronald, 1980.
—*Edward Granville Browne and the Bahá'í Faith.* Oxford: George Ronald, 1970.
—*Eminent Bahá'ís in the Time of Bahá'u'lláh: with some Historical Background.* Oxford: George Ronald, 1985.

Brown, Ramona Allen. *Memories of 'Abdu'l-Bahá.* Wilmette, IL: Bahá'í Publishing Trust, 1980.

Cole, Juan R. and Momen, Moojan, eds. *Studies in Bábí and Bahá'í History: From Iran East & West.* Los Angeles: Kalimát Press, 1984.

Compton's Encyclopedia, America Online edition, January 1, 1993.

Diary of Juliet Thompson, The. Los Angeles: Kalimát Press, 1983.

Gail, Marzieh. *Arches of the Years.* Oxford: George Ronald, 1991.
—*Bahá'í Glossary.* Wilmette, IL: Bahá'í Publishing Trust, 1976.
—*Summon Up Remembrance.* Oxford: George Ronald, 1987.

Green Acre on the Piscataqua. Eliot, Maine: Green Acre Bahá'í School Council, 1991.

Hannen Moe, Judy. *Aflame with Devotion, The Hannen and Knobloch Families and the Early Days of the Bahá'í Faith in America.* IL: Bahá'í Publishing Trust, 2019.

Harper, Barron. *Lights of Fortitude: Glimpses into the Lives of the Hands of the Cause of God.* Oxford: George Ronald, 1997.

Ḥaydar-'Alí, Ḥájí Mírzá. *Stories from the Delight of Hearts: The Memoirs of Ḥájí Mírzá Ḥaydar-'Alí.* Los Angeles: Kalimát Press, 1980.

Hollinger, Richard, ed. *'Abdu'l-Bahá in America: Agnes Parsons' Diary.* Los Angeles: Kalimát Press, 1996.

—ed. *Community Histories: Studies in the Bábí and Bahá'í Religions*, vol. 6. Los Angeles: Kalimát Press, 1992.

Ives, Howard Colby. *Portals to Freedom.* London: George Ronald, 1967.

Law, Jonathan, ed. *The Giant Book of 1000 Great Lives.* London: Magpie Books, 1996.

Metelmann, Velda Piff. *Lua Getsinger: Herald of the Covenant.* Oxford: George Ronald, 1997.

Momen, Moojan. *The Bábí and Bahá'í Religions, 1844–1944. Some Contemporary Western Accounts.* Oxford: George Ronald, 1981.

—ed. *Studies in Bábí and Bahá'í History*, vol. 1. Los Angeles: Kalimát Press, 1982.

Momen, Wendi. *A Basic Bahá'í Dictionary.* Oxford: George Ronald, 1989.

Morrison, Gayle. *To Move the World.* Wilmette, IL: Bahá'í Publishing Trust, 1982.

Nabíl-i-A'ẓam. *The Dawn-Breakers: Nabíl's Narrative of the Early Days of the Bahá'í Revelation.* Wilmette, IL: Bahá'í Publishing Trust, 1970

Nakhjavani, Violette. *The Maxwells of Montreal* vol. 1. Oxford: George Ronald, 2011.

—*The Maxwells of Montreal* vol. 2. Oxford: George Ronald, 2012.

Rabbaní, Rúḥíyyih. *The Guardian of the Bahá'í Faith.* London: Bahá'í Publishing Trust, 1988.

—*The Priceless Pearl.* London: Bahá'í Publishing Trust, 1969.

Rutstein, Nathan. *Corinne True: Faithful Handmaid of 'Abdu'l-Bahá.* Oxford: George Ronald, 1987.

—*He Loved and Served: The Story of Curtis Kelsey.* Oxford: George Ronald, 1982.

Shoghi Effendi. *God Passes By*. Wilmette, IL: Bahá'í Publishing Trust, rev. edn. 1974.

Star of the West. Rpt. Oxford: George Ronald, 1984.

Stockman, Robert. *The Bahá'í Faith In America*, vol. 1. Wilmette, IL: Bahá'í Publishing Trust, 1985.

—*The Bahá'í Faith in America, Early Expansion, 1900–1912*, vol. 2. Oxford: George Ronald, 1995.

Taherzadeh, Adib. *The Covenant of Bahá'u'lláh*. Oxford: George Ronald, 1992.

—*The Revelation of Bahá'u'lláh*, vol. 1. Oxford: George Ronald, 1974.

Ward, Allan L. *239 Days*. Wilmette, IL: Bahá'í Publishing Trust, 1979.

Whitehead, O.Z. *Some Bahá'ís to Remember*. Oxford: George Ronald, 1983.

—*Some Early Bahá'ís of the West*. Oxford: George Ronald, 1976.

Whitmore, Bruce W. *The Dawning Place*. Wilmette, IL: Bahá'í Publishing Trust, 1984.

REFERENCES AND NOTES

1. '. . . there hath appeared and above its horizon there hath shone forth the Orb of the beauty of the great, the Most Mighty Branch of God – His ancient and immutable Mystery . . .' Bahá'u'lláh, 'Lawḥ-i-Arḍ-i-Bá' (Tablet of the Land of Bá), *Tablets*, p. 227.

2. Since Maḥmúd wrote his diary, several books have been published of transcripts or notes of 'Abdu'l-Bahá's talks given on His travels to Europe and America. Among them are *The Promulgation of Universal Peace*, a collection of His talks in the United States in 1912, *Paris Talks* and *'Abdu'l-Bahá in London,* notes of His discourses in those cities in 1911–12.

3. See the Báb's address to the Letters of the Living: 'Such must be the degree of your detachment, that into whatever city you enter to proclaim and teach the Cause of God, you should in no wise expect either meat or reward from its people. Nay, when you depart out of that city, you should shake the dust from off your feet. As you have entered it pure and undefiled, so must you depart from that city.' Nabíl, *Dawn-Breakers*, pp. 92–3.

4. Thus far only the volume relating to 'Abdu'l-Bahá's journey in North America has been translated.

5. See *Paris Talks*, a collection of 'Abdu'l-Bahá's addresses in Paris and London in 1911–13.

6. The SS *Cedric* was built by Harland and Wolff, a Belfast firm.

7. 'Mashaeen' (the Peripatetics) were followers of the school of thought originated by Socrates, Plato and Aristotle; the 'Ishraq' (Illuminationists) followed the Sophists, such as the Persian philosopher and physicist Shahabidin Sohrehvardi, who lived in the 12th century.

8. See Shoghi Effendi, *God Passes By*, pp. 107–9.

9. In Persian, *tasbih*, a rosary of 95 beads for reciting the Greatest Name of God, Alláh-u-Abhá (God is the Most Glorious).
10. From Jalálu'd-Dín Rúmí, eminent Sufi mystic and poet (1207–73).
11. Maḥmúd states that 'Abdu'l-Bahá cited a poem of Ḥáfiẓ which says, 'Is there any relationship between piety and uprightness and hypocrisy?'
12. Three other sources indicate that the arrival of 'Abdu'l-Bahá to America was on April 11, 1912: Balyuzi, *'Abdu'l-Bahá*, p. 172; *Star of the West*, vol. 3, no. 3, p. 3; and 'Abdu'l-Bahá, *Promulgation of Universal Peace*, p. 3. It may be because the Muslim day begins and ends at sunset that April 11 was indicated by Maḥmúd as April 10.
13. 'Abdu'l-Bahá is reported to have said when He saw the Statue of Liberty, 'There is the new world's symbol of liberty and freedom. After being forty years a prisoner I can tell you that freedom is not a matter of place. It is a condition. Unless one accept dire vicissitudes he will not attain. When one is released from the prison of self, that is indeed a release.' *Star of the West*, vol. 3, no. 3, p. 4.
14. When 'Abdu'l-Bahá saw the New York City skyline He is reported to have said, 'These are the minarets of Western World commerce and industry . . .' *Star of the West*, vol. 3, no. 3, p. 4.
15. Juliet Thompson records that Edward Kinney 'was called to come on board the ship'. Although most of the Bahá'ís left the pier, Marjorie Morten, Rhoda Nichols and Juliet hid themselves to catch a glimpse of 'Abdu'l-Bahá. *Diary of Juliet Thompson*, pp. 233–4.
16. For a transcript of 'Abdu'l-Bahá's talk see *Promulgation*, pp. 3–4.
17. The events described here took place on Friday, April 12, 1912.
18. For a transcript of 'Abdu'l-Bahá's talk see *Promulgation*, pp. 4–7.
19. For a transcript of 'Abdu'l-Bahá's talk see *Promulgation*, pp. 7–9.
20. The events described here took place on Saturday, April 13, 1912.
21. At 141 East Twenty-first Street, New York. For a transcript of 'Abdu'l-Bahá's talk see *Promulgation*, pp. 9–11.
22. The events described here took place on Monday, April 15, 1912.
23. For a transcript of this interview see *Star of the West*, vol. 3, no. 7, pp. 4–5.

24. For a transcript of this interview see *Star of the West*, vol. 4, no. 7, pp. 5–11.

25. According to *Promulgation of Universal Peace*, the talk at the home of Mountfort Mills was on April 15, 1912. For a transcript of 'Abdu'l-Bahá's talk see *Promulgation*, pp. 16–18.

26. The sinking of the *Titanic* in the North Atlantic occurred on the night of April 14, 1912. The discrepancy in the date is no doubt due to the fact that Maḥmúd assembled and wrote the diary months later, using notes he hastily took at the time.

27. At Fifth Avenue and Tenth Street, New York. For transcripts of 'Abdu'l-Bahá's talk see *Promulgation*, pp. 11–13, and *Star of the West*, vol. 4, no. 1, pp. 7–8.

28. That is, they were awe-inspired. This is an allusion to a Persian proverb. When the iguana hunts flies, it sits on a rock facing the sun. In Persian, an iguana is called *aftab parast*, 'sun worshipper'.

29. Union Meeting of Advanced Thought Centers, Carnegie Lyceum, West Fifty-Seventh Street, New York. For a transcript of 'Abdu'l-Bahá's talk see *Promulgation*, pp. 14–16.

30. For a transcript of 'Abdu'l-Bahá's talk see *Promulgation*, pp. 23–5.

31. For a transcript of 'Abdu'l-Bahá's talk see *Promulgation*, pp. 25–9.

32. According to *Promulgation*, p. 32, 'Abdu'l-Bahá's visit to the Bowery Mission in New York City was on April 19, 1912. For transcripts of 'Abdu'l-Bahá's talk see *Promulgation*, pp. 32–4 and *Star of the West*, vol. 3, no. 7, pp. 11–12.

33. For a transcript of 'Abdu'l-Bahá's talk see *Promulgation*, pp. 29–32.

34. The celebrated lover of ancient Persian and Arabian lore whose beloved was Laylí.

35. Joseph Hannen notes that 'Receptions were held at the home of Mrs Parsons every afternoon at about 5:00 o'clock [sic], from Monday to Friday, inclusive'. *Star of the West*, vol. 3, no. 3, p. 7.

36. For a transcript of 'Abdu'l-Bahá's talk see *Promulgation*, p. 35.

37. Located at Thirteenth and L Streets, Washington DC.

38. For another transcript of 'Abdu'l-Bahá's talk see *Promulgation*, pp. 39–42.

39. 'Abdu'l-Bahá's talk was at the home of Mr and Mrs Arthur J. Parsons, 1700 Eighteenth Street, NW, Washington DC. For a transcript see *Promulgation*, pp. 43–4.

40. Agnes Parsons states in her diary that this talk was given on April 23, 1912 at the Parsons's home and this is confirmed by *Promulgation*, pp. 46–8, which is a transcript of the talk. Mrs Parsons states: 'From the Khan's we returned to this house where were found the place thronged. There were probably 250 people present, many standing. Abdul Baha [sic] spoke about the *Titanic* Disaster.' Hollinger, *Agnes Parsons' Diary*, p. 35.

41. This dinner party was held on April 22, 1912. Agnes Parsons states: 'A Persian dinner, cooked by Mirza Sohrab, was served by Abdul Baha about 8 o'clock . . . Abdul Baha served and talked while the others ate.' Also at the dinner were Siyyid Asadu'lláh-i-Qumí, Ali Kuli Khan, Mírzá 'Alí Akbar K͟hán, Dr Faríd, Edward Getsinger, Charles Mason Remey, Joseph Hannen, Ahmad Sohrab and Mírzá Maḥmúd. (Hollinger, *Agnes Parsons' Diary*, pp. 25–6.) Marzieh Gail notes that 'Mrs Parsons's house had a large ball-room that would seat around two hundred people, and a crowd of this size would be invited whenever He spoke in her home'. (Gail, *Arches of the Years*, p. 80.)

42. Howard University was founded in 1867 'to educate newly freed slaves' and was in 1912 'one of the foremost black universities in the country'. (Hollinger, *Agnes Parsons' Diary*, p. 29, note 42.) Allan Ward notes that 'well over a thousand students, faculty members, administrators, and guests jammed Rankin Chapel'. (Ward, *239 Days*, p. 40.)

43. For a transcript of 'Abdu'l-Bahá's talk see *Promulgation*, pp. 44–6.

44. Joseph Hannen notes that 'This was a most notable occasion, and here, as everywhere when both white and colored people were present, Abdul-Baha [sic] seemed happiest. The address was received with breathless attention . . .' *Star of the West*, vol. 3, no. 3, p. 7.

45. Ali Kuli Khan was the Chargé d'Affaires for the Persian Legation. Agnes Parsons states that there were 19 people present at the luncheon apart from 'Abdu'l-Bahá, including Ali Kuli Khan, his wife, Florence, and two children; 'Mrs Breede ' (probably Alice Ives Breed, Florence Khan's mother), Mrs Severance, Helen Goodall, Ella Cooper, Miss A Dorr, Edward Getsinger, Dr Faríd, Ahmad Sohrab, Juliet Thompson, Louis Gregory, Charles Mason Remey and Agnes

Parsons. (Hollinger, *Agnes Parsons' Diary*, p. 31.) It was at this luncheon that 'Abdu'l-Bahá rearranged the seating, asking Louis Gregory to sit beside Him, although Mr Gregory had not been invited to the luncheon. (See *Bahá'í World*, vol. 12, p. 688.) For Juliet Thompson's account of this luncheon see *Diary of Juliet Thompson*, pp. 269–70.

46. Juliet Thompson describes this as a 'reception' attended by the Turkish Ambassador Ḍíyá Páshá, Admiral Peary and Alexander Graham Bell. (*Diary of Juliet Thompson*, pp. 270–3.) Agnes Parsons indicates that the Turkish Ambassador went on with the party to the Parsons's home, where 'Abdu'l-Bahá spoke again. (Hollinger, *Agnes Parsons' Diary*, p. 34.) *Promulgation*, pp. 46–52, indicates that 'Abdu'l-Bahá gave three talks on April 23, 1912: at Howard University, at the home of Mr and Mrs Arthur J. Parsons and at the Bethel Literary Society.

47. *Promulgation*, pp. 46–8, indicates that 'Abdu'l-Bahá spoke about the tragedy of the sinking of the *Titanic* and the relationship between material and the spiritual worlds.

48. According to Mrs Parsons these were Mr and Mrs Arnault Belmont, Juliet Thompson and two Iranians. Hollinger, *Agnes Parsons' Diary*, pp. 35–6.

49. 'Abdu'l-Bahá addressed the Bethel Literary Society at the Metropolitan African Methodist Episcopal Church, M Street, NW Washington DC. For a transcript of 'Abdu'l-Bahá's talk see *Promulgation*, pp. 49–52. Joseph Hannen notes that 'again the audience taxed the capacity of the edifice in which the meeting was held'. *Star of the West*, vol. 3, no. 3, p. 7.

50. This was held at Studio Hall, 1219 Connecticut Avenue, Washington DC. For a transcript of 'Abdu'l-Bahá's talk see *Promulgation,* pp. 52–4. Joseph Hannen indicates that this was held in the afternoon, noting that it was 'one of the most beautiful functions of the week': '. . . more than 100 children, with as many adults, parents and friends, gathered. Abdul-Baha [sic] received and embraced each child, seeming most happy in their presence, and then delivered a wonderful address. Abdul-Baha presented each child, before he left, with a gift.' *Star of the West*, vol. 3, no. 3, p. 7.

51. 'Abdu'l-Bahá also spoke at the Parsons's home later in the afternoon. For a transcript of His talk see *Promulgation*, pp. 54–6.

52. Zia Bagdadi in his diary wrote of this event, 'In the evening, 'Abdu'l-Bahá addressed the white and colored believers and their friends at the home of Mrs Dyer, a member of the colored race.' Bagdadi, "Abdu'l-Bahá in America', *Star of the West*, vol. 19, no. 3, p. 89.

53. Alan Ward indicates that 'Abdu'l-Bahá took a streetcar to Mr Bell's home. Ward, *239 Days*, p. 43.

54. This passage was translated by Shoghi Effendi. See *God Passes By*, p. 293.

55. He was not the Ambassador but the Chargé d'Affaires.

56. 'Abdu'l-Bahá spoke to the Theosophical Society at the Parsons's home at 10:30 in the morning. For a transcript of this talk see *Promulgation*, pp. 58–60 and *Star of the West*, vol. 3, no. 3, pp. 22–3. Agnes Parsons notes that 'Abdu'l-Bahá 'addressed a small group of Theosophists in my large room. I have invited them here to save Abdul Baha having to go out so much. The Theosophists had asked Him to speak to them.' Hollinger, *Agnes Parsons' Diary*, p. 46.

    The Theosophical Society was founded in New York in 1875 by Madame Blavatsky and Colonel H. S. Olcott and is based on Hindu ideas of karma and reincarnation, nirvana being the eventual aim.

57. That is, the Parsons's home. For a transcript of 'Abdu'l-Bahá's talk see *Promulgation*, pp. 61–4 and *Star of the West*, vol. 3, no. 5, pp. 7–8. Agnes Parsons notes that the meeting took place in her 'large room', which was 'thoroughly filled'. Hollinger, *Agnes Parsons' Diary*, p. 47.

58. Agnes Parsons indicates that those at the dinner were 'the Ambassador, his son, his son's wife, his daughter, Mirza and Mme. Khan, Dr and Mrs Williams, Dr Fareed, the two visiting Persians, the Persian Secretary, Mr Parsons and myself.' (Hollinger, *Agnes Parsons' Diary*, p. 47.) 'Roses had been piled along the tables and formed a mound in the center where 'Abdu'l-Bahá and Ḍíyá Páshá sat.' (Ward, *239 Days*, p. 44.)

59. Theodore Roosevelt visited 'Abdu'l-Bahá at the Parsons's home on April 25, after the reception at the Turkish Embassy. He was not President at this time.

60. Agnes Parsons states that 'Abdu'l-Bahá spoke to the Woman's Alliance (Hollinger, *Agnes Parsons' Diary*, p. 50); the subject was the equal rights of men and women. Allan Ward confirms this, saying that 'Abdu'l-Bahá 'addressed the ladies of President Taft's All Saints

Unitarian Church; the room was completely filled'. (Ward, *239 Days*, p. 45.)

61. Agnes Parsons indicates that the meeting began at quarter to five in the afternoon and was held in the large room. 'It was filled with people eager to hear His last talk at our house. His subject was the Human and Divine Spirit in Man. He made a little farewell talk also, expressing His gratitude and happiness and added an admonition to all who had heard the Spiritual teachings to endeavor to gain something from them.' Hollinger, *Agnes Parsons' Diary*, p. 51.

62. This was the Continental Hall, the 'public hall of the Daughters of the American Revolution', 'perhaps the most prestigious meeting place in Washington, at the time'. (Hollinger, *Agnes Parsons' Diary*, pp. 51–2, note 73.) Samuel Gompers, president of the American Federation of Labor; Benjamin Trueblood, secretary of the American Peace Society; and A. C. Monohon of the United States Bureau of Education shared the platform with 'Abdu'l-Bahá.

63. Secretary of the United States Treasury, Lee McClung. Allan Ward says that 'Abdu'l-Bahá had breakfast with Mr McClung (Ward, *239 Days*, p. 44.) Juliet Thompson later asked Mr McClung how 'Abdu'l-Bahá had impressed him. She wrote, 'A shy look came into his face, and Mr McClung is anything but shy. "Well, I felt as though I was in the presence of one of the great old Prophets: Elijah, Isaiah, Moses. No, it was more than that! Christ . . . no – *now* I have it! He seemed to me my Divine Father."' (*Diary of Juliet Thompson*, p. 280.)

64. Agnes Parsons says: 'I went down at 9:30 p.m. and found everything looking very lovely. I had arranged for Abdul Baha to sit on the large sofa in the south eastern corner of the library, but others took possession of it and as I had to receive, I haven't yet heard in detail the way and where the people were presented to Him.' Hollinger, *Agnes Parsons' Diary*, p. 54.

65. Admiral Peary had attended the reception at Ali Kuli Khan's on 23 April. On that occasion 'Abdu'l-Bahá had told the Admiral, in the words of Juliet Thompson, that 'for a very long time the world had been much concerned about the North Pole, where it was and what was to found there. Now *he*, Admiral Peary, had discovered it and that *nothing* was to [be] found there; and so, in forever relieving the public mind, he had rendered a great service.' *Diary of Juliet Thompson*, pp. 272–3.

66. Edward Alfred Mitchell Innes was not the ambassador but rather an employee of the British Embassy in Washington DC. Agnes Parsons was present during the interview and remembers 'Abdu'l-Bahá saying, 'A man who has been injured should not retaliate – but that the Law should carry out retribution. In its doing so, there is not the spirit of revenge, for this that the Law does is for the safety of the Body Politic.' Hollinger, *Agnes Parsons' Diary*, p. 57.

67. Agnes Parsons states that she and Dr Faríd traveled with 'Abdu'l-Bahá in His carriage to the station. Others at the station included the Turkish Ambassador and his son, Ali Kuli Khan and Mme Khan, Mírzá Sohrab, Charles Mason Remey, Mrs Belmont and Leona Barnitz. Hollinger, *Agnes Parsons' Diary*, p. 58.

68. This may be a reference to the Síyáh-Chál (the Black Pit) in Ṭihrán where Bahá'u'lláh was imprisoned for eight months in 1852; to His banishment to Adrianople, 'this remote prison'; or to His exile in 1868 to the prison city of 'Akká.

69. Allan Ward records that the *Chicago Daily News* reported 'Abdu'l-Bahá missing in its April 29 edition. 'In the Corinthian hall in the Masonic Temple building 170 delegates attending the Bahai [sic] convention waited for the leader of the movement.' (Cited in Ward, *239 Days*, p. 47.) 'The delegates expected 'Abdu'l-Bahá to arrive in Chicago early on the twenty-ninth and "passed an anxious morning and afternoon meeting inward-bound trains".' (Whitmore, *Dawning Place*, p. 57.)

70. The part of European Turkey where Adrianople (Edirne) is situated. At the time it was under the rule of the Ottoman Empire.

71. Jane Addams, a sociologist and vice president of the National American Woman Suffrage Association, founded Hull House, one of the earliest community centers, in Chicago in 1889. For transcripts of 'Abdu'l-Bahá's talk at Hull House see *Promulgation*, pp. 67–9 and 'Wisdom Talks of Abdul-Baha', *Star of the West*, supplement to vol. 3, no. 3.

72. 'Abdu'l-Bahá spoke at the Fourth Annual Conference of the National Association for the Advancement of Colored People. For transcripts of His talk see *Promulgation*, pp. 69–70 and 'Wisdom-Talks of Abdul-Baha', *Star of the West*, supplement to vol. 3, no. 3.

73. 'Abdu'l-Bahá addressed the final session of the Convention held at Drill Hall, Masonic Temple. For transcripts of the talk see *Promulga-*

tion, pp. 65–7 and 'Wisdom-Talks of Abdul-Baha', *Star of the West*, supplement to vol. 3, no. 3.

74. Dawning-place of the praises or remembrances or mention of God. Generally, this term refers to the Baháʾí House of Worship or Temple and the dependencies clustered around it. (Momen, *Dictionary*, p. 148.) For accounts of ʿAbduʾl-Baháʾs visit to the Temple site in Wilmette see Whitmore, *Dawning Place*, pp. 60–5 and *Star of the West*, vol. 3, no. 4, pp. 5–6.

75. For transcripts of ʿAbduʾl-Baháʾs talk see *Promulgation*, pp. 71–2, 'Wisdom-Talks of Abdul-Baha', *Star of the West*, supplement to vol. 3, no. 3 and *Star of the West*, vol. 5, no. 16, p. 250.

76. Honore Jaxon reported: 'Abdul-Baha [sic] next called for the implements necessitated by the gravelly nature of the soil, and in response there was brought to him first an axe and then a shovel. With these tools of every-day life of the workers of the world, Abdul-Baha and friends from every race present, excavated a resting place for a stone . . .' *Star of the West*, vol. 3, no. 4, p. 6.

77. Pársís are Zoroastrian Persians who emigrated to India after the Arab conquest of Iran.

78. ʿAbduʾl-Bahá said as He set the stone in the ground, 'The Temple is already built.' Cited in Whitmore, *Dawning Place*, p. 65.

79. There does not appear to be a transcript of this talk in the English accounts, if indeed ʿAbduʾl-Bahá gave it.

80. For transcripts of ʿAbduʾl-Baháʾs talk see *Promulgation*, pp. 74–7 and *Star of the West*, vol. 3, no. 4, pp. 12–14.

81. From Maḥmúd's description, this appears to be the talk delivered at the Plaza Hotel on 2 May, transcripts of which can be found in *Promulgation*, pp. 79–83 and in *Star of the West*, vol. 3, no. 4, pp. 15–17. There is no indication that this was given to Unitarians.

82. This talk was given the following day, May 4, 1912. For a transcript of the talk see *Promulgation*, pp. 87–91.

83. According to *Promulgation*, ʿAbduʾl-Bahá went to this church at 935 East Fiftieth Street on May 5, which is supported by other sources (Ward, *239 Days*, pp. 55–6; *Star of the West*, vol. 3, no. 4, p. 22.) Balyuzi states that the talk was given on May 4. (Balyuzi, *ʿAbduʾl-Bahá*, p. 188.) For transcripts of the talk see *Promulgation*, pp. 93–6

and *Star of the West*, vol. 3, no. 4, pp. 22–4. The rector's name is variously spelled: Milburn and Melbourne in Ward, *239 Days*, pp. 56 and 57; Milburne in Balyuzi, *'Abdu'l-Bahá*, p. 188.

84. This was perhaps a visit to the grave of Corinne True's son Davis, who died shortly after 'Abdu'l-Bahá's arrival in Chicago. Rutstein, *Corinne True*, p. 103.

85. According to *Promulgation*, 'Abdu'l-Bahá's talk took place on May 5. Allan Ward confirms this, adding that 'The meeting was held, since the congregation had no building of its own, at the Abraham Lincoln Center at 700 East Oakwood, a building with a seating capacity of seven hundred.' (Ward, *239 Days*, pp. 56–7.) For transcripts of 'Abdu'l-Bahá's talk see *Promulgation*, pp. 97–100 and *Star of the West*, vol. 3, no. 4, pp. 24–7.

86. According to Allan Ward, 'Abdu'l-Bahá had 'especially invited the children to be brought to the Large Parlour. He talked to each one of them, held them in His lap, embracing and kissing them, whispering in their ears.' (Ward, *239 Days*, p. 55.) For an account of 'Abdu'l-Bahá's meeting with the children see *Star of the West*, vol. 3, no. 7, pp. 6–7. For other translations of 'Abdu'l-Bahá's talk see *Promulgation*, pp. 91–3 and *Star of the West*, vol. 3, no. 4, p. 22.

87. 'Abdu'l-Bahá's train arrived in Cleveland at 4:00 p.m. Ward, *239 Days*, p. 60.

88. For an account of 'Abdu'l-Bahá's visit and a transcription of His talk see *Star of the West*, vol. 3, no. 6, pp. 5–6. A different translation can be found in *Promulgation*, p. 104. Both accounts indicate that 'Abdu'l-Bahá's talk was given at Dr Swingle's sanatorium, 8203 Wade Park Ave. N.E.

89. For transcripts of 'Abdu'l-Bahá's talk see *Promulgation*, pp. 101–3 and *Star of the West*, vol. 3, no. 4, pp. 29–32.

90. For transcripts of 'Abdu'l-Bahá's talk see *Promulgation*, pp. 105–10 and *Star of the West*, vol. 3, no. 6, pp. 2–8.

91. Agnes Parsons states that Ali Kuli Khan and his wife, Mr and Mrs Hippolyte Dreyfus-Barney, Ahmad Sohrab, Joseph and Pauline Hannen and herself were at the train station to meet 'Abdu'l-Bahá. Hollinger, *Agnes Parsons' Diary*, p. 61.

92. The apartment belonged to the family of William P. Ripley, who temporarily vacated it for 'Abdu'l-Bahá and His party. Mrs Parsons

gives the address as 1336 Harvard Street N.W. (Hollinger, *Agnes Parsons' Diary*, p. 59, note 80.) According to Allan Ward, the address was 1340 Harvard Street. (Ward, *239 Days*, p. 64.)

93. Agnes Parsons notes that 'Abdu'l-Bahá 'had a ten o'clock dinner at Mrs Hemmick's'. Hollinger, *Agnes Parsons' Diary*, p. 65.

94. Agnes Parsons notes that the carriage to take 'Abdu'l-Bahá to the railway station did not reach His apartment in time, so 'Abdu'l-Bahá missed the train. Hollinger, *Agnes Parsons' Diary*, p. 66.

95. Hudson Apartment House, 227 Riverside Drive, New York, overlooking the Hudson River. Juliet Thompson notes: 'A few of us gathered in His rooms to prepare them for Him and fill the room with flowers; then to wait for His arrival: May Maxwell, Lua Getsinger, Carrie Kinney, Kate Ives, Grace Robarts, and I. Mr Mills and Mr Woodcock were waiting too . . . His flat is on one of the top stories, so that its windows frame the sky.' *Diary of Juliet Thompson*, p. 282.

96. Theodore Roosevelt was president from 1901 to 1909; William Howard Taft was president during the period of 'Abdu'l-Bahá's visit to the United States.

97. For other transcripts of 'Abdu'l-Bahá's talk see *Promulgation*, pp. 111–13 and *Star of the West*, vol. 3, no. 10, pp. 11–13.

98. See *Diary of Juliet Thompson*, p. 284 for a description of this event.

99. For the stenographic notes of this address taken by E. Foster see *Star of the West*, vol. 3, no. 10, pp. 12–13.

100. For transcripts of 'Abdu'l-Bahá's talk see *Promulgation*, pp. 113–16 and *Star of the West*, vol. 3, no. 7, pp. 13–14.

101. 'Ayn-'Ayn = 'Abdu'l-Bahá 'Abbás.

102. Meeting of the International Peace Forum held at the Grace Methodist Episcopal Church, West 104th Street, New York.

103. For another transcript of 'Abdu'l-Bahá's talk see *Promulgation*, pp. 116–22.

104. This meeting was held at the Hotel Astor, New York. For transcripts of 'Abdu'l-Bahá's talk see *Promulgation*, pp. 123–6 and *Star of the West*, vol. 3, no. 8, pp. 14–15. For transcripts of the other speeches made on this occasion see *Star of the West*, pp. 10–14.

Juliet Thompson notes, 'The Master was really too ill to have gone to this Conference. He had been in bed all morning, suffering from complete exhaustion, and had a high temperature. I was with Him all morning. While I was sitting beside Him I asked: "*Must* You go to the Hotel Astor when You are so ill?" "I work by the confirmation of the Holy Spirit," He answered. "I do not work by hygienic laws. If I did," He laughed, "I would get nothing done."' *Diary of Juliet Thompson*, p. 285.

105. A four-wheel carriage with a top divided into two sections that can be let down, thrown back or removed, with a raised seat outside for the driver.

106. The night before 'Abdu'l-Bahá left Lake Mohonk, He gave Dr Zia Bagdadi the key to His New York apartment, requesting him to bring back a Persian rug by 10:00 a.m. the following day. Since no trains ran at night, Dr Bagdadi jumped on the caboose of a moving train heading for New York. He collected the rug, caught an early morning train back to Lake Mohonk, hitched a ride with the mail carrier and arrived back at the conference site at 10:00 a.m., just as 'Abdu'l-Bahá was shaking hands with Mr Smiley in farewell. See Ward, *239 Days*, pp. 68–9.

107. *Promulgation*, pp. 126–9 and *Star of the West*, vol. 3, no. 9, pp. 9–12 indicate that this talk was given on Sunday, May 19, 1912.

108. For Ives's account of 'Abdu'l-Bahá's talk at his church see *Portals to Freedom*, pp. 80–7. Ives notes that 'it was one of the briefest of 'Abdu'l-Bahá's public talks' (p. 87). He further comments, 'To me 'Abdu'l-Bahá's talk in the Brotherhood Church and the address before the Unitarian Conference in Boston marked a new phase in my spiritual journey from self to God' (p. 90).

109. The Woman's Suffrage Meeting was held at the Metropolitan Temple, Seventh Avenue and Fourteenth Street, New York. For transcripts of 'Abdu'l-Bahá's talk see *Promulgation*, pp. 133–7 and *Star of the West*, vol. 3, no. 8, pp. 15–20.

110. For an account of this day see *Diary of Juliet Thompson*, pp. 288–93.

111. The name is unclear in the original. It could read Blake.

112. It was 'Abdu'l-Bahá's sixty-eighth birthday. He was born on May 23, 1844, the same date and year as the Declaration of the Báb.

113. For another account of this event see Gail, *Arches of the Years*, p. 89.

114. Also called the Unitarian Conference, held at Ford Hall, Boston. For a transcript of the talk see *Promulgation*, pp. 140–3.
115. For a transcript of 'Abdu'l-Bahá's talk and prayer see *Promulgation*, pp. 143–6.
116. For transcripts of 'Abdu'l-Bahá's talk see *Promulgation*, pp. 147–50 and *Star of the West*, vol. 3, no. 8, pp. 20–2. For another account of the evening see *Diary of Juliet Thompson*, p. 296.
117. For transcripts of 'Abdu'l-Bahá's talk, see *Promulgation*, pp. 150–3, and *Star of the West*, vol. 3, no. 7, pp. 14–21, both of which state that the talk took place on May 28.
118. For another transcript of 'Abdu'l-Bahá's talk see *Star of the West*, vol. 3, no. 7, p. 21.
119. The events described here took place on Thursday, May 30, 1912.
120. For transcripts of this talk see *Promulgation*, pp. 156–60 and *Star of the West*. vol. 4, no. 3, pp. 55–8.
121. Hoar's Sanitorium was located in Fanwood, New Jersey.
122. For a transcript of the talk given at the Fanwood Town Hall see *Promulgation*, pp. 161–3.
123. For other transcripts of the talk of 'Abdu'l-Bahá see *Promulgation*, pp. 163–71, *Star of the West*, vol. 3, no. 10, pp. 24–9 and *Star of the West*, vol. 5, no. 16, pp. 246–50.
124. The events described here took place on Tuesday, June 4, 1912.
125. For transcripts of 'Abdu'l-Bahá's answers to questions put to Him see *Star of the West*, vol. 7, no. 9, pp. 77–84.
126. Ashrafi, Persian gold coins (about 22 to 24 carats, weighing approximately 9 to 12 grams).
127. The house at 309 West 78th Street belonged to Mrs Champney.
128. This is in reference to Amín'u'lláh Faríd who often solicited money and gifts in the name of 'Abdu'l-Bahá despite the Master's explicit instructions to the contrary. Owing to his further disobedience to 'Abdu'l-Bahá, Faríd was later declared a Covenant-Breaker. See Smith, 'The American Bahá'í Community', *Studies in Bábí and Bahá'í History*, pp. 188–9.

129. Balyuzi notes that this was on Saturday, 8 June 1912. See Balyuzi, *'Abdu'l-Bahá*, p. 209.

130. For transcripts of 'Abdu'l-Bahá's talks in Philadelphia and an account of His visit there, see *Promulgation*, pp. 172–82, *Star of the West*, vol. 5, no. 6, pp. 83–90 and *Star of the West*, vol. 5, no. 7, pp. 99–106.

131. One was the Unitarian Church at 15th Street and Girard Avenue and the other the Baptist Temple, at Broad and Berks Streets, Philadelphia. According to *Promulgation*, both meetings took place on June 9, 1912. For a transcript of 'Abdu'l-Bahá's talk at the Unitarian Church see *Promulgation*, pp. 172–6; for a transcript of the talk at the Baptist Temple see *Promulgation*, pp. 176–82.

132. According to Balyuzi and Ward, the events recorded here took place on Monday, June 10, 1912. See Balyuzi, *'Abdu'l-Bahá*, p. 211 and Ward, *239 Days*, p. 88.

133. Bahá'u'lláh, *Kitáb-i-Aqdas*, para. 53 (translated by Shoghi Effendi).

134. The events described probably took place on Tuesday, June 11, 1912.

135. For transcripts of 'Abdu'l-Bahá's talks given on June 11, 1912 see *Promulgation*, pp. 183–7 and *Star of the West*, vol. 4, no. 6, pp. 99–101.

136. The events described probably took place on Wednesday, June 12, 1912.

137. For a transcript of one of 'Abdu'l-Bahá's talks given on June 12, 1912 see *Promulgation*, pp. 187–9.

138. The events described probably took place on Thursday, June 13, 1912. See Ward, *239 Days*, p. 90.

139. The events described probably took place on Friday, June 14 or Saturday, June 15, 1912.

140. Sultan of Turkey from 1876 until he was deposed in 1909.

141. A commission sent by the Ottoman government to investigate charges leveled against 'Abdu'l-Bahá by violators of the Covenant. See Balyuzi, *'Abdu'l-Bahá*, pp. 112–25.

142. This talk was given at 309 West Seventy-eighth Street, New York, on June 15, not June 13. For a transcript of the talk see *Promulgation*, pp. 189–90.

143. The events described probably took place on Saturday, June 15, 1912.
144. A believer mentioned in 'Abdu'l-Bahá's *Memorials of the Faithful*, pp. 54–7.
145. A quotation from the poet Rúmí.
146. The events described here took place on Sunday, June 16, 1912.
147. This meeting took place at the Fourth Unitarian Church, Beverly Road, Flatbush, Brooklyn. For transcripts of 'Abdu'l-Bahá's talk see *Promulgation*, pp. 190–4 and *Star of the West*, vol. 3, no. 10, pp. 30–2.
148. For translations of the prayer see *Promulgation*, p. 193 and *Star of the West*, vol. 3, no. 10, p. 32.
149. For 'Abdu'l-Bahá's address to the Sunday school children see *Promulgation*, pp. 193–4 and *Star of the West*, vol. 3, no. 10, p. 32.
150. 935 Eastern Parkway, Brooklyn. For transcripts of 'Abdu'l-Bahá's talk see *Promulgation*, pp. 194–7 and *Star of the West*, vol. 3, no. 10. pp. 17–19.
151. The Central Congregational Church, Hancock Street, Brooklyn. For transcripts of 'Abdu'l-Bahá's talk see *Promulgation*, pp. 197–203 and *Star of the West*, vol. 3, no. 10, pp. 19–22.
152. The events described here took place on Monday, June 17, 1912.
153. Although not identified, this is most likely Mírzá 'Alí-Muḥammad Varqá.
154. The events described took place on Tuesday, June 18, 1912.
155. For another description of this event see *Star of the West*, vol. 3, no. 10, pp. 2–4.
156. The events described here took place on Wednesday, June 19, 1912. Although not mentioned by Mírzá Maḥmúd, June 19 was the day 'Abdu'l-Bahá designated New York the City of the Covenant. See Balyuzi, *'Abdu'l-Bahá*, p. 220 and *Diary of Juliet Thompson*, pp. 311–16.
157. Also known as the Súriy-i-Ghuṣn, it was revealed by Bahá'u'lláh while in Adrianople. See Shoghi Effendi, *God Passes By*, p. 242.

158. Those following Mírzá Yaḥyá, also known as Subḥ-i-Azal, the half-brother of Bahá'u'lláh who claimed to be the successor of the Báb.
159. A believer who had been exiled with Bahá'u'lláh to 'Akká.
160. The events described here took place on Thursday, June 20, 1912. See Balyuzi, *'Abdu'l-Bahá*, p. 221 and *Diary of Juliet Thompson*, p. 317.
161. For transcripts of 'Abdu'l-Bahá's talk see *Promulgation*, pp. 206–9 and *Star of the West*, vol. 3, no. 10, pp. 23–4.
162. The events described here took place on Friday, June 21, 1912. See Balyuzi, *'Abdu'l-Bahá*, p. 221 and *Diary of Juliet Thompson*, pp. 317–21.
163. The events described here took place on Saturday, June 22, 1912.
164. The events described here took place on Sunday, June 23, 1912.
165. Mírzá Asadu'lláh of Khuy, on whom the Báb conferred the designation 'Dayyán' (lit. 'conqueror' or 'judge'). After the martyrdom of the Báb, a number of His followers turned to Dayyán for guidance. He went to the length of claiming to be 'He Whom God shall make manifest' but after meeting Bahá'u'lláh in Iraq, he retracted the claim. Mírzá Yaḥyá caused 'the murder of Dayyán, whom he feared and envied'. See Shoghi Effendi, *God Passes By*, p. 165.
166. For details of 'Abdu'l-Vahháb, see the chapter entitled 'The Story of a Shírází Youth' in Balyuzi, *King of Glory*, pp. 94–8.
167. Juliet Thompson relates in her diary: 'The Master's whole aspect suddenly changed. It was as though the spirit of the martyr had entered into Him. With that God-like head erect, snapping His fingers high in the air, beating out a drum-like rhythm with His foot till we could hardly endure the vibrations set up, He triumphantly sang "The Martyr's Song".

> 'I have come again, I have come again,
> By way of Shíráz I have come again!
> With the wine cup in My hand!
> Such is the madness of Love!'
> *Diary of Juliet Thompson*, pp. 320–1.

168. For a transcript of 'Abdu'l-Bahá's talk see *Promulgation*, pp. 210–13.

169. The events described here took place on Wednesday, June 26, 1912. See Ward, *239 Days*, p. 100.

170. This visit to Newark took place on Thursday, June 27, 1912. See Ward, *239 Days*, p. 100.

171. A Persian hat, brimless, of lambskin or felt, long worn by government officials, civilians, etc. The term 'hatted' refers to laymen while 'turbaned' indicates the clergy or learned class. Gail, *Bahá'í Glossary*, p. 27.

172. A 'para' was the smallest denomination of currency of the Ottoman Empire in the 1860s.

173. A reference to Bahá'u'lláh's withdrawal in April 1854 from Baghdád to Sulaymáníyyih, a small town about 200 miles away in Kurdistán, where He resided until March 1856. See Balyuzi, *King of Glory*, pp. 115–22.

174. 'O God, He Who is invoked.' The cycle of every Divine Dispensation. Specifically, the time of Mustagháth is the day of the Latter Resurrection, i.e. the Advent of Bahá'u'lláh. Gail, *Bahá'í Glossary*, p. 37. See also Bahá'u'lláh, *Kitáb-i-Íqán*, pp. 229, 248.

175. He was the sole companion of Bahá'u'lláh in Sulaymáníyyih. He was set upon by highwaymen or frontier patrols and was mortally wounded. When found near death, he gave his name and bequeathed all his possessions to Darvísh Muḥammad-i-Írání, the name Bahá'u'lláh had assumed. See Balyuzi, *King of Glory*, pp. 116–17.

176. The events described here took place on Saturday, June 29, 1912.

177. Roy Wilhelm's home, the venue of the Unity Feast, marks the only public memorial which the American Bahá'ís have been permitted to construct in observance of 'Abdu'l-Bahá's North American journeys. For another account of this event, see *Diary of Juliet Thompson*, pp. 322–5.

178. For transcripts of 'Abdu'l-Bahá's talk at the Unity Feast see *Promulgation*, pp. 213–15 and *Star of the West*, vol. 3, no. 8, pp. 16–18.

179. The events described here took place on Sunday, June 30, 1912.

180. Mr Topakyan, the Persian Consul General, resided in Morristown, New Jersey.

181. The events described here took place on Monday, July 1, 1912.
182. During His stay in New York, 'Abdu'l-Bahá resided at 309 West 78th Street.
183. For transcripts of 'Abdu'l-Bahá's talks on July 1, 1912 see *Promulgation*, pp. 216–18 and *Star of the West*, vol. 4, no. 6, pp. 102–3.
184. The events described here took place on Tuesday, July 2, 1912.
185. For transcripts of 'Abdu'l-Bahá's talks on 1 July see *Promulgation*, pp. 216–17 and 218.
186. The events described here took place on Wednesday, July 3, 1912.
187. The events described here took place on Thursday, July 4, 1912.
188. Juliet Thompson records that

    On the fourth of July, Mamma had her birthday dinner with the Master. He was so sweet to her . . . When we sat with Him after dinner, He spoke of tests. 'Even the sword,' He said, 'is no test to the Persian believers. They are given a chance to recant; they cry out instead: "Yá Bahá'u'l-Abhá!" Then the sword is raised,' – He shot out His arm as though brandishing a sword – 'they cry out all the more "Yá Bahá'u'l-Abhá". But some of the people here are tested if I don't say "How do you do?"' *Diary of Juliet Thompson*, pp. 326–7.

189. It is not clear on what day the events described here took place.
190. The National History Museum. For an account of this excursion see *Diary of Juliet Thompson*, p. 329–32.
191. For transcripts of 'Abdu'l-Bahá's two talks see *Promulgation*, pp. 218–25, *Star of the West*, vol. 3, no. 11, pp. 6–10 and *Star of the West*, vol. 4, no. 5, pp. 87–90.
192. For transcripts of 'Abdu'l-Bahá's talk see *Promulgation*, pp. 225–8 and *Star of the West*. vol. 3, no. 11, pp. 10–12.
193. 'Abdu'l-Bahá had asked Lua Getsinger to go to California to proclaim the Covenant. Juliet Thompson relates that as Lua was eager to remain with the Master, she delayed going and, in order to prevent her departure, had deliberately walked through some poison ivy during the Unity Feast at Roy Wilhelm's house, which made her feet swell. Lua said to Juliet Thompson, '*Look* at me, Julie. *Look* at my feet. Oh, please go right back to the Master and tell Him about

them and say: "How can Lua travel now?"'
   I did it, returned to the Master's house, found Him in His room and put Lua's question to Him. He laughed, then crossed the room to a table on which stood a bowl of fruit, and, selecting an apple and a pomegranate, gave them to me.
   'Take these to Lua,' He said. 'Tell her to eat them and she will be cured. Spend the day with her, Juliet.'
   O precious Lua – strange mixture of disobedience and obedience – and all from love! I shall never forget her, seizing first the apple, then the pomegranate and gravely chewing them all the way through till not even a pomegranate seed was left: thoroughly eating her cure, which was certain to send her to California. *Diary of Juliet Thompson*, pp. 323–6.

194. It has not been possible to identify either Siyyid 'Abdu'lláh's work or Mírzá Abu'l-Faḍl's refutation of it. Mírzá Abu'l-Faḍl's *The Brilliant Proof*, published in 1912 to refute the criticisms of the Christian missionary Peter Z. Easton, does not contain the passages cited.

195. Naisan is the name of a Hebrew month. It had been used in the ancient Egyptian calendar and was still in use in 1912. It originated in Babylonia before its adoption by other civilizations.

196. The guinea was one pound sterling and one shilling (i.e. one pound and five pence in today's currency). In 1912 the equivalent of 1,000 guineas was approximately $16,000.

197. O Ye Peoples of the World!
   Know, verily, that an unforeseen calamity followeth you, and grievous retribution awaiteth you. Think not that which ye have committed hath been effaced in My sight. By My beauty! All your doings hath My pen graven with open characters upon tablets of chrysolite. Bahá'u'lláh, *Hidden Words*, Persian no. 63.

198. The events described here took place on Friday, July 12, 1912.

199. For Juliet Thompson's description of Percy Grant's meeting with 'Abdu'l-Bahá and the meeting at her home see *Diary of Juliet Thompson*, pp. 339–46.

200. The events described here took place on Sunday, July 14, 1912.

201. For transcripts of 'Abdu'l-Bahá's talk at the All Souls' Unitarian Church, Fourth Avenue and Twentieth Street on July 14 see *Promulgation*, pp. 228–35 and *Star of the West*, vol. 3, no. 11, pp. 12–16.

202. The events described here took place on Monday, July 15, 1912.
203. For a transcript of 'Abdu'l-Bahá's talk at the Krugs' home see *Promulgation*, pp. 236–7. The text of this talk differs from the overview of it provided by Maḥmúd.
204. The events described here took place on Wednesday, July 17, 1912.
205. There are several accounts of this wedding. In her obituary of Grace Ober, Mabel Rice-Wray Ives writes:

> During the months of 'Abdu'l-Bahá's stay in America in 1912 Mrs Ober (Grace Robarts) had the honor of being indeed the 'servant' in His home in whatever city He was staying. He chose her to go ahead and secure an apartment for Him and have it in readiness upon His arrival. Then she would care for His home as a housekeeper and hostess while He and His secretaries and those Persians who had the privilege of serving Him in various capacities, remained there. She kept the home immaculate, and always ready for the constant stream of guests from morning to night, Bahá'ís and inquirers and souls in difficulty to whom 'Abdu'l-Bahá was always a loving Father. It was during one of the New York City visits of 'Abdu'l-Bahá that He suggested her marriage to Harlan Ober. Gaining the consent of these two devoted believers, who in His consummate wisdom He had drawn together, He, on the following day, July 17, 1912, married them in the morning according to the Bahá'í marriage.
>
> This infinite bounty of being chosen for each other and joined in marriage by the Centre of the Covenant Himself was a unique favor bestowed upon these two souls alone, out of all America. *The Bahá'í World*, vol. 8, p. 658.

* * *

Juliet Thompson writes in her diary:

> In the evening I returned from a wedding, Grace Robarts' and Harlan Ober's, where the Master, for me, as well as for the bride and bridegroom, turned the water of life into wine.
>
> Grace and Harlan stood together, transfigured; they seemed to be bathed in white light. Mr Ives, standing opposite, married them. Back in the shadow sat the Master. There were times when I, sitting at a little distance from Him, felt His lightning glance

on me. At the end of the service He blessed the marriage. *Diary of Juliet Thompson*, pp. 350–1.

* * *

Howard Colby Ives provides a long account of the wedding and discusses the nature of Bahá'í marriage. (See Ives, *Portals to Freedom*, pp. 92–113). Here he describes the Master at the ceremony:

> After the simple wedding ceremony and the bride and groom had resumed their seats, 'Abdu'l-Bahá rose. His cream-colored 'abá fell in graceful folds to His feet. Upon His head he wore a tarboosh, or fez, of the same color, beneath which His long white hair fell almost to His shoulders. Most impressive of all His impressive aspects were His eyes. Blue they were but so changing with His mood! Now gentle and appealing, now holding a deep, tranquil lambent repose as though gazing upon scenes of glory far removed.
>
> His brow above those wide-set eyes was like an ivory dome. His neatly clipped beard, snowy white, touched His breast, but around His mouth no straggling hairs obscured the mobile lips.
>
> He spoke through an interpreter, as was His custom . . . He swept the room with a glance at once enfolding and abstracted. He raised His hands, palm upwards, level with His waist, His eyes closed and He chanted a prayer for the souls united by Him and by me.

* * *

For another account of the wedding see *Star of the West*, vol. 3, no. 12, pp. 14–15.

206. The events described here took place on Thursday, July 18, 1912.

207. The events described here took place on Friday, July 19, 1912.

208. Mentioned in the *Dawn-Breakers*, chapter 5.

209. A doctor of Islamic law, who has authority to interpret and issue judgments.

210. Known as <u>Sh</u>ay<u>kh</u> Hindí, a poet from India.

211. Martha Root was among those in the audience that evening and was so taken by 'Abdu'l-Bahá's account of the martyrdom of Varqá and

his son Rúḥu'lláh that she later wrote her own moving account of the Varqá family, 'White Roses of Persia'. See Garis, *Martha Root*, pp. 53–4.

212. The events described here took place on Sunday, July 21, 1912.

213. It is customary in the East to show one's highest respect to a guest by apologizing for the lack of any service rendered.

214. A ruler of Egypt from 1867 to 1914, governing as a viceroy of the Sultan of Turkey.

215. For transcripts of 'Abdu'l-Bahá's talk see *Promulgation*, pp. 238–9 and *Star of the West*, vol. 4, no. 7, p. 122.

216. 'Abdu'l-Bahá spoke to the Theosophical Society at The Kensington, Exeter and Boylston Streets, Boston. For a transcript of His talk see *Promulgation*, pp. 239–43.

217. For transcripts of this brief address see *Promulgation*, p. 244 and *Star of the West*, vol. 7, no. 12, p. 116.

218. Yá Rasúlu'lláh, an invocation of Muslims to the Prophet Muḥammad.

219. For other accounts of 'Abdu'l-Bahá's visit to Dublin see Hollinger, *Agnes Parsons' Diary*, pp. 69–124 and Ives, *Portals to Freedom*, pp. 114–31.

220. Muslim clergymen, doctors of religion, by whose decisions Muslim life is regulated.

221. Bahá'u'lláh's Tablet to the Shah of Persia, dispatched from 'Akká, and His lengthiest to any single sovereign. The Shah put its bearer, Badí', to death.

222. Muḥammad 'Alí Mírzá succeeded Muẓaffaru'd-Dín Sháh to the throne of the Qájár dynasty in 1907 and abdicated in 1909.

223. From a Persian proverb, equivalent to 'home is where the heart is'.

224. For an account of the visit of the Bahá'ís to Dublin see *Star of the West*, vol. 3, no. 11, pp. 3–6.

225. It is possible that the events described as taking place on this date took place at some other time, as Joseph Hannen had provided transcripts of two talks 'Abdu'l-Bahá gave in Dublin, one 'at Abdu'l-Baha's house, Dublin, Wednesday morning, July 31st' and the other 'at 9:30 a.m., July 31st, Abdu'l-Baha, on the veranda of His house'. (*Star of*

the West, vol. 3, no. 11, pp. 4–6.) See also the entry in the diary of Agnes Parsons for Wednesday, July 31. (Hollinger, *Agnes Parsons' Diary*, pp. 85–8.) Mrs Parsons's diary suggests that the date of the visit to the summer school was August 1; however, there are two entries for August 1 in her diary (pp. 88–91).

226. Shoghi Effendi describes this incident:

    Even in the city of 'Ishqabád the newly established Shí'ah community, envious of the rising prestige of the followers of Bahá'u'lláh who were living in their midst, instigated two ruffians to assault the seventy-year old Ḥájí Muḥammad-Riḍáy-i-Iṣfahání, whom, in broad day and in the midst of the bazaar, they stabbed in no less than thirty-two places, exposing his liver, lacerating his stomach and tearing open his breast. A military court dispatched by the Czar to 'Ishqabád established, after prolonged investigation, the guilt of the Shí'ahs, sentencing two to death and banishing six others – a sentence which neither Náṣiri'd-Dín Sháh, nor the 'ulamás of Ṭihrán, of Mashhad and of Tabríz, who were appealed to, could mitigate, but which the representatives of the aggrieved community, through their magnanimous intercession which greatly surprised the Russian authorities, succeeded in having commuted to a lighter punishment. Shoghi Effendi, *God Passes By*, pp. 202–3.

227. The events described here took place on Sunday, August 4, 1912. See Hollinger, *Agnes Parsons' Diary*, p. 94.

228. The author says, '*shaghul ghamar*' (an impossible act).

229. 'Abdu'l-Bahá's half-brother, the archbreaker of Bahá'u'lláh's Covenant. See *God Passes By*, pp. 246, 249.

230. A notorious enemy of the Faith. See *God Passes By*, p. 146.

231. A comprehensive study of Islamic theology by Shaykh Ibn al-'Arabí, one of the most influential Sufi thinkers, much quoted by the 'ulamá. The work contains a full exposition of Sufi doctrine. 'Conquests' in a mystical context carries no military connotations but implies the opening of the heart to knowledge and understanding.

232. 'Abdu'l-Bahá spoke at the Dublin Inn on August 5, 1912. For transcripts of His talk see *Promulgation*, pp. 245–7 and *Star of the West*, vol. 3, no. 18, pp. 4–6.

233. This is possibly the talk recorded in *Promulgation*, pp. 247–52 and *Star of the West*, vol. 3, no. 18, pp. 6–10.
234. Before 'Abdu'l-Bahá went to the church He spoke with Howard Colby Ives. See Ives, *Portals to Freedom*, pp. 120–8.
235. A famous 14th-century Persian musician poet.
236. Herat is present-day Kabul in Afghanistan. Bokhara is an ancient city of Persia, now in Uzbekistan.
237. The river of Múliyán, near Bokhara.
238. Rúdakí, as translated by Edward G. Browne. See *A Literary History of Persia*, vol. 1, p. 16.
239. Sa'dí, the great 13th-century Persian poet, famous in the West for his 'Gulistan' or 'Rose Garden'.
240. A Persian Bahá'í woman, the first Persian woman to travel in the United States.
241. A Persian expression denoting one who passes round the wine cup at joyful gatherings.
242. For an account of 'Abdu'l-Bahá's arrival at Green Acre see *Star of the West*, vol. 3, no. 15, pp. 3–4. H. M. Balyuzi writes:

> Green Acre, an estate of nearly two hundred acres, lies on the banks of the Piscataqua river in Eliot, Maine, four miles from the shores of the Atlantic . . . In 1894 . . . Miss Sarah J. Farmer, a woman highly enlightened, had opened the estate as a conference center for people of advanced and liberal views. Two years later she embraced the Bahá'í Faith. And when she went on pilgrimage to 'Akká, she offered the facilities of Green Acre to 'Abdu'l-Bahá . . . Today the Green Acre property (the home of a well-famed Summer School) is administered by the National Spiritual Assembly of the Bahá'ís of the United States. It includes the Inn, the Fellowship House, the Arts and Crafts Studio and a holding on Monsalvat where 'Abdu'l-Bahá stood and commended the wish of Sarah Farmer that a 'university of the higher sciences' should be built on that height. Balyuzi, *'Abdu'l-Bahá*, pp. 240–1.

* * *

See also *Green Acre on the Piscataqua*, an account of Green Acre's 100-year history, chronicling its development from a resort hotel in 1890 to its present-day use as a Bahá'í school.

243. In fact, 'Abdu'l-Bahá visited Miss Farmer at the sanatorium in Portsmouth where she, an invalid, was a patient.

244. The Eirenian, the House of Peace.

245. For transcripts of 'Abdu'l-Bahá's talk see *Promulgation*, pp. 253–61 and *Star of the West*, vol. 3, no. 16, pp. 5–9. Balyuzi states that this was 'one of the longest talks of His entire tour'. Balyuzi, *'Abdu'l-Bahá*, p. 241.

246. 'Abdu'l-Bahá gave several talks in Green Acre on August 17, 1912. For transcripts of these talks see *Promulgation*, pp. 261–3, 263–4 and 270–5.

247. For transcripts of 'Abdu'l-Bahá's talk see *Promulgation*, p. 264–70 and *Star of the West*, vol. 8, no. 7, pp. 76–80.

248. For a transcript of 'Abdu'l-Bahá's talk see *Star of the West*, vol. 3, no. 15, pp. 4–7.

249. Then called Eliot House, now Staples Cottage.

250. For Fred Mortensen's own account of his meeting with 'Abdu'l-Bahá at Green Acre, see *Star of the West*, vol. 14, no. 12, pp. 365–7; Balyuzi, *'Abdu'l-Bahá*, pp. 247–51; and Ward, *239 Days*, pp. 127–9.

251. *Green Acre on the Piscataqua* gives two accounts of this unity feast:

After dinner He hosted a unity feast from the porch of what He called 'Bahá'í Home' . . . We have only a few descriptions of the feast. Alice Tobey Cummings remembered the round peppermints that Ella Robarts had brought at 'Abdu'l-Bahá's request for the refreshment table at the feast, some of which she and Louise Thompson saved and for years distributed to the friends on special occasions. She also remembered 'Abdu'l-Bahá saying that He had left enough spirit at Green Acre to bring dry bones to life. *Green Acre on the Piscataqua*, pp. 51–3.

After dinner 'Abdu'l-Bahá emerged from what was then known as the Eliot House and, standing on the porch, spoke to those gathered. So forceful and melodious was His voice that passers-by would stop to listen.

        One can imagine 'Abdu'l-Bahá, a man of sixty-eight years, wearing a long flowing, cream colored robe and a dark *'abá* or overcoat, a white turbaned headdress on his flowing silky white hair. As He talked, He walked back and forth across the porch gesturing with His hands. His voice strong and sure, His translator by His side. *Green Acre on the Piscataqua*, p. 58 (based on notes of Ivy Drew Edwards).

252. *Green Acre on the Piscataqua* provides several accounts of 'Abdu'l-Bahá's visit to Monsalvat, among them Harry Randall's:

        He went to the top of Mt. Salvat, which is a part of the Green Acre property there, and He told us that on this spot a great Mashreq'ul-Azkar [sic] would be built and that the whole hill would be covered with institutions of learning, science, and religion, and to impress us with the importance of this Center, He said already it had been created and was not a prophecy alone and the Mashreq'ul-Azkar hung low over that place. *Green Acre on the Piscataqua*, p. 59.

253. Maḥmúd describes the moving picture as a camera which rotated in two different directions when it took photographs. Its plate was about half a meter long.

254. 'That evening He dined with and spoke to nineteen guests at the home of Esther Annie Magee and her daughter Edith Inglis.' *Green Acre on the Piscataqua*, p. 59.

255. The Wilson house is today part of the endowments of the American Bahá'í community.

256. For transcripts of 'Abdu'l-Bahá's talk to the New Thought Forum at the Metaphysical Club in Boston see *Promulgation*, pp. 276–80 and *Star of the West*, vol. 4, no. 7, pp. 117–22.

257. For a transcript of 'Abdu'l-Bahá's talk at Franklin Square House, Boston, see *Promulgation*, pp. 280–4.

258. For a transcript of 'Abdu'l-Bahá's talk see *Promulgation*, pp. 284–9.

259. It is likely that the wedding of Ruby Breed, youngest daughter of Francis and Alice Breed, to Clarence Johnson took place on this date. 'Abdu'l-Bahá attended the wedding ceremony and afterwards gave a talk 'on marriage, on the union of the sexes in all four kingdoms – mineral, vegetable, animal and human – and passing on to the next life in the Heavenly Kingdom'. For a description of the wedding see

Gail, *Arches of the Years*, p. 90; for a newspaper account see Ward, *239 Days*, pp. 131–2.

260. This meeting took place at the home of Madame Morey, 34 Hillside Avenue, Malden on Thursday, August 29, 1912. For a transcript of 'Abdu'l-Bahá's talk see *Promulgation*, pp. 289–96. On August 31, a local newspaper, the *Transcript*, reported:

> Abdul Baha Abbas [sic] . . . was the guest of honor at a reception given on Thursday evening at her residence in Malden by Mme. Beale Morey, the musician. There were nearly a hundred guests present, for whom Mme. Morey played at the piano an introductory musical programme, following which Abdul Beha Abbas [sic] gave a talk on the 'Religions of the World', showing the points of similarity of beliefs of different nations and their relations in the forming of a universal brotherhood. Cited in Ward, *239 Days*, p. 132.

261. The Maxwell home at 1548 Pine Avenue West, Montreal, (indicated as 716 Pine Avenue West in *Promulgation*) is now a national Bahá'í endowment, given to the Faith by Amatu'l-Bahá Rúḥíyyih Khánum in 1948.

262. John Lewis, editor of the *Montreal Daily Star*. See Balyuzi, *'Abdu'l-Bahá*, pp. 256–8.

263. From Saná'í, 12th century, the first of the great Persian mystic poets.

264. Ahmad Sohrab, one of 'Abdu'l-Bahá's entourage.

265. For another translation of 'Abdu'l-Bahá's talk see *Promulgation*, pp. 297–302.

266. For transcripts of the talks of 'Abdu'l-Bahá, which were given at the home of Mr and Mrs Maxwell, see *Promulgation*, pp. 302–8.

267. For a transcript of 'Abdu'l-Bahá's talk see *Promulgation*, pp. 308–12.

268. This is probably a believer mentioned in *Memorials of the Faithful*, pp. 171–2, who at one time waited on Bahá'u'lláh.

269. The first Caliph of Islam after the passing of Muḥammad.

270. For a transcript of the talk by 'Abdu'l-Bahá's at the St James Methodist Church, Montreal, see *Promulgation*, pp. 312–19.

271. The child, Mary, was then two years old. In 1937 she married the Guardian of the Bahá'í Faith, Shoghi Effendi, and was given the

title Amatu'l-Bahá Rúḥíyyih Khánum. She was appointed a Hand of the Cause of God in 1952.

272. From the Persian proverb, 'Your place is vacant', meaning that you are missed.

273. A title of 'Abdu'l-Bahá: 'When the ocean of My presence hath ebbed and the Book of My Revelation is ended, turn your faces toward Him Whom God hath purposed, Who hath branched from this Ancient Root.' Bahá'u'lláh, *Kitáb-i-Aqdas*, para. 121.

274. Corinne True lived at 5338 Kenmore Avenue.

275. This is possibly Bernard Jacobsen, a prominent Bahá'í in Kenosha.

276. See *Tablets of Bahá'u'lláh*, pp. 99–134.

277. Shu'á'u'lláh, the son of 'Abdu'l-Bahá's faithless half brother Mírzá Muḥammad-'Alí, was in the United States at the same time as 'Abdu'l-Bahá. On May 4, 1912 he had written to the *Kenosha Evening News* denouncing 'Abdu'l-Bahá for trying to subvert the teachings of Bahá'u'lláh and proposing a meeting between himself and 'Abdu'l-Bahá to settle their differences. Kheiralla was also to attend. 'Abdu'l-Bahá ignored the letter. Kheiralla, on July 8, also wrote to the newspaper in support of Shu'á'u'lláh. Roger Dahl notes that 'Abdu'l-Bahá's visit to Kenosha 'seems to have been primarily intended by 'Abdu'l-Bahá as a means of uplifting the spirits of the Bahá'ís in Kenosha and raising the public prestige of that community in the face of opposition by the followers of Kheiralla'. Dahl, 'A History of the Kenosha Bahá'í Community, 1897–1980' in Hollinger, *Community Histories*, p. 1–57.

278. For another account of 'Abdu'l-Bahá's visit to Kenosha see Collins, 'Kenosha, 1893–1912' in Momen, *Studies in Bábí and Bahá'í History*, vol. 1, pp. 244–8. 'Abdu'l-Bahá was taken to the Bahá'í Center in Kenosha at Gronquist Hall, 616 Fifty-seventh Street.

279. A governor of Palestine during a period of the Ottoman Empire.

280. For a transcript of 'Abdu'l-Bahá's talk see *Promulgation*, pp. 320–4.

281. Martyred in Iṣfahán with his brother, the Beloved of Martyrs (Mírzá Muḥammad-Ḥusayn) on March 17, 1879. See *God Passes By*, pp. 200–1.

282. The Walker Art Gallery. See Ward, *239 Days*, p. 148.
283. 'Abdu'l-Bahá gave this talk at the home of Dr and Mrs Clement Woolson, 870 Laurel Avenue, St Paul, on September 20, 1912. For a transcript of the talk see *Promulgation*, pp. 329–33.
284. 'Abdu'l-Bahá spoke at the home of Albert Hall, 2030 Queen Avenue South, Minneapolis on September 20, 1912. For a transcript of His talk see *Promulgation*, pp. 325–8.
285. In the early days of Islam, on the recommendation of the Persian Salmán, ditches were dug to protect the believers from the onslaught of the enemies attacking the Prophet Muḥammad.
286. Anushírván was a Sásáníd king known for his just rule. The Prophet Muḥammad was born during his reign. Khusraw is the name of several Persian kings. Khusraw I (531–79 AD) was the greatest of the Sásáníd monarchs. He extended his rule east to the Indus River, west across Arabia, and north and northwest, taking part of Armenia and Caucasia from the Byzantines.
287. The Executive Committee of the Central Organization for a Durable Peace.
288. A low mountain near the village of Tákur, in the province of Núr, Persia, the summer residence of Bahá'u'lláh.
289. 'Abdu'l-Bahá here is speaking ironically in reference to His nephew Shu'á'u'lláh, whose name means 'ray of light', as being 'of darkness', for shortly after the passing of Bahá'u'lláh he became a Covenant-breaker, following in the footsteps of his father, Mírzá Muḥammad-'Alí, 'Abdu'l-Bahá's unfaithful half-brother.
290. 'Abdu'l-Bahá here is quoting a passage from the Kitáb-i-Aqdas, para. 37.
291. 'Abdu'l-Bahá spoke at the home of Mrs Sidney Roberts on September 24, 1912. For transcripts of His talk see *Promulgation*, pp. 334–7 and *Star of the West*, vol. 4, no. 13, pp. 219–26.
292. Although not identified, 'Abdu'l-Bahá is likely referring to Fujita, who accompanied Him on His journey westward.
293. 'Abdu'l-Bahá's talk at the Second Divine Science Church, 3929 West Thirty-eighth Avenue, Denver was given on September 25, 1912. For a transcript of His talk see *Promulgation*, pp, 337–42.

294. A story based on the Mathnaví of Rúmí.

295. Hajaru'l-asvad, a stone at the northeast corner of the Ka'bá, which is the holiest spot in the Islamic world, the center of pilgrimage for Muslims and the direction in which they face for their obligatory prayers.

296. See Qur'án 29:69 (Suríh of the Spider), a reference to the flight of Muḥammad and His son-in-law 'Alí to a cave outside Mecca because of persecution by the enemies of His Cause.

297. This was also the week of the State Fair and the Mormon Convention and the city was filled with people from Utah, adjoining states and beyond. For the account of Feny E. Paulson, a Bahá'í who met 'Abdu'l-Bahá and His entourage in Utah, see Ward, *239 Days*, pp. 159–63.

298. Siyyid Yaḥyáy-i-Dárábí, surnamed Vaḥíd, a devoted follower of the Báb.

299. He had been a servant of the Báb at Máh-Kú.

300. This event occurred at the home of Bahá'u'lláh when 'Abdu'l-Bahá was a child of five. See Nabíl, *Dawn-Breakers*, p. 432.

301. For another account of 'Abdu'l-Bahá's stay in San Francisco see *Star of the West*, vol. 3, no. 12, pp. 9–10 and vol. 3, no. 13, pp. 11–13.

302. This was Kanichi Yamamoto, the first Japanese Bahá'í. Ḥasan is the name of the second Imám and means 'good' while Ḥusayn, the name of the third Imám, is a diminutive form of Ḥasan.

303. David Starr Jordan, the president of Leland Stanford Junior University.

304. A different talk is recorded as taking place at the home of Mrs Helen S. Goodall on October 3, 1912 in *Star of the West*. See vol. 4, no. 11, pp. 190–4.

305. For a transcript of one of the interviews see *Star of the West*, vol. 4, no. 12, pp. 206–7.

306. 'Abdu'l-Bahá spoke to the Japanese Young Men's Christian Association at the Japanese Independent Church, Oakland on October 7, 1912. For a transcript of His talk see *Promulgation*, pp. 343–8. The talk was translated first into English and then into Japanese. See Ward, *239 Days*, p. 166.

307. Those portions of Dr David Starr Jordan's introductory and closing remarks included by Maḥmúd have been taken directly from *The Palo Altan*. The newspaper devoted its entire edition of November 1, 1912, to the visit of 'Abdu'l-Bahá to Stanford University and printed, in their entirety, 'Abdu'l-Bahá's talks at the university, the Emmanu-el Congregation and the Unitarian Church in Palo Alto.

308. For transcripts of 'Abdu'l-Bahá's talk at Leland Stanford Junior University see *Promulgation*, pp. 348–55 and *Star of the West*, vol. 3, no. 12, pp. 10–14.

309. This meeting was held on Monday, October 7, 1912. For a transcript of 'Abdu'l-Bahá's talk see *Promulgation*, pp. 343–8.

310. For a transcript of 'Abdu'l-Bahá's talk see *Promulgation*, pp. 355–61.

311. 'Abdu'l-Bahá's statement is recorded in *Promulgation* (p. 361) as:

> Strange indeed that after twenty years training in colleges and universities man should reach such a station wherein he will deny the existence of the ideal or that which is not perceptible to the senses. Have you ever stopped to think that the animal already has graduated from such a university? Have you ever realized that the cow is already a professor emeritus of that university? For the cow without hard labor and study is already a philosopher of the superlative degree in the school of nature. The cow denies everything that is not tangible, saying, 'I can see! I can eat! Therefore, I believe only in that which is tangible!' Then why should we go to colleges? Let us go to the cow.

312. For a transcript of 'Abdu'l-Bahá's interview on October 10, 1912, with Mr Tinsley, who was recovering from an accident, see *Star of the West*, vol. 4, no. 12, p. 205.

313. 'Abdu'l-Bahá spoke at Temple Emmanu-el, 450 Sutter Street, San Francisco.

314. For other transcripts of 'Abdu'l-Bahá's talk see *Promulgation*, pp. 361–70 and *Star of the West*, vol. 3, no. 13, pp. 3–11.

315. Mrs Hearst took the first group of Western pilgrims to visit 'Abdu'l-Bahá in 'Akká in 1898.

316. City and district of ancient Sumer in southern Babylonia.

317. Equivalent to about $10 in 1912 currency.

318. From the Sufi poet Rúmí.

319. Thornton Chase had died suddenly and unexpectedly on September 30, 1912.

320. Maḥmúd is probably referring to the San Francisco–Oakland Bay.

321. For a transcript of 'Abdu'l-Bahá's talk at the Nineteen Day Feat see *Star of the West*, vol. 4, no. 12, pp. 203–9.

322. For another account of the Nineteen Day Feast see Brown, *Memories of 'Abdu'l-Bahá*, pp. 54–7.

323. A town near Shíráz where many Bahá'ís were cruelly martyred by fanatic mobs and mullás during the ministry of 'Abdu'l-Bahá.

324. For another account of 'Abdu'l-Bahá's visit to Thornton Chase's grave see *Star of the West*, vol. 3, no. 13, pp. 14–15.

325. Shu'á'u'lláh was in Pasadena, California during 'Abdu'l-Bahá's travels in America.

326. And it was told him [by certain people] which said, Thy mother and thy brethren stand without, desiring to see thee. And he answered and said unto them, My mother and my brethren are these which hear the word of God, and do it. Luke 8:20–1.

327. Bahá'u'lláh, *Kitáb-i-Aqdas*, para. 53.

328. For a transcript of a talk 'Abdu'l-Bahá had with one of the friends on October 22, 1912, on the meaning of sacrifice see *Star of the West*, vol. 4, no. 12, p. 205.

329. For another account of the morning of October 23, 1912 see Brown, *Memories of 'Abdu'l-Bahá*, pp. 78–81.

330. This refers to Bahá'u'lláh's retirement to the mountains of Sulaymáníyyih between April 1854 and March 1856. See *God Passes By*, pp. 119–26.

331. Bahá'u'lláh's companion while in Sulaymáníyyih, who was 'set upon either by highwaymen or frontier patrols and was mortally wounded'. See Balyuzi, *King of Glory*, p. 116.

332. This paragraph was translated by Shoghi Effendi. See *God Passes By*, pp. 293–4.

333. For another account of the evening of October 24, 1912 see Brown, *Memories of 'Abdu'l-Bahá*, pp. 83–5.

334. This was Christine Fraser, who operated a 'Home of Truth' in Sacramento. The Homes of Truth were based on the teachings of New Thought developed by Emma Curtis Hopkins. Caton notes:

> 'Abdu'l-Bahá was met at the Central Pacific Arcade Station by Christine Fraser and Carrie Yoerk, a Sacramentan from a prominent family who was also associated with the Home of Truth. They took him, with his entourage, by car to the Home of Truth and invited him to remain for lunch and stay for the night. Goodall and Cooper, along with the other Americans, went directly from the train station to the Hotel Sacramento where they were to be staying and where 'Abdu'l-Bahá was to speak that night.
>
> . . . there were a number of New Thought people there, and they were very interested in the Bahá'í Faith. 'Abdu'l-Bahá retired to a private room to rest after lunch. At about 3:20 p.m., Cooper, Goodall, and others arrived from the Hotel Sacramento. It seems that his luncheon at the Home of Truth had come as a surprise to 'Abdu'l-Bahá, since Cooper later related that he called her into his room to scold her for arranging the meeting without consulting him, and so requiring that he separate himself from the other Bahá'ís and leave them waiting at the hotel. Caton, 'A History of the Sacramento Bahá'í Community, 1912–1987' in Hollinger, *Community Histories*, p. 245.

335. For a transcript of 'Abdu'l-Bahá's talk at the Hotel Sacramento see *Promulgation*, pp. 370–6.

336. For Lua Getsinger's notes of 'Abdu'l-Bahá's visit to Sacramento see Metelmann, *Lua Getsinger*, pp. 177–8.

337. For transcripts of 'Abdu'l-Bahá's talk in the Assembly Hall at the Hotel Sacramento at 9:30 a.m. see *Promulgation*, pp. 376–80 and *Star of the West*, vol. 5, no. 17, pp. 259–62.

338. 'And I say unto you, That many shall come from the east and west, and shall sit down with Abraham, and Isaac, and Jacob, in the kingdom of heaven. But the children of the kingdom shall be cast out into outer darkness; there shall be weeping and gnashing of teeth.' Matt. 8:11–12.

339. For a transcript of 'Abdu'l-Bahá's talk see *Promulgation*, pp. 381–3.

340. This incident took place on August 8, 1912, in Dublin, New Hampshire, between Mrs Agnes Parsons and her husband, Jeffrey. See Hollinger, *Agnes Parsons' Diary*, pp. 97–8.

341. For transcripts of 'Abdu'l-Bahá's talk see *Promulgation*, pp. 383–7 and *Star of the West*, vol. 5, no. 15, pp. 230–4.

342. There is nothing in the writings of Bahá'u'lláh which provides for musical instruments in Bahá'í Temples or rostrums for the delivery of addresses. Indeed, in the Kitáb-i-Aqdas Bahá'u'lláh states: 'Ye have been prohibited from making use of pulpits' (para. 154). In the Notes (note 168) to the Kitáb-i-Aqdas the Universal House of Justice has elucidated:

> These provisions have their antecedent in the Persian Bayán. The Báb forbade the use of pulpits for the delivery of sermons and the reading of the Text. He specified, instead, that to enable all to hear the Word of God clearly, a chair for the speaker should be placed upon a platform.
>
> In comments on this law, 'Abdu'l-Bahá and Shoghi Effendi have made it clear that in the Mashriqu'l-Adhkár (where sermons are prohibited and only the words of Holy Scripture may be read) the reader may stand or sit, and if necessary to be better heard, may use a low moveable platform, but that no pulpit is permitted.

343. The Tarbíyat Schools were highly acclaimed. The boys' school was established in 1898 and the girls' school was founded by Dr Susan Moody after her arrival in Ṭihrán in 1909. Both schools were owned and managed entirely by Bahá'ís, although children of all religions attended, particularly the children of government and civil officials. The schools closed in 1934.

344. This woman is not identified but may be Mrs Farmer.

345. For transcripts of 'Abdu'l-Bahá's talk given at the Grand Hotel in Cincinnati see *Promulgation*, pp. 388–9 and *Star of the West*, vol. 6, no. 11, pp. 81–2.

346. The 'Young Turk Revolution' of 1908 resulted in the reinstatement of the constitution, which the Sultan had suspended, and the release of all religious and political prisoners. See *God Passes By*, pp. 271–2.

347. Compare with *Selections from the Writings of 'Abdu'l-Bahá*, p. 270:

In the Orient scatter perfumes,
And shed splendors on the West.
Carry light unto the Bulgar,
And the Slav with life invest.

348. Maḥmúd is probably referring to the Súriy-i-Mulúk (Súrih of Kings) revealed by Bahá'u'lláh.

349. The Sultan of Turkey at the time of Bahá'u'lláh, one of the monarchs addressed by Bahá'u'lláh in His Súriy-i-Mulúk.

350. The revolution occurred in Ṭihrán in 1905, replacing the absolute monarchy of the Qájárs with a parliamentary monarchy. In 1921 the Qájár dynasty was overthrown by Reza Shah Pahlavi, who established the Pahlavi dynasty, which was in turn overthrown in 1979 by the Ayatollah Khomeini.

351. Mrs Parsons's account of the events of November 6, 1912 differ markedly from Maḥmúd's. See Hollinger, *Agnes Parsons' Diary*, pp. 127–8.

352. For Mrs Parsons's account of November 7, 1912 see Hollinger, *Agnes Parsons' Diary*, pp. 128–30. For transcripts of 'Abdu'l-Bahá's two talks given at the home of Mrs Parsons on November 7 see *Promulgation*, pp. 397–9, 400–2 and *Star of the West*, vol. 6, no. 3, pp. 19–21.

353. 'Abdu'l-Bahá spoke at the Church of Our Father (Universalist), Washington DC at 8:15 p.m. on November 6, 1912. For transcripts of His talk see *Promulgation*, pp. 390–7 and *Star of the West*, vol. 5, no. 13, pp. 195–9.

354. For Mrs Parsons's account of the events of November 8, 1912 see Hollinger, *Agnes Parsons' Diary*, pp. 130–2.

355. For transcripts of 'Abdu'l-Bahá's talk at the Eighth Street Temple (Jewish Synagogue) on November 8, 1912 see *Promulgation*, pp. 402–10 and *Star of the West*, vol. 6, no. 1, pp. 3–10.

356. For transcripts of 'Abdu'l-Bahá's talks given at the home of Mrs Parsons on November 9, 1912 see *Promulgation*, pp. 411–15, 415–18 and *Star of the West*, vol. 6, no. 2, pp. 11–16.

357. For transcripts of 'Abdu'l-Bahá's talk at the Bahá'í Banquet at Rauscher's Hall, Washington DC see *Promulgation*, pp. 418–21 and *Star of the West*, vol. 6, no. 13, pp. 97–9.
358. For Mrs Parsons's account of the events of November 9, 1912 see Hollinger, *Agnes Parsons' Diary*, pp. 132–5.
359. *The Brilliant Proof*, published in Chicago in 1912.
360. For transcripts of 'Abdu'l-Bahá's talk at the home of Mrs Parsons see *Promulgation*, pp. 421–5 and *Star of the West*, vol. 6, no. 3, pp. 21–4.
361. Joseph and Pauline Hannen lived at 1252 Eighth Street, NW, Washington DC. For transcripts of 'Abdu'l-Bahá talk see *Promulgation*, pp. 425–8 and *Star of the West*, vol. 6, no. 13, pp. 99–103.
362. For Mrs Parsons's account of the events of the day see Hollinger, *Agnes Parsons' Diary*, pp. 135–7. For transcripts of a talk given by 'Abdu'l-Bahá at 1901 Eighteenth Street, NW, Washington DC on November 10, 1912 see *Promulgation*, pp. 428–30 and *Star of the West*, vol. 6, no. 13, pp. 103–4.
363. For Mrs Parsons's account of the events of November 11, 1912 see Hollinger, *Agnes Parsons' Diary*, pp. 138–41.
364. Howard and Hebe Struven lived at 1800 Bentaloo Street, West Baltimore.
365. For an another account of 'Abdu'l-Bahá's visit to Baltimore see Clark, 'The Bahá'ís of Baltimore, 1898–1990' in Hollinger, *Community Histories*, pp. 125–9.
366. For another account of 'Abdu'l-Bahá's arrival in New York see *Diary of Juliet Thompson*, pp. 362–4.
367. For a transcript of 'Abdu'l-Bahá's Tablet to Andrew Carnegie see *Star of the West*, vol. 6, no. 11, pp. 82–3.
368. For another account of the events of November 12 see *Diary of Juliet Thompson*, pp. 364–7.
369. For transcripts of 'Abdu'l-Bahá's talks at 48 West Tenth Street see *Promulgation*, pp. 431–7 and *Star of the West*, vol. 8, no. 3, pp. 29–40. For Juliet Thompson's description of the events see *Diary of Juliet Thompson*, pp. 368–9.

370. Ḥaḍrát means 'his excellency' or 'his honor'. 'Abdu'l-Bahá may be referring to Ṭarázu'lláh Samandarí, appointed a Hand of the Cause of God by Shoghi Effendi on December 24, 1951.

371. For a another transcript of 'Abdu'l-Bahá's talk given at 309 West Seventy-eighth Street see *Promulgation*, p. 437.

372. See 'Abdu'l-Bahá, *Memorials of the Faithful*, pp. 39–41.

373. 'Abdu'l-Bahá spoke on November 17, 1912 at the Genealogical Hall, 252 West Fifty-eighth Street. For a transcript of His talk see *Promulgation*, pp. 437–42.

374. For other transcripts of 'Abdu'l-Bahá's talk at the home of Mr and Mrs Frank K. Moxey, 575 Riverside Drive, New York, see *Promulgation*, pp. 442–7 and *Star of the West*, vol. 6, no. 8, pp. 59–64.

375. For an account of the beginning of the Howard MacNutt affair, see Stockman, *The Bahá'í Faith in America*, vol. 1, pp. 168–78. For another account of the discussion between 'Abdu'l-Bahá and Howard MacNutt see *Diary of Juliet Thompson*, pp. 369–72.

376. See Matt. 5:17: 'Think not that I am come to destroy the law, or the prophets; I am not come to destroy, but to fulfil.'

377. For a transcript of 'Abdu'l-Bahá's talk see *Promulgation*, pp. 447–8.

378. For Juliet Thompson's account of the banquet see *Diary of Juliet Thompson*, pp. 375–6. For Howard Colby Ives's account see *Portals to Freedom*, pp. 149–50, 158.

379. Luke 18:16–17: 'But Jesus called them [unto him], and said, Suffer little children to come unto me, and forbid them not: for of such is the kingdom of God. Verily I say unto you, Whosoever shall not receive the kingdom of God as a little child shall in no wise enter therein.'

380. For another account of the events of November 25, 1912, see *Diary of Juliet Thompson*, pp. 376–80.

381. For a transcript of 'Abdu'l-Bahá's talk at the home of Mr and Mrs Kinney see *Promulgation*, pp. 449–52.

382. For transcripts of other talks of 'Abdu'l-Bahá delivered on Monday, December 2, 1912, at the home of Mr and Mrs Kinney see *Promulgation*, pp. 452–3, 453–7 and *Star of the West*, vol. 4, no. 15, pp. 253–8 and vol. 5, no. 1, pp. 7–10.

383. For other transcripts of 'Abdu'l-Bahá's talk see *Promulgation*, pp. 357–8 and *Star of the West*, vol. 7, no. 12, pp. 114–15.

384. 'Abdu'l-Bahá's talk this evening was given to Mrs Kinney's Bible class. For a transcript of His talk see *Promulgation*, pp. 458–60.

385. For the transcript of another of 'Abdu'l-Bahá's talks given on Tuesday, December 3, 1912 at the home of Mr and Mrs Kinney see *Promulgation*, pp. 460–1.

386. Qur'án, Súrih 48:23: 'Such is God's method carried into effect of old; no change canst thou find in God's mode of dealing.' Rodwell, *The Koran*, p. 462.

387. For other transcripts of 'Abdu'l-Bahá's talk at the Theosophical Society, 2228 Broadway, New York see *Promulgation*, pp. 462–8 and *Star of the West*, vol. 7, no. 8, pp. 69–76.

388. For other transcripts of 'Abdu'l-Bahá's farewell address see *Promulgation*, pp. 468–70 and *Star of the West*, vol. 3, no. 18, pp. 3–4.

389. Bahá'u'lláh, *Kitáb-i-Aqdas*, para. 53.

390. Early Zoroastrian Bahá'ís of India. Mr Bahrám had previously been a Zoroastrian priest.

INDEX

This index is alphabetized letter by letter, hence *churches* preceded *Church of the Ascension.*

'Abdu'l-Bahá, vii, 3-8, 159, 172-3, 229, 248, 348, 377-8, 401-2, 429, 457
   accommodation of, 37, 232, 261, 275, 292-3
   account of visit with, 173
   attitudes towards, 111
   baptism, 111, 352
   birthday of, 108
   Center of the Covenant, 125, 129, 156-7, 308
   departs from Alexandria, vii, 13
   departure of, from America, 413, 423-6
   desires martyrdom, 134-5
   desires to meet friends, 200
   does not accept funds for journey, 7, 62, 109, 159, 176, 260, 407-9
   drives of, 85, 137, 178, 188, 217, 223, 235, 237, 293, 321, 367
   economies made by, 234, 253, 350
   encourages Bahá'ís to teach, 131, 176, 207, 219, 283, 284, 292, 331, 337, 340, 372, 383, 395-6, 397, 414-5, 415
   enthusiasm of, 231
   exhaustion of, 7, 9, 15, 28, 39, 98, 100, 101, 111, 122, 127, 134, 146, 153, 165, 169, 214, 215, 221, 235, 245, 252, 275-6, 285, 286, 332, 336, 350, 377, 392, 396, 402, 406
   explanations of, 185-6, 416
   farewell address of, 423-6
   food of, 14, 17, 23, 23, 26, 28, 32, 33-4, 45, 57, 63, 106, 108, 109, 120, 139, 147, 150, 152, 161, 176, 199, 207, 207, 232, 247, 273, 325, 332, 411
   forbearance of, 122
   generosity of, 35, 46, 63, 103, 119, 210, 234, 247, 249, 251, 253, 260, 269, 286, 324, 325, 348, 407
   gifts offered to, 407-9
   happiness of, 291, 348, 402
   healing abilities of, 156, 207, 401
   health of, vii, viii, 7, 9, 10, 15, 24, 28, 34, 65, 97, 101, 114, 140-1, 146, 153, 154, 181, 207, 236, 241, 276, 279, 280, 290, 350, 352, 356
   imprisonment of, 9, 104, 144, 164, 244, 265, 361, 368, 410, 429
   influence of, 173
   instruments of destruction, 26
   interpreter of Word of God, 304
   jests of, 188, 196, 207, 306
   justice of, 251
   kindness of, 114
   knowledge of, 198
   love of children, 32, 40, 55
   luggage of, 34, 214, 222, 244, 250-1
   motion pictures of, 213

painting of, 135
photographs taken of, 35, 41, 74,
    80, 101, 120, 135, 147, 149, 170,
    183, 204, 276, 277, 399
poetry in praise of, 156, 158, 305,
    392
prayers of, 52, 89, 154, 214, 230,
    321, 322-3, 330, 366, 375, 381,
    401, 405, 409, 413, 414-5
'Prophet of the East', 38, 97, 98,
    112, 239, 246, 267, 277, 294,
    361, 401
respect shown to, 4, 5, 14, 8,29 33,
    42, 44, 47, 48, 53, 54, 56, 60,
    61, 61, 64, 81, 83, 87, 88, 97,
    99, 105, 106, 132, 161, 170, 172,
    219, 239, 257, 274, 281, 284,
    294, 299, 303, 305, 314, 340,
    344, 378, 387, 401-2
sadness of, 22, 125, 261, 264, 339
seal of, 327
selflessness of, 7, 62, 83, 103, 176,
    245, 275
significance of journey of, 44, 186,
    237, 238, 250, 253-4, 256, 276
simplicity of lifestyle of, viii, 14, 15,
    139, 141, 149, 152, 165, 207,
    217, 245, 247, 275, 332, 350
speaks in English, 86, 307
state of reverie, 264
station of, 38, 98, 111-2, 115, 176,
    206, 239, 305, 395, 401
stories of, 28, 100, 128, 136, 141-2,
    197, 200, 232-3, 259, 271, 282-3,
    289, 291, 293, 344-5, 349, 358,
    388
Tablets of, 28, 115, 135, 154, 179,
    186, 215, 218, 242, 392, 396,
    402
    'Abdu'l-Bahá will travel to California, 242
    America's response to the Faith, 272
    economics, 201-3
    in honor of Áqá Riḍáy-i-Shírází, Qannád, 135
    to Hippolyte Dreyfus, 124
talks and words of, regarding
    20th century, 85, 110, 128, 276,
        309, 317

'Abdu'l-Latíf, Mullá, 169
'Abdu'l-Vahháb-i-Shírází, 138
age of enlightenment, 362-3
'Akká, 222
Alexander the Great, 323
America, 40, 80, 96, 118, 119,
    144, 154, 230, 272, 290, 320,
    338, 371, 387, 392, 411
Americans, 86, 96, 119, 230, 299,
    371, 406, 409, 422
animals, 82, 92-3, 254, 284,
    294-5, 298, 419
Assemblies, 360-1
    the assistance of Bahá'u'lláh, 41,
    53, 54, 56, 124, 176, 182,
    186, 219, 235, 236, 238, 249,
    251, 253, 260, 262, 280, 288,
    353-4, 356, 390, 414, 426
astrology, 153
Azalis, 134, 336
backbiting, 424
Bahá'í Cause, 76, 132-4, 188,
    211, 217, 231, 260, 279, 290,
    299, 324, 353, 370, 426
Bahá'u'lláh, 20, 52, 66-8, 77,
    106-7, 121, 122, 124, 130,
    132-4, 150, 189, 206, 226-8,
    235, 262, 288, 296, 297, 300,
    319, 321, 326, 331, 336, 338,
    339, 341, 346, 353-4, 367-8,
    368, 370, 376, 377, 381, 388
Balkans, 367, 369, 424
Baltimore, 377-9
believers, 403, 411-12, 423-6
Browne, Edward G., 24, 271
Bryan, William Jennings, 273
calamities, 166
California, 326-7, 360
Cardinal in California, 349
Chase, Thornton, 335
Chicago, 65, 354, 356
children, 77-8, 92, 241, 296, 307,
    322, 324, 401-2
Christ, 266, 271, 291, 304, 308,
    314-16, 323, 331, 340, 349,
    351, 355, 367, 373, 389-90,
    397, 401, 410
Christ, disciples of, 139, 223,
    340, 389-90
Christians, 267

INDEX

cities, 40, 118, 216, 222, 276, 282, 372
City of God, 282
clergy, 24, 25, 39, 84, 86, 233, 249, 298, 301, 349, 370, 371, 372, 374, 410, 416
Constantine, 367
Covenant, 256, 287, 384, 403
Covenant-breakers, 333-4
creation, 24, 76, 105, 120, 152, 162, 248, 362, 400, 416-22
charity, 183
civilization, divine, 3, 38, 42, 44, 57, 63, 70, 74, 98, 119, 233, 254, 285, 299, 302, 302, 331, 351, 405
civilization, 178-9, 233, 285, 331, 405
commission of investigation, 328
congresses, divine, 288
consultation, board of (Assemblies), 360-1
detachment, 106, 283, 331, 384
dispensation of Bahá'u'lláh, 127-8, 161
disease, 81-2
distinction, 129
Divine Reality, 417
Dodge, Arthur Pillsbury, 381-2
dogma, 120, 232, 306, 310-12, 352, 359, 411, 416
dreams, 125, 419
economics, 80, 84, 301, 346, 376, 405
education, 71-2, 75, 120-1, 194, 222, 233, 291, 386, 401-2
equality of women and men, 61, 68, 71, 80, 104, 110, 184, 218, 228-9, 393, 402, 405
Esperanto, 175
eternal life, 171
Europe, 118, 139, 272
evil, 72, 76, 167, 195, 385-6
faith, 321
faithfulness, 218, 248
flowers, 26, 63, 190, 214, 295, 322
food, 30, 82, 93, 207, 207, 232, 306
furnishing one's home, 206

Ghafghazí, Mashhadí Amír, 184
gifts from believers, 407-8
God, 30, 71, 113, 152, 194, 213, 225-30, 265, 266, 320, 331, 346, 355, 390, 415, 417, 418, 419, 422, 423-5
Goodall, Helen, 326-7, 343
gratitude, 232
Greatest Holy Leaf, 402
habits, 162
Hands of the Cause, 25
happiness, 136, 140, 241, 253, 281, 284, 365, 384
healing, 207, 306
health, 10, 40, 82, 141-2, 247, 276, 279, 356, 396
heat and motion, 329
history of the Bahá'í Cause, 80, 346
Holy Spirit, 340
Honolulu, 302
hotels, 232, 262, 343
House of Justice, 261, 364, 366, 376, 385
how to live one's life, 211
humanity, 20, 31, 49-51, 66, 129
humility, 278, 320
idols, 20
ignorance of Baghdádís, 347
imitations, blind, 32, 37, 39, 43, 49, 51, 59, 63, 67, 71, 80, 91, 94, 120, 126, 131, 141, 195, 198, 225, 232, 306, 310-12, 359, 363, 364, 368, 411, 416
imprisonment, His, 244, 265, 410, 458
intelligence, 403
interpretation of Christ's words, 7, 48, 51, 123, 138, 142-3, 245, 354, 397
inventions, 57
Isfandíyár, 360, 377
Islam, 277, 301, 305, 308, 315, 318, 373
Japan, 252, 297
Japanese, 297, 319
Jerusalem, 265
journey, His, 27, 34, 37, 44, 71, 85, 173, 210, 237, 238, 253-4, 256, 258, 264, 268, 275, 325,

335, 338, 338, 347, 350,
350-1, 352, 356, 365, 367-8,
411, 413, 422
Kheiralla, 256
Krug, Grace, 177, 381, 413
laws of God, 266, 290, 312-14,
316
longevity, 172
Los Angeles, 336
love, 226-9, 247, 269-70, 300, 397
love for the believers, 64, 270,
342, 402, 408, 411-12, 423
MacNutt, Howard, 393-4
man, nature of, 158
man, reality of, 417-19
man created in the image of God,
61, 69, 257, 298, 415, 418,
419-20, 419-20
Manifestations, 19, 20, 30, 39,
49-52, 75-7, 83, 89-91, 96-7,
162, 168, 179, 197, 210, 217,
227, 243, 260, 280, 296, 300,
305, 309-18, 344, 345, 351,
359, 362, 369, 387, 389, 390,
403, 416-22
martyrs, 87, 139, 170, 178, 263,
328, 357, 367-8, 410
Mashriqu'l-Adhkár, 363-4, 385,
390, 392, 408
materialism, 268, 299
meat, 284
medicine, 82
Minneapolis, 265-70
Moody, Dr Susan, 360
morals, 80, 119, 183, 210, 243,
401
Muhájir, Áqá Riḍá Ghánad, 391
Muḥammad, 144, 238
museums, 267, 355
music, 200, 207, 210, 385
Muslims, 267, 316
nations, 76, 118, 168
nature, 15, 41, 50, 75, 82, 194,
234, 282, 304
newspapers, 263, 339
New York, 151, 384, 392, 411,
458
obedience, 156
opposition, 256
Palestine, 303

Parliament, international, 366-7
peace, universal, 35, 86, 90-7, 98,
168, 230, 272, 282, 304, 306,
308, 317-18, 330, 335, 336,
345, 346, 347, 351, 352, 356,
362, 409
peace congresses, 100, 238, 290
peace of mind, 407
Persians, 215, 281
philosophers, 188, 194, 331
philosophy, 328
physician, divine, 306
poor, the, 21, 80, 93, 106, 126,
197, 202-3, 241, 262, 270,
321, 380, 407
Portland, 325
poverty, 45, 106, 126
power of the Cause, 241
prediction of war, 233, 356
prejudice, 25, 48, 69, 80, 227,
304, 357, 368, 380, 398, 399-
400, 402, 423
president of the United States,
320
progress, 211-12, 299
property, 116, 263
prophecies, 83, 189, 317-18, 369,
415
purity, 335
Qur'án, 142
rabbis, 388
race unity, 55, 65, 69, 91-2, 254,
377, 399-400
rank, 203, 301, 357
reality, explanations of, 388
reincarnation, 19
religion, 24, 37, 39, 51-2, 67-9,
76, 80, 81, 90-7, 102, 138,
197, 225-30, 243, 265, 298,
301, 307, 309-18, 346, 349,
353, 359, 363, 382, 390, 397
Russia, 355
Sacramento, 344
sacrifice, 257, 410
San Francisco Bahá'ís, 341-2
scenery of America, 64, 65, 99,
106, 108, 134, 152, 187, 208,
286, 344-5, 348
science, 39, 56, 67, 107, 138,
227, 307

scripture, 415
Seattle, 329, 337
service to the Cause, 78-9, 140,
    176, 178, 181, 214, 268, 278,
    280, 284, 395, 408
Shu'á'u'lláh, 332-3
sins, 31
skyscrapers, 162, 396, 458
socialism, 116, 238, 263, 357
the soul, 26-7, 71-2, 110, 124,
    190-1, 193, 308, 376, 418
spirit, 328
spirituality, 64, 119, 136, 237,
    257, 262, 282
spiritual life, 294-5
spiritual world, 294-5
subways, 155
superstitions, 180-1, 208, 212,
    227, 411, 416
talks, His, 382
teaching, 340, 354, 372, 413-15
teachings of Bahá'u'lláh, 66-8,
    236, 279, 323, 335, 336, 362,
    371, 376, 388, 397
telepathy, 279
the Temple, 69
tests and trials, 66, 136, 208
Theosophists, 179, 237
Torah, 415
translations of Tablets, 383
transportation, forms of, 26, 32,
    65, 276
travelers, 231
truth, 206, 225-7, 309-10, 312,
    315, 316, 346, 398
Unitarians, 237
unity and oneness of humanity,
    76, 80, 94-6, 98, 168, 206,
    225-7, 230, 281, 300, 308,
    314, 316, 317-8, 323, 326,
    336, 347, 351, 353, 362, 371,
    378, 399, 401, 423-4
Unity Feast, 146
unity of believers, 78-9, 393, 395,
    397, 408, 409
universality, 171
universal language, 229
vegetable kingdom, 299
volcanoes, 20
war, 35, 89-96, 118, 227, 233,
    233, 272-3, 331, 337, 345,
    356, 367-8, 399
Washington dc, 372, 396
waterfalls, 246
work, 126
women, 162, 218, 358, 393, 402,
    405
workers' rights, 21
world, contingent, 285, 294-5
writing, His, 132
Yaḥyá, Mírzá, 223, 256, 261,
    336, 391
trains, 350
transformation of hearts effected by,
    6, 16, 61, 211, 212
transportation used by, *see* forms of
    transportation and individual
    names, e.g. trains
translations of talks, 60
tributes to, 40, 43, 48, 56, 75, 87-8,
    103, 105, 111, 112, 218-9, 224-5,
    235, 250, 257, 300, 301, 303,
    308, 309, 344, 361, 362
visits of, to
    Baltimore, 377-8
    Boston, 104-11, 174-6, 222
    Buffalo, 244-51
    Chicago, 64-79, 252-62, 260-2
    Cincinnati, 364-6
    Cleveland, 79-81
    Denver, 275-84, 349-50
    Dublin, New Hampshire,
        177-204
    Glenwood Springs, 285-7
    Green Acre, 141, 176, 204-15
    Kenosha, 258-260
    Lincoln, 271-5
    Los Angeles, 329-336
    Malden, 215-220
    Minneapolis, 262-9
    Montclair, New Jersey, 87, 135,
        137-46
    Montreal, 220-244
    museums, 155-9, 267, 355
    New Jersey, 87-9, 103, 115, 116,
        164, 170
    New York, 33-40, 85-101, 111-
        22, 123-36, 150-74, 380-426
    Niagara Falls, 251
    Oakland, 295, 326, 337-8

parks, 110, 122, 143, 144, 155, 158, 296, 299
Philadelphia, 122-3
Pittsburgh, 81-3
Pleasanton, 319-24
Sacramento, 341-7
St Paul, 267-8
Salt Lake City, 287-90
San Francisco, 292-320, 324, 327, 329, 336-8
site of Mashriqu'l-Adhkár, 70, 392
summer schools, 182-3, 209-10
technical school, 340
Washington dc, 47-64, 82-6, 368-78
walks of, 61, 150, 151, 158, 166, 180, 199, 206, 210, 235, 246, 247, 254, 256, 269, 277, 281, 285, 292, 293, 307, 322, 326, 329, 337, 339, 372, 380, 383, 392, 396
writes account of His visit, 351
'Abdu'l-Azíz, Sultán, 369
'Abdu'l-Ḥamíd, Sultán, 128, 328, 429
'Abdu'l-Ḥusayn, Shaykh, 176
'Abdu'lláh, Siyyid, 158-9, 475
'Abdu'l-Latíf, 169
'Abdu'l-Vahháb-i-Shírází, 138
Abraham, 67, 189, 227, 310
Abú Bakr, 238
Abu'l-Faḍl, Mírzá, 134, 158, 160, 179, 328, 376, 429, 447, 475
Abu'l-Qásim, Ḥájí, 14, 176
Abu'l-Qásim-i-Hamadání, Áqá, 145, 338, 430
Adrianople, 369
Advanced Thought Center, 42
Afnán-i-Yazdí, 28, 430
agriculture, 288-9
airplanes, 26
'Akká, 9, 67, 75, 145, 186, 222, 244, 286, 323
alchemy, 57
alcohol, 116, 141-2, 170
Alexander the Great, 323
Alexandria, vii, 9, 13, 15, 23, 66, 258
Algiers, 27
'all right', 86
All Saints Unitarian Church (Washington DC), 60
All-Souls Church (Chicago), 77
America, vii, 4-6, 8, 9-10, 36, 40, 57, 63, 80, 96, 108, 118, 119, 144, 155, 182, 371, 387, 401, 411
agriculture in, 288-9
government of, 118, 119, 230, 233, 320, 378, 392, 409
republics of, 272
teaching the Cause in, 270
Americans, viii, ix, 86, 96, 119, 173, 169, 188, 230, 278, 293, 299, 371, 406, 409, 428-9
American Unitarian Association Conference, 105, 109
animals, 82, 92-3, 235, 254, 284, 294-5, 298, 419
Ansonia, Hotel, 36, 37, 47, 103
Anushírván, 272
Arabia, 90, 98, 315
Arabic, 175, 323
armaments, 26, 35, 40, 87, 96, 233, 272
Armenians, 170
Asadu'lláh-i-Qumí, Siyyid, 13, 16, 22, 70, 220, 430, 460
asceticism, 208
Ashraf, Ghodsieh (Qudsíyyih) Khánum, 70, 203, 430
Ashton, Mr and Mrs, 275
Asia, 73, 76, 94-5, 98
Assemblies, Bahá'í, 156, 360-1
Astor, Hotel, 97, 467
astrologers, 387
astrology, 153
attar of rose, 147, 341, 359, 375, 399, 400
Austin, Mr and Mrs, 21, 22, 25
automobiles, 76, 104, 109, 110, 149, 153, 175, 183, 204, 209, 212, 217, 217, 237, 252, 258, 262, 268, 269, 274, 280, 293, 295, 296, 319, 321, 343, 362, 378, 396
Azalis, 24, 134, 138, 177, 336
Azíz'u'lláh Khán, Mírzá, 115

Báb, the, 67, 96, 130, 138, 177, 272, 291, 457
Declaration of, 107
Shrine of, 23, 322
backbiting, 424

INDEX 501

Badrí Páshá, 260
Bagdadi, Muhammad Mustafa, 83
Bagdadi, Dr Zia, 69, 70, 83, 430, 440, 462, 468
Baghdád, 23, 124, 137, 140, 145, 181, 183, 185, 223, 271, 273, 347, 473
Bahá'í Cause, 6-7, 73, 76, 77, 87
  history of, 80, 344
  spread of, 370
  teachings of, 4, 20,29 33, 57, 84, 112, 148, 162, 168, 197, 198, 217, 236, 240, 279, 323, 362, 371, 388, 397
Bahá'í House (Green Acre), 208, 210
Bahá'ís, 3-4, 115, 262, 270, 305, 374-5, 403
  duties of, 425
  people becoming, 106, 267, 346
  persecution of Persian, 389
  qualities of, 324, 326, 338, 411
  sorrow of, at 'Abdu'l-Bahá's departure, 413, 423, 426
  station of, 385
  steadfastness of, 258, 334, 337, 340
  unity among, 79, 129, 135, 147, 165, 170, 170, 334, 356, 361, 383, 395, 408, 409
Bahá'í Temple Unity, 69
Bahá'u'lláh, 3, 20, 66-8, 87, 89, 94-7, 99, 163, 266, 286, 300, 316, 321, 336, 346, 381, 429
  'Abdu'l-Bahá's article on, 343
  declaration of, 137
  persecution of, 33, 152, 169, 181, 259, 341
  power of, 128, 132-4, 151, 216, 353-4
  Shrine of, 144, 322, 342, 348, 352
  suffering of, 118, 122, 160, 189, 274, 326, 334, 339, 412
  teachings of, *see* Bahá'í Cause, teachings of
  withdrawal of, from Baghdád, 145, 338, 473
Bahrám, Mehtar Isfandíyár, 427
Balkans war, 271, 356, 367, 369, 380, 424
Baltimore, 377-8
baptism, 111, 352
Baptist Temple (Philadelphia), 123, 166

Barakatu'lláh, Mr, 158
baths, 15, 29, 145, 162, 247, 296
battleships, 233
Bell, Alexander Graham, 56-7, 430, 461
Berkeley, 305
  mayor of, 301
Berlin, 118
Bible, the, 18
blacks, 54-5, 153, 184-5, 235, 254, 360, 381, 339-40, 462
  animosity of whites towards, 44-45, 69, 399-400
  attend meetings with whites, 44, 68, 153, 377
  see also race unity
Blacks, Professor, 106
body, physical, 190-3, 282, 350, 376, 418-9
  care of, 142
  see also health
boats, 246, 295
Bosch, John, 47, 431
Boston, 104, 111, 174-6
  visit of 'Abdu'l-Bahá to, 104-11, 174-6, 222
Boston Hotel, 109
Boston Theosophical Society, 175
Bourgeois, Louis, 165, 431
Bowery Mission Hall, 45
Brahma, 24
Breed, Alice, 107, 174, 217, 431, 460, 482
Brilliant Proof, The (Mírzá Abu'l-Faḍl), 134, 376, 475
Brookline, 109
Brooklyn, 120, 121-2, 130-1, 132, 163, 166, 208
Brooklyn Eagle, 131
Brotherhood Church (New Jersey), 103, 161, 468
Browne, Edward G., 24, 271, 431
Bryan, William Jennings, 273, 274, 431
Bryan, Mrs William, 274
Buddha, 20, 24, 73, 307
Buddhism, 180
Buddhists, 159
Buffalo, visit of 'Abdu'l-Bahá to, 244-51
buildings, 34, 162, 282, 285, 295
  see also skyscrapers
Bulletin (San Francisco), 298

calamities, 166
California, 32, 154, 156, 166, 220, 242, 245, 268, 276, 368, 382
  Baháʼís of, 338, 356
cameras, 41, 183, 277
Carnegie, Andrew, 380, 432
carpet, Persian, 101, 157, 468
carriages, 26, 38, 40, 41, 55, 60, 69, 99, 102, 130, 163, 164, 178, 215, 221, 223, 224, 234, 396
Catholics, 25, 236, 410
cause and effect, 191-2
Cedric, S.S., 13, 457
Celtic, S.S., 423
Central Park (New York), 385, 396
Central Organization for a Durable Peace, 272
century, 20th, 85, 110, 276, 309, 317
Century Club (San Francisco), 325
Champney, Mrs, 380
charity, 183
Charles, Hotel (Boston), 104
Chase, Thornton, 287, 325, 330, 330, 335, 365-6, 432
Chicago, vii, 32, 44, 64, 64, 65, 73, 86, 249, 356, 379
  visits of ʻAbduʼl-Bahá to, 67-81, 252-62, 261-3, 353-64
children, 40, 92, 120, 131, 133, 162, 183, 241, 263, 269, 322, 324, 348, 395, 400-2, 461
  brought to see ʻAbduʼl-Bahá, 32, 77, 104, 146, 259, 293, 295, 335, 339, 359, 376, 383, 466
  conferences of, 55, 121, 307
Chinese, 107
Christ, 7, 19, 31, 48, 52, 63, 67, 73, 86, 90, 111, 111, 123, 138, 142, 192, 197, 227, 239, 245, 251, 253, 266, 271, 291, 304, 308, 323, 355, 380, 389-90, 404, 408, 417
  disciples of, 139, 182, 193, 223, 389
Christianity, 160, 367
  proofs of veracity of, 6, 304
Christians, 229, 243, 251, 315, 318, 373
Christian Scientists, 385, 387
chrysolite, Tablets of, 160
churches, 6, 9, 23, 42, 43, 55, 60, 75, 77, 89-91, 102, 103, 105, 111, 122-3, 131, 164, 222, 224, 237, 239, 249, 259-60, 276, 277, 280, 281, 294, 300, 301, 304, 349-50, 353, 361-2, 378
  ʻAbduʼl-Bahá contributes to, 55, 103, 210
  a symbol of the Covenant, 117
Church of Our Father (Universalist), 370, 491
Church of the Ascension (New York), 42, 43, 117-8, 161
Church of the Divine Paternity (New York), 102
Church of Divine Science (Denver), 276, 279-80
Church of the Messiah, 248-50, 350
Cincinnati, visit of ʻAbduʼl-Bahá to, 364-7
cities, 118, 217, 222, 276, 282, 372, 401
  effects of, 40
civilization, 178-9, 233, 285, 331, 405
  divine, 3, 38, 42, 44, 57, 63, 70, 74, 80, 98, 119, 183, 231, 233, 254, 265, 285, 302, 304 331, 351, 405
Clark, Mr and Mrs, 161
Clark, Mrs (Denver), 277-8
clergy, 4, 6, 25, 25, 39, 40, 44, 63, 74, 75, 86, 103-4, 103, 110, 111, 128, 142-3, 161, 184, 198, 211, 216, 221, 233, 235, 239, 240, 248-9, 259, 264, 265, 268, 277, 277, 280, 281, 294, 298, 300, 301, 307, 352, 353, 355-6, 361-2, 370, 371, 373, 397-8, 401, 410, 415
Cardinal, 290, 349
opposition of, to ʻAbduʼl-Bahá, 62, 84, 109, 157, 371, 372
climate, 15, 181
Cleveland, 82
  visit of ʻAbduʼl-Bahá to, 82-3
clothing, Persian, vii, 21, 27, 97, 143, 152, 173, 233, 248, 273, 277, 280, 384-5, 380
Cochran, Mrs, 402
Collins, Mr, 248
Colombo, Professor, 416
Colorado, Hotel (Glenwood Springs), 285
colours, 160
Columbia University, 46
Columbus, Christopher, 28, 182, 210

INDEX 503

Commercial Club (Minneapolis), 266
Commission of Inquiry, 128, 244, 328, 429
Committee of Union and Progress, 144
congresses,
  agricultural, 289
  divine, 288
  peace, 3, 9,29 37, 80, 83, 99-101, 174, 237, 290
constancy, 211
Constantine, 367
Constantinople, 163
consultation, board of, 360
Confucius, 73
Congregational Church (Brooklyn), 131
Congregational Church (Kenosha), 259
conscience, freedom of, 131
Cooper, Ella, 161, 208, 292, 293, 295, 307, 318, 320, 337, 337-8, 342, 343, 409, 433, 460, 489
courage, 171
Covenant, 3, 125, 134, 162, 287, 332-4, 384
  Feast of the, 374-5
  firmness in, 384, 395, 399, 403
  power of the, 113, 182, 256, 344
Covenant-breakers, 3, 16, 24, 28, 274, 332-4, 386-7, 394, 429, 469
cow, the, 188, 306, 487
creation, 24, 77, 105, 120, 152, 153, 162, 179, 184, 220, 248, 362, 400, 416-22
cursing, prohibition of, 127, 148, 162, 168
customs house, 221, 244

dancing, 210
Daniel, 382
Davies, Mrs, 363
Day of the Covenant, 374-5, 398
Dayyán, Mírzá Asadu'lláh-i-Khuy, 138, 433, 472
death, 153-4, 190-3
Denison House (Boston), 106
Denver, 344
  visit of 'Abdu'l-Bahá to, 277-85, 349-50
detachment, 106, 120, 126, 155, 283, 331, 384
D'Evelyn, Dr Frederick, 292, 433

diet, 306
  see also food, healing and health
dirigibles, 26
disabled, the, 202
disease, 81
dispensation, of Bahá'u'lláh, greatness of, 127-8, 161, 178, 240
disunity, effects of, 189
Divine Knowledge Club, 387
Díyá Páshá, Yúsuf, 58, 433, 461, 464
Dodge, Arthur Pillsbury, 44, 381, 394, 433, 442
dogma, 119, 232, 307, 309-12, 352, 359, 411, 416
Donner party, 291
dreams, 125, 208, 376, 418-19
Dreyfus, Hippolyte, 124, 171, 433-4, 466
Dreyfus-Barney, Laura, 85, 434, 438, 466
Drill Hall (Chicago), 69
Dublin, New Hampshire, 168, 169, 172, 174, 176-209, 215
Dyer, Mr and Mrs Andrew J., 55

Earl Hall, Columbia University, 46
earthquake, 299
East, the, 171
Easterners
  attitude of Westerners towards, see Westerners
economics, 80, 84, 181, 199, 201-3, 236, 238, 301, 346, 376, 405
Edsall, Charles, 87, 88, 137, 139, 141, 143-4, 145
education, 38, 45, 55, 72, 75, 104, 113, 120, 146, 148, 162, 183, 198, 386, 401-2
  divine, 121, 194, 222, 233, 263, 291
  of girls, 109, 148
  of women, see women, education of
ego, 127, 157, 211-12
Egypt, 7, 9, 10, 98, 144, 176, 328
Egyptians, 14
Eirenion, the (Green Acre), 214
electricity, 247, 328
elements, 169, 190-1, 213
Emery, Mrs Marshall, 45, 406
enemies, 127, 148, 162
England, 405

Englehorn, Miss, 220
enlightenment, age of, 362-3
entertainments, 246, 247, 259
equality, 263
   of women and men, 61, 68, 109, 148, 162, 163, 184, 228-9, 358, 393, 402, 405
Esperanto, 175
Euclid Hotel (Cleveland), 79, 80
Europe, 9, 98, 118, 139, 252, 272, 426-7, 429
evil, 72, 76, 167, 195, 385-6

faithfulness, 218, 258
Fanwood, New Jersey, 115
Faraj, Áqá, 235
Faríd, Dr Amínu'lláh, 13, 22, 122, 234, 434, 460, 462, 464, 469
Farmer, Mrs (Cincinnati), 365
Farmer, Sarah, 205, 210, 215, 434, 438, 441, 480
farmers, 201-2, 203
Federation of Women's Clubs, 71
ferries, 87, 170, 342
fidelity, 135
Fikr (Thought), 216
First Congregational Church (Oakland), 298, 301
First Unitarian Church (San Francisco), 300
Fletcher, Rabbi, 110
flowers, 26, 63, 74, 78, 97, 104, 120, 146-7, 164, 190, 252, 259, 285, 290, 295, 322, 330, 359, 365, 374, 398, 400
food, 30, 82, 93, 106, 108, 195, 207, 232-3, 284, 289, 306
   see also, 'Abdu'l-Bahá, food of
Ford Hall (Boston), 108
Forde, Dr, 75
forgiveness, 51-2, 79, 127, 148, 163, 216
fortune tellers, 206, 208
Fourth of July celebration, 137, 152, 474
France, 96, 118, 252
Fraser, Christine, 343, 489
Free Religious Association, 108
friends, 196
Fujita, Saichiro, 252, 263, 434-5, 485
Futúḥát-i-Makkíyyih, 185

Georgi, Dr, 111
Germany, 118
Getsinger, Edward, 47, 220, 435, 435, 460, 460
Getsinger, Lua, 156, 156-7, 435, 435, 448, 467, 474
Ghafghazí, Mashhadí Amír, 184
Gibraltar, 27
gifts, offered to 'Abdu'l-Bahá, 407-8
Glenwood Springs, 285-7
God, 30, 91, 94-5, 113, 152, 167, 179, 194, 213, 219, 225-30, 355, 390, 423-6
   Kingdom of, 416-22
   love of, 205, 408
   nearness to, 219
   proofs of existence of, 6, 71, 305, 346
   unity of, 57, 88
   word of, 178, 278, 295
Golden Circle, 111, 175
Golden Gate Park, 296
Goodale, Mrs Henry, 259, 435
Goodall, Helen, 161, 208, 292, 293, 295, 296, 307, 318, 326-7, 336, 337, 342-3, 409, 433, 435, 446, 460
Goshtasp, Javan Mard, 427
governance, 118, 119, 230, 252, 320
Grace Methodist Church (New York), 89
Grand Central Station, 47
Grand Hotel (Cincinnati), 365, 366
Grand Northern Hotel (New York), 398
Grant, Dr Percy Stickney, 42, 43, 97, 117, 161, 436, 475
gratitude, 196, 232
Great Britain, 96
Greatest Holy Leaf, 24, 402, 407, 436
Greatest Name, symbol of, 374, 398
Greece, 98, 151, 222, 331
Greeks, 14, 151, 155, 311, 312, 314, 345
Greek-Syrian Relief Society, 106
Green Acre, 141, 201, 205, 206-11, 215, 434, 438, 480
   visits of 'Abdu'l-Bahá to, 176, 204-15, 481-2
Green Acre Fellowship and Society, 205, 207
Gregory, Louis, 69, 184, 436, 442, 445, 461

Hague, the, 272
Hall, Albert Heath, 264, 268, 436
Hall, Dr Frank Oliver, 102
Hall, Professor, 107
Handel Hall (Chicago), 69
Hands of the Cause, 29
Hannen, Pauline and Joseph, 377, 436-7, 440, 459, 460, 466
happiness, 136, 140, 241, 253, 281, 284, 365, 384
Harmon, W. W., 178, 179-81, 437
Harris, Mr, 143
Harris, Hooper, 382, 393, 394, 395, 437, 445
Harvey, Rev Leon A., 164
Ḥasan, Mullá, 169
Ḥaydar-'Alí, Ḥájí Mírzá, 238, 326, 327, 437-8
healing, 306
health, 15, 40, 82, 142, 156, 186, 195, 306, 396
  of 'Abdu'l-Bahá, *see* 'Abdu'l-Bahá, health of
Hearst, Phoebe, 24, 319-20, 322, 438, 442, 487
heat, 329
Hemmick, Alice Barney-, 85, 438, 467
Henderson, Mr, 182-3
Hidden Words, 160, 300
Hill, Dr, 112
Hindi, S͟hayk͟h, 169
Hindus, 24, 73, 208
Hoar, William H., 115, 157, 390, 394, 399, 438
Holmes, Miss, 70
Holy Land, 144, 309-11, 391
Holy Spirit, 157
  influence of, 111, 340
Honolulu, 302
Hoover, Mr, 61
House of Justice (Universal), viii, 115, 125, 129, 148, 163, 261, 263, 364, 366, 376, 385
Howard University (Washington DC), 54, 460
Hudson building (New York), 85, 467
Hudson River, 114, 119, 163, 380
Hull House (Chicago), 68, 464
humanity
  capacities of, 324
  oneness of, 29, 31, 80, 99, 113, 119, 135, 163, 168, 184, 225-7, 230-1, 268, 281, 300, 316, 314, 317, 317-8, 323, 326, 353, 369, 371, 378, 399, 401, 423-4
  prosperity of, 77, 135, 353
  reality of, 417-19
  superiority over nature, 41, 82, 158, 234, 304
  unity of, 35, 42, 43, 59, 63, 67, 69, 89, 95-6, 148, 193, 206, 351
human nature, 46, 158
human rights, 119
humility, 16, 320
humor, 306, 350
Huntington Chambers (Boston), 110
Ḥusayn K͟hán, Mírzá, 163, 438-9

imitations, blind, 3, 32, 37, 39, 43, 49, 52, 59, 63, 67, 71, 80, 91, 94, 119, 126, 131, 141, 195, 198, 225, 225-7, 232, 306, 309-11, 352, 359, 363, 364, 368, 411, 416
immortality, of the soul, *see* soul, immortality of
Independence Day, 137, 152, 474
India, vii, 73, 98, 427
Indians, 73-4, 98, 293, 300, 307
Innes, Edward Alfred Mitchell, 64, 464
intelligence, 403
International Peace (Frederick Lynch), 112
International Peace Society, 99
International (Supreme) Tribunal, 148, 229-30
inventions, 56-7
Isaac, 189, 310
Isaiah, 224, 317, 371
Isfandíyár, 360, 377, 439
'Is͟hqábád, 184
Is͟hráqát, Tablet of, 256
Ishraq doctrine, 18, 457
Islam, 27, 103, 132, 141-2, 156, 158, 185, 261, 271, 277, 301, 308, 315, 318
  proofs of veracity of, 6, 312, 308, 373
Israelites, history of, 309-14
Italian Consul, 33
Italians, 14, 23

Italy, 87
Ives, Dr Howard Colby, 103, 161, 167, 439, 468, 477
Ives, Kate, 212, 467

Jack, Dr, 110
Jackson, Mr, 254, 259
Jackson, Mrs, 109
Jackson, Professor William, 97
Jacob, 189, 310
Jahrum, martyrs of, 328
Jání, Ḥájí Mírzá, 24, 439
Japan, 252, 297, 302, 434
Japanese, 98, 107, 252, 256, 278, 293, 297, 319, 434
Japanese Club, 305
Jerusalem, 265
Jews, 81, 158, 211, 229, 243, 251, 303, 308-9, 318, 352, 346, 373, 374, 388
Jones, Mr, 383
Jones, Musette 'Rouhieh', 383
Jordan, David Starr, 303, 304, 486
Joseph, 189, 310
journalists, 6, 29 34, 37, 38, 66, 66, 79-80, 81, 106, 109, 149, 174, 222, 239, 246, 254, 260, 263, 266, 272, 274, 275, 283, 288, 294, 296, 331, 332, 344, 349, 353, 362, 378
Judaism, 308-16

Kaufman, Mr, 171
Kaufman, Mrs, 153
Kenosha, 259-60
Keynon Hotel (Salt Lake City), 290
Kerry, Mrs, 143
Khan, Ali Kuli, 54, 56, 431, 439, 441, 460, 463, 464, 466
Khedive of Egypt, 172
Kheiralla, Ibrahim George, 15-16, 256, 258, 333, 387, 394, 429, 435, 439-40, 484
Killius, Mr and Mrs Albert C., ix, 74, 440
King of Martyrs (Mírzá Muḥammad-Ḥasan), 263
Kings and rulers, 229, 337, 362
Kinney, Carrie, 103, 103, 114, 206, 208, 385, 393, 397, 400, 406, 409, 411, 415, 416, 440, 467
Kinney, Edward, 36, 36, 45, 103, 103, 111, 176, 381, 383, 393, 395, 397, 416, 440
Kitáb-i-Aqdas, 334
Knobloch, Fanny, 186, 204, 437, 440
Krishna, 20
Khusraw, 272
Khusraw, Áqá, 13-14, 22, 33
knowledge, 128, 228
Krug, Dr Florian, 141, 177, 441
Krug, Grace, 141, 165, 177, 208, 381, 385, 394, 497, 403, 413, 441

Lake Dublin, 178, 184, 199
Lake Michigan, 256
Lake Mohonk, Hotel, 99
Lake Mohonk, peace conference at, 99-102, 113, 468
landaus, 99
language, 305
  universal, 29 175, 229
Lankershim, Hotel (Los Angeles), 330
LaSalle Hotel (Chicago), 71
laws, 302, 378
  natural, 136
  obedience to, of one's country, 137
  of God, 266, 290, 312-4, 316
  of religion, 186, 207, 243
Lawḥ-i-Sulṭán, 177
Leland Stanford University (Palo Alto), 303
Leroy, Dr, 210
Liberty, Statue of, 34, 458
life, 190-3
  eternal, 210
  see also soul, immortality of
  longevity of, 172
  spiritual, 294-5
light, spiritual, 113
lights, electric and gas, 65, 163, 247, 300, 302, 372, 405
Lincoln, Nebraska, 273-5, 273-5
London, 9
Los Angeles, 287, 325, 336, 365
  visit of 'Abdu'l-Bahá to, 330-6
love, 32, 193, 225-9, 247, 261, 269-70, 300, 397
Luce, Robert, 105
Lunt, Alfred E., 205, 441
Lynch, Frederick, 112, 441

INDEX 507

MacNutt, Howard, 38, 131, 132, 166, 179, 386, 393-4, 440, 441
Magee, Esther Annie, 213
Máh-Kú, 291
Malden, Massachusetts, 215
   visit of 'Abdu'l-Bahá to, 215-20
Manifestations, 19, 20, 30, 39, 67, 76, 77, 89-91, 96, 109, 126, 129, 137, 168, 179, 185, 197, 207, 227, 243, 260, 300, 305, 305, 309-18, 344, 345, 351, 359, 362, 369, 387, 388, 390, 403, 404, 416-22
mankind, *see* humanity
marriage, 162, 167, 184
martyrs, 87, 139, 169-70, 178, 263, 328, 357, 367, 410
Mashriqu'l-Adhkár, 363-4, 385, 392, 408, 409, 416
   in Chicago, 69, 74, 252, 340, 431
   dedication of, 70, 430
   in 'Ishqábád, 70, 430
materialism, 19, 39, 41, 299
materialists, 6, 126, 165
Mathew, Louisa, 21, 22, 184, 436, 442
Maxim, Hudson, 40
Maxwell, Mary (Rúḥíyyih Khánum), 241, 443, 447, 483
Maxwell, May, 221, 231, 234, 238, 241, 442-3, 448, 467
Maxwell, Sutherland, 221, 222, 231, 238, 241, 443
Mázindarán, 246
McClung, Lee, 64, 463
McKinney, Edna, 207
meat, 284
medicine, 82, 238
Medina, 238
Merriman, Isabel, 304
Messina, 20-1, 25
Methodist Church (Montreal), 239
Metropolitan Temple (New York), 112
Mikado, 252
Milburn, Dr Joseph A., 75, 77, 86, 356, 362
Milburn, Mrs, 356
Milford, 118, 119
Military Park, Newark, 143
Mills, Mountfort, 40, 43, 104, 249, 443, 459
Minneapolis, 209, 273

   visit of 'Abdu'l-Bahá to, 264-70
Mississippi River, 269
Monsalvat, 212, 480, 482
Montclair, New Jersey, 135
   visits of 'Abdu'l-Bahá to, 87-9, 137-46
Montessori, Mrs, 25
Montreal, 232, 236
   Bishop of, 239
   visit of 'Abdu'l-Bahá to, 220-54
Moody, Dr Susan, 359-60, 443
Moore, Dr and Mrs, 212
morals, 80, 120, 121, 183, 210, 249, 266, 401
Morey, Mrs, 219, 483
Mormons, 289
Morristown, New Jersey, 149
Morten, Mrs Alexander, 39
Mortensen, Fred, 209, 443, 481
Moses, 67, 90, 96, 189, 197, 211, 227, 243, 310-7, 397
Moss, Mrs, 64
Most Great Prison, 9, 70, 164, 243-4, 259, 412
motion, 329
motion pictures, 132-3, 213
Mount Carmel, 130
Mount Morris Baptist Church (New York), 111
Moxey, Mrs, 392
Moxey, Frank K., 156, 159, 392
Muhájir, Áqá Riḍá Ghánud, 391
Muḥammad, 67, 73, 90-1, 96, 144, 185, 189, 197, 227, 238, 243, 267, 272, 272, 288, 308, 313, 315-16
Muḥammad-'Alí, Mírzá, 185, 429, 444, 447, 485
Muḥammad 'Alí Mírzá, 178, 444
Muḥammad-'Alí Páshá, Prince, 173
Muḥammad-Ḥasan, Mírzá (King of Martyrs), 263
Muḥammad Qulí, 145
Muḥammad-Taqí, Ḥájí, the Afnán, 30, 177
Muḥammad-Taqí Iṣfahání, Áqá, 176
Muḥammad-Taqí Manshádí, Siyyid, 129, 444
Munír-i-Zayn, Mírzá, 13, 15, 22, 33
murder, 93
museums, 155, 267, 355-6

music, 28, 80, 142, 203, 207, 261, 320, 326, 354, 375, 375, 385
   effect of, 199-200, 210
   spiritual, 142
Muslims, 73, 229, 243, 315, 318, 374
Nabíl-i-Zarandí, 28, 444
Nakhjavání, Mírzá 'Alí-Akbar, 121, 182, 186, 220, 263, 348, 444
Naples, 18, 21, 22
Napoleon, 182, 252
Nashua, New Hampshire, 205
Náṣiri'd-Dín Sháh, 15, 140, 177, 439
nations, 76, 118, 168
nature, 50, 75, 82, 194, 234, 282, 304, 306
   and humanity, 41, 82
   laws of, 17
Newark, New Jersey, 142-3, 146
New Jersey, 390
   visits of 'Abdu'l-Bahá to, 87-8, 103, 115, 119, 164, 170
newspapers, 6, 43, 81, 82, 101, 110, 131, 149, 156, 173, 174, 216, 235, 236, 241, 251, 246, 247, 248, 251, 260, 263, 267, 277, 284, 297, 331, 339, 366
newspapermen, *see* journalists
New Thought Forum, 215, 216
Newton, Mrs, 121, 163
New York, 13, 81, 146, 163
   arrival in, 30, 33
   banquet in, 398-9
   City of the Covenant, 471
   departure from, 411
   purpose of 'Abdu'l-Bahá's visit to, 395, 413
   railways in, 396
   skyscrapers, vii, 34, 162, 372-3, 396, 458
   traffic in, 396
   visits of 'Abdu'l-Bahá to, 33-46, 85-99, 101-4, 111-15, 116-20, 123-36, 150-74, 380-426
   weather in, 160-1
New York Peace Society, 40, 97
Niagara Falls, 246, 251
Nichols, Mrs, 109
Nineteen Day Feast, 208, 326, 363
North Pole, 28, 63, 120, 182, 446
Notre Dame Roman Catholic Cathedral (Montreal), 222
Nutt, Dr William Frederick, 258, 387

Oakland, 295, 325, 337-9, 339
Ober, Harlan, 167, 445, 446, 476
obedience, 156-7
Omaha, Nebraska, 271-80
oneness, divine, 160
Open Forum (San Francisco), 306
opposition, 256, 376
Orient-Occident Unity Conference, 48
Orient-Occident Unity Society, 62
orphans, 202
Ottawa, 248

Pacific Ocean, 292
painting of 'Abdu'l-Bahá, 135
Palestine, 265
Palo Alto, 294, 303-5
parades, 152
Paris, 9, 118
parks, visits of 'Abdu'l-Bahá to, 110, 122, 143, 144, 155, 158, 296, 299
Parliament, international, 366-7
Parsis, 243
Parsons, Agnes, 47, 53, 58, 61, 62, 64, 83, 84, 84, 169, 176, 178, 180, 181, 182, 183, 185, 186, 190, 198, 201, 203, 208, 220, 358, 369, 370, 374, 376, 445, 459, 460, 461, 462, 464, 467
Parsons, Arthur Jeffrey, 178, 182, 183, 185, 186, 190, 198, 203, 358, 445, 462
Parsons, Jeffrey, 201
Patent Office, United States, 63
peace,
   of mind, 407
   universal, 29 34-5, 37, 38, 44, 46, 54, 63, 68, 77, 86, 90-7, 98, 99, 112, 119, 148, 168, 197, 230, 234, 272-3, 282, 300, 304, 309-18, 323, 339, 351, 353, 362, 378, 409
peace congresses, 7, 9, 29, 37, 81, 83, 99-101, 174, 238, 290
Peace Forum, 89
Peary, Admiral Robert Edwin, 63, 120, 182, 445-6, 461, 463
Penfield, Mrs, 104
Penshoe, Mr, 118

Peripatetics, 18, 457
Persia, 29 66, 95-6, 141-2, 144, 161,
    163, 178-9, 263, 268, 272
  governance of, 215-6
Persians, 163, 178-9, 188-9, 215-6, 268,
    281, 339, 389
Peter, 291, 390, 410
Philadelphia, 379
  visit of 'Abdu'l-Bahá to, 123
Phillips, Miss, 38
philosophers, 6, 81, 109, 110, 151, 188,
    194, 206, 210, 268, 277, 281, 306,
    311, 328, 331
philosophy, divine, 115, 123, 211
photographs, 35, 41, 74, 80, 101, 120,
    135, 147, 149, 170, 183, 204, 276,
    277, 286, 399
physicians, 306
  divine, 306
  Italian, 13-14, 22, 33
Pittsburgh, 81-3
Plato, 194, 457
Plaza Hotel (Chicago), 65, 70, 71, 353
Plaza, Hotel (Minneapolis), 265
Plaza Hotel (New York), 152
Pleasanton, visit of 'Abdu'l-Bahá to,
    319-23
Plymouth Congregational Church (Chicago), 65, 356, 362
poetry, 156, 158, 200, 261, 305, 392
poets, 111, 156, 200, 261
Police Journal, 263
politicians, 272
politics, 137, 180, 216, 324-5
polygamy, 38, 289
pomegranate preserve, 156, 475
poor, the, 7, 21, 45-6, 62, 79, 80, 85,
    93, 103, 106, 210, 241, 260, 263,
    321, 380, 407
  see also poverty
Portland, 325, 329, 337
Port Said, 5, 9
Portsmouth Church, 211
Portsmouth, New Hampshire, 210
Post, The (Denver), 279
Post, The (San Francisco), 297-8
Potomac River, 64
poverty, 45-6, 106, 126, 197
  see also, poor, the
prayers, 52, 154, 330, 405

Shoghi Effendi chants, 15, 17
prejudice, 25, 68, 226-8, 229, 398, 399-
    400, 423
  against 'Abdu'l-Bahá's entourage,
    13-14, 380
  effects of, 32, 43, 59, 68, 148, 137,
    304-5, 357
  elimination of, 80, 87, 92, 162-3,
    214, 221, 368, 402
presidents, election of, 320
'Prince of the East', 248
professions, engagement in, 126
property, 116
prophecies, 83, 167, 189, 317-8, 369-
    70, 415
'Prophet of the East', 38, 97, 98, 112,
    239, 246, 248, 267, 277, 294, 361,
    401
Protestants, 410
Pumpelly, Mr and Mrs, 198
purity, 329

Qá'im, 128
Qur'án, 141-2

rabbis, 103, 388, 415
race unity, 44-5, 54, 65, 91-2, 153, 168,
    184, 214, 254, 377, 399-400
Ralston, Georgia, 157, 292, 293, 342,
    446
Ralston, William, 292, 293, 446
Ramleh, 13, 24, 34
Randall, Dr John H., 102
rank, 203, 301, 357
reality,
  criteria for establishing, 266
  explanations of, 388
  investigation of, 195
reincarnation, 19, 143
religion, 24, 37, 86, 90-7, 125, 148,
    168, 186, 225-30, 243, 305, 308-18,
    359, 382, 389
  and science, 39, 43, 68, 138, 213,
    227, 306
  unity of, 43, 68, 73, 76, 80, 90-7,
    102, 109, 112, 131, 185, 189,
    197, 243, 272, 301, 309-18, 346,
    350, 353, 363
Remey, Charles Mason, 205, 375, 446,
    448, 460, 461, 464

reporters, newspaper, *see* journalists
Riḍáy-i-S͟hírází, Qannád, Áqá, 135, 446
Riger, Judge, 240
Rivers, Mrs, 121, 163
Riverside Drive, New York, 85, 101, 380, 383, 467
Robarts, Grace, 167, 445, 446, 467, 476
Roberts, Mrs Sidney, 276, 283, 350
Rocky Mountains, 287
Roosevelt, Theodore, 60, 86, 447, 462, 467
Rúdakí, 200
Rúḥá K͟hánum, 13, 447
Rúḥu'lláh, 115, 170, 449
Russell, Mrs, 359
Russia, 96, 355
Russian Consul, 18

Sacramento, 343-6
Sacramento, Hotel, 343
sacrifice, 196, 256, 410
St Helena, 252
St Paul, 268-9, 270
Salmán, S͟hayk͟h, 177, 447
Salt Lake City, 288-90, 347-8
Samandarí, Mr, 389
Sámání, Amír Náṣir, 200
San Francisco, 201, 242, 297, 305, 373
  earthquake, 299
  visit of 'Abdu'l-Bahá to, 292-320, 327, 329, 336-41
Sayyáḥ, Mírzá 'Alíy-i-, 291
scenery, 64, 65, 69, 99, 106, 108, 119, 134, 149, 152, 177, 187, 208, 218, 237, 245, 246, 251, 285, 296, 287, 295, 344-5, 348
Schenley, Hotel (Pittsburgh), 81
scholars, 109
science, 56-7, 107, 114
  and religion, *see* religion, and science
Seattle, 325, 329, 337
self-mortification, prohibition of, 142
senses, the, 192
service, to humanity, 120, 126
ships, 10, 13-14, 15, 17, 21, 22, 26, 31, 34, 41, 423, 426
shipyard, 210
Shirley, Hotel (Denver), 275, 283
Shoghi Effendi, viii, 13, 15, 17, 22, 23, 33, 433, 447

Short, W. H., 40
S͟hu'á'u'lláh, Mírzá, 274, 332-4, 447, 484, 485
Sieglar, Mrs, 165
sign language, 57
Silverman, Rabbi, 113
sin, 31, 216
skyscrapers, vii, 34, 162, 285, 372-3, 396
  see also buildings
sleep, 191
Smiley, Mr, 99-100
Smith, Mrs, 135
socialism, 262-3, 272
Socialist Club (Montreal), 236
socialists, 6, 116, 165, 181, 201, 238, 239, 262, 346, 357
society, 201-3
Society of Indians Residing in Chicago, 72
Socrates, 210, 311, 457
Sohrab, Mírzá Ahmad, 7, 83, 220, 223, 460, 461, 464, 466
soul, 123-4, 153-4, 234, 376, 418-19
  capacities of the, 57, 71-2, 113-4
  immortality of the, 6, 110, 175, 180, 187, 190-3, 199, 200, 205, 231, 308
  see also life, eternal
  nature of the, 18, 26-7
Spain, 27, 98
Spencer, Anna Garland, 97
spirit, 328
spirit, the, 114
  see also soul
spiritualists, 237, 387
spirituality, 39, 40, 41, 57, 119, 127, 136, 142, 183, 180, 183, 193, 237, 299, 299
Spokane, 248
Star of the West, 352
Statue of Liberty, 34
Struven, Howard and Hebe, 378, 446, 448
subway, 155
suffrage movement, 61, 104
Sufism, 18, 143, 300
Sulaymáníyyih, 145, 185, 338-9, 473
summer schools, 183
  for boys, 182-3

for girls, 209
The Sun (New York), 155
superstitions, 25, 49, 51, 59, 68, 80, 92, 94, 180-1, 198, 207, 208, 212, 221, 227, 411, 416
Supreme (International) Tribunal, 148, 229
Surúsh, Mihtar Ardishír Bahrám, 70
Swingle, Dr, 80, 466
Switzerland, 9, 63
synagogues, 5, 9, 132, 265-6, 373
Syria, 98
Syrians, 90, 111

Tablet of the Branch, 134
Tabríz, 161
Taft, President William Howard, 63, 105, 462, 467
Ṭáhirih, 178, 448
Tarbíyat Schools, 365, 490
Tatum, Mrs, 209, 211
taxi, 235
Taylor, Miss, 208
teaching, the Bahá'í Cause, 131-2, 157, 176, 270
telegrams, 32, 33, 34, 47, 70, 81, 154, 178, 268, 287, 297, 329, 364, 379
telepathy, 180, 279
telephone, 56, 57, 221, 274, 343
Temple, Bahá'í, *see* Mashriqu'l-Adhkár
Temple Emmanu-el (San Francisco), 308, 339
tests and trials, 66, 136, 196
theists, 165
Theosophical Society, 74, 114, 175, 218, 219, 257, 416, 462
Theosophists, 57, 114, 175, 178-9, 180, 237, 219, 237, 462
Thompson, Juliet, 135, 155, 161, 208, 388, 395, 436, 448, 458, 461, 463, 467, 468, 472, 474-5, 476-7
Ṭihrán, 23, 140, 215, 369
time, 163
Titanic, sinking of the, 10, 41, 53, 213, 258, 459, 460, 461
tithe, the, 202
Topakyan, Consul General, 97, 125, 149, 170, 387, 399
Torah, 19, 168, 251, 311-16, 313, 314, 315, 415

traffic, 396
trains, 26, 47, 64-5, 79, 81, 83, 85, 87, 116, 201, 209, 221, 245, 251, 264, 270-1, 275, 276, 277, 284, 287-8, 329, 336, 342-3, 344-5, 346, 347, 348, 350, 351, 352, 353, 365, 378, 379
  accident, 258
  in New York, 396
  snow sheds over, 291
  see also transportation, forms of
trams, 76, 144, 146, 170, 234, 235, 246, 247, 289, 330
translators, 83, 112, 383
transportation, forms of, 26, 32, 47, 64-5, 76, 79, 81, 83, 85, 87, 99, 104, 109, 116, 144, 146, 149, 153, 155, 170, 175, 178, 183, 201, 205, 209, 209, 212, 215, 217, 221, 222, 224, 234, 235, 237, 245, 246, 247, 251, 258, 261, 264, 268, 269, 270-1, 274, 275, 276, 277, 278-80, 284, 287-8, 289, 293, 295, 296, 319, 321, 329, 330, 336, 342-3, 344-5, 346, 347, 348, 350, 351, 352, 353, 362, 365, 378, 379, 396, 423, 426
treasury, village, 202-3
Tremont Temple (Boston), 105
Trinity, 300
Tripoli, 92
True, Corinne, 77, 171, 252, 253, 261, 359, 360, 365, 434, 448
trustworthiness, 245
truth, 63, 67-8, 91, 96, 180, 195, 206, 225-7, 309-10, 312, 316, 317, 398
truthfulness, 245
Turkey, 180, 329, 345, 380
Turkish Revolution, 9, 259, 429, 490
Turks, 23, 107, 231, 348, 380

Unitarian Church (Baltimore), 378
Unitarian Church (Brooklyn), 130
Unitarian Church (Dublin), 184, 198
Unitarian Church (Montreal), 221-2, 224
Unitarian Church (New York), 164
Unitarian Church (Palo Alto), 304
Unitarian Church (Philadelphia), 123
Unitarians, 13, 71, 105, 109, 110, 237
United States, *see* America

unity, 32, 43, 47, 54, 73, 97, 99, 168, 212, 237, 247, 300, 304, 397
Unity Church (Montclair), 137
Unity Club, 120, 121
Unity Feast, 146-9
Universal House of Justice, the, *see* House of Justice
Universalist Church (Washington DC), 48-53, 370
University of New York, 115
Utica, 208

Vaḥíd, Áqá Siyyid Yaḥyá, 291
Varqá, Mírzá 'Alí-Muḥammad, 115, 170, 449, 471
Varqá, Mírzá Valíyu'lláh Khán-i-, 97, 115, 161, 170, 220, 449
vegetable kingdom, 299
vengeance, 194
Viceroy of Christ, chair reserved for, 42, 43
Victoria, Hotel, 174
Virginia, 64
Visitation, Tablet of, 330
volcanoes, 20

Waite, Louise (Shahnáz Khánum), 261, 354-5, 449
war, 26, 35, 39, 41, 68, 77, 80, 89-97, 118, 224, 225-7, 229, 233, 331, 345, 367, 368, 399
  'Abdu'l-Bahá predicts war, 233, 337
  Balkans, 271, 356, 367, 369, 380, 424
  between Turkey and Italy, 21
  between Turkey and Greece, 345
  prohibition of, 148
Washington DC, 7, 47, 65, 185, 283, 367, 372
  banquet in, 374-5, 398-9
  visits of 'Abdu'l-Bahá to, 47-64, 84-5, 368-78
waterfalls, 246-7
wealth, 145, 165
weapons, *see* armaments
West Englewood, New Jersey, 146-50, 164-5
Westerners, 260, 268
  attitude to Easterners, 5, 13-14, 18, 21, 23, 41
  excessive eating habits of, 14

unity of, with Easterners, 23, 48, 59, 81, 121, 175, 210, 247, 278, 295, 374-6, 368, 368-9, 424-5
White, Mrs, 109
White Star Line, 13
Wiers, Dr Edgar S., 87
Wilhelm, Roy, 147, 165, 386, 449-50
Wilson, Marie P. 215, 220
Wilson, Woodrow, 274, 432, 450
Windsor, Hotel (Montreal), 232, 234, 235, 241
Windust, Albert, 352, 450
wine, 116, 141-2, 170
Wise, Dr Stephen S., 98
Woolson, Dr Clement, 268-9, 270
women, 141, 162, 208, 387
  education of, 38, 54, 61, 68, 71, 80, 85, 104, 120, 165, 218, 228-9, 393, 402, 405
  equality with men, 61, 68, 71, 80, 109, 148, 162, 163, 183, 228-9, 358, 402, 405
  rights of, 38, 80, 85, 104, 218, 325
Women's Club (New York), 402
Women's Union, 120
work, 126, 165
Workers' Union, 255
world, contingent, 285, 294-5
Woodcock, Miss, 21, 22
Woodcock, Mr and Mrs Percy, 21, 22, 26, 236, 467
Worcester, 106, 107
workers' rights, 21

Yaḥyá, Mírzá, 24, 138, 223, 256, 261, 336, 391, 433, 450, 472
  followers of, *see* Azalis
Yamamoto, Kanichi, 450, 486
Young Turk Revolution, 9, 259, 429, 490
Zarqání, Mírzá Maḥmúd-i-, vii-ix, 4-5, 8, 13, 22, 36, 278, 283, 427, 437, 451, 457, 460
Zaytoun, 9
Zoroaster, 243
Zoroastrians, 142, 158, 229, 243

www.ingramcontent.com/pod-product-compliance
Lightning Source LLC
Chambersburg PA
CBHW042224010526
44111CB00044B/2939